WRITING DOWN THE MYTHS

Previously published volumes in this series are listed at the back of the book.

VOLUME 17

Writing Down the Myths

Edited by

Joseph Falaky Nagy

BREPOLS

British Library Cataloguing in Publication Data

Writing down the myths. -- (Cursor mundi ; 17)
  1. Myth--History.
  2. Mythologists--History.
I. Series
II. Nagy, Joseph Falaky editor of compilation.
809.9'15-dc23

ISBN-13: 9782503542188

© 2013, Brepols Publishers n.v., Turnhout, Belgium

D/2013/0095/79
ISBN: 978-2-503-54218-8
e-ISBN: 978-2-503-54259-1
Printed in the E.U. on acid-free paper

CONTENTS

ILLUSTRATIONS

Figures

Tables

EDITOR'S PREFACE

Joseph Falaky Nagy

Contemporary scholarly definitions of and approaches to myth, though profoundly affected over the last two hundred centuries by the fieldwork and findings of anthropologists and folklorists who have worked with living oral traditions, are still to a great extent indebted to classical Greek and Roman, and medieval European masterpieces of mythography — literary compendia that purport to sum up ancient traditional stories about gods and goddesses, heroes and heroines, primal events, and/or the beginnings of the world. Such texts, which weave narrative materials from oral tradition and from earlier literature into mythologies, have in some cases become canonical formulations serving as sources, templates, and inspirations for other literary and scholarly works, both within their own literary-historical contexts and well beyond them. There are cases, however, where these codified mythologies served as epitaphs, seemingly marking the end of particular (oral) traditions instead of their (literary) revival. The essays in this volume examine the various agenda (literary, cultural, political) that led to the production of mythological collections in the classical and late antique world, and the extent to which the agenda that produced comparable works in certain medieval cultures of northwest Europe (Ireland, Wales, Iceland, Denmark) operated along similar or even historically related lines. Some of the essays, on the other hand, offer fascinating *comparanda* from non-European literary traditions: Hittite, Japanese, and Indic.

As all of those know who participated in the 2009 UCLA conference on 'Writing Down the Myths' that gave birth to this publication, medievalists, classicists, and scholars from a variety of disciplines can all learn a great deal from each other's expertise in regard to the establishment of mythological canons in earlier times. The questions we invited those participants and the contributors to this volume to address include: How 'authentic' are classical and medieval mythographies, and how do we determine that authenticity? To what uses were they put in the ancient and medieval worlds? What was the transmission history of pre-medieval mythographic works in the Middle Ages, and to what extent and to whom were they available as models to the post-classical world? What and whence was the 'mythographic urge' behind medieval works such as the Welsh *Mabinogi* and Snorri's *Edda*? Are such compositions attempts to negotiate received or developing concepts of history, or are they revivals of meta-historical poetics? What are the differences in function, approach, and subtext between these premodern 'write-ups' of myth and modern popular handbooks of mythology? And is mythography to be found in every culture that develops a written tradition, or is it a particular characteristic of Greek, Roman, and classically influenced cultures?

The above-mentioned conference, 'Writing Down the Myths: The Construction of Mythology in Classical and Medieval Traditions' (16–18 April 2009) was sponsored by the Ahmanson Foundation and by the UCLA Center for Medieval and Renaissance Studies. I wish to thank the Director of the CMRS, Brian Copenhaver, its staff, Karen Burgess, Benay Furtivo, and Brett Landenberger, and the co-organizer of the conference, Kendra Willson, for their unstinting support, as well as Dr Blair Sullivan, Publications Director of the CMRS, for her genial encouragement and sage advice. Thanks are also due to all the participants, who generously offered the essays contained herein and patiently tolerated the queries of their editor. I also note with gratitude the moral and logistical support given to the conference by the members of the teaching staff of the UCLA General Education Cluster Course GE 30, 'Neverending Stories: Multidisciplinary Perspectives on Myth': Malcolm Harris, Stephanie Jamison, Gregory Kendrick, Eric Kristensson, Katherine McLoone, Anna Pagé, Timothy Tangherlini, and Elizabeth Thornton. What we all learned from the conference served us in good stead indeed as we launched the course in the Fall of 2009, and the memory of the conference still inspires those of us involved in GE 30 as we prepare to teach the course once again in the upcoming year.

ARE MYTHS INSIDE THE TEXT
OR OUTSIDE THE BOX?

Joseph Falaky Nagy*

A t the end of the older surviving version of the Irish *Cath Maige Tuired* (Battle of Mag Tuired), one of the outstanding examples of 'writing down the myths' — that is, of mythographic literature — to have come down to us from the early Middle Ages,[1] the author adds a prosimetric coda that reinforces the profundity of the story just told. This coda follows an account of the monumental battle between two larger-than-life communities: the Túatha Dé Danann (Tribes of the Goddess Danu), possessors of wondrous powers and objects said in our medieval sources to have been the earlier occupants of Ireland before they were displaced by the 'sons of Míl', the human ancestors of the Irish; and the Fomoiri, sinister transmarine invaders closely intertwined by marriage with the Túatha Dé and seeking to wrest control of Ireland away from them. The text concludes:

* Joseph Falaky Nagy (jfnagy@humnet.ucla.edu) is Professor in the Department of English and the Indo-European Studies Program at the University of California, Los Angeles. He has authored books and articles on medieval Irish literature, Celtic mythology, and the comparative study of oral tradition.

[1] *Cath Maige Tuired*, ed. and trans. by Gray, from which all quoted passages of the Irish text and translations are taken. Gray's indispensable commentary on the text unfolds in the three installments of an article, Gray, 'Cath Maige Tuired (1–24)'; Gray, 'Cath Maige Tuired (24–120)'; and Gray, 'Cath Maige Tuired (84–93, 120–67)'. See also Ó Cathasaigh, '*Cath Maige Tuired* as Exemplary Myth'. An Early Modern Irish telling of the story, different in many respects from the earlier version, has also survived: *Cath Muighe Tuireadh*, ed. by Ó Cuív. A much briefer account of the battle is given in the *Lebor Gabála Érenn*, ed. and trans. by Macalister (Book of the Taking of Ireland), a huge work that embodies the mixture of traditional and learned lore characteristic of medieval Irish literary accounts of the island's past (see pp. 118–20). Other literary references to the narrative material contained in *Cath Maige Tuired* as well as to tradition concerning a 'First Battle of Mag Tuired' are examined in Murphy, 'Notes on *Cath Maige Tuired*'.

Writing Down the Myths, ed. by Joseph Falaky Nagy, CURSOR 17, (Turnhout: Brepols, 2013)
pp. 1–18   BREPOLS 🖳 PUBLISHERS   10.1484/M.CURSOR-EB.1. 100844

Then after the battle was won and the slaughter had been cleaned away, the Morrígan, the daughter of Ernmas, proceeded to announce the battle and the great victory which had occurred there to the royal heights of Ireland and to its síd [supernatural dwelling]-hosts, to its chief waters and to its rivermouths. And that is the reason Badb [= the Morrígan] still relates great deeds. 'Have you any news?' everyone asked her then. [Here follows a poem obscurely detailing the cosmic and social benefits resulting from the victory of the Morrígan's people, the Túatha Dé.]

She also prophesied the end of the world, foretelling every evil that would occur then, and every disease and every vengeance; and she chanted the following poem [and here the text ends with a fragment of a poem detailing the breakdown in morals that will occur in the end-time].[2]

Both the seasoned scholar of medieval Celtic literature and the reader encountering *Cath Maige Tuired* for the first time would probably agree that the note on which this story of hard-won triumph ends is peculiarly grim. The Morrígan (also known as Badb), monopolizing the end of the text, barely allows any time for the Túatha Dé to savour the fruits of their triumph over their enemies, or for the latter-day audience of the story to derive satisfaction from her poetic foretelling of good times to come. Rather, she extends the arc of her prophecy dramatically, casting a pall not only over the proceedings of the story but even over the future in or beyond the lifetime of the reader or hearer of the textualized story, purportedly transmitted all the way from the ancient past to the ninth century, when the text appears to have been written down. True, the Morrígan's vaguely biblical prediction of the end of the world may have struck an eschatologically-minded Christian reader as reassuringly familiar, or even as a pleasant surprise, vindicating a hunch widely shared throughout the Irish literary tradition that native pre-Christian tradition had intuited the Christian shape of things to come.[3] Still, it must have startled the original readership of a story of ancient times newly recounted and available in written form, just as it still strikes the modern reader as odd, that with

---

[2] *Cath Maige Tuired*, ed. and trans. by Gray, pp. 71, 73.

[3] In reference to a story he recounts about a native seer's anticipation of Christ before the coming of Christianity, the seventeenth-century Irish historian Geoffrey Keating expresses a sensibility perfectly consonant with that of Irish men of letters going back to the beginnings of Irish literary tradition: 'In case anyone is amazed that Bacrach or some other druid, (albeit) pagans, could prophesy the death of Christ, why would it be more appropriate for the Sibyls (also pagans) to foresee Christ before his birth than for Bacrach or his like?' (my translation of the passage from the Irish text as given in *Stories from Keating's History of Ireland*, ed. by Bergin, p. 8 (bk II, sect. 33)). Compare the other major Celtic premodern literary tradition, that of Wales, where the Christianity-predicting Sibyl, Marged Haycock observes, 'was well-known by medieval translators and poets in Wales': Haycock, '*Sy abl fodd, Sibli fain*', p. 129.

the abrupt intrusion of an ominous future, the story is rendered more than just 'old', and the voices heard in it no longer fit comfortably in a file marked 'past'.

The Morrígan is not the only possessor of a poetic voice that turns the *Cath Maige Tuired* into a remarkable literary vehicle for time travel. There is also the poet Lóch Lethglas,[4] who, unlike the Morrígan, is actually designated a *fili* in the text, a term for the most prestigious kind of poet in medieval Irish society (usually a male). Unlike the Morrígan, who has already appeared and played an important role in the part of the story leading up to the final confrontation between the Túatha Dé and Fomoiri, Lóch is introduced in the narrative towards the end of the battle, when he is summoned by his patron, Indech, a royal leader of the invaders and one of the champions on the field of Mag Tuired. (Although the cause for which he fights is unjust, and his people symbolize the forces that undermine proper social relations, Indech, like any person of power and high visibility in medieval Ireland, requires the presence and services of a poet.)[5] He calls for 'my *fili*' after he has been grievously injured by the falling corpse of his towering colleague Balor, another leader of the Fomoiri, who is downed by a slingshot and collapses catastrophically on his own people. The cast that brings about both Balor's and Indech's demise comes from Balor's daughter's son Lug, the leader of the forces of the Túatha Dé (including the Morrígan, who not only poetizes but fights against the enemy with her own powerful magic). With this cast, perhaps evocative for the medieval audience of David's celebrated feat of defeating the Philistine giant, Lug fatally takes out Balor's magically destructive single eye and knocks him down. When Indech, collaterally damaged, demands that Lóch ascertain 'who hurled this cast at me', Lóch proceeds to make inquiries, engaging in poetic dialogue with Lug, who freely and proudly identifies himself to the poet. Slightly later in the text, after the Fomoiri have been routed by the Túatha Dé (incited, we note in passing, by a poem sung by the Morrígan), Lug and Lóch meet again and resume their conversation. Now that the Túatha Dé have unquestionably triumphed, the *fili* begs for mercy from the leader of the victorious forces. Lug, ever the shrewd negotiator, demands the fulfillment of three wishes as the price for sparing Lóch's life. What those three wishes are is not

---

[4] *Cath Maige Tuired*, ed. and trans. by Gray, pp. 60–65.

[5] Lóch, however, is not your garden-variety *fili* (or perhaps he is, in a very unusual way): the poet is *lethglas* (half-green), the text elaborates, 'from the ground to the crown of his head' (*Cath Maige Tuired*, ed. and trans. by Gray, pp. 62–63). The much lower-ranked poetic performer, the *cáinte* 'satirist' Cridenbél, a figure as villainous as the Fomoiri, is distinguished by his own freakishness: his mouth is in his chest (*Cath Maige Tuired*, ed. and trans. by Gray, p. 28). These grotesque and liminal features reflect the essential 'strangeness' of the enemies of the Túatha Dé.

spelled out in the text, but Lóch eagerly assents to the deal, and, either granting Lug's requests or throwing bonuses into the bargain, proclaims: 'I will remove the need to guard against the Fomoire from Ireland forever; and whatever judgement your tongue will deliver in any difficult case, it will resolve the matter until the end of life.'[6] The text continues: 'So Lóch was spared. Then he chanted The Decree of Fastening to the Gaels [here follows another obscure poem].'

This 'decree' (the word *dá[i]l* can also mean 'agreement') seems to elaborate upon the assurance of a Fomoiri-free Ireland, but, as the editor of the text points out, the *astud* 'fastening' that the poem celebrates also pertains to the sturdiness of Lug's judicial decisions as guaranteed by Lóch. Whatever and however much power the poem ratifies and conveys, it is clearly an important prize to be taken away from the battle.[7] A puzzling detail, however, is the matter of *to whom* the poem is conveyed by means of performance: the text says *do Gaídelaib* 'to the Gaels'. There are, however, no 'Gaels' in the world of this text. These — that is, the Irish — are a people who, in the legendary schema within which *Cath Maige Tuired* and many other medieval Irish stories operate, enter the scene as the *successors* to the Túatha Dé, who are forced by these newcomers to the island literally to go underground (into the *síde* — the mounds, caves, and souterrains with which they are traditionally associated). So Lóch's poem of ratification is presumably addressed both to an audience of his time (Lug) and also, quite pointedly, to a posterity that includes the readers, hearers, and beneficiaries of this text. If we imagine the latter theatrically, it is as if Lóch on stage had turned to the audience and in Brechtian fashion sung the 'Decree' to us.

Returning to the Morrígan and re-examining the prose introduction to her pair of prophetic poems, we find an even more dramatic breaking of the proscenium of chronology. Let us recall that, in this passage as quoted above, the poetess-herald proclaims the victory of her people to both the inhabitants of Ireland at the time (not yet underground, but proleptically referred to as '*síd*-hosts') and the landscape of the island itself. After presenting her proclamation, the text says:

---

[6] Kim McCone points out the possible continuation of the Davidic correspondence here (David slaying the Philistine giant with his sling, defeating the Philistines generally, and subsequently maintaining rule and judgement over the Israelites) in McCone, 'A Tale of Two Ditties', p. 139.

[7] As noted by the text's editor, 'the bargaining between Lug and Lóch illustrates the role of contractual exchange as a process which complements warfare in establishing order' (Gray, 'Cath Maige Tuired (84–93, 120–67)', p. 251). Lug's role as negotiator on behalf of his people and their interests is also on display in another episode concerning the aftermath of the battle, discussed in Sayers, 'Bargaining for the Life of Bres'.

'And that is the reason Badb still relates great deeds'. *Badb* (scald-crow) is an alternative designation for the Morrígan, who sometimes does appear in stories in the form of this bird. Thus, in this case of linkage established between the past of the story and the present of its reception, it is not only *what is sung or told* that lives on into the present but *the singer or teller herself*. Even if deprived of her erstwhile human or supernatural form and now existing 'just' as a bird (should this be the point of the text's switching to the name *Badb*), the Morrígan proves an extraordinarily hardy survivor. And unlike other legendary living relics of the hoary past who are celebrated in medieval Irish literary tradition, but specifically for what they know and can tell about that past, Badb, the text implies, can also proclaim *contemporary* 'great deeds still' (*airdgníomha beus*).[8]

Could this seemingly parenthetical comment be a major point being made by the author of *Cath Maige Tuired* about the tenacity of the 'old' stories he is telling? In a text as self-conscious as this, surely it would not be surprising to find corroboration of what over the last few decades has become axiomatic in medieval Irish studies: namely, that any native tale preserved in our sources was added to the written record because it could be told or read as having some implicit application to political and social circumstances of the time of its composition or recension.[9] For example, scholars have noted a historical subtext to the mythological *Cath Maige Tuired*, having to do with the Vikings (as latter-day Fomoiri), their settlement in Ireland, and their impact on Irish power struggles of the late first millennium.[10] Perhaps these are the kinds of contemporary 'great deeds' that the Morrígan now in the form of a bird — or as the mascot of *Cath Maige Tuired* itself — still proclaims as effectively as ever.

[8] Yet another kind of 'survivor into the present' featured in *Cath Maige Tuired* (both the earlier and later versions, and also in its 'prequel', about a supposed 'First' Battle of Mag Tuired) are the '"proto-textual" stones' that 'do not merely anchor the warriors on the field of battle and provide perches for poets — they also inscribe the memory of the warriors and the story of the battle itself into the landscape, linking history, poetry, land, battle, and narrative' (Blustein, 'Poets and Pillars in *Cath Maige Tuired*', p. 23). These monuments are enshrined in the place-name itself, *Mag Tuired* (Field of Pillars).

[9] An example of this reflexivity is the following comment made in the text, after it tells of Lug's proving himself among the Túatha Dé by triumphing in the board game known as *fidchell*: 'But if *fidchell* was invented at the time of the Trojan war, it had not reached Ireland yet, for the battle of Mag Tuired and the destruction of Troy occurred at the same time' (*Cath Maige Tuired*, ed. and trans. by Gray, p. 41).

[10] On the historical subtext pertinent to the Viking era in Ireland, see Carey, 'Myth and Mythography in *Cath Maige Tuired*'. Later historical resonances acquired by the myth as retold in oral tradition are examined in Radner, 'The Combat of Lug and Balor'. On the timely messages imparted in a sequel of sorts to *Cath Maige Tuired*, see Breatnach, '*Oidheadh Chloinne Tuireann*'.

As all of the studies gathered here demonstrate in regard to different ancient, classical, medieval, and even modern literary traditions, mythography — the project of 'writing down the myths' — entails a re-evaluation of the relationship between a hypothetical past and present, as well as requiring the concomitant transference of authority of various kinds from one medium or text into another. Claiming a contemporary relevance as does *Cath Maige Tuired* for Lóch's poem 'to the Gaels', mythographic works typically purport to convey information of lasting value, even if it needs to be fine-tuned to fit new religious, cultural, and social circumstances that inevitably develop between the 'then' of the stories in question and the 'now' of the composition of the work itself. Writing down the myths does not automatically foster a sceptical or agnostic attitude towards the materials, but it does present opportunities for contracting and expanding an existing mythology, creating new myths and a new systematization of them alto-gether, or even for generating 'myths about myths' that offer keys to understand-ing the material as presented. In fact, mythography, cousin to if not identical with the problematic process of *translatio* as discussed in Katherine McLoone's con-tribution to this volume, represents the beginnings of the scholarly discipline of comparative mythology.[11] Whether a professed or secret devotee of the mythi-cal beings whose achievements he chronicles, a learned antiquarian rummaging among the artefacts stowed away in the attic of culture, or a lover of what others may consider *outré* or even subversive stories, but who operates freely after issuing a 'Kids, don't try this at home!' warning about the material he is presenting, the mythographer, from the ancient writer of Hittite texts to the twentieth-century packager of ancient Greek mythology for students and the general public, joins in the mission of the Irish Badb as she proclaims 'the great deeds' of the past in terms meaningful and useful to the people of the present.

* * *

But do the myths selected and fashioned by the mythographer for his text always behave in their new literary environment as he intends them to? What strate-gies of containment do those undertaking to commit myths to a written form employ in order to ensure that these tales will fulfil the agenda authorizing this sea-change in the first place? And can myths ever break loose or out of the mythographic text, endangering its seal of cultural approval? A return to medi-eval Celtic literary tradition, a laboratory justly celebrated for its experiments in trying to encompass the lore of the past, may provide us with the beginnings of answers to these difficult questions.

[11] See below, pp. 181–200.

Many if not most vernacular Irish and Welsh texts of the Middle Ages that are primarily narrative in nature, in addition to their own story structure and themes, prominently feature one or more characters with tales to tell. In her contribution to this volume, 'Vessels of Myth',[12] Kimberly Ball, analysing a notable example of this syndrome, demonstrates that such 'stories-within-the-story' are typically far more than textual window-dressing and cannot be easily jettisoned from the critical reader's consideration of what the main story the text tells is all about. In fact, the outcome of the 'host' tale sometimes actually hinges on the telling of the introduced tale(s). The latter can be an actual personal-experience narrative (as it is in the Irish 'Phantom Chariot' text examined by Ball), but, in any case, this embedding technique as practised in medieval Celtic literary traditions dictates that there has to be some direct connection between the events told in the tale and the teller (as a participant, eyewitness, or unique inheritor of the knowledge of 'what happened'). The storyteller, in other words, must have special credentials in order to vouchsafe with authority for the 'truth' of the story (or version of a story) he or she tells.

The character assigned the role of storyteller is not necessarily a professional performer, the telling may be incomplete or allusive, and the story's performance may be just mentioned in passing as opposed to described in any detail. Along these lines, in *Cath Maige Tuired*, when Lug introduces himself at the court of Tara as *samíldánach* (possessing all the arts), he is in effect *implying* a story or a whole series of stories about the remarkable accomplishment of acquiring all of these skills, including that of tradition-bearer — a background narrative to which Lug and the text tantalizingly may be alluding, but which *Cath Maige Tuired* does not include.[13] Or when Bres, the inadequate king of the Túatha Dé, is banished from the throne, he and his mother go to his father's people, the sinister Fomoiri, and his mother tells them about what has happened (an act mentioned but not described). This account probably followed the story as told in the text so far, although one might imagine that Bres's mother would have given the story a slant more sympathetic to her son. For a finale, as we have seen, *Cath Maige Tuired* presents the Morrígan's two eschatological poems, one with a good outcome, the other with a bad one. These anticipate perhaps the most important story of all, that of human destiny itself. Given the basically non-narrative nature of poetic

---

[12] See below, pp. 137–55.

[13] *Cath Maige Tuired*, ed. and trans. by Gray, pp. 38, 40. Among the arts over which Lug claims mastery are those of the 'poet' (*fili*) and the 'historian' (*senchaid*) (p. 41), both of whom are professionally involved in the preservation and performance of traditional stories.

discourse in Celtic traditions, her verses relate future events obliquely, giving us only hints — a pre-story, as it were — about things to come.

It is no coincidence that the type of character whom the medieval Celtic author invites into the text in order to tell his or her story in the midst of a larger story — characters such as Lug, Bres, and the Morrígan in *Cath Maige Tuired* — usually comes with a dossier we would identify as 'mythic' without much hesitation. This featured storyteller is usually identified as a member or descendant of an otherworldly community (such as the Túatha Dé or the Fomoiri), a possessor of mysterious supernatural powers, a lone survivor from a remote past, or an *incognito* stranger whose true identity the mythic audience fully discovers only after the storyteller has told his story or left the premises.[14] Even if the story is a first-person narrative having to do with events that are recent in the context of the larger tale in which the narrator appears, the fact that the story is told by a character possessed of (what is ultimately revealed to be) such conspicuous mythic valence confers a special quality upon the story as well.

A famous example of 'myth by association', whereby the storyteller's distinctiveness lends a cachet to his story as passed on to posterity via the written tradition, is the massive twelfth- or thirteenth-century *prosimetrum* Irish text titled the *Acallam na Senórach* (Dialogue of the Ancients).[15] The 'ancients' in question are the warrior Caílte mac Rónáin and his fellow members of the fabled war-band of old known as the hero Finn's *fían*. Instead of passing away, as did their larger-than-life leader Finn and most of their companions (at the centre of a cycle of tales known today as the Fenian or Ossianic), Caílte and friends take refuge in a distinctly pre-Christian otherworld and find themselves, after departing from their supernatural host, in an era more than a hundred years after their own. Their re-emergence coincides with the coming of the missionary St Patrick, a historical figure of the fifth century, who happens to meet with Caílte and the other ancient warriors during the initial stage of his proselytizing journey across Ireland. After some legitimizing preliminaries (such as the baptism of these survivors from a

---

[14] MacQuarrie, 'Recognizing Gods in Guises' examines how the conceit of the mysterious vanishing storyteller operates in a text from late medieval/early modern Irish tradition. The 'Kern' is an avatar of a character that earlier sources clearly viewed as a member of a pre-Christian pantheon — namely, Manannán mac Lir, who may well have been the Irish counterpart to the Welsh figure of Manawydan fab Llyr, discussed below in connection with the Third Branch of the *Mabinogi*.

[15] *Tales of the Elders of Ireland*, trans. by Dooley and Roe. On the text as frame tale, see below, Ball, 'Vessels of Myth', pp. 139–41; on the multilayered nature of the text, see Parsons, 'The Structure of *Acallam na Senórach*'.

mythic world), Caílte and Patrick join forces to become a travelling 'cultural performance', a cross between question-and-answer and show-and-tell that both spreads the new religion (courtesy of Patrick) and (courtesy of the old warrior) reintroduces formerly lost lore about the people, events, places, and values of olden times back into the mainstream.[16] All the characters living in the time frame of the story of the *Acallam* (which, we should remember, is set several centuries before the era in which this text was composed) realize how special Caílte is, and what a unique opportunity he presents for learning about the past through the stories he can tell and the poems he can recite. The infusion of this new-yet-old information is a cause for celebration in the past portrayed in the *Acallam*, almost as much as the coming of the 'true' religion, which provides a new means for transmitting this lore to future generations: that is, the technology of writing. Thanks to the latter, even those living long after the time of Patrick can eavesdrop on these conversations, since, as the text repeatedly makes clear, Patrick's scribe dutifully recorded them. Thus the medieval audience of *Acallam na Senórach* enjoyed a triple-layered entertainment, the nostalgic focus of which alternates among the legends concerning Patrick's missionary work in Ireland, the pluperfect adventures of the characters of Fenian story as recounted by Caílte, and the *new* adventures undertaken by the still-heroic Caílte, both the designated storyteller and the leading protagonist of the *Acallam*. The monumental task of writing down the myths Caílte still remembers, a recovery operation that becomes as important to the frame tale of the *Acallam* as the premise of the Dialogue itself, is initiated after Patrick's guardian angels assure him that, provided he look after

---

[16] *Acallam*, the title given to this text packed with stories, allusions to stories that remain untold, and poems, is a noun formed from a verb meaning 'speaks to, converses with' (*Dictionary of the Irish Language*, ed. by Royal Irish Academy, under *ad-gládathar*). The designation not only aligns this work with other Irish texts so designated, but also resonates with a label applied to certain kinds of text or performance in medieval Welsh literature. Sioned Davies, one of the contributors to this volume, says of the character Cynon's account of his adventure in *Owein* (the Welsh adaptation of the French romance *Yvain*): 'Thus the tale is [described in the text as] an *ymddiddan* (= conversation) in so far as Cynon addresses another character, and also speaks in the first person. In a *cyfarwyddyd*, however, the narrator is totally divorced from the tale — he himself took no part in the action of the story. A *cyfarwydd* (storyteller), of course, could also narrate *ymddiddaneu* — Gwydion entertains the court with "ymdidaneu digrif" (pleasant dialogues). [...] It seems to me that an *ymddiddan*, therefore, was a short anecdote recited by a speaker, probably concerning his or her own experiences. [...] But in his performance, a storyteller could also make use of *ymddiddan* in its original sense: he could re-create conversation and dialogue in order to vary his rendering and to create a dramatic atmosphere' (Davies, 'Storytelling in Medieval Wales', p. 239).

the transcription of every story and poem Caílte offers him, Patrick's pleasurable listening to what the old warrior has to say will not be a sinful distraction from his mission. What he preserves, the angels tell Patrick, will provide entertainment (literally a 'shortening (of time)') for future generations.[17]

This compositional technique, on display in *Acallam na Senórach*, of embedding the older and more valuable story within a larger narrative structure also operates in medieval Celtic texts completely different in format, which on the surface hardly seem to invite the designation 'frame tale'.[18] The Middle-Welsh *Mabinogi*, roughly contemporary with or slightly earlier than the *Acallam*, and consisting of four separate prose tales or 'Branches', might strike the modern reader as a collection of narratives sorely lacking a frame tale, given the text's refusal to supply any guidance to the reader as to what to make of these stories, or in what historical context to view them, apart from a vague, even mythic past.[19] As meaningful as the *Mabinogi*'s main tales might have been to their original audience, the stories told within these stories (or the outlines of the Branches themselves as narrativized by characters privileged with special insight into what has happened) provide the modern reader with some of the most salient clues about what the *Mabinogi* was supposed to convey to its audience.[20]

In the latter part of the First Branch, for example, the important character of Teyrnon, the foster father of Pryderi (the only character to appear in all four Branches), contributes most significantly to the story by piecing together the back-story of his mysterious young ward. (That Teyrnon is a more important personage than the rather plodding way he goes about the task might sug-

---

[17] *Tales of the Elders of Ireland*, trans. by Dooley and Roe, p. 12; *Dictionary of the Irish Language*, ed. by Royal Irish Academy, under *gairtiugud*.

[18] Observing similar strategies for framing certain kinds of narrative is not to prove that one text specifically borrowed from another, even though it may reinforce our sense that medieval Celtic literary traditions, along with northern European literary cultures of the Middle Ages in general, frequently reflect the contiguity of the peoples and institutions that created and sustained them. An ambitious attempt to argue for structural influence on the most famous medieval frame tale of all, Chaucer's *Canterbury Tales*, emanating from Snorri's *Edda* (particularly the 'Deluding of Gylfi' section, which employs a frame for the telling of myths) and *Acallam na Senórach*, is presented in McTurk, *Chaucer and the Norse and Celtic Worlds*, pp. 1–33, 76–105.

[19] *The Mabinogion*, trans. by Davies, pp. 3–64; *The Mabinogi*, trans. by Bollard; *The Mabinogi*, ed. and trans. by Ford, pp. 35–109.

[20] On the importance of storytelling as both a recurring reflexive activity in the *Mabinogi* and as a heuristic model for a modern scholarly understanding of the text, see Davies, 'Storytelling in Medieval Wales', and Davies, '"He was the best teller of tales"'.

gest is signalled by his name, which at an earlier stage of its history would have denoted a god.)[21] Pryderi, a child Teyrnon accidentally rescues from a monster and subsequently raises as his own, turns out to be the lost son of Pwyll, the main character in the first half of the Branch, and of his supernatural wife Rhiannon, whom Pwyll woos and wins (albeit with considerable difficulty) in the first half. Teyrnon learns that Pwyll's wife, unjustly and incredibly accused of having eaten her son (who mysteriously disappears almost as soon as he is born), is condemned to a punishment of having to tell the story of her purported crime to any visitor to the court who will listen, as well as offering to give the visitor a ride to the court on her back.[22]

In the climactic final scenes of this Branch, Teyrnon visits his old friend Pwyll's court, rescues Rhiannon from her outlandish punishment, and returns the lost-but-now-found child to his parents, much to their long-delayed relief and joy. Teyrnon also tells the story of the finding and fostering of Pryderi, as he has pieced it together from his having rescued and raised the boy, from what he learned from those who had travelled to the court, as well as from what he remembered about Pwyll's distinguishing features, knowledge that enabled Teyrnon to recognize the growing boy as Pwyll's son. True, this is an act of storytelling only mentioned and not fully represented in the text, but it is safe to infer that Teyrnon's 'side of the story' would have accorded with the tale as already told in the latter part of the First Branch. His version of the events, like that of the First Branch itself, would have left some key questions unanswered, such as who was the monstrous kidnapper of Rhiannon's newborn child, and why did he take him from his mother

---

[21] On Teyrnon 'Great, or Divine, Lord', see *The Mabinogion*, trans. by Davies, p. 231.

[22] The story of Rhiannon's cannibalism comes from the women who had been left in charge of caring for Rhiannon and her newborn child. Having neglected their duty and fallen asleep, the women awoke to find the baby missing. Fearful of being blamed, they slew a newly born litter of pups and smeared the blood and tossed the bones onto the sleeping Rhiannon, and then accused her of having eaten her child, despite their attempts to stop her (*The Mabinogion*, trans. by Davies, pp. 16–17). It has long been noted that Rhiannon's plight is hardly unique, being an example of the international tale motif 'The Calumniated Wife' (K2110.1), while the women's attempt to implicate Rhiannon echoes the traditional ruse (K2155.1), 'Blood smeared on innocent person brings accusation of murder', and the falsehood (K2116.1.1.1), 'Innocent woman accused of eating her new-born children'. On the other hand, as Jessica Hemming has noted, the combination of these motifs is rare, if not unique to the story of Rhiannon: 'The situation in *Pwyll* is given its very own designation [in the Motif Index], K2116.1.1.1.1, "Bones of puppies as false evidence of wife's having eaten her new-born child"; not that this is very helpful from a comparative point of view, as this appears to be the only example of its kind' (Hemming, 'Reflections on Rhiannon', p. 22). See Thompson, *Motif-Index of Folk-Literature*.

— two of the mysteries of the *Mabinogi* that today's readers are still pondering. Unanswered questions notwithstanding, we know Teyrnon's story to be true, as opposed to the account of Rhiannon's purported savage crime, the explanatory value of which at least some members of the court had accepted, and which poor Rhiannon was forced to rehearse as part of her punishment.

And yet, even though Rhiannon's assertion that she never harmed her child is proven correct, can we altogether dismiss the alternative story of what happened to the baby — that is, the tale Rhiannon was forced to tell to those she would meet at the entrance to the court? Could this 'false' story promulgated as part of the punishment of the innocent heroine, and deemed believable by at least some of Pwyll's subjects if not by Pwyll himself, be pointing to a 'different' Rhiannon and an alternative account of her relationship with her husband and her son? Perhaps the horrible accusation of filicidal cannibalism, along with the meaning of her name (Divine Queen) and her persistent association with horses (including the magical mount on which she first appears in the story),[23] are clues pointing to a murky, even sinister aspect of her mythological profile, and to a multiform of her story that once may have existed, but that the author chose to show only through a glass darkly.[24]

A prominent translator and scholar of the *Mabinogi* has speculated that originally Teyrnon the 'Divine Lord' was the consort of the 'Divine Queen' Rhiannon, and Pryderi was their son.[25] The fact, moreover, that Teyrnon and Rhiannon are the characters in the First Branch with the most crucial stories to tell also suggests a special bond between them. It is therefore more than a coincidence that the Second Branch of the *Mabinogi* assigns its two pivotal storytelling performances to a husband-and-wife pair: Matholwch, an ancient sovereign of Ireland, and the British princess Branwen, whom he successfully seeks in marriage from her brother Bendigeidfran, the ruler of Britain, in order to strengthen the relationship between the two island kingdoms. At the wedding feast, Matholwch's telling the story of how he came to be familiar with the original owners of the special cauldron given to him by his brother-in-law Bendigeidfran provides us with all we need to know about just how bad a king Matholwch is: someone who will prove to be a craven spouse to his bride and a treacherous host to her kinsmen. The Irish monarch's personal-experience narrative, relayed at length by the text, is

---

[23] *The Mabinogion*, trans. by Davies, pp. 8–11.

[24] On Rhiannon and the Celto-Roman horse-goddess Epona, see *The Mabinogi*, ed. and trans. by Ford, pp. 4–5.

[25] *The Mabinogi*, ed. and trans. by Ford, pp. 12, 15. See also *The Mabinogi*, trans. by Bollard, p. 34.

also an aetiological tale, featuring a race of beings who are descended from a giant and his even more gigantic as well as alarmingly fecund wife. This grotesque pair, who had emerged out of a lake in Ireland (with the cauldron) during Matholwch's reign, before long becomes, together with their offspring (fully armed at birth!), a nuisance for Matholwch and his people. Ironically, after a failed attempt on their lives and their escape to Britain, the giant couple come to be viewed in their new home as valued and productive citizens of the realm. This surprising outcome, which completely changes the picture of the giants painted by Matholwch in his account, is supplied by Bendigeidfran, who finishes his brother-in-law's story. Clearly the conclusion to be drawn is that Matholwch incompetently handled the challenge posed by the introduction of the giant couple into the sphere of his putative control, while Bendigeidfran could not only accommodate them but also harness their powers and skills.

Later in this Branch, Matholwch's spouse Branwen — like Rhiannon, a calumniated wife — receives the chance to tell her story, of how she has been mistreated by the Irish, whom her husband cannot or will not control. We the readers, however, are not the recipients of her version of the story of what has happened, although we can assume that it probably would have accorded with what the text (sympathetic to both Branwen and the British) has already told us. But the details of *how* Branwen conveys her tale of woe (a call to arms to her brother) are made clear. This unusual act of transmission stands out as unique in the Four Branches — and, more generally, as extraordinarily reflexive in the context of medieval Celtic literature — because Branwen is said to write down (or to have someone else write down) her 'myth', the tale of her abuse and urgent need for deliverance. As if to draw even more attention to this anachronistic resort to a 'new' medium in the story, the letter is said to be borne across the sea to her brother by a starling whom Branwen in her misery had taught how to speak. Arguably, in an earlier version of the story about the conveyance of a story, it would have been the talking bird and not a written letter that delivered Branwen's urgent message.[26]

---

[26] On the broader cultural implications of Branwen's use of writing, see Davies's remarks: 'Much research remains to be done on the actual relationship between orality and literacy in medieval Wales; the boundaries between oral and literate cultures are difficult and perhaps impossible to identify. This is highlighted in an episode in *Branwen*, the second branch of the *Mabinogi*. Branwen is mistreated on her return to Ireland; she rears a starling, teaches it language, and instructs the bird what manner of man is her brother, the king of the Island of the Mighty. She ties a letter to the bird's wings and sends it off to Wales to seek her brother. Perhaps the two boundaries touch here; in an oral culture, the starling, having been taught words, would

The Third Branch, continuing the story in the wake of Bendigeidfran's disastrous expedition to Ireland and the return of a few survivors to Britain, employs the character Manawydan, the late Bendigeidfran's brother, as a detective, casting him in a role similar to the one played by Teyrnon in the First Branch. On the surface confirming but in fact belying his reputation as an exceptionally easy-going ruler,[27] Manawydan tries to force out into the open the perpetrator *and* the story behind the disappearance of his people, his wife Rhiannon (whose first husband Pwyll passed away at the end of the First Branch), and his stepson Pryderi (Rhiannon's son, who disappears as easily in this story as he did in the First Branch). The quest on which Manawydan sets out, after he and Pryderi's wife find themselves seemingly the last humans in the kingdom, is motivated by a curious combination of the personal (he is trying to rescue people he cares about), the pragmatic (he is also trying to sustain himself with a livelihood, first going back to working as a craftsman, as he did earlier in the same Branch, and then becoming a farmer), and the dispassionate: at the climax of the story, he seems determined to carry out the formal execution of the single rodent he succeeds in capturing of the many who have been devastating his crop, instead of just killing it outright. The solution to the mystery of the disappearances that have taken place in this Branch (climaxing in the theft of wheat) is supplied by a magical shapeshifter, whom Manawydan finally coaxes out into the open when the magician attempts to save his pregnant wife (the captured mouse) from the execution being prepared by Manawydan. Putting aside his disguises, Llwyd confesses to being the mastermind behind the kidnappings and depredation, and under duress agrees to free his prisoners and never bother them again. The explanation he gives for why he has so relentlessly targeted Pryderi and company leads back to the First Branch — to an episode in which Pwyll humiliatingly turned the tables on Gwawl, the rival suitor for Rhiannon's hand who nearly succeeded in winning her back from Pwyll, and whose humiliation his kinsman Llwyd had set out to avenge.

The Fourth Branch introduces a character specifically noted for his storytelling skills, a trickster who brings about the deception of Pryderi and his death (Pryderi's final 'disappearance') with the tales he tells. This character, Gwydion, and his brother Gilfaethwy insinuate their way into Pryderi's confidence in the guise of *cyfarwyddiaid* 'possessors of lore, storytellers'. Later, Gwydion and his

surely have delivered the message by mouth; in a literate culture spoken words are not enough — the message has to be written down. When Branwen's brother receives the letter, it is read out loud to him — even in a literate culture, the aural has its place' (Davies, 'Storytelling in Medieval Wales', pp. 252–53).

[27] *The Mabinogion*, trans. by Davies, p. 35.

foster son Lleu use the same cover when they visit Lleu's mother and Gwydion's sister Aranrhod, offering narrative entertainment as a way to disguise their identities and to gain access to a kinswoman who has become their enemy. On both occasions of Gwydion's assuming this disguise, the text goes out of its way to declare him as good at storytelling as the best *cyfarwydd*.[28] Tantalizingly, while we know what Gwydion's devious intention is in each case, we do not hear the stories he tells on these occasions of performance.

The second time Gwydion performs, teaming up with his nephew Lleu as his sidekick, his plan is to make a future narrative about the younger man possible, by trapping Aranrhod into giving her offspring (the seeming product of parthenogenesis whom Aranrhod is too embarrassed to acknowledge as her child) that which he needs in order to acquire and maintain a heroic reputation: arms. The storytelling, in effect 'weaponized' by Gwydion, creates a situation in which it becomes possible for him to override the wrathful Aranrhod's earlier declaration that Lleu would never receive the gear that any self-respecting warrior-hero would need for his unfolding story to conform to traditional expectations about such characters. The mission proves successful, after Aranrhod supplies the *incognito* Lleu with weapons, just as in an earlier episode she had unwittingly given him a memorable name, despite her having put a curse upon him to remain nameless. To provide the third *sine qua non* of which Aranrhod's powerful words had seemingly deprived the hero-under-construction, Gwydion turns to his king and fellow magician Math to help create a wife for Lleu out of flowers (since his mother had with her three-part curse put human wives beyond his reach).

Gwydion's work completed, Lleu's wondrously fashioned bride Blodeuedd should have been a trophy of his having, heroically speaking, 'arrived', but instead she deceitfully lures her husband, a Samson to her Delilah, into revealing the plot of a story that should have been suppressed: namely, the convoluted recipe for how Lleu, clearly a supernatural and seemingly invulnerable being, may be slain. Subsequently, the cat having been let out of the bag, Lleu is slain by Blodeuedd's lover, and the story seems permanently derailed from its expected course. Gwydion, however, intervenes decisively once again and saves the day, as well as our narrative expectations. In this, the concluding Branch, we see that a storyteller as proficient as Gwydion in his craft or avocation can subvert the truth as much as uphold it, just as Gwydion's making an 'artificial' wife threatens to make a treacherous artifice out of the institution of marriage itself, and to destroy the bridegroom for whom the bride was intended. So too, 'life', the framing narrative

---

[28] *The Mabinogion*, trans. by Davies, pp. 48, 57.

of the Fourth Branch, follows the pattern set by 'myth', the framed narrative, at its own peril. As marvelous, precious, and entertaining as it is, storytelling within a story, especially of the deceitful or treacherously provoked kind, can send the frame tale careening off into uncharted territory.

* * *

Commonly, 'mythography' refers to the writing down of purportedly old stories that tell of gods and heroes, origins and creations, the order of things and their ultimate destinies. Perhaps these medieval Celtic examples of the long-lived and widespread practice of mythography as sampled in this collection of studies provide us with a new (or is it old?) way of defining the stories this practice strives to preserve, enshrine, and display. They are tales that, like specimens of rare value, require protective insulation, an embedding that affords some distance between the world in which these stories play out and the world of the consumers for whom the written text is manufactured. Yet these (let us call them) 'myths', as fragile, fragmentary, and in need of protection as they might seem, are stories that refuse to stay within the 'quaint' frame in which the mythographer presents them. Indeed, their relevance sometimes reaches into or even beyond the milieu encompassing the author and audience of the myth-encasing text.

A mythographic work, such as the many examples featured in the following studies, typically has its own controlling (hi)story into which its author undertakes to set the narrative gems he has chosen, and from which it is meant for the latter to acquire additional layers of meaning. There is, however, always the danger that, rebelliously resisting the frame, the embedded narratives, albeit obscure or fragmentary, redirect the master narrative or wear down its original agenda, just as the mysterious narrative subtext at work in the *Mabinogi* succeeds in eliminating virtually the entire cast of characters by the end of the Third Branch, temporarily replacing the people of the realm with a ravenous horde of mice. Not just in the cases of *Cath Maige Tuired* and the *Mabinogi* do myths, the stories told within a story, escape from confinement, open up the text like the jar associated with Pandora in Greek myth, or the chest in which Lleu is originally hidden after he is born,[29] and give licence to the users of the mythographic text to think of and with these stories 'outside the box'. May the readers of *Writing Down the Myths*, as they encounter stories and texts from a wide variety of sources, traditions, and cultures, experience this liberating effect.

---

[29] On the various appearances of this particular motif in medieval Welsh literature, see Jones, 'Boys in Boxes', pp. 216–25.

Works Cited

Primary Sources

Cath Maige Tuired: The Second Battle of Mag Tuired, ed. and trans. by Elizabeth A. Gray, Irish Texts Society, 52 (Naas: Irish Texts Society, 1982)

Cath Muighe Tuireadh: The Second Battle of Magh Tuireadh, ed. by Brian Ó Cuív (Dublin: Dublin Institute for Advanced Studies, 1945)

Lebor Gabála Érenn: The Book of the Taking of Ireland. Part IV, ed. and trans. by R. A. Stewart Macalister, Irish Texts Society, 41 (Dublin: Irish Texts Society, 1941)

The Mabinogi and Other Medieval Welsh Tales, ed. and trans. by Patrick K. Ford (Berkeley: University of California Press, 1977)

The Mabinogi: Legend and Landscape of Wales, trans. by John Bollard, photography by Anthony Griffiths (Llandysul: Gomer, 2006)

The Mabinogion, trans. by Sioned Davies (Oxford: Oxford University Press, 2007)

Stories from Keating's History of Ireland, ed. by Osborn Bergin, 3rd edn (Dublin: Royal Irish Academy, 1930)

Tales of the Elders of Ireland, trans. by Ann Dooley and Harry Roe (Oxford: Oxford University Press, 1999)

Secondary Studies

Blustein, Rebecca, 'Poets and Pillars in Cath Maige Tuired', in *Myth in Celtic Literatures*, ed. by Joseph Falaky Nagy, Celtic Studies Association of North America Yearbook, 6 (Dublin: Four Courts, 2007), pp. 22–38

Breatnach, Caoimhín, '*Oidheadh Chloinne Tuireann* agus *Cath Maige Tuired*: dhá shampla de mhiotas eiseamláireach', *Éigse*, 32 (2000), 35–46

Carey, John, 'Myth and Mythography in *Cath Maige Tuired*', *Studia Celtica*, 24–25 (1989–1990), 53–69

Davies, Sioned, '"He was the best teller of tales in the world": Performing Medieval Welsh Narrative', in *Performing Medieval Narrative*, ed. by Evelyn Birge Vitz, Nancy Freeman Regalado, and Marilyn Lawrence (Cambridge: Brewer, 2005), pp. 15–26

—— , 'Storytelling in Medieval Wales', *Oral Tradition*, 7 (1992), 231–57

Gray, Elizabeth A., 'Cath Maige Tuired: Myth and Structure (1–24)', *Éigse*, 18 (1981), 183–209

—— , 'Cath Maige Tuired: Myth and Structure (24–120)', *Éigse*, 19 (1982), 1–35

—— , 'Cath Maige Tuired: Myth and Structure (84–93, 120–67)', *Éigse*, 19 (1983), 230–62

Haycock, Marged, '*Sy abl fodd, Sibli fain*: Sibyl in Medieval Wales', in *Heroic Poets and Poetic Heroes in Celtic Tradition: A Festschrift for Patrick K. Ford*, ed. by Joseph Falaky Nagy and Leslie Ellen Jones, Celtic Studies Association of North America Yearbook, 3–4 (Dublin: Four Courts, 2005), pp. 115–30

Hemming, Jessica, 'Reflections on Rhiannon and the Horse Episodes in "Pwyll"', *Western Folklore*, 57 (1998), 19–40

Jones, Leslie Ellen, 'Boys in Boxes: The Recipe for a Welsh Hero', in *Heroic Poets and Poetic Heroes in Celtic Tradition: A Festschrift for Patrick K. Ford*, ed. by Joseph Falaky Nagy and Leslie Ellen Jones, Celtic Studies Association of North America Yearbook, 3–4 (Dublin: Four Courts, 2005), pp. 207–25

MacQuarrie, Charles, 'Recognizing Gods in Guises: Identity, Performance, and Performative Reading in O'Donnell's *Kern*', in *Narrative in Celtic Tradition: Essays in Honor of Edgar M. Slotkin*, ed. by Joseph F. Eska, Celtic Studies Association of North America Yearbook, 8–9 (Hamilton: Colgate University Press, 2011), pp. 147–56

McCone, Kim, 'A Tale of Two Ditties: Poet and Satirist in *Cath Maige Tuired*', in *Sages, Saints and Storytellers: Celtic Studies in Honour of Professor James Carney*, ed. by Donnchadh Ó Corráin, Liam Breatnach, and Kim McCone, Maynooth Monographs, 2 (Maynooth: An Sagart, 1989), pp. 122–43

McTurk, Rory, *Chaucer and the Norse and Celtic Worlds* (Aldershot: Ashgate, 2005)

Murphy, Gerard, 'Notes on *Cath Maige Tuired*', *Éigse*, 7 (1953–55), 191–98, 204

Ó Cathasaigh, Tomás, '*Cath Maige Tuired* as Exemplary Myth', in *Folia Gadelica: Aistí ó iardhaltaí leis a bronnadh ar R. A. Breatnach, M.A., M.R.I.A. i ndeireadh a théarma mar Ollamh le Teanga agus Litríocht na Gaeilge i gColáiste Ollscoile Chorcaí*, ed. by Pádraig de Brún, Seán Ó Coileáin, and Pádraig Ó Riain (Cork: Cork University Press, 1983), pp. 1–19

Parsons, Geraldine, 'The Structure of *Acallam na Senórach*', *Cambrian Medieval Celtic Studies*, 55 (2008), 11–39

Radner, Joan N., 'The Combat of Lug and Balor: Discourses of Power in Irish Myth and Folktale', *Oral Tradition*, 7 (1992), 143–49

Royal Irish Academy, ed., *Dictionary of the Irish Language: Based Mainly on Old and Middle Irish Materials*, compact edn (Dublin: Royal Irish Academy, 1983)

Sayers, William, 'Bargaining for the Life of Bres in Cath Maige Tuired', *Bulletin of the Board of Celtic Studies*, 34 (1987), 26–40

Thompson, Stith, *Motif-Index of Folk-Literature: A Classification of Narrative Elements in Folktales, Ballads, Myths, Fables, Mediaeval Romances, Exempla, Fabliaux, Jest-Books and Local Legends*, 2nd edn, 6 vols (Bloomington: Indiana University Press, 1955–58)

Packaging Greek Mythology

William Hansen*

W hat is Greek mythology? The real Greek mythology consisted of traditional, mostly oral stories about supernatural beings and mortals that circulated among ancient speakers of the Greek language. The narratives constituted a sort of system, the individual stories being linked with one another by the genealogical ties of their characters, by chronology, and by a backdrop of familiar landscapes and conventional fantasy-lands; but the system was a loose one, for the stories were also characterized by inconsistency, redundancy, and other kinds of messiness. Since narratives were constantly being added, dropped, and reshaped, the system was also in a constant state of change. And it was large. Like the animal a thousand miles long imagined by Aristotle in his *Poetics*, a creature so great that no human being could take it all in at one time, Greek mythology was too immense to be apprehended in its fullness by any single mind.[1]

But something so large and unwieldy is not what comes to mind when most people think of Greek mythology. For them, Greek mythology is a fixed corpus of stories about gods, monsters, and heroes that can be accommodated comfortably within the compass of a single printed volume. The persons responsible for this transformation are the mythographers, who in the course of selecting and retelling Greek mythological stories have converted the real Greek mythology from a huge and slippery mass fantasy into a manageable corpus of unchanging stories, the Greek mythology of the handbooks. Greek, and subsequently classi-

* William Hansen (hansen@indiana.edu) is Professor Emeritus of Classical Studies and Folklore at Indiana University, the author of *Classical Mythology: A Guide to the Mythical World of the Greeks and Romans* (Oxford: Oxford University Press, 2005), and is a specialist in the folklore of the classical world.

[1] Aristotle, *Poetics*, VII. 1451a.

Writing Down the Myths, ed. by Joseph Falaky Nagy, CURSOR 17, (Turnhout: Brepols, 2013)
pp. 19–43   BREPOLS ❦ PUBLISHERS   10.1484/M.CURSOR-EB.1. 100845

cal, mythography flourished throughout the classical, Hellenistic, and imperial periods, continued into Late Antiquity, the Middle Ages, and the Renaissance, and thrives today.[2]

In the present essay I wish to look at American and British mythographers of the past two centuries and consider what they actually do when they go about their work. I focus on popular mythography because most persons get their mythology from popular and semi-popular presentations.

The Myth of Pandora

I take as a sample myth the well-known narrative of the first woman, Pandora, because the story is likely to be included in every compilation of Greek mythology and because, as we shall see, it offers mythographers some challenges. The Pandora story is part of a larger myth that represents the creation of the first human beings as taking place in two stages. Males are created first (the surviving sources do not tell how), and females, led by Pandora, come into being later. In this myth women are not part of the original divine plan, such as it may have been.

In the larger myth, then, the primordial human community consists only of men. Gods and men constitute two different groups, but they share a life of ease and abundance and appear to have a neighbourly relationship. This happy condition changes after gods and men convene in order to decide how meat shall be distributed between the two groups. Prometheus slaughters an ox and tricks the Olympian gods into choosing the less-desirable parts of the animal, which thereby become forever the gods' portion. In his anger at this deception and loss, Zeus withdraws from the soil its *bios*, or 'life', its vital energy, which previously allowed the earth to produce abundant crops of food with little effort on the part of men. Now men will have to work hard to extract their food from the soil. In addition, Zeus withdraws (or withholds) fire from men. Although men have the better portion of meat, they will not be able to cook it. At this juncture Prometheus steals fire from the gods and gives it to mankind. Zeus, now doubly enraged, punishes Prometheus by having him bound to a mountain, and punishes mortal men by introducing into their community the first woman, the prototype of human females. These are the events that lead into the Pandora myth.

---

[2] For texts and testimonia of the early mythographers see *Early Greek Mythography*, ed. by Fowler. The term 'mythography' (*mythographia*) is not attested until Strabo, *Geography* (I. 2. 35, VIII. 3. 9); see *Early Greek Mythography*, ed. by Fowler, p. xxvii.

The two principal texts of the myth in ancient Greek sources appear in works composed by the poet Hesiod, who flourished around 700 BC.[3] The content of the two texts differs somewhat, since the concern that calls forth each telling is different and the narrator slants his narration to his theme.

Here, from Hesiod's *Theogony*, is Version One (as we can call it), beginning with the creation of Pandora.[4] Words in brackets are probably interpolations; words in parentheses are my own, added for clarification.

> 570 In exchange for fire, he (Zeus) quickly made an evil for humans.
> For the famous Lame One (Hephaistos) made from earth the likeness
> of a modest virgin by the plans of Kronos' son (Zeus).
> Owl-eyed Athena girded her and adorned her
> in silvery clothes; she drew down with her hands a
> 575 decorated veil over her head, marvelous to see;
> [and Pallas Athena put around her head
> lovely, fresh-budding garlands, the flowers of a meadow],
> and she placed upon her head a golden headband,
> which the famous Lame One (Hephaistos) himself had made,
> 580 working it with his hands to please father Zeus.
> On it were wrought many designs, marvelous to see.
> Of all the dread beasts the land and sea nourish,
> he included most, amazing, like living
> animals with voices; and charm breathed over them all.
> 585 But when he had made the lovely evil in exchange for the good thing (fire),
> he led her out to where the other gods and men were.
> She delighted in the adornment from the great father's
> owl-eyed daughter (Athena); awe filled immortal gods and mortal men
> when they saw the sheer deception, irresistible for human beings.
> 590 For from her is the stock of female women,
> [from her is the deadly stock and tribes of women]
> a great woe to mortals, dwelling with men,
> companions not of baneful poverty but of luxury.

In this version Zeus orders the creation of the first human maiden. Two deities discharge the task, Hephaistos fashioning her from earth and Athena attiring and ornamenting her. Hephaistos then leads her to the assembled gods and men, who are awestruck.

---

[3] For a convenient overview of the ancient, medieval, and Renaissance sources, see Panofsky and Panofsky, *Pandora's Box*, pp. 3–13.

[4] Hesiod, *Theogony*, ll. 570–593. The translation is mine. The standard commentary is Hesiod, *Theogony*, ed. by West, pp. 325–31.

In another poem, the *Works and Days*, Hesiod recounts the myth differently and at greater length.[5] Here is Version Two.

> Cloud-gatherer Zeus was angered and said to him,
> 'Son of Iapetos (Prometheus), knowing counsels beyond all others,
> 55   you rejoice, having stolen fire and deceived my mind —
> a great woe to you yourself and to human beings hereafter.
> In exchange for fire I will give them an evil, for all
> to enjoy in their heart, as they embrace their own evil.'
> So he spoke, and the father of men and gods laughed.
> 60   He ordered famous Hephaistos as swiftly as possible
> to mix earth with water, and to put in a human voice
> and strength, to make it like immortal goddesses in face,
> a beautiful, lovely maiden's image; and Athena
> to teach her crafts, to weave the intricate web;
> 65   and golden Aphrodite to pour charm over her head
> and painful longing and limb-consuming cares;
> and he ordered the messenger Hermes Argeiphontes
> to put in her a dog's mind and deceitful behaviour.
> So he spoke, and they obeyed lord Zeus, Kronos' son.
> 70   Immediately the famous Lame One (Hephaistos) formed from earth
> the likeness of a modest virgin by the plans of Kronos' son (Zeus);
> owl-eyed Athena girded her and adorned her;
> the divine Graces and mistress Persuasion put
> golden necklaces on her skin, and on her head the
> 75   lovely-haired Hours put a garland of spring flowers;
> and Pallas Athena arranged each adornment on her skin.
> And in her chest the messenger Argeiphontes (Hermes)
> wrought lies and sly stories and deceitful behaviour
> by the plans of deep-sounding Zeus; the herald
> 80   of the gods put in a voice, and named this woman
> Pandora (All-Gifts), since all who have Olympian homes
> had given her a gift, a woe to barley-consuming men.

Next, the gods induce a member of the community of men to accept their new creation.

> And when he had finished the sheer irresistible deception,
> the father sent famed Argeiphontes (Hermes), swift messenger of the gods,
> 85   to take the gift to Epimetheus; and Epimetheus

---

[5] Hesiod, *Works and Days*, ll. 53–105. Basic commentaries include Hesiod, *Works and Days*, ed. by West, pp. 155–72, and Verdenius, *A Commentary on Hesiod*, pp. 46–75.

did not think about how Prometheus had told him
never to accept a gift from Olympian Zeus, but to send it
back, lest it turn out to be some evil for mortals.
But he accepted it and perceived the evil only when he had it.

Finally, we learn the implications.

90   For earlier the tribes of humans used to live on the earth
apart from and without evils and without toil
and harsh diseases, which bring death to men.
[For mortals straightaway grow old in misery.]
But the woman removed with her hands the great lid of the storage jar,
95   and scattered these; she devised sad cares for humans.
Hope alone, there in the unbreakable home,
remained within, under the rim of the storage jar, and did not
fly out; for before this she replaced the lid of the storage jar
by the plans of aegis-holder, cloud-gatherer Zeus.
100   But the rest, uncounted miseries, wander among humans;
the earth is full of evils, the sea is full.
By day and by night diseases of their own accord
visit humans, bringing evils to mortals in
silence, since crafty Zeus took away their voice.
105   So there is no way at all to evade the mind of Zeus.

In this text Hesiod tells how, on the orders of Zeus, a group of deities creates the first woman, Pandora. Hermes takes this maiden to the community of men, offering her to Prometheus's foolish brother Epimetheus, who accepts her. Pandora takes the lid off a large jar, and out of it fly the spirits of diseases, which now populate the earth bringing misery and death to humans. Hesiod says nothing about where this jar of evils comes from, and he is vague about Pandora's motive for opening it.

The two versions obviously differ. In the latter, the *Works and Days*, Hesiod focuses upon the quality of the human condition: why life is so hard, why misery is inescapable. In this telling of the myth the emphasis is on the jar that Pandora opens and the evils that escape from it to change the quality of human life permanently and irreversibly for the worse. In the former, the *Theogony*, Hesiod recounts the myth otherwise. There is no foolish Epimetheus who accepts Pandora as his wife, and there is no jar of evils. The concern of the poem is not the quality of human life but the origin and nature of the individual elements that make up the world — the sky, the gods, human females, and so on. Here the narrator is concerned to say how women came to be part of the world, and what they are like.

So we have the myth of Pandora in two forms, a version in which the emphasis is on the first woman herself as evil and a version in which the emphasis is on a jar of evils. The two versions are impossible to reconcile.[6] The first woman is created either by a pair of gods or by a large committee of gods. Once created, she is brought either to an assembly of gods and mortal men or to Epimetheus alone. Then either she opens a jar or she does not. That is, either the new misery that is introduced into the primordial, all-male community of mortals is the maiden herself, the prototype of mortal women, the spoiler of men's paradise, or the new misery is the contents of the jar. You can combine the two versions, but all you get is a third version, one that may never have existed in ancient Greece. Since the telling of a traditional oral story answers to a specific occasion, the one that called it forth, there is no neutral, or default, version.

Bulfinch's 'Age of Fable'

During the nineteenth century the best-known and most influential handbook of Greek mythology in the English language was *Bulfinch's Mythology*. Written by the well-educated Boston bank-clerk Thomas Bulfinch and published in 1855 under the title *The Age of Fable; or, Stories of Gods and Heroes*, it became an American best-seller as well as a classic of popular scholarship.[7] You can still buy the book today; indeed, it has probably not been out of print since the day it was published.

After relating how Prometheus fashions the first man, Bulfinch continues as follows:

> Woman was not yet made. The story (absurd enough!) is that Jupiter made her, and sent her to Prometheus and his brother, to punish them for their presumption in stealing fire from heaven; and man, for accepting the gift. The first woman was named Pandora. She was made in heaven, every god contributing something to perfect her. Venus gave her beauty, Mercury persuasion, Apollo music, etc. Thus equipped, she was conveyed to earth, and presented to Epimetheus, who gladly

---

[6] Jensen, 'Fjendtlige guder', p. 314 and n. 8; and Hansen, 'Reading Embedded Narration', pp. 117–18.

[7] On the life and work of Thomas Bulfinch (1796–1867) see Cleary, *Myths for the Millions*; and for an evaluation see Feldman and Richardson, *The Rise of Modern Mythology*, pp. 505–10. The title by which the book is now familiarly known, *Bulfinch's Mythology*, seems to have been devised by Edward Hale for an edition published in 1881: Bulfinch, *The Age of Fable*, rev. by Hale (Cleary, *Myths for the Millions*, p. 319).

accepted her, though cautioned by his brother to beware of Jupiter and his gifts. Epimetheus had in his house a jar, in which were kept certain noxious articles for which, in fitting man for his new abode, he had had no occasion. Pandora was seized with an eager curiosity to know what this jar contained; and one day she slipped off the cover and looked in. Forthwith there escaped a multitude of plagues for hapless man, — such as gout, rheumatism, and colic for his body, and envy, spite, and revenge for his mind, — and scattered themselves far and wide. Pandora hastened to replace the lid! but, alas! the whole contents of the jar had escaped, one thing only excepted, which lay at the bottom, and that was *hope*. So we see at this day, whatever evils are abroad, hope never entirely leaves us; and while we have *that*, no amount of other ills can make us completely wretched.[8]

In retelling the story, what does Bulfinch do? First of all, proceeding from his Christian perspective, he condemns the myth of Pandora as being absurd. Bulfinch implies a contrast with the Hebrew myth of Eve, although, as it happens, with little justification, since the Hebrew myth of the first woman is not greatly different from the Greek myth of the first woman.[9] Each is a misogynistic story in which man is represented as primary and woman comes along later, only to ruin man's primordial paradise.

Confronting the problem of their being two versions of the Hesiodic myth, Bulfinch implicitly opts for Version Two, that in which the jar appears. In a nod to the conventions of the day and to his own Latin schooling, the mythographer converts the names of the Greek gods to their Roman counterparts.

As he recounts this version, Bulfinch casually adds a detail of his own here and there. Thus he says that Apollo gave music to Pandora, whereas the original Greek version does not mention Apollo at all. He supplies the mysterious jar of evils with a prehistory, explaining that it was something that Epimetheus kept in his house but had no particular use for. Carrying on, Bulfinch gives Pandora a motive for opening it: she takes the lid off of the jar because of her 'eager curiosity'. That is, Bulfinch's Pandora is a weak-willed and foolish woman, for there is not a word about curiosity, let alone eager curiosity, in Hesiod's text. Next, the

---

[8] Bulfinch, *Bulfinch's Mythology*, pp. 16–17. Bulfinch goes on to give the myth of Pandora in a different and happier form ('Another story is that [...]'), but this narrative appears to be Bulfinch's free rewriting of an Aesopic fable (*Babrius and Phaedrus*, ed. and trans. by Perry, nr 58, pp. 74–75) whose main character in the original is not Pandora but an anonymous and genderless 'human being' (*anthropos*). There is, however, an epigram by Macedonius the Consul in the so-called *Greek Anthology*, x. 71, that alludes to a version of the story in which Pandora releases good things rather than bad (see *The Greek Anthology*, ed. and trans. by Paton, IV, 40–41).

[9] The comparison of Pandora and Eve was often made by the Fathers of the Church; see Panofsky and Panofsky, *Pandora's Box*, pp. 11–13.

modern narrator elaborates upon the evils that escape from the jar, taming down the original miseries, since for Hesiod the evils include fatal diseases. Death was not part of the original community of happy men; now it is. Bulfinch concludes by making explicit the implications of Hope's being trapped in the jar, ending his myth on a happy note rather than with the curmudgeonly pessimism of Hesiod.

Edith Hamilton's 'Mythology'

In the century following Bulfinch the two best known and most widely-read handbooks of Greek mythology in English were Edith Hamilton's *Mythology* and Robert Graves's *The Greek Myths*.[10] Hamilton, headmistress of the Bryn Mawr Preparatory School in Baltimore, Maryland, began her writing career after she retired from education. Her *Mythology* came out in 1942 and, like Bulfinch's *Age of Fable*, is a work that, once it was published, has probably never gone out of print.

Hamilton explains that the Greeks had more than one mythic account of how mankind was created. According to one myth, Prometheus fashions them, and according to another the gods create them, beginning with the men of the Golden Age. But then Prometheus angers Zeus. Hamilton continues:

> The father of Men and of Gods was not one to put up with this sort of treatment. He swore to be revenged, on mankind first and then on mankind's friend. He made a great evil for men, a sweet and lovely thing to look upon, in the likeness of a shy maiden, and all the gods gave her gifts, silvery raiment and a broidered veil, a wonder to behold, and bright garlands of blooming flowers and a crown of gold — great beauty shone out from it. Because of what they gave her they called her *Pandora*, which means 'the gift of all'. When this beautiful disaster had been made, Zeus brought her out and wonder took hold of gods and men when they beheld her. From her, the first woman, comes the race of women, who are an evil to men, with a nature to do evil.

> Another story about Pandora is that the source of all misfortune was not her wicked nature, but only her curiosity. The gods presented her with a box into which each had put something harmful, and forbade her ever to open it. Then they sent her to Epimetheus, who took her gladly although Prometheus had warned him never to accept anything from Zeus. He took her, and afterward when that dangerous thing, a woman, was his, he understood how good his brother's advice had been. For Pandora, like all women, was possessed of a lively curiosity. She *had* to know what was in the box. One day she lifted the lid — and out flew plagues innumerable,

---

[10] On the life and work of Edith Hamilton (1867–1963) see Reid, *Edith Hamilton* and Hallett, 'Edith Hamilton'.

sorrow and mischief for mankind. In terror Pandora clapped the lid down, but too late. One good thing, however, was there — Hope. It was the only good the casket had held among the many evils, and it remains to this day mankind's sole comfort in misfortune. So mortals learned that it is not possible to get the better of Zeus or ever deceive him.[11]

Unlike Bulfinch, Hamilton attempts to distinguish the two ancient versions of the Pandora myth, the maiden of evil and the jar of evils, and mostly succeeds in doing so, except that Hamilton's Pandora opens not a jar but a box. But, after all, isn't our proverbial expression 'Pandora's box'? Indeed it is, but we say 'Pandora's box' because of the careless narration of another modern mythographer, the Dutch humanist Erasmus of Rotterdam, who in 1508 retold the Pandora myth in Latin, substituting the word *pyxis* (box) for the rather similar word *pithus* (storage jar). The influence of Erasmus was extensive both on other mythographers and on popular speech, so that to this day nearly every European language employs the proverbial expression 'Pandora's box'.[12] In the present case, the familiarity of the proverbial phrase presumably induced Edith Hamilton, perhaps unconsciously, to change Pandora's vessel from Hesiod's jar to Erasmus's box.

Like Bulfinch, Hamilton supplies a back-story for the mysterious vessel, about whose origin Hesiod says nothing at all. For Bulfinch the vessel was something that Pandora's husband Epimetheus kept in his house, and it contained noxious things for which Epimetheus had no use. For Hamilton the gods each placed something harmful into the vessel and presented it to Pandora before she was given to her husband. So the vessel must have originated among the gods.

Further, like Bulfinch, Hamilton provides Pandora with a motive for opening the vessel. Bulfinch mentions her 'eager curiosity'; Hamilton, her 'lively curiosity'. The characterization of Pandora as a pitiful victim of her own curiosity appears not only at the opening of the vessel but also at its closing. Bulfinch's Pandora 'hastened to replace the lid! but, alas!' Hamilton writes: 'In terror Pandora clapped the lid down, but too late'. Hesiod himself treats the matter of motive vaguely. The pertinent line in the *Works and Days* says that 'she devised [ἐμήσατο] sad cares for men', implying that she knew full well what she was doing when she lifted the lid of the jar; for the verb μήδομαι denotes agency and usually implies intent.[13] But even if one renders the verb more blandly as 'she wrought', as some scholars

---

[11] Hamilton, *Mythology*, pp. 70–72.

[12] Harrison, 'Pandora's Box', pp. 99–101; and Panofsky and Panofsky, *Pandora's Box*, pp. 14–26.

[13] Hesiod, *Works and Days*, l. 95.

do, the fact remains that Hesiod's Pandora is not *manifestly* a weak-willed woman overcome by curiosity.[14] On the contrary, for Hesiod women are sly, treacherous, and untrustworthy.[15]

In addition to providing a prehistory for the vessel and a motive for Pandora, Hamilton sharpens the tension of the narrative by inserting a prohibition against the opening of the vessel, saying that the gods forbade Pandora ever to open it. The narrative function of the tabu is to pique Pandora's curiosity, but it also serves to convert Hesiod's strong Pandora into a weak Pandora, for it places her in a position like that of a child, someone for whom others make domestic rules.

Finally, both Bulfinch and Hamilton introduce changes of detail here and there. Bulfinch has Apollo give Pandora a musical education, and Hamilton converts her jar of evils to a box.

Robert Graves's 'Greek Myths'

The other twentieth-century handbook of Greek mythology that has achieved the status of a standard is *The Greek Myths* by the eccentric poet, novelist, translator, and scholar Robert Graves. Commissioned by E. V. Rieu for Penguin Books, it appeared in 1955 and, like Bulfinch's and Hamilton's books, became a huge success that has gone through countless editions.[16]

Graves, like Hamilton, gives the myth of Prometheus's creation of man and the Myth of the Ages as alternative myths of the origin of man. Rather later in his presentation he brings in the story of Pandora.

> Zeus swore revenge. He ordered Hephaistos to make a clay woman, and the four Winds to breathe life into her, and all the goddesses of Olympos to adorn her. This woman, Pandora, the most beautiful ever created, Zeus sent as a gift to Epimetheus, under Hermes's escort. But Epimetheus, having been warned by his brother to accept no gift from Zeus, respectfully excused himself.

After describing how Zeus punishes Prometheus, Graves continues.

---

[14] Scholars are divided on the question of Pandora's motive: Is her act malicious? Is she overcome by curiosity? See for example Hesiod, *Works and Days*, ed. by West, pp. 168–69; Verdenius, *A Commentary on Hesiod*, p. 65; and Lyons, 'The Scandal of Women's Ritual', pp. 46–47. Since Hesiod himself does not say, all modern attributions of motive are conjectural.

[15] Hesiod, *Works and Days*, ll. 67–68, 77–79, 373–75.

[16] For a glimpse into Graves's workshop see Lowe, 'Killing the Graves Myth'.

Epimetheus, alarmed by his brother's fate, hastened to marry Pandora, whom Zeus had made as foolish, mischievous, and idle as she was beautiful — the first of a long line of such women. Presently she opened a box, which Prometheus had warned Epimetheus to keep closed, and in which he had been at pains to imprison all the Spites that might plague mankind, such as Old Age, Labor, Sickness, Insanity, Vice, and Passion. Out these flew in a cloud, stung Epimetheus and Pandora in every part of their bodies, and then attacked the race of mortals. Delusive Hope, however, whom Prometheus had also shut in the box, discouraged them by her lies from a general suicide.[17]

So Graves joins his predecessors in adding a back-story for the vessel (Prometheus imprisoned in it all the evils that might plague mankind), a prohibition (Prometheus instructed Epimetheus not to open it), and a characterization of Pandora. She is, Graves declares, 'foolish, mischievous, and idle'.

Like his predecessors, moreover, Graves silently introduces changes of detail here and there as it suits him, such as that the Four Winds breathe life into Pandora, that Epimetheus declines to marry Pandora the first time around, that Pandora's vessel is a box, that the evils therefrom sting everybody like insects,[18] and, strangest of all, that were it not for the spirit of Hope, everyone would have committed suicide.

H. J. Rose's 'Handbook'

Still other authors of mythological handbooks take silent liberties with the ancient myth. I mention only H. J. Rose, author of *A Handbook of Greek Mythology*, a semi-scholarly compendium published in 1929, who writes: 'She had brought

---

[17] Graves, *The Greek Myths*, I, 34–36 (creation of man), pp. 144–45 (Pandora).

[18] The cloud of insects that, according to Graves, flew out of Pandora's box may owe its origin to Graves's memories of his childhood reading of Hawthorne, *A Wonder-Book*, which was first published in 1852. Panofsky and Panofsky, *Pandora's Box*, pp. 110–11, comments that Hawthorne's paraphrase left 'an ineffaceable impression on the minds of countless Anglo-Saxon readers'. According to Hawthorne, Pandora, driven by curiosity, lifts the lid of the box, whereupon 'a sudden swarm of winged creatures' flies out. They sting Epimetheus, who cries out. The 'thunder-cloud' of insects so darkens the room that Pandora can scarcely see. 'But she heard a disagreeable buzzing, as if a great many huge flies, or gigantic mosquitoes, or those insects which we call dor-bugs, and pinching-dogs, were darting about' (Hawthorne, *A Wonder-Book*, pp. 92–93). Insects also appear memorably in the Pandora retelling in a mythological compendium published in 1934 by the British classicist, W. H. D. Rouse: 'In a moment, out flew a swarm of horrid things, looking like bluebottle flies, and beetles, and wasps, fat and black and ugly, buzzing and darting about everywhere' (Rouse, *Gods, Heroes and Men*, p. 20).

Figure 1. The author beside a *pithos*. Author's own.

Figure 2. *Pithoi* in the Minoan palace at Knossos, Crete. Author's own.

with her a jar, containing all manner of evils and diseases.'[19] That is, like Bulfinch, Hamilton, and Graves, Rose offers his own back-story for the mysterious jar of evils, saying, in his case, that Pandora brings it along with her.

Now, although Hesiod himself says nothing of the origin of the jar, I can assure you that Pandora does *not* bring it with her. The Greeks possessed a large vocabulary for different sorts of clay pots, and the kind that Pandora opens is called by Hesiod a *pithos*, which is a very large storage jar.[20] An ordinary *pithos* ranges from four to seven feet in height (Fig. 1). It is used to store such things as oil, wine, or grains in a house or in the cellar of a palace (Fig. 2). Even when it is empty, it is heavy. One does not casually carry it around anymore than one would lug around a heavy chest. Indeed, a *pithos* is so large a vessel that you could live in one, as the Cynic philosopher Diogenes is said to have done,[21] and the dead were sometimes buried in them. The one thing you can say for sure about Pandora's *pithos* is that she will not have carried it along with her.

[19] Rose, *A Handbook of Greek Mythology*, p. 55.

[20] Harrison, 'Pandora's Box', p. 101; Panofsky and Panofsky, *Pandora's Box*, p. 8 n. 10; Cullen and Keller, 'The Greek Pithos through Time'.

[21] Lucian, *How to Write History*, trans. by Kilburn, pp. 4–5 (chap. 3).

Figure 3. Dante Gabriel Rossetti, *Pandora* (1869). Public Domain.

So the popular mythographers face a problem of too little information in the myth of Pandora: where does the vessel of evils come from? what precisely does it contain? why does Pandora open it? Their solution for the most part is to fill in the gaps with their own inventions. For Bulfinch, the vessel is something that Epimetheus has in his house; for Hamilton, the gods present it to Pandora; for Graves, Prometheus imprisons in it all the evils that may plague mankind; and Rose's Pandora brings it with her. Bulfinch, Hamilton, and Graves describe the contents of the vessel variously, Hamilton with restraint, Bulfinch and Graves with considerable invention, although all of them suppress, or do not perceive, the grim Hesiodic detail that the ills that escape from Pandora's jar include fatal diseases, which now introduce death into the world.[22] As for motive, Bulfinch's and Hamilton's Pandora is a victim of her own curiosity, while Graves's Pandora is, somewhat indecisively, 'foolish, mischievous, and idle', suggesting that she acts from folly or maybe malice or maybe boredom.

A Glance at Iconography

From antiquity to the present day the verbal tradition of Greek mythology has been paralleled by an iconic tradition in which visual artists have portrayed different moments in the mythological narratives. Among the favoured scenes of the Pandora myth is the dramatic moment in which she opens the vessel.[23] Here, in a small sampling of the visual tradition, I select three treatments by British and American painters who are contemporaries of Bulfinch, Hamilton, and Graves.

The Pre-Raphaelite artist Dante Gabriel Rossetti portrayed Pandora on several occasions, with relatively minor variations.[24] In them, as in this chalk drawing of 1869, she is a voluptuous *femme fatale* who unconcernedly looks slightly past the viewer as she opens, or is about to open, a splendid box from which a cloud of evil smoke is in the process of escaping (Fig. 3).

Towards the end of the nineteenth century the English painter John William Waterhouse imagines quite a different, weak-willed Pandora. She is shown kneeling on the ground in profile as, overcome by curiosity, she strives to peek into a chest whose lid she is lifting. As in Rossetti's painting, the evils that slowly emerge from the box have the form of smoke or vapour (Fig. 4).

---

[22] Hesiod, *Works and Days*, l. 92.

[23] Panofsky and Panofsky, *Pandora's Box*, pp. 34–113.

[24] See Panofsky and Panofsky, *Pandora's Box*, pp. 108–09, 161–62.

Figure 4.
John William Waterhouse,
Pandora (1896).
Public Domain.

In the next century the illustrator Kelly Freas paints a mischievous Pandora for the cover of a mass-market science-fiction novel, *Pandora's Planet*, published in 1972. His Pandora opens the small box she is holding, and looks directly at the viewer with malicious glee, indicating that she is thoroughly enjoying her role. Ethereal figures surround her that presumably represent the evils she is releasing (Fig. 5).

The paintings of Pandora are not illustrations of the ancient Greek myth so much as they are of the later mythographic tradition — in the case of Freas's painting, an illustration of a modern work of fiction inspired by mythography. The painters show the jar version, treating the container of evils as an attribute of Pandora, and following the tradition initiated by Erasmus they imagine the container as a box. They convert Pandora into a more definite character than Hesiod's, each portrayal implying a particular motive for the opening of the vessel, either malice (Rossetti, Freas) or curiosity (Waterhouse). So the three visual art-

Figure 5. *Pandora's Planet*, cover illustrated by Kelly Freas (Daw, 1972).

ists treat the myth of Pandora as freely as do their literary counterparts Bulfinch, Hamilton, and Graves, and in similar ways.

Myths of the First Humans

Bulfinch, Hamilton, and Graves are, as we have seen, faced not only with too little information but also with too much information. Is the evil given by the Olympian gods to mankind Pandora herself, or is it the ills that reside in the jar she opens? Hamilton elects to give both forms of the story, while Bulfinch and Graves opt without comment for the version with the colourful jar of evils.

The problem of too much information is not, however, limited to the fact that the myth of Pandora is found in more than one version. The real Greek mythology is redundant also in having multiple accounts of the origin of human beings more generally. According to a familiar myth Prometheus forms the first human beings, male and female, out of clay.[25] According to the Pandora myth the original human community consists only of males; females, beginning with Pandora, come along only later. In the Myth of the Ages the gods create first a golden generation of humans, then a silver generation, and so on, in a succession of separate creations. And although popular mythographers are content to pass over them, the real Greek mythology includes also many other anthropogonic myths.[26] The difficulty for the compiler of a handbook is that these myths offer competing accounts of human origins. To take just the best-known myths, either the first man and woman are created at the same time (the one-stage myth of Prometheus), or men are created first and women are created later (the two-stage myth of Pandora), or there is a succession of discrete creations (the four- or five-stage Myth of the Ages).

How do Bulfinch, Hamilton, and Graves handle the fact that Greek myth was awash in anthropogonies? The short answer is that each of them resorts to sleight-of-hand. They impose upon the stories a harmony that the real Greek mythology did not have. Thus Bulfinch writes:

> But a nobler animal was wanted, and Man was made. It is not known whether the creator made him of divine materials, or whether in the earth, so lately separated from heaven, there lurked still some heavenly seeds. Prometheus took some of this

---

[25] Apollodorus, *Library*, I. 7. 1; Pausanias, *The Description of Greece*, x. 4. 4; Ovid, *Metamorphoses*, I. 76–88.

[26] On Greek myths of human origins see in general Guarducci, 'Leggende dell'antica Grecia'.

earth, and kneading it up with water, made man in the image of the gods. He gave him an upright stature, so that while all other animals turn their faces downward, and look to the earth, he raises his to heaven, and gazes on the stars.[27]

Readers surely understand 'Man' here in the gender-neutral sense of 'human' until, a paragraph later, Bulfinch announces that 'Woman was not yet made' and begins his account of the myth of Pandora, at which point it becomes apparent that by 'Man' Bulfinch means rather 'human male'. But this is a falsification of the myth of Prometheus, who fashions the first human *couple* from clay.

Hamilton exploits the same ambiguity in the English language and in the same way. She says that the time for the appearance of mankind came, adding that there was more than one account of how men were created. Either Prometheus and his brother Epimetheus fashioned them or, according to another myth, the gods created them, beginning with the men of the Golden Age.[28] Here too it is reasonable to understand each of these creations as referring to both men and women, but the author presently disabuses us of this interpretation:

> These two stories of the creation, — the story of the five ages, and the story of Prometheus and Epimetheus, — different as they are, agree in one point. For a long time, certainly throughout the happy Golden Age, only men were upon the earth; there were no women.[29]

Hamilton's statement that these narratives concern the genesis only of males entirely misrepresents the ancient myths.

Graves's solution is different but no more honourable. Like Hamilton, he presents the Promethean creation story and the Myth of the Ages (which he mixes with myths of autochthony) as alternatives. When he comes to Pandora, he slyly substitutes one superlative for another ('This woman, Pandora, the most beautiful ever created'), demoting her from first woman to most beautiful woman and thereby sidestepping a conflict between the Pandora story and other myths of human origins.[30]

In sum, Bulfinch, Hamilton, and Graves manifestly wish to include more than one Greek anthropogonic myth, but recognize that to do so would result in an inconsistency in their presentation. They evade this awkwardness by rewriting the ancient myths.

---

[27] Bulfinch, *Bulfinch's Mythology*, p. 16.

[28] Hamilton, *Mythology*, pp. 68–69.

[29] Hamilton, *Mythology*, p. 70.

[30] Graves, *The Greek Myths*, I, 34–36 (creation of man), pp. 144–45 (Pandora).

Ancient Popular Mythographers

Are the popular mythographers of the present day representative of the tradition? Let us compare how ancient popular mythographers handle the Pandora tradition. The two best-known works of prose mythography to survive from classical antiquity are Pseudo-Apollodorus's *Bibliotheke* (or *Library*) and Hyginus's *Fabulae* (or *Traditional Stories*). Although their authorship and dates are uncertain, these handbooks were likely composed in the first or second century AD. Both handbooks have the feel of popular digests.[31]

According to Pseudo-Apollodorus:

> Prometheus fashioned human beings (*anthropous*) out of water and earth, and gave them fire, which unknown to Zeus he had concealed in a stalk of fennel [...]. Prometheus had a son, Deukalion. He reigned in the regions around Phthia and married Pyrrha, the daughter of Epimetheus and Pandora, the first woman fashioned by the gods.[32]

What Pseudo-Apollodorus does is to summarize the Prometheus myth very briefly and then allude to the Pandora myth. Declining to reject one tradition or the other wholly, he acknowledges them both, one after the other: the one-stage tradition according to which a single god Prometheus fashions the first humans, and the two-stage tradition according to which men come into being first and the gods cooperatively create the first woman later. Pseudo-Apollodorus avoids mentioning the part of the Pandora tradition that most obviously conflicts with the Prometheus tradition, namely, the first stage, according to which men exist for a while without women.

As it happens, the Latin mythographer Hyginus handles the myth of human origins in essentially the same way, summarizing the Prometheus version in a single line and following it with an abbreviated account of Pandora. According to him:

> Prometheus was the first to fashion human beings (*homines*) out of clay. Acting on Jupiter's orders Vulcan later shaped from clay a woman, to whom Minerva gave life and the rest of the gods gave other gifts, for which reason they named her Pandora.[33]

---

[31] On the character and nature of the works by Pseudo-Apollodorus and Hyginus see Cameron, *Greek Mythography in the Roman World*.

[32] Apollodorus, *Library*, I. 7. 1–2. My translation.

[33] Hyginus, *Fabulae*, 142. My translation.

Although Pseudo-Apollodorus and Hyginus feature Pandora, they abbreviate her myth almost to the point of non-existence. They make no mention of the jar, which possibly seemed childish to them; indeed, they entirely omit the idea of Zeus's introducing misery into the primordial human community. No woman full of evil, no jar full of evils; just a first woman.

If giving two different anthropogonies one after the other seems like a strange procedure, consider that the editor of the Hebrew book of Genesis adopts precisely the same strategy. Genesis begins with the so-called Priestly document, according to which god, called Elohim, creates humans, both male and female, on the sixth day.[34] The book continues with the J (or JE) document, according to which god, here called Yahweh Elohim, fashions a human male from the soil and blows the breath of life into his nostrils; later, after he has created animals as possible companions for the man, god decides that they will not do, so that he forms a woman, creating her from the man's rib.[35] Here, as in the Greco-Roman mythographers, a one-stage anthropogony in which god fashions the first humans, male and female, at the same time, is followed immediately by a two-stage anthropogony in which the fashioning of the first woman takes place later, not being part of the original divine plan. The Greek Pseudo-Apollodorus, the Roman Hyginus, and the anonymous Hebrew editor agree in giving two versions, one after the other, without either reconciling them or calling the reader's attention to the inconsistency.[36] The practice of ordering competing or variant traditions serially lends perspective to what surely is its most striking ancient expression, the four canonical Gospels, arranged one after the other, in the New Testament, where one might have expected only one such account.[37]

Pseudo-Apollodorus and Hyginus handle Pandora differently from their modern successors but perhaps not more straightforwardly. For them, Pandora has no myth other than to be fashioned by the gods and to marry. She is simply

---

[34] Genesis, 1. 27–28.

[35] Genesis, 2. 7; 2. 20–22.

[36] Notice that in ancient mythography anthropogonies that occur subsequent to the initial appearance of human males and females do not compete with the original one. In the lineages of Inachos and of Agenor human beings simply develop genealogically from the mating of a god and a nymph, the river-god Inachos and the Okeanid Melia in one case, and the god Poseidon and the nymph Libya in the other (Apollodorus, *Library*, II. 1, III. 1). Hyginus tells the story of how, on a particular occasion for a particular need, Jupiter transformed certain ants into human beings (Hyginus, *Fabulae*, 52). The principle of human beings has long been established, so that subsequent subsidiary lines are not of cosmic significance.

[37] See Metzger, *The Canon of the New Testament*, pp. 262–64.

the first woman. They do not acknowledge the mythic tradition of the primordial community of human males, and they do not interest themselves in the mythic origin of human miseries.

Conclusion

Modern popular mythographers, as we have seen, handle the Pandora myth with surprising and unannounced freedom. Doubtless some persons will wish to come to their defence, pointing out that they merely do what the ancients themselves did: innovate on the basis of tradition, treating Greek mythology creatively as an open and living system rather than as a closed one. Since however innovations introduced by modern British and American retellers are neither Greek nor traditional, one cannot justifiably label the resultant narratives as either 'Greek' or 'mythology', so that the modern narratives cannot qualify as Greek mythology, alive and well and adapting to new conditions.

That is not of course to say that writers and artists should not behave as writers and artists. Bulfinch's contemporary Nathaniel Hawthorne, referring to his own handling of classical mythology in his *Wonder-Book for Girls and Boys* (1852), serves his readers clear notice that he does not

> plead guilty to a sacrilege, in having sometimes shaped anew, as his fancy dictated, the forms that have been hallowed by an antiquity of two or three thousand years. No epoch of time can claim a copyright in these immortal fables. They seem never to have been made; and certainly, so long as man exists, they can never perish; but, by their indestructibility itself, they are legitimate subjects for every age to clothe with its own garniture of manners and sentiment and to imbue with its own morality.[38]

As Hawthorne sees the matter, the traditions are neither his nor anyone else's, so that they are fair game for whatever he may wish to do with them. In the same spirit, the painters Rossetti, Waterhouse, and Freas aim, not for faithfulness to a distant tradition, but for artistic effect.

But Bulfinch, Hamilton, and Graves do not frame their works as belletristic in any respect. Rather, in their titles — Bulfinch's *The Age of Fable; or, Stories of Gods and Heroes*; Hamilton's *Mythology*; Graves's *The Greek Myths* — and in their statements of their individual aims they lead their readers to expect, not free treatments, but practical expositions of Greek mythology. Bulfinch says he

---

[38] Hawthorne, *A Wonder-Book*, p. v.

has chosen as his province 'mythology as connected with literature'. Hamilton's aim is 'to keep distinct for the reader the very different writers from whom our knowledge of the myths comes'. And in his introduction Graves speaks of 'true myth' and the 'study of Greek mythology' and states in part that his own 'method has been to assemble in harmonious narrative all the scattered elements of each myth'.[39] These declarations lead the reader to believe that the principal aim of the handbooks is to inform.

Popular mythography, supplemented by the visual arts, brings to ordinary moderns what they commonly think of as Greek mythology. Peering at the tradition from the outside, authors and artists negotiate their own representations of the ancient myths and legends, packaging Greek mythology conveniently in handbooks that are congenial to modern readers and in visual representations that appeal to modern viewers.[40] In the case of Pandora, at least, it would be a stretch to classify the representations — after so much personal, situational, and cultural conditioning — as authentic. As Richard Bentley allegedly remarked about Pope's translation of the *Iliad*, 'It's a very pretty poem, Mr Pope, but you must not call it Homer.' It would be truer to say that the Pandoras of the popular mythographers and the artists represent silent compromises between ancient and modern contexts, between the fantasies of the past and the fantasies of the present.

---

[39] Bulfinch, *Bulfinch's Mythology*, p. 5 (original is italicized); Hamilton, *Mythology*, p. 4; Graves, *The Greek Myths*, I, 10, 11, 22.

[40] I adapt the thought from the introduction to *Apollodorus' 'Library' and Hyginus' 'Fabulae'*, trans. by Smith and Trzaskoma, p. xx.

Works Cited

Primary Sources

Apollodorus: The Library, ed. and trans. by J. G. Frazer, Loeb Classical Library, 2 vols (London: Heinemann, 1921)

Apollodorus' 'Library' and Hyginus' 'Fabulae': Two Handbooks of Greek Mythology, trans. by R. Scott Smith and Stephen M. Trzaskoma (Indianapolis: Hackett, 2007)

Babrius and Phaedrus, ed. and trans. by Ben Edwin Perry, Loeb Classical Library (Cambridge, MA: Harvard University Press, 1965)

Bulfinch, Thomas, *The Age of Fable; or, Beauties of Mythology*, rev. by Edward Everett Hale, 2nd edn (Boston: Tilton, 1881)

——, *The Age of Fable; or, Stories of Gods and Heroes* (Boston: Sanborn, Carter, and Bazin, 1855)

——, *Bulfinch's Mythology: The Age of Fable, the Age of Chivalry, Legends of Charlemagne* (London: Lane, [n.d.])

Early Greek Mythography, I: Text and Introduction, ed. by Robert L. Fowler (Oxford: Oxford University Press, 2000)

The Greek Anthology, ed. and trans. by W. R. Paton, Loeb Classical Library, 5 vols (Cambridge, MA: Harvard University Press, 1916–18)

Hawthorne, Nathaniel, *A Wonder-Book for Girls and Boys* (Boston, MA: Mifflin, 1892)

Hesiod, *Theogony*, ed. with commentary by Martin Litchfield West (Oxford: Clarendon, 1966)

——, *Works and Days*, ed. with commentary by Martin Litchfield West (Oxford: Clarendon, 1978)

Hygini Fabvlae, ed. by H. J. Rose (Leiden: Sijthoff, 1934)

Lucian, *How to Write History*, trans. by K. Kilburn, in *Lucian*, trans. by A. M. Harmon and others, Loeb Classical Library, 8 vols (Cambridge, MA: Harvard University Press, 1913–67), VI (1959), pp. 2–73

Secondary Studies

Anvil, Christopher, *Pandora's Planet* (Garden City: Doubleday, 1972)

Cameron, Alan, *Greek Mythography in the Roman World*, American Classical Studies, 48 (Oxford: Oxford University Press, 2004)

Cleary, Marie Sally, *Myths for the Millions: Thomas Bulfinch, His America, and His Mythology Book*, Kulturtransfer und Geschlechterforschung, 4 (Frankfurt a.M.: Lang, 2007)

Cullen, Tracey, and Donald R. Keller, 'The Greek Pithos through Time: Multiple Functions and Diverse Imagery', in *The Changing Roles of Ceramics in Society: 26,000 B.P. to the Present*, ed. by W. D. Kingery, Ceramics and Civilization, 5 (Westerville: American Ceramic Society, 1990), pp. 183–209

Feldman, Burton, and Robert D. Richardson, *The Rise of Modern Mythology 1680–1860* (Bloomington: Indiana University Press, 1972)

Graves, Robert, *The Greek Myths*, 2 vols (London: Penguin, 1955)

Guarducci, Margherita, 'Leggende dell'antica Grecia relative all'origine dell'umanità e analoghe tradizioni de altri paesi', in *Atti della Reale Accademia Nazionale dei Lincei*, 6th ser., Memorie della classe di scienze morali, storiche e filologiche, 2 (1926), pp. 379–459

Hallett, Judith P., 'Edith Hamilton', *Classical World*, 90 (1996–97), 104–47

Hamilton, Edith, *Mythology: Timeless Tales of Gods and Heroes* (New York: New American Library, [n.d.])

Hansen, William, 'Reading Embedded Narration', in *Myth and Symbol II: Symbolic Phenomena in Ancient Greek Culture,* ed. by Synnøve des Bouvrie, Papers from the Norwegian Institute at Athens, 7 (Bergen: Norwegian Institute at Athens, 2004), pp. 111–21

Harrison, Jane Ellen, 'Pandora's Box', *Journal of Hellenic Studies*, 20 (1900), 99–114

Jensen, Minna Skafte, 'Fjendtlige guder: Hesiods to versioner af Prometheus-historien', in *Gudar på jorden: Festskrift till Lars Lönnroth*, ed. by Stina Hansson and Mats Malm (Stockholm: Symposion, 2000), pp. 311–21

Lowe, Nick, 'Killing the Graves Myth', *Times Literary Supplement,* 20 December 2005, pp. 12–20

Lyons, Deborah, 'The Scandal of Women's Ritual', in *Finding Persephone: Women's Rituals in the Ancient Mediterranean*, ed. by Maryline G. Parca and Angeliki Tzanetou (Bloomington: Indiana University Press, 2007), pp. 29–51

Metzger, Bruce M., *The Canon of the New Testament: Its Origin, Development, and Significance* (Oxford: Oxford University Press, 1987)

Panofsky, Dora, and Irwin Panofsky, *Pandora's Box: The Changing Aspects of a Mythical Symbol*, 2nd edn (New York: Harper and Row, 1965)

Reid, Doris Fielding, *Edith Hamilton: An Intimate Portrait* (New York: Norton, 1967)

Rose, Herbert Jennings, *A Handbook of Greek Mythology, including its Extension to Rome* (New York: Dutton, 1929)

Rouse, William Henry Denham, *Gods, Heroes and Men of Ancient Greece: Mythology's Great Tales of Valor and Romance* (New York: New American Library, 1957)

Verdenius, Willem Jacob, *A Commentary on Hesiod: Works and Days, vv. 1–382* (Leiden: Brill, 1985)

THE 'MYTH BEFORE THE MYTH BEGAN'

Richard Martin[*]

... The clouds preceded us.

There was a muddy centre before we breathed.
There was a myth before the myth began,
venerable and articulate and complete.

From this the poem springs: that we live in a place
that is not our own and, much more, not ourselves
And hard it is in spite of blazoned days.

(Wallace Stevens, *Notes Toward a Supreme Fiction*)[1]

T wo decades ago, a contextual analysis of the Greek noun that gives us
the word 'myth' led me to the claim that it means, in Homeric poetry,
an 'authoritative utterance', and that *muthos* represents a unitary speech-
act term comprising subcategories of rebuke, command, and recollection.[2] This
paper is an attempt to fill out the rest of the story. How does one travel, in terms
of the semantics of *muthos*, from its Homeric meaning to the more familiar
sense in which the word signifies something much more like our 'myth' — an
unverifiable, probably fictional, account of gods and heroes, supernatural beings,
or distant ancestors? Such is the sense that the word seems to bear already in the
fifth century BC, at least in the work of the historian Thucydides, if not that of

* Richard Martin (rpmartin@stanford.edu) is Antony and Isabelle Raubitschek Professor
of Classics at Stanford University, the author of the definitive study of the word *muthos* as used
in Homeric diction, *The Language of Heroes: Speech and Performance in the Iliad* (Ithaca, NY:
Cornell University Press, 1991), and the editor/annotator of *Bulfinch's Mythology* (New York:
Harper Collins, 1991).

[1] Stevens, *Collected Poems*, p. 383.

[2] Martin, *The Language of Heroes*, pp.10–88.

Writing Down the Myths, ed. by Joseph Falaky Nagy, CURSOR 17, (Turnhout: Brepols, 2013)
pp. 45–66   BREPOLS PUBLISHERS   10.1484/M.CURSOR-EB.1. 100846

Pindar and others. While the full story still remains to be told in detail, here is an initial mapping of the territory for such a future project.[3]

The semantic history of the term 'myth' is relevant to the present collective volume for several reasons. Mythography, first of all, does not occur in a vacuum. Whatever the medium — writing, acting, singing, or oral story-telling — those urges that motivate people to gather, fix, record, propagate, and employ mythic stories must be investigated in terms of context and social function. Semantic analysis, in this regard, is nothing less than the investigation of culture, in this case, that of the so-called 'archaic' period (roughly 750–500 BC) in Greek-speaking lands. When recording or transmitting a *muthos*, how did the individual distinguish the relevant piece of lore or verbal art from other utterances, and what was the result, in terms of the development of 'myth' collections?

Second, mythography implies *myths*, plural: telling one tale does not make a mythographer. As it happens — perhaps surprisingly, to those bound up in print culture — circumstances for the accumulation and agglomeration of myths *do* exist *prior* to any writing down of the myths. In other words, there are sociopoetic templates and protocols even in an illiterate culture that shape the recording and selection of myths (and even what to call myths) once that culture turns to the new technology of writing. The gradual transformation of the semantics of *muthos* from the sense of 'authoritative utterance' to 'fiction' should be seen as part of this social process. Essentially, the process illustrates the reinterpretation of an (older) speech-act as a (newly recognized) genre of speaking. But the genre itself — as such things do — gets attached to particular people and situations, determined far in advance of any categorization.

These particularities we can see at work in stylized form already in Homeric epic in the archaic period. But traces of the sociopoetic processes that transform the meaning of *muthos* can still be detected in the writings by and about the first Greek mythographers, those authors of the fifth and fourth centuries BC whose work survives only in fragmentary condition. These men, the earliest of those we know to have been engaged in collecting and collating stories of the past, are usually considered from a retrospective viewpoint grounded in the brilliant 'intellectual revolution' that centred on fifth-century Athens. Thus, they are more often heralded as proto-historians (albeit of a primitive type).[4] But if we choose instead

[3] I am thankful to Joseph Nagy and Kendra Willson for accommodating my slow thought processes, providing in the form of the April 2009 conference at UCLA the ideal venue in which to present ideas that have been simmering for the past twenty years.

[4] For an account of Hellanicus and Hecataeus from this vantage point, see Pearson, *Early Ionian Historians*.

to see them in relation to the eras that precede them, the mythographers turn out to display the habits, motivations, and methods that one sees already in Homeric depiction of myth — or, more specifically, of *muthos*-telling. In short, one can detect a continuity between the dynamics of *muthos*-as-speech act and the eventual, static product, a 'myth' in a book — a familiar modern artefact, but already, an ancient invention.

Let us, then, think first of *muthos* as constituting the 'myth before the myth began'. A *muthos* was 'venerable and articulate and complete' inasmuch as the various speech acts by this term in Homeric poetry seek the tone of authority, are never open-ended, and always have a point. They *aim* for completeness, for a conclusion. It is probable, in fact, that the root underlying the noun form *muthos* is that found in the Greek verb *muô* — meaning 'to close' the eyes or mouth. From the same root we have the words *mystêrion* (mystery) and *mystês* (initiate), in both of which the notions of closure, and of being closed off or excluded, are operative.[5] In *muthos*, in the proposed sense of 'authoritative utterance', one sees a slightly different growth out of the action of 'closure': that found in English 'conclusion' (from Latin *con-claudo*, 'close up') — a speech-act that trumps and prevents further speech-acts.[6]

Now, of the 160 or so speeches designated *muthos* in Homer, about two-thirds seem to have nothing to do with storytelling, and so the *muthos*-to-myth linkage looks at first sight rather unlikely. The regularly employed kernel form of a *muthos* in the *Iliad* or *Odyssey* is a command, of the sort Agamemnon makes to the old priest Chryses at the start of the *Iliad*, ordering him to leave and never come back begging for his daughter in the Achaean camp.[7] 'He enjoined a *krateros muthos* [a hard speech] upon him', which Chryses obeyed'.[8] Out of the larger group of speeches identified by the poet or his characters as *muthos*, however, we can specify a smaller subgroup that one could just as easily translate with 'story' rather than 'speech'. Or more accurately, they can be viewed as speeches with supporting evidence. When Agamemnon tells a disappointed Chryses to go home, he does not have to indulge in details. Agamemnon is commander of Greek forces and holds the rod of power, the *skêptron*; although the priest holds the *skêptron* of Apollo, might beats right in this case. But in other cases, the stylized poetic repre-

---

[5] On these connections see Nagy, *Pindar's Homer*, p. 32.

[6] On the parallel semantics of Latin *concludo* see *Oxford Latin Dictionary*, ed. by Glare, under 1a, 'confine, keep secret' in conjunction with 5b, 'define, state expressly'; and *Dictionnaire étymologique de la langue Latine*, ed. by Ernout and Meillet, pp. 125–26.

[7] Homer, *Iliad*, I. 26–32.

[8] Homer, *Iliad*, I. 25; see also, I. 33.

sentations show that one has to explain *why* he or she has the authority to speak or act in a certain way, including the giving of commands. Thus, 'speech' or 'utterance' segues into 'story', and often leads to a story about the past that shores up one's present positioning in society. Another way of putting this is to say that no *muthos* in the sense of 'story' (straightforward as the tale may seem) ever comes unaccompanied by the force of *muthos* in the sense of authoritative speech-act. Myth-stories *do* something *for* you and against your opponent.

It is interesting, speaking of the *skêptron*, that this material symbol of power in the imaginary world of Homeric poetry has its own relationship to *muthos* meaning command, but also to storytelling. For instance, Odysseus, the good lieutenant for the bad commander Agamemnon, acts as enforcer and sets about beating those who refuse to fall into line after the abortive troop-rousing attempt in Book 11 of the *Iliad*. He tries to get the rank-and-file to listen to their leader. The poet says: 'Whatever man of the common people he found yelling, that man he kept driving with the *skêptron* and kept berating with a *muthos*, saying "strange man [*daimoni*] — sit still and listen to the *muthos* of other people".'[9] A bit earlier in the poem, we had learned that this very sceptre had a back-story of its own. Hephaestus the smith god made it; the first recipient, Zeus, gave it to Hermes. From him it passed to the mortal hero Pelops, who gave it to Atreus, who upon his death left it to Thyestes, from whom Agamemnon got it.[10] In short, when a common grunt gets hit with a stick and an order, there is a story to back this up — if the *skêptron* could talk it could tell quite an authoritative, venerable tale. Surely its owner, Agamemnon, can *recite* the same story, whenever it is called for, but usually he does not have to. Put another way, behind every *muthos*-command is such a latent, explanatory *muthos*-story, detailing why the speaker commands consent. The story, detached from its context, will eventually look and feel, to later Greeks and then to us, like 'myth'. Imagine the 'genealogy' of the sceptre, for instance, removed from the immediate context within which the story clearly undergirds kingly authority: it sounds like an innocuous tale, useful for establishing relative chronology, and the prestige of an artefact, but not much more.

In Homer, these *muthoi* that precede and create the 'myths' are finely articulated, usually long, tales. Their venerable quality comes from being put into the mouths of sage figures like Phoenix, the advisor of Achilles, and Nestor, the preternaturally aged warrior from Pylos. I will touch on two stories by these men, whom I shall name 'sages', then on two stories by warriors. (Of course, Phoenix

---

[9] Homer, *Iliad*, 11. 198–200.

[10] Homer, *Iliad*, 11. 102–08.

and Nestor and almost everyone else in the *Iliad* are warriors as well, but it is their role as sage advisors that becomes foregrounded in the poem.) This rather artificial division of tales by the status of their tellers will function as a heuristic device when we then turn to the corpus of early Greek mythography. What will emerge is in part a tale of continuity, but one with an interesting breakpoint.

* * *

To begin with the ultimate storyteller, Nestor: in Book XI of the *Iliad*, he is in his hut recovering from battle when Patroclus, the companion of Achilles, enters to find out the latest news about who has been wounded. Nestor proceeds to entertain or harangue Patroclus with a speech 150 lines long, in which he recalls in great detail a cattle raid, a reprisal move against the men of Elis, and evidently his first experience of fighting.[11] This is an initiatory tale, the reflection in Greek epic of a sub-genre of 'boyhood deed' stories such as we find incorporated into the Old Irish saga *Táin Bó Cuailnge*.[12] Usually, the *Iliad* chooses to suppress such tales of pre-Trojan War conflict.[13] After describing how he was forced to go to the post-raiding battle on foot, because his father thought him too young to fight in a chariot, Nestor draws the paradigmatic conclusion: *he* fought for his community, but Achilles is refusing to battle for the greater good. Patroclus is expected to relay this story to his companion. And to seal the message, Nestor brings up another recollection: how at the start of the Trojan expedition he and others went to the home of Achilles and Patroclus, and what their respective fathers had said. In other words, Nestor is ventriloquizing — almost morphing into the form of — the young fighters' fathers. Achilles had been told to excel and be superior to others; Patroclus (says Nestor) had been told to act as advisor to Achilles.[14] Nestor's own advice is for Patroclus to recall this function, so that he might beg Achilles to let him wear the hero's armour and enter the fray as a sort of decoy. Of course, this sage advice of Nestor will soon get Patroclus killed.

* * *

[11] For a thematic analysis of the speech, see Martin, 'Wrapping Homer Up'.

[12] On the origins of the Greek tales of raids, see Walcot, 'Cattle Raiding, Herioc Tradition, and Ritual'. For the relationship of Homeric epic to the Irish material, see Melia, 'Some Remarks on the Affinities of Medieval Irish Saga'. On the later development of this subgenre, see Nagy, *The Wisdom of the Outlaw*.

[13] The *Odyssey* does deploy one such story of initiation, to great effect, in the famous flashback concerning how Odysseus acquired his scar: Homer, *Odyssey*, XIX. 392–466.

[14] Homer, *Iliad*, XI. 783–90.

To be as transparent as possible: like many speeches in the *Iliad*, this one is *not* framed with reference to either *muthos* or its contrasting lexical item, *epos* (word). What justifies including Nestor's speech here as *muthos*? The overall typological study of the 160 or so thus designated speeches shows that long recollection, along with commands and flyting (the exchange of blame language) are the speech genres marked by the term.[15] By extension, with attention to its function and similarities to other such utterances that are explicitly marked, we can safely call Nestor's recollection a *muthos*. Supporting this point is the fact that when Nestor himself refers, within the speech, to his earlier attempt to persuade Achilles and Patroclus to join the expedition, he calls that utterance a *muthos*.[16] We can imagine his signature rhetoric as it would have unfolded in that episode, and thereby extend the term he has applied to it to this example of the same rhetorical act.

It may be significant that persuasion in the *Iliad*, even in the form of a *muthos* like Nestor's, so often goes wrong. Very often, persuasive rhetoric half works. I am still not sure what that means.[17] Another example, even more elaborate than Nestor's, is by the sage figure Phoenix, who makes his one and only speaking appearance in Book IX. He fails to get Achilles to agree to re-enter battle, but at least prevents him from storming off in his ship within hours, as he had threatened. Phoenix begins his *muthos* (again not explicitly so designated) with autobiography, as had Nestor — a Faulkneresque tale of sleeping with his father's concubine and having to leave town, then of his service as Achilles' guardian, getting spit up on by the baby hero, and so forth.[18] He turns next to an allegorical paradigm: Achilles should not reject the Achaeans' gifts and entreaties, because Prayers personified (the *Litai*) are daughters of Zeus and deserve honour.[19] Finally, Phoenix brings up a tale not related to his personal biography — the story of Meleager, who hid himself away in anger at his kin during an attack by the Curetes, and, despite the entreaties and promised gifts of his family and his community of Calydon, did not emerge until it was too late. He never got the gifts — re-enter battle now, says Phoenix to Achilles, and *you* at least won't miss getting paid.[20]

---

[15] Details in Martin, *The Language of Heroes*, pp. 45–70.

[16] Homer, *Iliad*, XI. 78.

[17] The Homeric poet's attention to failed rhetoric seems to be of a piece with his concern for differentiation in speech-style, even across ethnicities, on which see Mackie, *Talking Trojan*.

[18] Homer, *Iliad*, IX. 434–95.

[19] Homer, *Iliad*, IX. 502–14.

[20] Homer, *Iliad*, IX. 524–605.

These are examples, then, of tales about the past being recollected by persons at least partly involved, in order to persuade a listener about the right course of action. Phoenix's speech is the more interesting because — like many story-telling events recorded by ethnographers — it is a messy combination of folkloric genres: autobiography, parable, and what actually resembles 'myth' — a story of a hero, Meleager, whom he did not personally know, but whose story has become emblematic of how one should not act.[21] We easily detect the 'myth' within the *muthos* in scenes like this: such a tale, denuded of the surrounding context and its rhetorical framework, could slide without alteration into a handbook of 'Myth'. But what needs stressing is the tale's function as language-in-use: it is not a static set-piece but a constituent of various dynamic speech-acts.[22]

Next to these figures of older men who dispense advice to Achilles, we can place two scenes involving younger warriors. Diomedes in the *Iliad* is explicitly a neophyte, one whom Nestor identifies as not yet having reached the perfection of speaking *muthoi*.[23] In Book Four, Agamemnon picks on him. The troops are preparing for battle. The commander says to the young Diomedes, in winged words 'why are you cowering?'. That was not the way Tydeus acted (Tydeus being the father of Diomedes): Agamemnon proceeds to tell how Tydeus had once visited his own home city, Mycenae 'but I never met him or saw him'. In other words, for Agamemnon this story is already folklore, if not myth. Tydeus, he goes on to say, later went to Thebes, annoying the inhabitants by challenging them all to deeds of strength and winning, thus so enraging the Thebans that they ambushed him on the way home. Tydeus killed forty-nine out of the fifty sent against him. Agamemnon does not elaborate on Tydeus's later career at Thebes — how for instance he was caught gnawing the skull of a dead enemy. But he leaves the sting in Diomedes: such a man was better than you in battle, though you are better at talking. Diomedes does not deign to reply.[24]

The point is that Agamemnon uses a *muthos*/command and a *muthos*/story to back it up in the mode that scholars of Old English and Norse saga call 'flyting' — this is elaborate blame, meant to spur on the addressee to fight.[25] A similar flyting event comes in Book VI when the same Greek Diomedes enters the battle and

---

[21] On the combination of genres marking typical Egyptian epic tale-telling events, for example, see Reynolds, *Heroic Poets, Poetic Heroes*.

[22] An excellent further survey on oral storytelling in Homer, with broader discussion of innovation, and an extended folklore bibliography is Edmunds, 'Myth in Homer'.

[23] Homer, *Iliad*. IX, 55–56.

[24] Homer, *Iliad*. IV, 364–400.

[25] A useful summary is Parks, 'Flyting and Fighting'.

confronts Glaucus, an ally of the Trojans. Diomedes speaks first, asking Glaucus whether he is a god (as he is not supposed to fight divinities). Even a mighty hero of the past, Lycurgus, lost grievously when he tried to fight the divine Dionysus, observes the young Diomedes. He proceeds to tell the tale, in a dozen lines.[26] It sounds like myth, a story of gods and humans in the past, yet it has a context and a point. Even though it is not personal history, it remains highly relevant to the personal situation at hand. (One can, by the way, understand the whole sequence as ironic, basically 'trash-talking' on the part of Diomedes). He ends up saying 'if you are not a god — come and fight, so that you sooner enter the coils of destruction'.[27]

Now the camera shifts to Glaucus, who, instead of being rattled, has his own *muthos* and myth to tell. He traces the lineage of the trickster of Argos, the mortal Sisyphus, and then talks about the grandson of Sisyphus, Bellerophon, the Chimera, and the ancient hero's experience with a seductive woman, the whole tale sounding like it comes from a handbook of mythology. Only at the end of the long story do we learn that Bellerophon is in fact Glaucus's own grandfather.[28] So myth — in the sense of tale-telling about the heroic past — is employed in the service of self-presentation in the heroic present.[29] It is also meant to take the wind out of Diomedes. Remarkably, the Greek has a comeback: he claims that his own grandfather Oineus acted as host for Bellerophon long ago in Argos, for twenty days, and they gave each other gifts. This makes the grandsons guest-friends, too, and therefore they should avoid one another's spear, says Diomedes.[30] The scene can be read as all the more brilliant if it is in fact 'myth' in the later Greek sense of lying fiction, an improvization (unverifiable on the spot by Glaucus) that saves his opponent's skin. Diomedes is the one who, after all, appears to rook Glaucus right after this speech, cornering him into giving up his gold armour in exchange for Diomedes' bronze gear worth slightly more than one-tenth its value.

In sum, the *Iliad* shows us story-telling tied to *muthoi*, whether of long sage recollections that act as paradigms or slightly shorter genealogical tales that function to challenge warriors. A fairly straightforward conclusion about Greek

---

[26] Homer, *Iliad*, vi. 130–41.

[27] Homer, *Iliad*, vi. 142–43.

[28] Homer, *Iliad*, vi. 206.

[29] Note that Glaucus in his tale quotes his father Hippolochus (son of Bellerophon) as having told him to excel and be superior to others (Homer, *Iliad*, vi. 208), exactly the words that Nestor quoted as having been uttered by Peleus to Achilles (Homer, *Iliad*, xi. 784), in a speech where Nestor mythologized his own past by way of offering a paradigm for behaviour.

[30] Homer, *Iliad*, vi. 215–26.

mythography can be made at this juncture. Whether the *Iliad* records conditions in the twelfth, eighth, or sixth centuries BC, or some amalgam thereof, we glimpse a world in which there are living, breathing myth anthologies. Sage-advisor figures must possess a repertoire, based partly on their own experience, but including famous precedents of the past. One story alone does not suffice; persuasion requires versatility and variety. Not surprising, that. But warriors, it emerges, are *also* men of *muthoi*, walking tale anthologies, and they, too, must have a ready stock of stories, at least relating to their own genealogies and their claims to authority. The latter requirement is illustrated most strikingly in the wonderful opening scene of the Old Irish story of Mac Dathó's Pig, in which the awarding of the champion's portion has to wait until every hero has had his say about how his own tribe defeated the others. The talk runs something like this: 'Our people killed your brother.' 'Oh, well I cut off your friend's head.' 'Yes, well I'm the one who cut off your father's hand', says another warrior. 'Forget that — I'm the one who put out your eye with my javelin', and so on until the warrior Conall Cernach arrives, just as another, Cét, is about to carve the animal and award the 'hero's portion':[31]

> 'Get up from the pig now', said Conall. 'But what should bring you to it?' asked Cét. 'It is quite proper', said Conall, 'that you should challenge me! I accept your challenge to single combat, Cét', said Conall. 'I swear what my tribe swears, that since I took a spear in my hand I have not often slept without the head of a Connaughtman under my head, and without having wounded a man every single day and every single night'. 'It is true', said Cét. 'You are a better hero than I am. If Anlúan were in the house he would offer you yet another contest. It is a pity for us that he is not in the house'. 'He is though', said Conall, taking the head of Anlúan from his belt, and throwing it at Cét's breast with such force that a gush of blood burst over his lips. Cét then left the pig, and Conall sat down beside it.[32]

Laconic rhetorical statement is topped with a visceral flourish, the corporal evidence to back up Conall's assertion.

The Greek material is less direct, and its warrior *muthoi* are more prone to cite a more distant past, the deeds of father and grandfathers. But the upshot is the same: fighters need the equivalent of a handbook knowledge of stories, their own and their opponents', to rate as players. Warriors turn out to be as much transmitters of 'myth' as bards and wise men are.

---

[31] The tale is most readily available in *Early Irish Myths and Sagas*, ed. and trans. by Gantz, pp. 180–87; Irish text in *Scéla Mucce Meic Dathó*, ed. by Thurneysen.

[32] Translation from *An Early Irish Reader*, ed. by Chadwick, pp. 22–23.

It is time to turn now from the roots of the mythographic enterprise, as glimpsed in Homeric poetry, to the branches and flowers, appearing in fragmentary writings of the classical period attributed to men collectively known as mythographers. In Greek they are called various things, and since the citations of their words and works are usually in much later authors, it is hard to know what a contemporary term would be to describe them. *Logopoios*, 'account-maker' (as used in Herodotus, *The Persian Wars*, v. 125.1) would probably be the best bet.[33] I pass over with only a sideways glance the all-important sixth century, but it is in that era that the transformation of *muthoi* (in the sense of stylized speech-acts) into 'myths' (in the sense of pure stories of the past) must have gained ground. Marcel Detienne, in *The Creation of Mythology*, would go so far as to suggest that the spread of writing, which enabled the recording and comparison of widely varying versions of what people had previously thought their own true stories, brought about a new semantic development, in which *muthos* came to mean something like our modern 'myth' in its sense of *false* story.[34] But Detienne's analysis has to be revisited, especially since his reading of Pindar's use of *muthos* in his fifth-century victory odes just does not hold up. Pindar, instead, can be seen to use *muthos* as a neutral 'story' or even as in Homer, as an act of speaking. But that is another story.[35] Relevant to Pindar and to the development I have been mentioning is the survival into the fifth century of a genre of speaking based on the advising function of *muthos* that we have seen at work in the *Iliad*. Leslie Kurke usefully lists all the compositions that we know about in which a mythical advisor figure instructed someone.[36] These include the Instructions of Cheiron the Centaur; sayings of Rhadamanthus and Pittheus; and a logos of Nestor to Neoptolemos, composed by the sophist Hippias of Elis.[37] From the perspective of Homeric poetry, this shows a continuity of presentational technique: it is the

[33] On this word and the later *logographos*, see *Early Greek Mythography*, ed. by Fowler, pp. xxiii–ix; Hecataeus, *Fragmenta*, ed. by Nenci, p. xxii; Pearson, *Early Ionian Historians*, pp. 6–9; and Calame, *Mythe et histoire dans l'Antiquité grecque*, pp. 41–45.

[34] Detienne, *The Creation of Mythology*, trans. by Cook. See also Calame, *Mythe et histoire dans l'Antiquité grecque*, pp. 9–18.

[35] The few instances in Pindaric poetry, *pace* Detienne, only acquire the sense of false story by being modified by negative adjectives (for example Pindar, *Olympian Odes*, I. 29: *dedaidalmenoi pseudesi poikilois* — *muthoi*, 'stories elaborately adorned with variegated lies'; see also Pindar, *Nemean Odes*, VII. 24–25). For further detail, see Martin, '*Nemean 7* and Pindaric Hymnologic'. Note that even Aristotle in the fourth century BC can preserve a neutral sense of *muthos* as simply plot or story: Calame, *Mythe et histoire dans l'Antiquité grecque*, pp. 26–28.

[36] Kurke, 'Pindar's Sixth *Pythian*'.

[37] See Plato, *Greater Hippias*, 286a5.

act of speaking, set in a distant past, that authorizes the content of these directive utterances, usually rather bland but useful stuff like 'be good to your friends' and 'respect your parents'. Once again, a medieval Irish parallel comes to mind in the genre of *tecosca* or 'instructions', attributed to various mythic and heroic characters such as Morann.[38]

Given the symbiotic relation of *muthos* to myth, of command, recollecting, and flyting to the deployment of actual 'mythic' stories, already at an early period, can we see any survivals of these contexts of utterances when real mythography — the writing down of stories — actually starts in the late sixth or early fifth century BC? The following investigation involved reading through the authors contained in Robert Fowler's excellent new edition of the mythographers (while feeling very much in need of the promised second volume, containing notes and commentary). Ninety per cent of the citations from the twenty-nine mythographers collected by Fowler are not particularly helpful in answering the question of the continuity of performance or presentation habits. We usually learn, often via later marginal notes to authors like the third century BC poet Apollonius Rhodius, that a certain mythographer had told a different version of some story. Sometimes all we discover is that mythographer *X* had also used the unusual word *Y* in his version of events. That is the nature of the fragmented ancient evidence. But on other occasions we can glean something of the circumstances, methods, motivations, and reception of the mythographers. And when we do, the picture looks remarkably like the Homeric depiction of *muthos*-deployment. That is to say, sages and warriors are the predominant templates, if only metaphorically. Even when writing down myths, from whatever their sources, these authors, almost all prose writers, are working with the problems and urges of the Homeric *muthos* speakers. Here is a brief mythographic dossier that can illustrate the point.

The figure of the sage advisor is represented by at least one fifth-century mythographer, Pherecydes of Athens, who flourished around 465 BC.[39] The Byzantine encyclopedia known as *Suda* 'Fortress' dates from the tenth century AD, but has been shown to contain good information dating back at least to Hellenistic scholars of the third century BC, and earlier to Aristotle.[40] According to the *Suda*, Pherecydes is credited with inventing prose — a new art form, to which the canonical poetic tradition gradually yielded in the course of the fifth

---

[38] See *Audacht Morainn*, ed. by Kelly, and on the parallels with Hesiodic and Homeric embedded passages of the advice genre, see Martin, 'Hesiod, Odysseus, and the Instruction of Princes'.

[39] The most complete study is now Pherecydes, *Testimonianze e frammenti*, ed. by Dolcetti.

[40] *Suidae lexicon*, ed. by Adler.

century.[41] He wrote about Athenian history — which is to say, largely Athenian genealogy — in a book appropriately called *Earth-Born Men*, (as the Athenians considered themselves autochthonous). Like many, he is tied to the transmission of Orphic traditions, which are all-pervasive in the sixth and fifth centuries. But most interesting is the *Suda*'s note that links Pherecydes to a composition in hexameter verse called *Paraineseis*, or 'Advisings'. For this word can describe the sort of speeches made in the *Iliad* by Nestor and Phoenix, as well as the later poetic work attributed to Theognis of Megara in the sixth century.[42] The *hupothêkai* (instructions) and related works surveyed by Kurke are in the same tradition (although she does not mention Pherecydes). In other words, we have a figure writing down the lore of his native city-state, involved in religious or ritual lore (tied to Orpheus) and also penning the sort of *muthoi* one can find in Homer, in the same metre as Homeric verse. Pherecydes of Athens strikes one as being like a verbal equivalent of the so-called 'bilingual' pots, those vases from the early fifth century BC that feature the newer technique of red-figure painting on one side and the older black-figure on the other, sometimes depicting the same mythological scene.[43] I list him as 'sage' because his genre of *parainesis* is that of the advisors we have seen.

Another famous mythographer from about a generation earlier (*c.* 560–480 BC), flourishing around the time of the Persian Wars, is Hecataeus. The historian (and part-time mythographer) Herodotus has something of a competition going with Hecataeus, since he, too, is an Ionian, from Asia Minor, and also travelled to places Hecataeus went. As we see in a passage from Book Two, Herodotus is pleased to take Hecataeus down a notch.[44] When his predecessor went to Egypt, and told the priests he could recite his own genealogy extending back for sixteen generations, they smiled indulgently (so we imagine) as they led him through their own line-up of statues of past eminences, by which they reckoned back twice as long. *Their* lineage did not go back to a god; so how could that of Hecataeus? At least, that seems to be their point. We never learn what Hecataeus responded, but this is a neat example of deflation through multicultural contact. Is the *muthos* cherished by Hecataeus, regarding genealogical self-presentation, a lie? Or just an unfortunate example of Hellenic naiveté?[45] Another signifi-

---

[41] *Suidae lexicon*, ed. by Adler, IV, 713, l. 23 (*phi*, 216).

[42] For the social context and poetics of Theognis, see *Theognis of Megara: Poetry and the Polis*, ed. by Figueira and Nagy.

[43] On the pottery type, see Cohen, *Attic Bilingual Vases*.

[44] Herodotus, *The Persian Wars*, II, 143. 1–4.

[45] The contemporary philosopher Heraclitus, also an Ionian, apparently thought the latter, as he lumped Hecataeus with Pythagoras, Hesiod, and Xenophanes in a set of those whose

cant point arises from the tale: we see the mythographer Hecataeus doing what Homeric heroes did in their own self-presentation, toting up their own heroic past, tracing their lineage back to the gods whenever possible, and boasting about it. Either Diomedes and company possessed the mythographic habit *avant la lettre* in the form of an oral-traditional accomplishment, or, to be open-minded about dating, the composer of the Homeric epics was already in touch with the developing mythographic habits of local writers, perhaps in Athens of the sixth century BC.

If a Greek mythologized himself, by recording an ancestry that reached back sixteen generations to the gods, this might seem harmless enough, albeit an obvious power-play in performance, from our vantage point. In the absence of documentation — that is, in any oral culture — the assertion of Hecataeus can go unchallenged (like that story Diomedes tells about his grandfather). It is 'sage' behaviour inasmuch as it is venerable and complete — not subject to the warrior-style of flyting and counter-myths. When the person doing the genealogizing is a doctor, however, we are on the cusp of another style. As we know from the work of Geoffrey Lloyd and others, doctoring in the ancient world was a competitive activity, making use of public display and agonistic diagnosing.[46] Thus, when Hippocrates of Kos traces his lineage twenty generations all the way back to Heracles, son of Zeus, and Asclepius, son of Apollo, we are looking at some serious credential claims. The mythographer who steps onto this playing field is putting into action something more like a warrior use of *muthos*. Pherecydes (among others such as the learned Eratosthenes) apparently approved the Hippocratic boast.[47] Pity those poor doctors who could not enlist their own genealogists to document similar bloodlines. Again, we are talking about self-assertion and self-presentation, by means of ancestry tracing — not unlike the proud statement of Glaucus in the *Iliad*, that he descends from Sisyphus, son of Aiolos, who was grandson of the original post-Flood human survivor, Deukalion.

With this mention of the other prominent *muthos* style, let me turn to some more noticeable 'warrior' traits in classical mythographers. Perhaps the most famous declaration of the allegedly new Ionian spirit in enquiry comes from Hecataeus of Miletus, as preserved in the later work of Demetrius.[48] 'Hecataeus

broad erudition (*polumathiē*) did not impart intelligence (*Die Fragmente der Vorsokratiker*, ed. by Diels and Kranz, 22 B 40; see also Hecataeus, *Fragmenta*, ed. by Nenci, p. 3, test. 1).

[46] Lloyd, *The Revolutions of Wisdom*, pp. 83–108.

[47] Soranus of Ephesus, *Vita Hippocratis secundum Soranum*, ed. by Ilberg, p. 175, l. 3.

[48] Demetrius, *On Style*, ed. by Roberts, 12 (pp. 75–76).

of Miletus thus declares with authority (*hôde mutheitai*): I write these things as they seem to me to be true. For the tales told by the Greeks are, as it appears to me, many and absurd'. We should translate the verb *mutheitai*, which derives from *muthos*, with the full force of that noun as we see it in Homeric poetry. Otherwise, if we translate as 'makes a fiction' or even more neutrally 'tells a story', the mythographer's opening manifesto loses its force. What he means to say is that what we will read in his work on genealogies is true — the opposite of *muthos* in the later sense of 'fiction'. For 'tales' (the untrue stories that he finds absurd) he uses the Greek word *logoi*. At the same time, however, we should note the slight dissonance between his declarative *mutheitai* — in the third person — and the phrase 'as they appear to me' (*hôs emoi phainontai*) with its reference to the first person. Part of this style we come to see later in Herodotus and Thucydides, both of whom refer to themselves in the third person in the *prooimia* of their historical accounts. But in those authors, there is no 'me' in close vicinity. The effect in Hecataeus might be to increase the emphasis on the authority of his utterance. It sounds legalistic, more like 'Hecateuas *attests*' to the following.[49]

One man's silly stories, of course, are another's truths — always the problem with myth. We wonder, when reading passages like Hecataeus's history of the early Aetolian kingship, how many other somewhat implausible events got seriously recorded by Hecataeus as part of his *Genealogies*. According to this narrative, Orestheus, son of Deukalion, on his way to assume the kingship, found that a dog of his gave birth to a stalk (*stelekhos*).[50] He ordered the stick to be buried and from it there grew a vine with many clusters of grapes. He therefore called his son Phytios (Productive); a grandson was named Oineus (Winey) after the vine, who became father of Aitolos, the eponymous ancestor of the region's people. Perhaps the stick the bitch birthed has significance beyond its apparent role in the story — after all sceptres too are sticks. Achilles in the *Iliad* talks about Agamemnon's as if it were a dead branch, that will never more produce (*phusei*) leaves and branches.[51] The stalk produced by Orestheus's dog, on the other hand, is marvelously productive. Who would defend this story? Plenty of Aetolians, no

---

[49] On the paradoxical expression, see further Calame, *Mythe et histoire dans l'Antiquité grecque*, p. 30. Hecataeus, *Fragmenta*, ed. by Nenci, pp. xxiv-vi, explains the sentence as referring to the absurdity of there being multiple versions of each story, all posing as true: polyphony is the mark of the phoney. Pearson, *Early Ionian Historians*, p. 98, sees an allusion to Hesiod's Muses (Hesiod, *Theogony*, ll. 27–29) who tell both truth and fictions like the truth.

[50] Athenaeus, *Epitome*, ed. by Kaibel, 2. 1 (I, p. 81, l. 7); also in *Early Greek Mythography*, ed. by Fowler, frag. 15, p. 129.

[51] Homer, *Iliad*, I. 234–39.

doubt. What does Hecataeus owe *them*? We do not precisely know, but one can easily imagine the flyting of myths and counter-myths in which this sort of story makes sense, claims to kingship being pretty serious things.

The evidence suggests that Hellanicus, another mythographer of the fifth century, is entangled in just such claims and counter-claims.[52] This time they are not about kingship but about a kin-slaying queen. The *scholia* (marginal notes) to line 9 of Euripides' *Medea* (produced 431 BC) include an apparently widespread story, that Euripides got paid five talents by the Corinthians to blame Medea for killing her own children. Previous versions of the tale, we are meant to conclude, blamed the Corinthians themselves — or, if you believe Didymus (the 'Bronze-Gutted' scholar almost exactly contemporary with the Augustan poet Horace), it was the relatives of Creon (Medea's victim) who had the children killed and then blamed Medea for infanticide. The existence of a reparation ritual at Corinth seems to argue for an old version in which the Corinthians are to blame — or, at least, blamed themselves. The story as given in *scholia* ad *Medea* line 273, citing the grammarian Parmeniscus, is an aitiological tale, according to which it was the women of Corinth who slew the children at an altar of Hera.[53] When a plague struck the city, an oracle specified expiation to appease the wrath of Medea's children and Hera through the annual sending of a delegation of seven boys and seven girls who were to live and sacrifice in the goddess's precinct.[54] Now the *scholia* tell us that the mythographer Hellanicus as well as the mysterious writer Hippys are sources for details of the life of Medea in Corinth. Could Hellanicus also have promoted this story about Medea's guilt, which absolves the Corinthians and puts an Athenian playwright — Euripides — in a bad light? Both authors are named two sentences after the mention of the bribery tale, although it is not directly attributed to them. Perhaps this is a fetch too far, but if we consider the motives and opportunities of the case, it is not insignificant that Hellanicus comes from Lesbos. He is said to have lived from about 490 to 405 — that is, he was almost exactly contemporary with Euripides. And we should not forget that Athens did some cruel things to Lesbos in the later fifth century. After the unsuccessful revolt by Mytilene from the Athenian empire in 427 BC, the Athenians voted to slaughter the entire male population. Only second thoughts and a last-minute

---

[52] On his mythographic, as opposed to ethnographic and chronographic writing, see Pearson, *Early Ionian Historians*, pp. 157–93.

[53] *Scholia* to Euripides, *Medea*, l. 273, in *Scholia Graeca in Euripidis tragoedias*, ed. by Dindorf, IV, 25–26.

[54] On the associations of this cult with apotropaic and initiatory rites, see Johnston, 'Corinthian Medea'.

intervention saved the town. Even at that, one thousand rebels were executed.[55]
There were several important citizens of Lesbos, which is a big, rich island. But it
is interesting that Hellanicus is said to have come specifically from Mytilene. The
Athenians had their own reasons for demonizing Medea, ancestress of the Medes,
after the Persian War. But Hellanicus (whose *polis* was nearly destroyed by the
Athenians) would have excellent reasons to believe that the Athenians were corrupt and not to be trusted.

The agonistic use of myth, then, continues the flyting, blaming, agonistic use
of *muthos* as we see it in epic. You might object that the world of the early fifth
century BC is not that of heroic duels. Yet, in a way, it is so even more. Consider
the normal conditions in which someone setting out to record 'myths' in that
century would find himself. It is a commonplace that all politics is local: so is
myth. Pausanias reports that the land of Corinth is named after Corinthus. 'That
Corinthus was a son of Zeus, I have never known anybody to say seriously —
except the majority of the Corinthinas'.[56] Pausanias says further that Eumelus,
a member of the powerful Bacchiad family, and the supposed author of an epic
poem *Corinthiaca* (though Pausanias is hesitant about the attribution) explained
that Corinth had formerly been named Ephyraea (after a daughter of Ocean) but
Marathon, an Athenian who had fled to the area and lived there some time, allot-
ted the land to his son, after whom it got its new name. We do not know how or
why Eumelus switched the paternity of Corinthus from a god to a mortal (albeit
a heroized mortal, in Attica, to which he later returned).[57] Perhaps this represents
a convenient compromise, or even a minority ideology fostered by the ruling
Bacchiad family: note Pausanias's phrase 'the majority' of the Corinthians when
referring to the belief in Corinthus as son of Zeus. It has the advantage of linking
an ancestral figure with Attica, a way of making a claim either of guest-friend-
ship or territorial ownership. As great-grandson of the Sun (Helios), Marathon
is related to Medea, whom, as we have seen, at least one segment of Corinthian
society desired to disown. Most likely, we are viewing dimly a faction fight fought
on the mythopoeic level, in which every small readjustment of the story packs a
punch for some interests: myth once more as *muthos*.

---

[55] Thucydides, *History of the Peloponnesian War*, III. 50.

[56] Pausanias, *The Description of Greece*, II. 1. 1; also in *Early Greek Mythography*, ed. by
Fowler, frag. 1 (p. 105).

[57] There may be a further rationalizing urge at work, as a story was also attributed to
Eumelus that pinpointed a location in human terrain (in Lydia) for the birth of Zeus (Lydus,
Ioannis Lydi liber de mensibus, ed. by Wünsch, IV. 71). Fowler attributes the *testimonium* to
Eumelus 'Pseudepigraphus' (*Early Greek Mythography*, ed. by Fowler, p. 109).

In these conditions, it is inevitable that mythographers either take sides, or eventually are perceived as doing so. This is no doubt a commonplace in medieval studies, when every minor kingdom, monastic site, and bishopric jostled for authority and used saga to establish its claims. Glastonbury and Arthurian myth come to mind. The city-state configuration of classical Greece is not much different in discursive practices. Spreading literacy, shifting political tides, and the need to claim land all collaborate in putting mythographers on a rather hot seat. Why would a Hellanicus or Hecataeus even attempt to construct a universal Greek genealogy of all city states? We have no explicit reference to their motives. But just as Homer is depicted in the *Lives* tradition (*c.* sixth century BC in origin) as a poet who wanders into town and produces a composition about local history, for which he is rewarded, so too mythographers must either have, or expect to gain, patronage.[58] Eumelus, the poet and member of a powerful clan, is a sort of aristocratic gun-for-hire. The prose-writing *logopoioi*, on the other hand, might be of middling origin but they no doubt learn from their poetic brethren. And the poets themselves are still in the game, by the way, through the fifth century. At the end of *Nemean* 7, a complex ode written for a victorious athlete from the island of Aegina, the poet Pindar says, 'I do not have to keep repeating myself, like people forever babbling "Dios Korinthos" ['Corinthus comes from Zeus's'].'[59] Pindar thereby aligns himself with people who are tired of Corinthian propaganda or inimical to the city's power, and at the same time, with a segment of Corinth's population (represented at one stage by Eumelus) who felt the same way, when they demoted Corinthus from son of Zeus to son of Marathon.

That mythography was never neutral can be imagined from the few examples already given. One senses that sometimes rather strange variations in detail — not obviously involving the claim to power — were concocted simply to give myth-recorders more status. How else might one explain the information given us by the mythographer Acusilaus that the Golden Fleece, affirmed by most people to have been golden, was in fact purple?[60] Does Acusilaus know something most people do not? Does he have a privileged source for this minority view? Or is this a case of providing authentic, realistic detail (as he apparently said it *became* purple 'from the sea')? On other occasions, mythographers seem to be picking fights with poetic predecessors just to appear more rational, or even simply for the sake of differentiation from tradition. Hecataeus, for instance, writes with

---

[58] For the 'Homeric' practice, see Martin, 'Read on Arrival'.

[59] Pindar, *Nemean Odes*, VII. 104–5.

[60] *Scholia* to Apollonius of Rhodes, *Argonautica*, 14.1146–48, in *Early Greek Mythography*, ed. by Fowler, frag. 37 (p. 24).

some disdain: 'Aigyptos did not go to Argos, but his children did — fifty of them, as Hesiod has it [literally 'made it', that is in poetry: *epoiêse*], but, as I think, not even twenty.'[61] Whatever the motive behind that move — rejecting as it does the common poetic trope of fifty offspring (Nereids, daughters of Thespius, etc.) — it makes life easier for the genealogist to get rid of thirty extraneous characters.

In some cases, nevertheless, already in antiquity the mythographers' cover was blown. Strabo the geographer lived more than three centuries after Hellanicus, yet he may have a reliable tradition at his disposal when he fingers his predecessor as gratifying (*kharizomenos*) the inhabitants of Troy who were the mythographer's contemporaries by writing that their little settlement was actually the same as the great city of Priam.[62] Hellanicus, in gratifying the audience of Ilium, acts in a manner that is hardly different from the hired praise-poet's relationship with the commissioning patron, a relationship of *kharis* or reciprocal gratitude.[63] We need not attribute this interpretation to Strabo, who writes with considerable hindsight. It is not unlikely that the ideology of 'reciprocal gratitude' was operative in the world of the fifth-century prose writers as it was of poets.

Pindar, as his odes show, was highly conscious of avoiding the appearance of paid partisanship. Praise has to look natural, acclaim must seem immediate and universal. His solution was to resort to an elaborate rhetorical system in which the athletic victories that he was paid to celebrate somehow organically and spontaneously elicited his exertions as laudator. He strove and exercised his art as hard as did his victors because their glory demanded his poetry and *vice versa*.[64] Here it seems we can find another parallel with the mythographers, but one that takes us in a different, unexpected direction. If, as I have been suggesting, the *muthos*-asserting tactics of Homeric imagination actually structure the later writing down of myths, we might think that the force of self-assertion, the threat of a live performance with its power to overwhelm opposition and gain consent, is somehow diminished or even defused by the use of the new technology. Doesn't writing change everything? Is not the 'graph' in mythography a key? Not necessarily. We are far enough now from the Great Divide theories of orality and literacy, as prop-

---

[61] *Scholia* to Euripides, *Orestes*, l. 872, in *Early Greek Mythography*, ed. by Fowler, frag. 19 (p. 113).

[62] Strabo, *Geography*, XIII. 1. 42; also in *Early Greek Mythography*, ed. by Fowler, frag. 25b, p. 165.

[63] On the representations in literature of this archaic notion, see MacLachlan, *The Age of Grace*. For analysis of the *kharis* relationship in Pindaric praise-poetry, see Kurke, *The Traffic in Praise*.

[64] Salient examples of these tropes are discussed in the classic study by Bundy, *Studia Pindarica*.

agated especially by Eric Havelock and Walter Ong, to begin to appreciate phenomena that in fact jump the gap, continuing oral habits into the written world.
Mythography is one such phenomenon. Starting from oral-performative roots,
it flourishes even in the allegedly harsher climate of script. Eventually *muthoi* get
stripped of their immediate contexts of use, with all the original pragmatic vari-
ables of speaker and setting, and become pretty stories — hero-tales and genealogies. But, as should appear from the examples already cited, that eventual outcome
— the purely cleaned-up and motiveless tale — has not yet come about by the
fifth century BC. Sides are still being taken, 'myth' has still the immediacy and
authority of *muthos*, and it fits the gratification culture of *kharis* in patron-client
relations, provided we substitute, on occasion, city-states and their factions in the
place of aristocratic individuals and families. And of course, the former are in most
poleis simply transformations of the latter, as the history of Athens well shows.

Looking at the situation in this way may help us understand two final and
rather odd stories. You could call these myths of mythography. They both have
to do with writing, and they crop up in the biographies of mythographers.
Pherecydes — whether the Athenian or the earlier man of the same name from
the Cycladic island Syros — is said to have taught Pythagoras, but was himself
an autodidact. Or, not quite. Pherecydes acquired knowledge, and trained himself (*heauton askêsai*) by the book: specifically, the secret books (*apokrupha biblia*) of the Phoenicians.[65] We learn from the *Suda* as well that Acusilaus of Argos
had a similar experience.[66] His composition called *Genealogies* was written 'from
bronze tablets' (*ek deltôn khalkôn*) which emerged in the course of a building project involving the excavation by his father of part of his house.

It is not the historical or archaeological likelihood of these discoveries that
fascinates one so much as the insistence on *distance* in the myth-learning process,

---

[65] *Suidae lexicon*, ed. by Adler, IV, 713, l. 23; see also *Early Greek Mythography*, ed. by Fowler,
frag. 1 (p. 272). Schibli, *Pherekydes of Syros*, p. 81, believes the story is about the man from Syros
and sees the reference to Phoenician books as part of a doxographic tradition that argued for
general Near Eastern influence on Greece, stemming from Philo of Alexandria (20 BC–AD 50).
Early Greek Mythography, ed. by Fowler, following Jacoby, places the *Suda testimonium* under
'Pherecydes Atheniensis' (see frag. 1, p. 272). In Pherecydes, *Testimonianze e frammenti*, ed.
by Dolcetti, pp. 28–31, Dolcetti outlines what she sees as the 'funzione politica precisa' of the
genealogical work by Pherecydes of Athens in connection with the politics of Cimon. If the
story of knowledge from books does relate to the Athenian (rather than the man of Syros), it
could act as a protective device to defend the mythographer's genealogical work against charges
of partisanship. The immediate context in the *Suda* passage, however, is about eschatological
and cosmogonic writings.

[66] *Suidae lexicon*, ed. by Adler, I, 87, l. 20 (*alpha*, 942).

spatial in the case of Pherecydes, temporal for Acusilaus. Such distancing makes sense if the closeness and the personal self-assertiveness of archaic myth-telling has indeed remained a problem for slightly later myth-writers. Saying 'I say this' sets you up to be challenged. On the other hand, finding the story already packaged, whether written down in *biblia* by Phoenicians or engraved on tablets by previous residents of your property in the Bronze Age, lets you tell the untrammelled and depersonalized truth. Even the opening sentence of the work of Hecataeus (*hôde mutheitai*) encapsulates this paradox: to hold off challenges, the writer distances himself, using the third-person instead of the first, while employing a verb that must retain the sense of 'makes an authoritative assertion'.

If mythography, finally, results in the endless stripping away of situation, a denuding of speech-acts in favour of pure plot-lines, we have to recognize the roles and motivations of mythographers in the process. They are not ethnographers, and certainly not interested in providing thick descriptions of the tale-telling event. The tales survive precisely because they *are* deracinated, made available for public consumption and reperformance in a number of contexts, defused for purposes of entertainment; and they get that way because writers no doubt wanted to avoid charges of self-interest. In the poem with which I began, from Wallace Stevens, the narrator asks:

> 'Do I press the extremest book of the wisest man
> Close to me, hidden in me day and night?'

To which our mythographers would no doubt answer — yes; do so; provided it is someone *else's* volume.

Works Cited

Primary Sources

Athenaeus, *Epitome*, in *Athenaei Naucratitae deipnosophistarum libri XV*, ed. by Georg Kaibel, 3 vols (Stuttgart: Teubner, 1965–66; orig. publ. Leipzig, 1887–90), I, 1–171

Audacht Morainn, ed. by Fergus Kelly (Dublin: Dublin Institute for Advanced Studies, 1976)

An Early Irish Reader, ed. by Norah Kershaw Chadwick (Cambridge: Cambridge University Press, 1927)

Die Fragmente der Vorsokratiker, ed. by Hermann Diels and Walther Kranz, 6th edn, 3 vols (Berlin: Weidmann, 1966–67)

Early Greek Mythography, I: Text and Introduction, ed. by Robert L. Fowler (Oxford: Oxford University Press, 2000)

Early Irish Myths and Sagas, trans. by Jeffrey Gantz (Harmondsworth: Penguin, 1981)

Hecataeus, *Hecataei Milesii Fragmenta*, ed. by Giuseppe Nenci, Biblioteca di studi superiori, 22 (Firenze: Nuova Italia, 1954)

Lydus, *Ioannis Lydi liber de mensibus*, ed. by Richard Wünsch (Leipzig: Teubner, 1967; orig. publ. 1898)

Pherecydes, *Testimonianze e frammenti: Ferecide di Atene; introduzione, testo, traduzione e commento*, ed. by Paola Dolcetti (Alessandria: Edizioni dell'Orso, 2004)

Scéla Mucce Meic Dathó, ed. by Rudolf Thurneysen, Mediaeval and Modern Irish Series, 6 (Dublin: Stationery Office, 1935)

Scholia Graeca in Euripidis tragoedias, ed. by W. Dindorf, 4 vols (Oxford: Oxford University Press, 1863)

Soranus of Ephesus, *Vita Hippocratis secundum Soranum*, in *Sorani Gynaeciorum libri IV; De signis fracturarum; De fasciis; Vita Hippocratis secundum Soranum*, ed. by Johannes Ilberg, Corpus medicorum Graecorum, 4 (Leipzig: Teubner, 1927), pp. 175–78

Stevens, Wallace, *Collected Poems* (New York: Knopf, 1961)

Thucydides, *History of the Peloponnesian War*

Secondary Studies

Adler, Ada, ed., *Suidae lexicon*, 5 vols (Stuttgart: Teubner, 1967–71)

Bundy, Elroy L., *Studia Pindarica* (Berkeley: University of California Press, 1986)

Calame, Claude, *Mythe et histoire dans l'Antiquité grecque: la Création symbolique d'une colonie*, 2nd edn (Lausanne: Payot, 1996)

Cohen, Beth, *Attic Bilingual Vases and their Painters* (New York: Garland, 1978)

Detienne, Marcel, *The Creation of Mythology*, trans. by Margaret Cook (Chicago: University of Chicago Press, 1986)

Ernout, Alfred, and Antoine Meillet, eds., *Dictionnaire étymologique de la langue Latine*, 4th edn (Paris: Klincksieck, 1959)

Figueira, Thomas J., and Gregory Nagy, eds, *Theognis of Megara: Poetry and the Polis* (Baltimore: Johns Hopkins University Press, 1985)

Glare, Peter Geoffrey William, ed., *Oxford Latin Dictionary* (Oxford: Oxford University Press, 1968)

Edmunds, Lowell, 'Myth in Homer', in *A New Companion to Homer*, ed. by Ian Morris and Barry Powell (Leiden: Brill, 1997), pp. 415–41

Johnston, Sarah Iles, 'Corinthian Medea and the Cult of Hera Akraia', in *Medea: Essays on Medea in Myth, Literature, Philosophy, and Art*, ed. by James J. Clauss and Sarah Iles Johnston (Princeton: Princeton University Press, 1997), pp. 44–70

Kurke, Leslie, 'Pindar's Sixth *Pythian* and the Tradition of Advice Poetry', *Transactions of the American Philological Association*, 120 (1990), 85–107

——, *The Traffic in Praise: Pindar and the Poetics of Social Economy* (Ithaca: Cornell University Press, 1991)

Lloyd, Geoffrey Ernest Richard, *The Revolutions of Wisdom: Studies in the Claims and Practice of Ancient Greek Science*, Sather Classical Lectures, 52 (Berkeley: University of California Press, 1987)

Mackie, Hilary, *Talking Trojan: Speech and Community in the Iliad* (Lanham: Rowman & Littlefield, 1996)

MacLachlan, Bonnie, *The Age of Grace: Charis in Early Greek Poetry* (Princeton: Princeton University Press, 1992)

Martin, Richard P., 'Hesiod, Odysseus, and the Instruction of Princes', *Transactions of the American Philological Association*, 114 (1984), 29–48

——, *The Language of Heroes: Speech and Performance in the Iliad* (Ithaca: Cornell University Press, 1989)

——, '*Nemean* 7 and Pindaric Hymnologic' (forthcoming)

——, 'Read on Arrival', in *Wandering Poets in Ancient Greek Culture: Travel, Locality and Pan-Hellenism*, ed. by Richard L. Hunter and Ian Rutherford (Cambridge: Cambridge University Press, 2009), pp. 80–104

——, 'Wrapping Homer Up: Cohesion, Discourse, and Deviation in the *Iliad*', in *Intratextuality: Greek and Roman Textual Relations*, ed. by Alison Sharrock and Helen Morales (New York: Oxford University Press, 2000), pp. 43–65

Melia, Daniel F., 'Some Remarks on the Affinities of Medieval Irish Saga', *Acta antiqua Hungarica*, 27 (1979), 255–61

Nagy, Gregory, *Pindar's Homer: The Lyric Possession of an Epic Past* (Baltimore: Johns Hopkins University Press, 1990)

Nagy, Joseph Falaky, *The Wisdom of the Outlaw: The Boyhood Deeds of Finn in Gaelic Narrative Tradition* (Los Angeles: University of California Press, 1985)

Parks, Ward, 'Flyting and Fighting: Pathways in the Realization of the Epic Contest', *Neophilologus*, 70 (1986), 292–306

Pearson, Lionel Ignacius Cusack, *Early Ionian Historians* (Oxford: Oxford University Press, 1939)

Reynolds, Dwight Fletcher, *Heroic Poets, Poetic Heroes: The Ethnography of Performance in an Arabic Oral Epic Tradition* (Ithaca: Cornell University Press, 1995)

Schibli, Hermann S., *Pherekydes of Syros* (Oxford: Clarendon Press, 1990)

Walcot, Peter, 'Cattle Raiding, Heroic Tradition, and Ritual: The Greek Evidence', *History of Religions*, 18 (1979), 326–51

Starving the Slender Muse:
Identity, Mythography, and
Intertextuality in Ovid's *Ibis*

Darcy Krasne*

A
lthough the Roman poet Publius Ovidius Naso, or Ovid, is well known,
some of his poems have fared better than others in the annals of scholarship. One poem in particular, the *Ibis*, has suffered serious neglect over
the years and, as a result, is little-known (or at least little-valued), even among
Ovidian scholars. Consisting primarily of a long catalogue of mythological
figures, the *Ibis* is (as I shall argue) akin to a mythographic text; since ancient
mythography was a prose genre, this is an interesting feature in its own right.
Additionally, this mythographic veneer proves to be a useful starting ground for
further investigation of the poem. Given the interdisciplinary nature of this volume and its intended audience, I shall begin by devoting some space to Ovid's
background and the context of his poetry, material which will prove directly relevant to my discussion of the *Ibis*.

Born in 43 BC, Ovid composed his poetry under the first Roman emperor,
Augustus. His best-known work today is a fifteen-book epic, the *Metamorphoses*,
which narrates numerous stories of metamorphosis from Greek and Roman
mythology. In ancient times, however, he was viewed primarily as an elegiac
poet, the difference being one of both genre and metre. In the field of classics,
'elegy' does not imply mournful poetry of lamentation, although the etymology
of the term was indeed seen to lie in expressions of lament.[1] Instead it serves as a

---

* Darcy Krasne (dkrasne@gmail.com) completed her PhD dissertation in Classics at the
University of California, Berkeley, in 2011, and has subsequently held visiting positions at the
University of Arkansas and the University of Missouri-Columbia.

[1] 'Elegy' was thought to be derived from ἒ ἒ λέγειν (*e e légein*), 'to say "alas"'.

Writing Down the Myths, ed. by Joseph Falaky Nagy, CURSOR 17, (Turnhout: Brepols, 2013)
pp. 67–85   BREPOLS ⬛ PUBLISHERS   10.1484/M.CURSOR-EB.1. 100847

metrical term, referring to any poetry written in elegiac couplets.[2] These are, as the name implies, constructed in pairs; odd lines are identical to dactylic hexameter, the metre used for epic, while even lines are shorter by one foot (*pes*), the term used by Roman poets and grammarians for a line's metrical divisions. Although the Greeks were flexible in their generic applications of the elegiac metre, the Romans used it primarily (although not exclusively) for love poetry.

The majority of Ovid's early work fits into this broadly-construed category, and he was viewed as a love-poet by his contemporaries.[3] His later elegiac work, however, written after his exile by Augustus in AD 8 to the shores of the Black Sea, professes a return to elegy's roots in lamentation and deals almost exclusively with the travails of his life in that barbarous region. His two major exilic works, the *Tristia* (Sad Things) and the *Epistulae ex Ponto* (Letters from the Black Sea), are both collections of verse epistles written to friends and associates back at Rome.

The main difference between the *Tristia* and *Ex Ponto* lies in their mode of address. Nearly all of the *Tristia*'s epistles anonymize their addressees, ostentatiously suppressing their names, while the *Ex Ponto* poems are addressed in a more typical epistolary fashion, such that the recipients are specified by name. This shift from anonymous to named addressees is an explicit part of Ovid's programme; in the proem to the *Ex Ponto*, he asserts that the only real difference between the collections is that in the latter, *epistula cui sit | non occultato nomine missa docet* (the letter professes to whom it is sent without hiding the name (Ovid, *Ex Ponto*, I. 1. 17–18)).[4] Ovid's professed reason for eschewing names in the earlier *Tristia* is that names can be dangerous, to both addresser and addressee. Stephen Hinds has commented that Ovid is 'programmatically obsessed [...] with the dangers that come from naming people's names'.[5] This danger lies not just in identifying those who should remain nameless, but also in confusing individuals who share names.[6]

---

[2] The metrical pattern is:

—⏑⏑|—⏑⏑|—⏑⏑|—⏑⏑|—⏑⏑|—— (*dactylic hexameter*)
—⏑⏑|—⏑⏑|—||—⏑⏑|—⏑⏑|— (*pentameter*)

[3] See Harrison, 'Ovid and Genre', on Ovid's generic experimentation.

[4] All translations are my own.

[5] Hinds, 'Ovid among the Conspiracy Theorists', p. 207.

[6] As Hinds has also noted (Hinds, 'Review of *Publica Carmina*'), the first two poems of the *Ex Ponto* (along with several others) make explicit or implicit comparisons between their addressees and famous (or infamous) homonymous historical individuals, often with little apparent regard for the effect this will have on public (or Augustan) perception of the addressee. Similar blurring of identity has been discussed by Ahl, *Lucan*, pp. 140–45, and Feeney, 'History

The *Ibis* also comes from the period of Ovid's exile. Its neglect derives primarily from the highly periphrastic and allusive mode in which it is written. Even a casual attempt at reading the poem turns, of necessity, into a prolonged exercise of scholarly research and investigative cross-referencing.[7] Moreover, nothing is known of the poem's true context. If we are to take Ovid's assertions within the *Ibis* at face value, the poem was written as an attack against an ex-friend at Rome who had been blackening Ovid's name in his absence and making hay with his misfortunes (Ovid, *Ibis*, ll. 7–22). Ovid conceals the name of this enemy under the pseudonym 'Ibis', following in the footsteps of the Alexandrian poet Callimachus, who had also written a curse poem entitled Ἶβις (*Ibis*) against an anonymous enemy (Ovid, *Ibis*, ll. 55–62);[8] nothing of Callimachus's poem survives.

The *Ibis* consists of two major parts. There are 250 lines of introductory ritual cursing of Ibis, followed by a further nearly four hundred lines of catalogue in which Ovid wishes on Ibis the fates suffered by mythological and historical figures, citing one or more per couplet. The majority of these figures are named only through extreme periphrasis. Reactions to this catalogue of *exempla*, or mythological examples, have been generally unfavourable — A. E. Housman, while praising the poem's first 250 lines as a 'masterpiece',[9] dismissed the remainder as 'merely a display of erudition'.[10] Gareth Williams, although defending the catalogue as a piece that 'cannot be dismissed [...] simply as a self-indulgent show of learning',[11] sees it primarily as the mark of an 'obsessive mentality' as demonstrated by Ovid's 'selection and disjointed ordering of *exempla*'.[12] To his mind, the catalogue is 'intended [...] to fascinate Ibis with the mysteriously ill-defined but

---

and Revelation in Vergil's Underworld', in the context of the parade of heroes in Virgil, *Aeneid*, VI; I thank John McDonald for suggesting to me this correspondence.

[7] Requiring a reader to supply extra information that is necessary for understanding the narrative is a technique familiar from Hellenistic epigram; see Bing, 'Ergänzungsspiel in the Epigrams of Callimachus', who labels the practice 'Ergänzungsspiel', essentially 'a game of supplementation'.

[8] Following the convention established by Watson, *Arae*, and Williams, *The Curse of Exile*, I retain Greek characters for Callimachus's title so as to distinguish it easily from Ovid's. In both cases, 'Ibis' refers to the bird.

[9] Housman, 'The *Ibis* of Ovid', p. 317.

[10] Housman, 'The *Ibis* of Ovid', pp. 317–18.

[11] Williams, *The Curse of Exile*, p. 81.

[12] Williams, *The Curse of Exile*, p. 91. Most of Williams's work on the poem confronts it as a study in obsession.

endlessly generated circumstances of his own death, which always lies [*sic*] outside the easy grasp of his understanding'.[13]

So we have a riddling and wide-ranging mythological catalogue in which some scholars have seen more worth than others. I would suggest that Ovid's arrangement of *exempla* in this catalogue is meant to resemble, on the surface, a series of mythographic catalogues, particularly in his clustering of mythological figures who share a single fate or another pertinent feature.[14] Within the *Ibis*, however, it is possible to detect further catalogues that run counter to the apparent organization of *exempla*. Moreover, despite structuring his work along mythographic lines, Ovid ultimately goes far beyond the mythographic urge to summarize. Rather than simply stripping away any narrative padding from the bare bones of the myths, leaving a compressed but still intelligible account, he creates a catalogue of *exempla* which are so desiccated that it is difficult to identify their subjects, much less any coordinating links between them, without doing one's own investigative research.

This mythic over-compression, which is tantamount to an obfuscation of identity, can be likened both to the suppression of Ibis's own identity and to the anonymous addressees of the *Tristia*. Here we see one small part of a pervasive parallelism and intertextuality which is detectable between Ovid's *Ibis* and his other exilic work, an issue to which I shall return later. Given such correspondences, it is not unreasonable to speculate that the *Ibis* is less a direct derivative from its professed model, Callimachus's Ἶβις, and more a functional part of Ovid's exile poetry.[15]

Most scholars perceive a basic lack of structural coherence in the *Ibis*. Williams (one of the few to comment at all on the catalogue's organizational principles) calls it 'a dream-like fantasy in which all temporal distinctions cease to apply'[16] as 'Ovid's need to feed his malice with more and more *exempla* takes precedence over any respect for literary chronology or narrative consistency'.[17] He tantaliz-

---

[13] Williams, *The Curse of Exile*, p. 90.

[14] The catalogue, a staple of ancient prose mythography, survives in works such as Hyginus's *Fabulae* and a number of papyrus fragments. For a comprehensive collection of these, see Van Rossum-Steenbeek, *Greek Readers' Digests?*; also see Cameron, *Greek Mythography in the Roman World*, pp. 268–303, for suggestions on Ovid's use of mythographic catalogues as research tools.

[15] A small amount of work has been done in this direction, primarily by Gareth Williams — see Williams, 'On Ovid's *Ibis*'; Williams, *The Curse of Exile*; Williams, 'Ovid's Exile Poetry'; Williams, 'Ovid's Exilic Poetry'. In a recent article (Battistella, 'Momenti intertestuali nell'*Ibis*'), Chiara Battistella discusses the intertextuality of the 250-line prologue.

[16] Williams, *The Curse of Exile*, p. 101.

[17] Williams, *The Curse of Exile*, p. 92.

ingly refers to its 'seemingly random sequence'[18] but does not expound upon what possibly less random sequence might be lurking in the catalogue's 'only loose coherence'.[19] This is exactly where perceptions of the *Metamorphoses* stood barely fifty years ago, when it was still seen by many as 'a disjointed succession of disparate, unrelated, and irrational incidents'.[20] In the face of this, some work has been done on the internal cohesion of the *Ibis*, particularly by Ursula Bernhardt,[21] who has shown how the catalogue is thematically grouped, breaking the text into fifty-one mini-catalogues[22] and thirty-five 'Einzelexempla'. María García Fuentes has examined how themes recur throughout the catalogue, suggesting twenty-nine categories (some broader and some more specific) into which many or most of the *exempla* fall.[23] Neither approach functions perfectly in isolation. García Fuentes makes no explicit mention of the various *exempla* which she includes in more than one category, nor of Ovid's frequent localized groupings of *exempla* from a single category. At the same time, Bernhardt's paring down of *exempla* to only their apparent overriding aspect (manner of death, name, etc.) serves to suppress the bridges between mini-catalogues and ultimately results in her need for *Einzelexempla*.[24] Even so, both approaches serve as useful tools, and considering the component mini-catalogues is the best way to begin an investigation of the catalogue. These mini-catalogues range, in fairly unbroken succession, from clusters of just two or three couplets to, arguably, a full twenty-four couplets in one location (Ovid, *Ibis*, ll. 365–412).

I shall start with a sample stretch of catalogue (Ovid, *Ibis*, ll. 469–500).[25] Most visibly, this passage comprises four mini-catalogues, each of which Ovid

---

[18] Williams, *The Curse of Exile*, p. 92, italics mine.

[19] Williams, *The Curse of Exile*, p. 92.

[20] Steiner, 'Ovid's *Carmen Perpetuum*', p. 218.

[21] Bernhardt, *Die Funktion der Kataloge*, pp. 328–99. The catalogue is analysed similarly in Ovid, *Ibis*, ed. by La Penna, pp. xlvi–xlix, although La Penna simply passes over in silence the *exempla* that do not 'fit'.

[22] My term, rather than a technical one, but Gordon, 'Poetry of Maledictions', which makes some useful remarks on the structure of the *Ibis*, uses the same term.

[23] García Fuentes, 'Mitología y maldición, ɪ'; García Fuentes, 'Mitología y maldición, ɪɪ'.

[24] She does give a more in-depth discussion of eight mini-catalogues (Bernhardt, *Die Funktion der Kataloge*, pp. 352–75), but her observation of actual overlaps between mini-catalogues is limited. In a list of mini-catalogue themes (pp. 336–38) she notes only the *exemplum* of Phoenix in two consecutive categories ('Von d. Stiefmutter Verleumdete' and 'Geblendete').

[25] In an effort to conserve space and avoid repetition, I do not quote the text in its entirety, but fig. 6 gives a schematized form of the whole passage.

Those struck by lightning (469–76)
>   Capaneus: struck by lightning
>   Demonax: struck by lightning
>   Semele: struck by lightning
>>   Iasion: struck by lightning + destroyed by his team of horses
>>   Phaëthon: struck by lightning + destroyed by his team of horses
>>   Salmoneus struck by lightning + destroyed by his team of horses
>   Lycaon's son: struck by lightning
>   Macelo & husband: struck by lightning

Those killed by dogs (477–80)
>   Thasus: torn apart by dogs
>   Actaeon: torn apart by dogs
>   Linus: torn apart by dogs

Those killed by snakes (481–84)
>   Eurydice: killed by a snake
>   Opheltes-Archemorus: killed by a snake
>   Laocoön: killed by a snake

Those who fell to their deaths (485–500)
>   Elpenor: fell to his death
>>   [the Dryopians: killed by Hercules + 'fell' to their death (verb *cadere*, 'to die/fall')]
>>   [Cacus: killed by Hercules + 'fell' to his death (verb *cadere*, 'to die/fall')]
>   Lichas: killed by Hercules + fell to his death

Those who fell to their deaths, take 2 (493–500)
>   Cleombrotus: fell to his death
>   Aegeus: fell to his death
>   Astyanax: fell to his death
>   Ino: fell to her death
>   Perdix: fell to his death
>   the †Lindian girl: fell to her death [+ possibly killed by Hercules]*

* The text of l. 499 is corrupt. If we read Lindia, however, there is certainly some connection with Hercules.

Figure 6. Lines 469–500 of Ovid's *Ibis* in schematized form.

begins by actually stating its linking element. Although such explicitness is not unique to this part of the poem, it is still the exception rather than the rule. The order of mini-catalogues here goes: 'Those struck by lightning', 'Those killed by dogs', 'Those killed by snakes', and 'Those who fell to their deaths'. These sound very much like the titles of catalogues in some mythographic texts, and indeed we have a mythographic catalogue preserved in Hyginus that corresponds nicely to 'those killed by dogs'.[26] We also have record in Hyginus of a mythographic 'those struck by lightning',[27] although the catalogue itself unfortunately does not survive. While neither Hyginus nor any of our papyrus fragments preserves a catalogue matching 'those killed by snakes' or 'those who fell to their deaths', it is easy to imagine such catalogues existing in a mythographic text.

[26] *Qui a canibus consumpti sunt* (Hyginus, *Fabulae*, 247).

[27] *Qui fulmine icti sunt* (Hyginus, *Fabulae*, 264).

Ovid's first mini-catalogue here, occupying eight lines, is more fully set off than those that follow:

aut Iovis infesti telo feriare trisulco,

470   ut satus Hipponoo Dexitheaeque pater,

ut soror Autonoes, ut cui matertera Maia,

ut temere optatos qui male rexit equos,

ut ferus Aeolides, ut sanguine natus eodem,

quo genita est liquidis quae caret Arctos aquis.

475   ut Macelo rapidis icta est cum coniuge flammis,

sic precor aetherii vindicis igne cadas.

(Ovid, *Ibis*, ll. 469–76)

(Or may you be struck by the three-grooved weapon of hostile Jupiter, as was Hipponoüs's son [= *Capaneus*] and the father of Dexithea [= *Demonax*], as was the sister of Autonoë [= *Semele*], as was the one whose aunt was Maia [= *Iasion*], as was the one who poorly guided the longed-for horses [= *Phaëthon*], as was the wild son of Aeolus [= *Salmoneus*], as was the one born from the same blood from which Arctos, who is deprived of the liquid waters, was born [= *any son of Lycaon*]; as Macelo was struck, along with her spouse, by the swift flames — thus, I pray, may you fall by the fire of a heavenly avenger.)

Both the opening *and* closing lines of the four couplets make it very clear what fate Ovid is wishing on his enemy, namely death by lightning. On the surface this is, I think, the most clearly identified and 'coherent' mini-catalogue of the entire text. Contained within it, however, there is yet another catalogue. Ovid consecutively mentions Iasion, Phaëthon, and Salmoneus, who were all struck by lightning (thus their inclusion in this section); but thanks to Hyginus we know that these three have another commonality, as they all appear in his catalogue of 'Teams of horses which destroyed their drivers':

QVAE QVADRIGAE RECTORES SVOS PERDIDERVNT
Phaethonta Solis filium ex Clymene. [...] Iasionem Iouis filium ex Electra Atlantis filia. Salmoneus, qui fulmina in quadrigas sedens imitabatur, cum quadriga fulmine ictus.

(Hyginus, *Fabulae*, 250)

(TEAMS OF HORSES WHICH DESTROYED THEIR DRIVERS
Phaëthon, son of the Sun by Clymene. [...] Iasion, son of Jupiter by Electra the daughter of Atlas. Salmoneus, who was sitting in his chariot making fake claps of thunder, was struck by a thunderbolt along with his chariot.)

Thus here in the *Ibis* we have, in essence, an overlapping Venn diagram of mythographic catalogues (see fig. 7), one labelled and one not, although Ovid may signpost the unlabelled catalogue by identifying the central figure, Phaëthon,

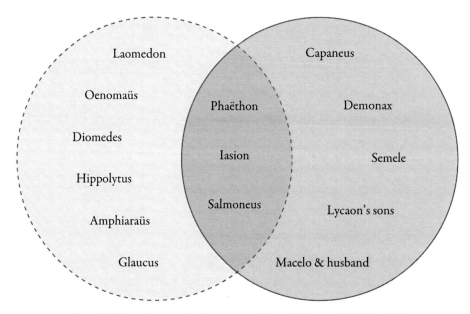

Figure 7. 'Those destroyed by their teams of horses' (Hyginus, *Fabulae*, 250)
and 'Those struck by lightning' (Ovid, *Ibis*, ll. 468–76).

through his fatal inability to control the horses which pull the chariot of the Sun
(Ovid, *Ibis*, l. 472).

The second mini-catalogue of the section, those eaten by dogs, closely parallels a catalogue in Hyginus:

> praedaque sis illis, quibus est Latonia Delos
> ante diem rapto non adeunda Thaso,
> quique verecundae speculantem labra Dianae,
> 480   quique Crotopiaden diripuere Linum.
> (Ovid, *Ibis*, ll. 477–80)

(And may you be prey for those who must not go to Latonian Delos because of
Thasus being snatched away before his time, and for those who tore apart the
one watching the bath of chaste Diana [= *Actaeon*], and for those who tore apart
Crotopus's descendant Linus.)

QVI A CANIBVS CONSVMPTI SVNT
Actaeon Aristaei filius. Thasius Delo, Anii sacerdotis Apollinis filius; ex
eo Delo nullus canis est. Euripides tragoediarum scriptor in templo con-
sumptus est.   (Hyginus, *Fabulae*, 247)

(THOSE WHO WERE EATEN BY DOGS
Actaeon the son of Aristaeus. Thasius, on Delos, the son of Apollo's priest
Anius; this is why there is no dog on Delos. Euripides the writer of tragedies
was eaten in a temple.)

The consonance between the two catalogues is impressive (we may note particularly their shared emphasis on the aetiological aspect of Thasus's death), but the
last figure in each differs. Where Hyginus names the tragedian Euripides, Ovid
gives pride of place to the child Linus. This is an important divergence, and the
exemplum of Linus — who proves to be at the centre of a web of associations
— is particularly intriguing for what it says about the interconnections between
mini-catalogues in the *Ibis*. Linus, as represented here, is the son of Apollo and
Psamathe; this is made indisputable by the patronymic *Crotopiades*. As with
Thasus, Linus's death has an aetiological element — he was exposed by his grandfather Crotopus, the king of Argos, and subsequently torn apart by dogs. In anger
at his death, Apollo sent a plague to punish Crotopus and the Argives, the ritual expiation for which included singing the eponymous linus-song (a kind of
dirge). Callimachus dealt with the story in Book 1 of the *Aetia* (Callimachus,
Aetia, frr. 26–31), and Ovid includes two other relevant couplets elsewhere in the
Ibis (Ovid, *Ibis*, ll. 573–76). Linus obviously fits into the immediate context of
the *Ibis* because of his manner of death (torn apart by dogs), but there are much
broader-reaching connections.

Greek mythology does not always present Linus as a baby, although whether
this is due to the existence of more than one Linus was debated even by the
Greeks (see Table 1). The only constant is his association with music and poetry,
sometimes as a musician himself and sometimes simply in providing an *aition* for
the linus-song. He is typically either the son of or killed by Apollo. This sort of
variability of narrative is an inherent part of Greek mythology, together with the
resultant nominal confusion or conflation. Linus is also often connected with
Orpheus and a number of other famous mythical figures (generally the sons of the
Muses) to whom are attributed the inventions of various musical, poetic, and rhe-

Table 1. Variations on the parentage and death of Linus.

Mother	Father	Killed by	Musician	Connected Figure	Source (e.g.)
Psamathe	Apollo	Dogs	No		Pausanias 1.43.7, 2.19.8
Calliope	Oiagros/Apollo	Hercules	Yes	Orpheus (brother)	Apollodorus 1.3.2§14
Calliope	Apollo	?	Yes	Other sons of Muses	Asclepiades *FGrH* 12 F 6b
Ourania	Amphimarus	Apollo	Yes		Pausanias 9.29.6
Ourania	Hermes	Apollo	Yes	Other genre-inventors	Diogenes Laertius 1.4

torical skills. Besides these strong ties to Orpheus and Apollo, Linus is frequently associated with Hercules — he was the hero's music teacher until Hercules killed him in a fit of pique by braining him with a lyre.

The version of Linus who appears in the *Ibis* is clearly Psamathe's son Linus, who was torn apart by dogs as a baby — at least on the surface. But the following mini-catalogue, a set of those killed by snake-bites, begins to activate associations with other versions of Linus.

> neve venenato levius feriaris ab angue,
>   quam senis Oeagri Calliopesque nurus,
> quam puer Hypsipyles, quam qui cava primus acuta
>   cuspide suspecti robora fixit equi.
>   (Ovid, *Ibis*, ll. 481–4)

(Or may you be struck by a snake no more lightly than was the daughter-in-law of old Oeagrus and Calliope [= *Eurydice*], than was Hypsipyle's boy [= *Opheltes-Archemorus*], than was he who first fixed the hollow oak of the suspected horse with a sharp spear-point [= *Laocoön*].)

The first victim in this catalogue is Eurydice, the wife of Orpheus. As can be seen in Table 1, Orpheus is the brother of 'another' Linus. As Eurydice's identity is revealed here through the names of her parents-in-law, Oeagrus and Calliope, she is therefore identified specifically with reference to the parents of that other Linus. Opheltes-Archemorus, the catalogue's second *exemplum*, is another figure who, like the first version of Linus, was killed as an infant.

Ovid then appears to begin a list of those who fell to their deaths (Ovid, *Ibis*, ll. 485–500), starting with Elpenor (Ovid, *Ibis*, ll. 485–86), but again he employs misdirection. Although he follows the opening couplet of the list with *tamque cadas* (and so may you fall) in an apparent continuation of the list of those who fell, he segues, with the next *exemplum*, into a list that employs the figurative meaning of *cadas* (may you die), specifically naming a trio of those killed by Hercules (Ovid, *Ibis*, ll. 487–92).[28] With the exception of Laocoön (Ovid, *Ibis*, ll. 483–84) and Elpenor, we can see Ovid spinning out the catalogue along the alternate threads provided by the name of Linus. One strand points to the tradition of Linus as Orpheus's brother, another follows the tradition of Linus dying as a baby, and a third strand reminds the reader that Hercules could also have been Linus's killer.

---

[28] Hercules' third victim here is Lichas, whom Hercules killed by throwing him off a cliff; this provides a transition back into 'those who fell'. The intersection of 'those who fell' and 'those killed by Hercules' has also been noted by Bernhardt, *Die Funktion der Kataloge*, pp. 366–70.

Within mythology, shared names sometimes create an actual shared identity.[29] In the section we just looked at, it is clear that whether Ovid is thinking of one Linus or several, the *name* of Linus is what really matters, prompting that particular collocation of mini-catalogues to occur.[30] Elsewhere in the *Ibis* (ll. 555–58), however, three Glauceses are explicitly named in conjunction, each suffering a distinctly different fate and never confused with each other in poetry or myth. Linus's name and identity are polyvalent; the three Glauci (despite sharing a name) retain their integrity. Still elsewhere (Ovid, *Ibis*, ll. 539–40), the poet Cinna is mistaken for another Cinna and, on no more grounds than this coincidence of their name, is torn apart by an angry mob.[31] Three modes of sharing a name, three possible results.[32]

Does Ovid's emphasis on the suppression and coincidence of names in the *Ibis* underscore the poetics of his anonymous mode of address as featured in the *Tristia*?[33] There, names (and the ability to avoid them or not) possess an obvious power. In the *Ibis*, Ovid makes clear the control he can retain over names if he so desires. Who is *conditor* [...] *tardae, laesus cognomine, Myrrhae* (the creator of slow Myrrha, harmed by his surname (Ovid, *Ibis*, l. 539))? It is Cinna-the-poet and *not* Cinna-the-conspirator. Ovid both identifies *and* specifies without saying the name at all, perhaps because history had already proven the danger of naming that particular name. Alternatively, he explicitly names more than one Glaucus while still managing to keep confusion at bay. But although he appears to specify a single version of Linus through his patronymic, context and the flexibility of myth serve to make available all of Linus's possible identities. Three modes of naming, and three resultant readings. Perhaps it is this demonstration of the control that

---

[29] Scylla (either the dog-waisted monster or the hair-cutting daughter of Nisus who became a halcyon) and Atalanta (daughter of Schoeneus or Iasius, wife of Melanion or Hippomenes) are standard examples of this.

[30] This nominal connection can be followed even further; according to Hyginus, *Fabulae*, 273. 6, and Apollodorus, *Library*, I. 9. 14, III. 6. 4, Opheltes-Archemorus was the son of Lycurgus and *Eurydice*. In the *Ibis*, the mother's name is misleadingly suppressed in favour of the nurse's — Hypsipyle replaces Eurydice, all but severing a link between contiguous *exempla*. And Actaeon, who immediately precedes Linus in the catalogue, was the son of Aristaeus, who in Augustan poetry (following Virgil, *Georgics*) was connected with the death of Orpheus's wife Eurydice. The threads here are thickly interconnected.

[31] An event familiar to non-Classicists from Shakespeare, *Julius Caesar*, III. 3.

[32] See Hinds, 'Ovid among the Conspiracy Theorists', p. 208, on nominal transference (and its dangers) in the exile poetry.

[33] See above, 68, 70.

Table 2. Catalogue opening by theme.

Lines	Mythic Figure	Lamed	Blinded	Adultery with Father's Wife* [False]	[True]	Vates†	Slays Guest
253–54	Philoctetes						
255–56	Telephus						
257–58	Bellerophon						
259–60	Phoenix						
261–62	Oedipus						
263–64	Tiresias						
265–66	Phineus						
267–68	Polymestor						
269–70	Polyphemus						
271–72	Sons of Phineus						
	Thamyras						
	Demodocus						

* Really, an *accusation* of adultery (true or false) with a father's *or* a host's wife *or* mistress. For Thamyras's inclusion in this category, a connection of which Ovid may or may not have been aware, see Devereux, 'The Self-Blinding of Oidipous in Sophokles', p. 41.

† In the case of Polyphemus, a prophet is involved in his story rather than his being a *vates* himself. In the case of Phineus's sons, they themselves are not *vates*, but of course their aforementioned father is. This column can be further broken down into prophet-*vates* (Tiresias and Phineus), *vates* associates (Polyphemus and Phineus's sons), and poet-*vates* (Thamyras and Demodocus) as indicated by the varying shades of grey.

Ovid possesses over naming and not naming which allows him to move from the *Tristia*'s anonymous addressees to a nominal mode of address in the *Ex Ponto*.

To return to the catalogue, we have seen how the text of the *Ibis* both seemingly reflects and ultimately confounds the cataloguing principles of ancient mythography. While this duality functions throughout much of the *Ibis* catalogue, sometimes it goes beyond the simple concealment of additional catalogues and alternate identities. The opening of the catalogue is a good demonstration of this. Here again we can make use of ancient mythographies as a parallel and even as an aid to identification. After beginning with *Troianis malis* (the sufferings of the Trojans (Ovid, *Ibis*, l. 252)), Ovid wishes on his enemy the fates of Philoctetes and Telephus, both of whom became lame:

> quantaque clavigeri Poeantius Herculis heres,
>   tanta venenato vulnera crure geras.
> 255 nec levius doleas quam qui bibit ubera cervae
>   armatique tulit vulnus, inermis opem.   (Ovid, *Ibis*, ll. 253–56)

(And may you endure just as many wounds in your envenomed leg as Poeas's son [= *Philoctetes*], the heir of club-bearing Hercules, endured. Nor may you be more lightly pained than he who drank at the hind's udder [= *Telephus*] and endured the armed man's wound, the unarmed man's aid.)

These references are periphrastically constructed and are somewhat abstruse at best, but a confused Roman reader (whether Ibis or anyone else) would have recourse to mythographic texts for clarification.

Although the closest that Ovid comes to identifying Telephus is in calling him *qui bibit ubera cervae* (the one who drank at the hind's udder (Ovid, *Ibis*, l. 255)), which might seem incomprehensibly obscure,[34] in Hyginus we find a catalogue entitled *Qui lacte ferino nutriti sunt* (Those who were nourished by the milk of wild animals (Hyginus, *Fabulae*, 252)), which gives Telephus, nursed *ab cerua* (by a deer), as the first entry. Additionally, the periphrasis is in fact a bilingual pun, being a Latin translation of the perceived etymology of Telephus's name:

Τήλεφος· [...] ἐκλήθη δὲ διὰ τὸ θηλάσαι αὐτὸν ἔλαφον.
[*Télephos: [...] eklēthē dè dià tò thēlásai autòn élaphon.*][35]

(Telephus: [...] and he was called that on account of a deer nursing him.)

Such wordplay is not infrequent among Ovid's contemporaries.[36]

Following Philoctetes and Telephus, the next nine *exempla* serve as an unbroken catalogue that is tantamount to 'those who became blind' (Ovid, *Ibis*, ll. 257–72). Although there are no surviving parallels for a list of blind men, it is easy to imagine based on extant catalogues that such might well have existed. Williams refers to 'the generic diversity of Ovid's *exempla* of blindness, their seemingly random sequence within this tableau',[37] but in fact there is a great deal of coherence and associative logic to their ordering (see Table 2, which gives a limited set of the connections between the *exempla* in lines 253–72). The later couplets all feature *vates*, or poet-prophets, a particularly loaded concept in Augustan poetry;[38] there

[34] And indeed, the reference thoroughly stumped medieval scholiasts. Most branches of the scholiastic tradition confusedly report this to be a tyrant named Dareus, but the P-scholia fabricate a figure called Caridion who bears some resemblance to Telephus in the details of his life (see *Scholia in [...] Ibin*, ed. by La Penna, pp. 23–24). See Cameron, *Greek Mythography in the Roman World*, pp. 180–83, for some recent discussion of the *Ibis* scholia's possible origins.

[35] *Etymologicon Magnum*, ed. by Gaisford, 756K. 54–55.

[36] See, for example, O'Hara, *True Names*, pp. 79–88; Hendry, 'Three Propertian Puns'.

[37] Williams, *The Curse of Exile*, p. 92.

[38] See, particularly, Newman, *The Concept of Vates in Augustan Poetry*. Polymestor's couplet

is juxtaposition of those who slew their guests, juxtaposition of parricides, and so on. It is possible to see how the fates suffered by the exemplary figures form one catalogue, while their crimes form an entirely separate string of catalogues. Although some of these are not quite contiguous, this is generally due to the constraint of yet another salient connective detail forcing the couplets into their seemingly disjoint ordering.

Overlapping catalogues of those who became lame and those who became blind are perhaps mythographically pertinent, but why should these figure as Ovid's first *exempla*? Augustan poets usually put forward certain elements of their programme in the first poem of a book or in the opening few lines of a stand-alone poem,[39] and as the start of the *Ibis* catalogue essentially functions as a restarting of the poem,[40] the same may be true here.

Early on in the *Ibis* prologue, Ovid threatened to wrap his poem in *caecae historiae*, or 'obscure stories' — literally, '*blind* stories':

55   nunc, quo Battiades inimicum devovet Ibin,
             hoc ego devoveo teque tuosque modo,
      utque ille, historiis involvam carmina caecis,
             non soleam quamvis hoc genus ipse sequi.
                        (Ovid, *Ibis*, ll. 55–58)

(Now, in the same mode as Battiades [= *Callimachus*] cursed his enemy Ibis, I curse you and yours, and as he did, I shall wrap my songs in 'blind' stories, although I myself am not used to writing in this genre.)

Most scholars apply the label to all of Ovid's riddling *exempla*, but Williams points out that the nine blind men to whom Ovid alludes at the start of the catalogue literally exemplify those promised blind stories, creating a link (one of many) between the two halves of the poem.[41] The emphasis on blindness also

intrudes in the vatic chain, but this is presumably so as to set him with Polyphemus; both violate *xenia*, and both have names beginning with *Poly-*.

[39] For a bibliography, see Keith, 'Amores 1.1', pp. 327–28.

[40] The catalogue begins following the parodic invocation of a Muse (in this case, the 'invocation' of a Fate); in proclaiming himself her *vates* (Ovid, *Ibis*, l. 247), Ovid makes clear the prooemial nature of the invocation. For discussion of this transitional passage between prologue and catalogue (Ovid, *Ibis*, l. 247), see Hinds, 'After Exile'.

[41] 'At an early stage in the catalogue (ll. 259–72) Ovid wishes on his enemy the blindness which afflicted such figures as Tiresias, Phineus, and Polyphemus, thereby adducing mythological *exempla* which literally bring about the *historiae caecae* promised earlier' (Williams, 'On Ovid's *Ibis*', p. 181). See also Ingleheart, 'What the Poet Saw', p. 68, n. 6. The catalogue actually begins

activates what Jennifer Ingleheart terms 'the vocabulary of sight which permeates the exilic *corpus*',[42] with the result that further traces of Ovid's greater exilic programme can be seen.

There are three or four couplets (Ovid, *Ibis*, ll. 251–56 or 251–58) before the mini-catalogue of blind men begins, however, and these lines engage no less with the prologue of the *Ibis* and the overarching themes of Ovid's poetry. Williams notes that 'as the catalogue begins, Ovid sets out to intimidate the enemy by ostentatiously displaying its epic credentials. [...] The stage is set for an epic performance in the catalogue, and Ovid duly obliges by taking his starting-point from Troy',[43] by which Williams means Ovid's first curse: *neve sine exemplis aevi cruciere prioris, | sint tua Troianis non leviora malis* (Or that you may not be tortured without the examples of an earlier age, may your misfortunes be no lighter than the Trojans (Ovid, *Ibis*, ll. 251–52)). Ovid has had epic openings to his various works before now. In the *Amores*, he began with the epic *arma* (weapons) and metre of Virgil's *Aeneid* — only to find that Cupid was crippling his poetry by stealing a foot and thus turning epic metre into elegiac:[44]

> arma graui numero uiolentaque bella parabam
> edere, materia conueniente modis.
> par erat inferior uersus: risisse Cupido
> dicitur atque unum surripuisse pedem.
> (Ovid, *Amores*, i. 1. 1–4)

(Of arms and violent wars I was preparing to write in weighty verse, with subject matter suiting metre. The lower line was equal — Cupid is said to have laughed and filched one foot.)

A short-footed and limping elegiac Muse subsequently reared her head in Book iii of the *Amores*: *uenit odoratos Elegia nexa capillos, | et, puto, pes illi longior alter erat* (Elegy came, her scented hair bound up, and, I think, one of her feet was longer than the other (Ovid, *Amores*, iii. 1. 7–8)). Similar metrical jests appear elsewhere in the Ovidian corpus.

---

one couplet earlier, however; Bellerophon serves as a lynchpin between the lamed Philoctetes and Telephus and the blind men who follow, depending on which version of Bellerophon's story is followed.

[42] Ingleheart, 'What the Poet Saw', p. 67.

[43] Williams, *The Curse of Exile*, p. 91.

[44] For *arma* in the same metrical position and the assonance of the first words, see Kenney, 'Ovid'. The metrical pattern of elegiac couplets is given above, in n. 2.

Early in the *Ibis*, Ovid drew attention to his metre's inappropriateness for the poem's content (again using the loaded word *pes*, both an anatomical and a metrical foot):[45] *prima quidem coepto committam proelia versu,* | *non soleant quamvis hoc pede bella geri* (Indeed, having commenced my verse, I shall undertake the first battles, although wars are not typically waged in this foot [= metre] (Ovid, *Ibis*, ll. 45–46)). Elegiac metre, he has said both here and elsewhere, is unsuitable for bellicose poetics of any sort. So the catalogue's seemingly epic opening, in a work by Ovid, especially reduced to a single non-epic pentameter, should ring alarm bells.

Philoctetes and Telephus, who follow hot on the heels of the Trojans at the 'epic' beginning of the catalogue, occur as a pair elsewhere in Ovid's poetry, given as *exempla* of incurable wounds. They also appear together in Hyginus, as consecutive entries in the section summarizing stories from the epic Trojan War cycle. But they have something else in common — they were both wounded in the foot or leg.[46] I submit that this is in fact another metrical foot joke. Ovid, who loves to mention the 'foot' of his metre, can scarcely have ignored the location of the wounds given to his first two *exempla*.[47]

This opening, therefore, repeats the opening of the *Amores*, but in obscure terms and with an incurable wound replacing Cupid's playful theft. Elsewhere in the exile poetry, Ovid likens the same incurable wound, borne by Telephus or Philoctetes, to his own exilic wound.[48] Just as we saw earlier that the confu-

---

[45] '[In the exile poetry] Ovid calls attention to his choice of meter in various ways, to make sure the reader realizes its role as a constant. He uses puns on the word *pes* as he did in the *Amores*, thereby emphasizing the metrical similarity. [...] All Ovid's *pes*-puns contain a statement of poetics' (Nagle, *The Poetics of Exile*, p. 22).

[46] These two, plus Bellerophon, form an archetypal trio of tragic lame men. The scholia to Aristophanes' *Frogs* claim that Aristophanes called Euripides a 'cripple-maker' because he portrayed Bellerophon, Philoctetes, and Telephus as lame (*Scholia in Ranas*, l. 846), no doubt strongly influencing future portrayals of those three.

[47] Although Telephus was technically wounded in the thigh, it was the result of catching his foot in a vine-shoot. Furthermore, Ovid refers obliquely to the location of Philoctetes' wound as his *crus*, or leg in general, and the basic limping gait is of equal importance. The very absence of the word *pes* from these couplets underscores its programmatic presence.

[48] Ovid, *Tristia*, v. 2. 9–20 (Telephus and Philoctetes); Ovid, *Tristia*, i. 1. 97–100 (Telephus); Ovid, *Tristia*, ii. 19–22 (Telephus, possibly following a *pes* pun at ii. 15–16); Ovid, *Ex Ponto*, i. 3. 3–10 (Philoctetes). Previously, their wounds had been likened to the wounds of love (Ovid, *Remedia amoris*, 111–16 (Philoctetes), Ovid, *Amores*, ii. 9. 7–8 (Telephus), Ovid, *Remedia amoris*, 47–48 (Telephus)); here their programmatic replacement of Cupid echoes the replacement of love's pain with exile's pain that allows Ovid his justification for maintaining the elegiac metre in his exilic lamentations.

sion of names in the *Ibis* finds a parallel in Ovid's greater exilic corpus, and just as the pervasive 'vocabulary of sight' is reflected in the next stretch of catalogue, here too we have an echo of Ovid's other poetry. However, without knowledge of Ovid's standard literary jests, or without knowledge of the traditional affiliation of Telephus and Philoctetes, the reference and poetic gesture are lost, and the *exempla* revert to mere *tela* (missiles) of Ovid's (or Ibis's) outrageous fortune.

In this way, as in so many others, the *Ibis* ultimately contradicts its deceptively mythographic appearance. Mythography's reductive prose stands alone and serves to make sense of other works. The *Ibis*, however, with its lines of poetry that are reduced far beyond any prose text and far beyond simple comprehension, relies on other works to make sense of it.

Works Cited

Primary Sources

Callimachus, *Aetia*, in *Callimachus*, ed. by Rudolf Pfeiffer, 2 vols (Oxford: Clarendon Press, 1949–53), I: *Fragmenta* (1949), pp. 1–160

Etymologicon Magnum: seu verius lexicon saepissime vocabulorum origines indagans ex pluribus lexicis scholiastis et grammaticis anonymi cuiusdam opera concinnatum, ed. by Thomas Gaisford (Amsterdam: Hakkert, 1962)

Hyginus, *Fabulae*, ed. by Peter K. Marshall, 2nd edn (München: Saur, 2002)

Ovid, *Amores*, in *Carmina Amatoria*, ed. by Antonio Ramírez de Verger (München: Saur, 2006), pp. 1–140

——, *Ex Ponto libri quattuor*, ed. by J. A. Richmond (Leipzig: Teubner, 1990)

——, *Ibis: prolegomeni, testo, apparato critico e commento*, ed. by Antonio La Penna, Biblioteca di Studi Superiori, 34 (Firenze: 'La Nuova Italia' Editrice, 1957)

Scholia in Ranas, in *Scholia Graeca in Aristophanem cum prolegomenis grammaticorum*, ed. by Friedrich Dübner (Hildesheim: Olms, 1969; orig. publ. Paris: Didot, 1877), pp. 273–314

Scholia in P. Ovidi Nasonis Ibin: Introduzione, testo, apparato critico e commento, ed. by Antonio La Penna, Biblioteca di studi superiori, 35 (Firenze: Nuova Italia, 1959)

Secondary Studies

Ahl, Frederick M., *Lucan: An Introduction*, Cornell Studies in Classical Philology, 39 (Ithaca: Cornell University Press, 1976)

Battistella, Chiara, 'Momenti intertestuali nell'*Ibis*', *Studi italiani di filologia classica*, 4th ser., 8 (2010), 179–202

Bernhardt, Ursula, *Die Funktion der Kataloge in Ovids Exilpoesie*, Altertumswissenschaftliche Texte und Studien, 15 (Hildesheim: Olms-Weidmann, 1986)

Bing, Peter, 'Ergänzungsspiel in the Epigrams of Callimachus', *Antike und Abendland*, 41 (1995), 115–31

Cameron, Alan, *Greek Mythography in the Roman World*, American Classical Studies, 48 (Oxford: Oxford University Press, 2004)

Devereux, G., 'The Self-Blinding of Oidipous in Sophokles: *Oidipous Tyrannos*', *Journal of Hellenic Studies*, 93 (1973), 36–49

Feeney, D. C., 'History and Revelation in Vergil's Underworld', *Proceedings of the Cambridge Philological Society*, 32 (1986), 1–24

García Fuentes, María Cruz, 'Mitología y maldición en el *Ibis*, I', *Cuadernos de filología clásica*, n.s., 2 (1992), 133–53

——, 'Mitología y maldición en el *Ibis*, II', *Cuadernos de filología clásica*, n.s., 3 (1992), 103–16

Gordon, Carol Jean, 'Poetry of Maledictions: A Commentary on the *Ibis* of Ovid' (unpublished doctoral thesis, McMaster University, 1992)

Harrison, Stephen, 'Ovid and Genre: Evolutions of an Elegist', in *The Cambridge Companion to Ovid*, ed. by Philip Hardie (Cambridge: Cambridge University Press, 2002), pp. 79–94

Hendry, Michael, 'Three Propertian Puns', *Classical Quarterly*, n.s., 47 (1997), 599–603

Hinds, Stephen, 'After Exile: Time and Teleology from *Metamorphoses* to *Ibis*', in *Ovidian Transformations: Essays on Ovid's 'Metamorphoses' and its Reception*, ed. by Philip Hardie, Alessandro Barchiesi, and Stephen Hinds, Cambridge Philological Society Supplement, 23 (Cambridge: Cambridge University Press, 1999), pp. 48–67

——, 'Ovid among the Conspiracy Theorists', in *Classical Constructions: Papers in Memory of Don Fowler, Classicist and Epicurean*, ed. by S. J. Heyworth, P. G. Fowler, and Stephen Harrison (Oxford: Oxford University Press, 2007), pp. 194–220

——, 'Review of Harry B. Evans, *Publica Carmina: Ovid's Books from Exile*', *Journal of Roman Studies*, 76 (1986), 321–22

Housman, A. E., 'The *Ibis* of Ovid', *Journal of Philology*, 35 (1920), 287–318

Ingleheart, Jennifer, 'What the Poet Saw: Ovid, the Error and the Theme of Sight in *Tristia 2*', *Materiali e discussioni per l'analisi dei testi classici*, 56 (2006), 63–86

Keith, Alison M., 'Amores 1.1: Propertius and the Ovidian Programme', in *Studies in Latin Literature and Roman History VI*, ed. by Carl Deroux, Collection Latomus, 217 (Brussels: Latomus, 1992), pp. 327–44

Kenney, Edward John, 'Ovid: A Poet in Love with Poetry', *Omnibus*, 8 (1984), 11–14

Nagle, Betty Rose, *The Poetics of Exile: Program and Polemic in the 'Tristia' and 'Epistulae ex Ponto' of Ovid*, Collection Latomus, 170 (Brussels: Latomus, 1980)

Newman, John Kevin, *The Concept of Vates in Augustan Poetry*, Collection Latomus, 89 (Brussels: Latomus, 1967)

O'Hara, James J., *True Names: Vergil and the Alexandrian Tradition of Etymological Wordplay* (Ann Arbor: University of Michigan Press, 1996)

Rossum-Steenbeek, Monique van, *Greek Readers' Digests? Studies on a Selection of Subliterary Papyri*, Mnemosyne Supplement, 175 (Leiden: Brill, 1998)

Steiner, Grundy, 'Ovid's *Carmen Perpetuum*', *Transactions and Proceedings of the American Philological Association*, 89 (1958), 218–36

Watson, Lindsay, *Arae: The Curse Poetry of Antiquity*, ARCA, Classical and Medieval Texts, Papers and Monographs, 26 (Leeds: Cairns, 1991)

Williams, Gareth D., *The Curse of Exile: A Study of Ovid's 'Ibis'*, Cambridge Philological Society Supplement, 19 (Cambridge: Cambridge University Press, 1996)

——, 'On Ovid's *Ibis*: A Poem in Context', *Proceedings of the Cambridge Philological Society*, n.s., 38 (1992), 171–89

——, 'Ovid's Exile Poetry: *Tristia, Epistulae ex Ponto* and *Ibis*', in *The Cambridge Companion to Ovid*, ed. by Philip Hardie (Cambridge: Cambridge University Press, 2002), pp. 233–45

——, 'Ovid's Exilic Poetry: Worlds Apart', in *Brill's Companion to Ovid*, ed. by Barbara Weiden Boyd (Leiden: Brill, 2002), pp. 337–81

MEDIEVAL LATIN MYTHOGRAPHY AS DEATH AND RESURRECTION OF MYTH

Jan Ziolkowski*

The collocation of death and renewed life in the title to this essay is wholly deliberate. The idea that myth exists at all is not at present unthreatened and has probably seldom been entirely so. Indeed, the adjective 'mythical' is often applied in reference to the bygone, so that it borders on the trite to speak of the mythical past, and sometimes the past is what has effectively died or at least is thought to have died.

To make matters worse, myth has been under assault for at least two and a half millennia. It can be spurned for conflicting with both reality and reason. When opposed to reality, myth is synonymous with fiction. When set against reason, it is irrational gibberish. For these and other causes, efforts have long been made to desacralize myth and to strip it of the significance that lends it its special legitimacy. But make no mistake: myth lives on. Since the process of demythologization is far from complete, the supposed mythlessness of our culture or of any past one is itself nothing but a myth, what has been called 'the myth of mythlessness'.[1]

Among the many lasting legacies of the Latin Middle Ages to Western culture is to have brought together the Greco-Roman and Judeo-Christian traditions. Were the two traditions not set next to each other so often in so many contexts as to make their relationship seem natural or familiar, they would seem exceedingly

* Jan Ziolkowski (ziolkowskij@doaks.org) is Arthur Kingsley Porter Professor of Medieval Latin at Harvard University, the Director of the Dumbarton Oaks Research Library and Collection, and the author of *Fairy Tales From Before Fairy Tales: The Medieval Past of Wonderful Lies* (Ann Arbor: University of Michigan Press, 2007), and numerous other studies of folklore and mythology in medieval European literature.

[1] Coupe, *Myth*, p. 9.

Writing Down the Myths, ed. by Joseph Falaky Nagy, CURSOR 17, (Turnhout: Brepols, 2013) pp. 87–106   BREPOLS ⚇ PUBLISHERS   10.1484/M.CURSOR-EB.1. 100848

odd bedfellows. In fact, the merging of the two could be considered in mythic terms the equivalent of interbreeding — serious mythcegenation. In this sense the title makes an effort to capture and highlight the peculiarity of embedding classical myth in a Christian context.

In comparison with fields such as Classics or various vernacular languages and literatures, myth and mythography have received relatively short shrift in medieval Latin studies. Thus the contrast with Scandinavian studies and Celtic studies is telling. Three chief explanations for the relative dearth of scholarship (a missed — or unmythed — opportunity) present themselves. One is that the Middle Ages are viewed correctly as having been a profoundly religious era, and the underpinnings of the Christian faith tend generally in the still predominantly Christian cultures of Europe and North America not to be presented as mythic. It seems to be nearly axiomatic that a person's own myths pass as religion or faith, while those of others run the risk of being relegated to the class of untruths — of myths.

Another reason the reception of classical mythography has been understudied is that the juxtaposition of medieval and mythography may induce thoughts of Celtic, Scandinavian, and Slavic myths, but not of Greco-Roman ones and their immediate offshoots. By dint of being Greco-Roman, myths so designated qualify as being ancient rather than as medieval. To this way of thinking they may have been transmitted in the Middle Ages, but they were not created then: classical mythography as received and even as modified in the Middle Ages would not pass muster as medieval mythography per se.

A third factor for the disproportionately little scholarship on Medieval Latin mythography, which may seem somehow to contradict the second factor, is that classical myths were preserved and transmuted so extensively in writings of the Latin Middle Ages as to overwhelm any aspiration to an exhaustive treatment. Mythography pervaded vast sweeps of culture altogether outside schools, but its special home was within teaching contexts. For this reason records of it abound in the glosses and commentaries that poured forth from and for medieval education. To this day myths carry associations with childishness, partly because mythological compendia have a way of being refashioned for the use of children, if they were not in fact targeted at that audience from the outset. In the Middle Ages books for young learners were perforce didactic, didacticism was rampant in schools, and thus myth was solidly entrenched in didactic schoolishness.

For all the reasons that have been adumbrated, those who have tracked the reception of classical myths have approached it most often on a classical-poet-by-classical-poet or myth-by-myth basis, so that we have monographs on Virgil,

Ovid, and other classical authors whose writings incorporate myths or on Venus, Hercules, Saturn, Medusa, and other characters of Greco-Roman myth.

In contrast, this contribution attempts a synthetic overview *in breve* rather than a comprehensive exposition of Latin mythography. This bird's eye view, perhaps from riskily Icarian altitudes, focuses particularly on what survived from the classical tradition into the Middle Ages and how such survival took place. Two dauntingly long volumes by Jane Chance have barely scratched the surface, since medieval mythography, even when delimited as the interpretation of classical myths, forms a body of materials nearly as forbiddingly large and complex as the corpus of medieval biblical exegesis.[2] At the same time, Chance's roughly 1250 pages would not be navigable for the individual in search of practical orientation. For such guidance those with a command of German could consult a brief history of classical mythology during the Middle Ages and Renaissance that was published in 1921 as an appendix to a famous mythological lexicon.[3] A how-to guide that sets forth strategies for coping with situations that are likely to arise in research can be found in the chapter on classical mythology included (perhaps counter-intuitively) in R. E. Kaske's *Medieval Christian Literary Imagery: A Guide to Interpretation.*[4] Last but not least, Michael Herren has produced a series of articles that have established not only which mythographic works were known but also the routes of transmission that made possible the incorporation of Greco-Roman mythology into early medieval Christian culture.[5]

Producing an overview of Latin mythography requires touching upon not only systematic treatises on mythology but also sources containing sporadic mentions of it.

Into the first category, of systematic treatment, would fall Ovid's *Metamorphoses* (completed in AD 8), Hyginus's *Fabulae* and *De astronomia* (also written early in the first century AD), the three treatises ascribed to the so-called Vatican Mythographers (which have been dated from the last quarter of the ninth century to the mid-twelfth century), Petrus Berchorius's *Ovidius moralizatus* (1340), Giovanni Boccaccio's *Genealogia deorum gentilium* (completed in various versions between 1360 and 1374), and others.

---

[2] Chance, *Medieval Mythography*.

[3] Gruppe, 'Geschichte der klassischen Mythologie'.

[4] Kaske, *Medieval Christian Literary Imagery*, pp. 104–29.

[5] Herren, 'The Earliest European Study of Graeco-Roman Mythology'; Herren, 'Literary and Glossarial Evidence'; Herren, 'The Transmission and Reception of Graeco-Roman Mythology'.

What was the transmission history of pre-medieval mythographic works in the Middle Ages, and to what extent and to whom were they available as models to the post-classical world? Our picture has clarified only very recently, since Hyginus did not receive a proper edition until 1997 and since the vast expanse of other ancient Roman mythographic sources elicited a thorough consideration only in 2004.[6] The transmission of full-blown mythographic works is notably thin in the early Middle Ages, as may be demonstrated by the case of Ovid's *Metamorphoses* (with no complete MSS extant from before the second half of the eleventh century).[7]

Beyond the systematic treatises sprawls a daunting jungle of sporadic mentions that make the *Metamorphoses* look restrained by comparison. In this category would be subsumed sources such as glosses and commentaries on myth-rich classical poets, with the obvious candidate being Virgil, who deserves notice because of the canonical importance in medieval Western learned culture that his poems held. Then as now, the first half of the *Aeneid* elicited a disproportionate share of attention. Texts that abound in this way in references to myths have been termed mythophoric.

Outside these two groupings, various post-classical authors and texts warrant mention for less orderly presentations of mythographic material. Under this heading would fall the first two books of Martianus Capella's *De nuptiis Philologiae et Mercurii* (fifth century) and the *Eclogue of Theodulus* (tenth century or earlier).[8] The profusion of codices and commentary from Late Antiquity onwards alone proves that 'the cosmic pantheon of the *De nuptiis* was authoritative for the middle ages'.[9] Parsing the notion of 'the cosmic pantheon' further, it has been observed that 'In the universe of the *De nuptiis* cosmology and mythology are precisely integrated, and mythographical analysis involves no more than a translation from one set of terms to the other'.[10] The *Eclogue of Theodulus* is equally precise in its dis-integration. It purveys myths in the voice of a character tellingly named Pseustis (Falsehood), whose choices are refuted by equal and opposite episodes from Scripture delivered by (predictably) Alethia (Truth).[11]

---

[6] See, respectively, Hyginus, *Fables*, ed. and trans. by Boriaud, and Cameron, *Greek Mythography in the Roman World*.

[7] *Texts and Transmission*, ed. by Reynolds and others, p. 276.

[8] Martianus Capella, *De nuptiis Philologiae et Mercurii*, ed. by Dick; Theodulus, *Ecloga*, ed. by Casaretto.

[9] Wetherbee, *Platonism and Poetry*, p. 90.

[10] *The Middle Ages*, ed. by Minnis and Johnson, p. 106.

[11] Theodulus, *Ecloga*, ed. by Casaretto.

Definitions

If no myth exists to recount the challenge of defining myth, we should take upon ourselves collectively in this volume the responsibility for creating one. In it the would-be definer would play a role similar to that of Prometheus — in this case, we could call him Promytheus — while myths themselves would have to be cast as resembling hydras, since whacking off the head of myth accomplishes nothing beyond causing mythology and mythography to replace it.

Rhetorically it would be feasible first to distract many readers (although no doubt not one as high-powered as whoever you are who are now perusing these words) with a show of joking and then to pirouette away from the difficulty of definition, but rhetoric and honesty are two different matters. So what *can* we say about myths? Three stock contentions would be that myths pass as sacred and true, that myths take place in the past, and that myths are narratives transmitted at least initially through oral tradition. An essential fourth dimension is that myths relate to intersections between the human and the divine. This vague statement is a way of signifying that myths tell individual tales of gods, supernatural figures, heroes, and so forth.

The challenge of determining what myth is makes even more problematic the definition of compounds such as mythology and mythography.[12] But rather than linger any longer over the definition of myth, I will compound temerity with temerity by discussing ever so briefly the meaning of mythology. The term 'mythology' serves most commonly to designate not the study of myth (as the -logy element might imply) but rather the totality of the myths of a culture or people. One trite observation I would venture is that myth is often regarded as prehistoric, mythology as historic. Consequently myth passes for being more authentic than mythology.[13] And what holds true of mythology applies even more aptly to mythography. The Heisenberg principle obtains with full force: merely by interpreting myths — or by existing at the stage of cultural development where such interpretation would seem necessary or legitimate — the mythographer alters myths irreparably. But alteration and execution (in the sense of putting to death) are not synonymous.

Whatever the present-day usage of myth and mythology, we face the customary difficulty that confronts philologists of medieval languages in reconciling the understandings of myth today, both specialist and general, with those that prevailed in the Middle Ages. In other words, we need to find out if myth and its

---

[12] Chance, *Medieval Mythography*, I, 2.

[13] Bies, 'Mythologie', p. 1074.

relatives belonged to the lexicon of medieval writers and if there were other terms from different roots that designated tales which we would recognize as being myths by our lights.

Investigation confirms that in Medieval Latin the Greek derivatives *mythus* or *mythos, mythicus, -a, -um; mythologia, mythologizare, mythologus, mythographus,* and *mythopoeius* were sesquipedalian words that existed mainly in glossaries, etymological dictionaries, and other reference works but that were otherwise not in common currency.

In perpetuating an understanding of *mythus* or *mythos*, a short passage in Martianus Capella was particularly influential: in it we are told that the leading character Philology 'had a fear [...] that [...] she would forgo altogether the myths and legends of mankind, those charming poetic diversities of the Milesian tales'.[14] The noun was construed in this spirit by lexicographers, especially those who flourished in the twelfth century and later. Thus both Osbern of Gloucester, a twelfth-century monk-encylopedist, and Hugutio of Pisa, author of an etymological dictionary who died in 1210, define myth as 'a playful tale, sweet in the telling'.[15] This definition constitutes a powerful affirmation of a view that no longer repudiates myths as the fake figments of pagans but instead celebrates them as the entertaining fictions of poets. With any threat of a pagan revival centuries in the past, readers (and writers) had gained the freedom to enjoy stories of bygone gods.

On the rare instances when the word *mythus* was used, it was routinely equated to the native Latin *fabula* or *narracio*.[16] In antiquity *fabula* referred to talk and story of many sorts. In one important range of meaning it denoted types of tales that are transmitted in literature. In the *Soliloquies* (probably composed in late 386) Augustine defined it as 'a falsehood composed for usefulness or delight'.[17] The corpus of such lying stories comprised Aesopic fables, Milesian

---

[14] Martianus Capella, *De nuptiis Philologiae et Mercurii*, ed. by Dick, p. 43, ll. 1–4 [2.100]: 'Mythos, poeticae etiam diuersitatis delicias Milesias historiasque mortalium [...] se penitus amissuram [...] formidabat [Philologia]'; Martianus Capella, *The Marriage of Philology and Mercury*, trans. by Stahl and Johnson, p. 35.

[15] Osbern of Gloucester, *Derivazioni*, ed. by Bertini and Ussani, p. 412, M 24. 4: 'et hec mithus thi .i. fabula iocosa et relatu dulcis, unde Martianus [2.220] nunc ergo mithos terminatas infiunt'. Uguccione da Pisa, *Derivationes*, ed. by Cecchini and others, II, 792, M 129. 19: 'hic mittus, mitti, fabula iocosa, dulcis relatu'.

[16] *Dictionary of Medieval Latin*, ed. by Latham and Howlett, VI, 1879, *mythologia* and *mythus, -os*.

[17] 'Compositum ad utilitatem delectationemve mendacium'. Augustine, *Soliloquiorum*

tales, dramatic narratives, and, last but not least, what would pass muster today as myths.[18] Augustine states the matter succinctly in *The City of God* (written between 413 and 427): 'If usage allowed it in Latin, we would call the genre fabular, but we call it fabulous; for mythic is so called from fables, seeing that fable is called *muthos* in Greek'.[19] This broader Latinate sense of fable was without doubt in the mind of the American writer, Thomas Bulfinch (1796–1867), when he entitled his extraordinarily successful mythography *The Age of Fable; or, Stories of Gods and Heroes* (1855). He was not thinking of Aesop's cock-and-bull stories. In belles-lettres the Latin *mythus* in all its multitudinous orthographies makes almost no appearance in early texts, with a single ninth-century appearance in a poem of Walahfrid or Pseudo-Walahfrid Strabo.[20] A century later the compound *mythographus* is attested in prose, in the mid-tenth-century *Phrenesis* by Rather of Verona.[21]

Mythologia, as its elements would seem to suggest, signified the narration or explication of myth. Even if the word had not figured in glosses and glossaries, it would have been widely known owing to its prominence in the title of a book (*c.* AD 500) by the Late Antique mythographer, Fulgentius.[22] Consequently Fulgentius lent his name eponymously to any allegorical interpretation of myth.[23] The noun was also familiar from the commentary tradition. Notably, Servius,

---

libri duo, ed. by Hörmann, p. 70, II. 11. 16–17.

[18] *Thesaurus linguae Latinae*, VI. 1. 27.40–28.79, especially pp. 27.40–28.17.

[19] Augustine, *City of God*, ed. by Dombart and Kalb, I, 252, 6. 5. 20–23: 'Latine si usus admitteret, genus, quod primum posuit, fabulare appellaremus; sed fabulosum dicamus; a fabulis enim mythicon dictum est, quoniam μῦθος Graece fabula dicitur' (If Latin usage allowed, the type that he placed first we would call fabular; but let us say 'fabulous'; for 'mythical' is so called from fables, seeing that fables are called mythos in Greek). See also Augustine, *City of God*, ed. by Dombart and Kalb, I, 255, 6. 6. 4–5: 'De theologia mythica, id est fabulosa, et de civili contra Varronem' (Of mythical — that is, fabulous — theology, and of civil, against Varro).

[20] Walahfrid Strabo, *Carmina*, ed. by Dümmler, p. 397, 50. 1. 15: 'Laudent concordes sueto te more sorores, | Est quorum numerus bis quater atque semel, | Quae, testante mytho, volitantes alite multo | Auricomo comites intonuere polis'.

[21] Ratherius Veronensis, *Phrenesis*, ed. by Reid, p. 209, 13. 410–11 (composed April 955–May 956): 'de cupido et inuido noster uti narrat mytographus'. Ratherius Veronensis, *The Complete Works*, trans. by Reid, p. 254: 'as our mythographer tells us about the envious miser'.

[22] *Hermeneumata pseudodositheana*, ed. by Goetz, p. 500, l. 31: 'matologia fabularum ratio'. On knowledge of Fulgentius's text see Laistner, 'Fulgentius in the Carolingian Age'. Cited by Orderic Vitalis, *Ecclesiastical History*, ed. by Chibnall, IV, 44, 7. 8. On his date and identity, see Hays, 'The Date and Identity of the Mythographer Fulgentius'.

[23] Lehmann, *Pseudo-antike Literatur des Mittelalters*, p. 20.

the late fourth-century grammarian, uses it in an observation on *Aeneid*, IV. 295, where he says that 'he means Acheron as it were being born from lowermost Tartarus [...] and this is the explication of the myth'.[24] In general *mythologia* comes to the fore infrequently in medieval Latin. In verse it appears in Eberhard of Béthune's *Graecismus* (*c.* 1212), a versified grammar that thrived as a textbook in the grammar schools from the thirteenth century on. Eberhard resorts to *mythologia* as a near synonym for *mythos*, a circumstance dictated by his desire to impose parallelism by resorting to terms with the suffix *-ia*.[25] Still rarer is the verb *mythologizare*, which emerges as a Grecism in the translationese of Henry Aristippus in his Latin rendering of Plato's *Phaedo* (1160).[26] The rhetorical figure of *mythopoeia* was so restricted in its circulation as not to have earned a place in Heinrich Lausberg's exhaustive *Handbook of Literary Rhetoric*.[27] However, its existence is attested in Cassiodorus's *Exposition of the Psalms* (late sixth century), and it entered into the glossaries from some such source.[28]

By and large myth and its derivatives survived only as quarantined in a scholastic lazaretto, where they were seen as being associated above all with poets. This sequestering began in Antiquity. For instance, Augustine in *The City of God* quotes a fragment of Varro (second century BC) to the effect that 'They call [that type of theology] mythical which the poets in particular employ; physical, which the philosophers employ; and civil, which the people employ'.[29] Whenever the

---

[24] Servius, *Aeneidos librorum VI–XII commentarii*, ed. by Thilo and Hagen, II, 53, commentary on Virgil, *Aeneid*, IV. 295: 'Acheronta vult quasi de imo nasci Tartaro [...]; et haec est mythologia'.

[25] Eberhard of Béthune, *Graecismus*, ed. by Wrobel, pp. 86–87, 10. 246–49: 'Castigat satira, sed elegia cantat amores, | Mythologia quod est fictum, comoedia uillas, | Uera dat historia, tragoedia turpia regum. | Est, mihi crede, mitos filum, sed fabula mythos, | A mitos hexamitum est, a mythos mythologia'.

[26] Plato, *Phaedo*, ed. by Minio-Paluello, p. 10, ll. 23–24: 'Decet eum qui debet illuc peregrinari pervalde inspicere et mithologizare de peregrinacione' (It befits him who ought to make a pilgrimage there to examine and mythologize thoroughly about pilgrimage).

[27] Lausberg, *Handbook of Literary Rhetoric*, ed. by Orton and Anderson.

[28] Cassiodorus, *Expositio Psalmorum*, ed. by Adriaen, 4. 30: 'Sub figura mythopoeia ecclesiam dicamus loqui' (We should say that the Church speaks in the figure of mythopoeia [which is to say, contriving myths]). For *figura metapoea*, see *Glossaria Leidensia*, 28. 34, in *A Late Eighth-Century Latin-Anglo-Saxon Glossary*, ed. by Hessels, p. 23.

[29] Varro, quoted in Augustine, *City of God*, ed. By Dombart and Kalb, I, 252, 6. 5. 25–27: 'Mythicon [genus theologiae] appellant, quo maxime utuntur poetae; physicon, quo philosophi; civile, quo populi'.

pagan poets came under assault, myth suffered along with its makers and broad-casters. Thus Peter Riga in a preface to his paraphrase of the Bible entitled *Aurora* (last quarter of the twelfth century) asked that 'mythologists give way and that this one [God] should occupy the first and foremost place among the training grounds of the prophets'.[30]

In the globalized present the differences between (and within) Greek and Roman mythologies may have been blurred even more than centuries of effort in Antiquity to make them closely parallel may have achieved. The members of the Greek pantheon bear different names from those of the Roman, but their equivalence is or was made strong. Nonetheless, the Romans had their own rich mythic tradition apart from Greek mythography.[31] In considering the medieval Western reception of myths we must take into account the balkiness or disin-terest that people may have felt about differences between Greek and Roman, high and low, urban and rustic, widespread and local, and so forth that would have mattered keenly in Antiquity. It was within the context of mythography that Greek and Roman myths were gathered to form what is designated collectively as mythology. The underlying aim was to equip an elite with the knowledge neces-sary to interpret and apply the myths within a specific code. This code — what could be called a literary etiquette — served to differentiate the cultured from the uncultured, the literate from the illiterate, the educated from the uneducated, and eventually the Latinate from the un-Latinate.

The 'Mythographic Urge'

Forty years ago the classicist G. S. Kirk asserted persuasively that 'the genuine mythopoeic urge lay in the hidden past; even Homer and Hesiod were working with a long, selective and formalized tradition'.[32] It may be axiomatic that the sys-tematic recording of mythography takes place only when faith in the myths has waned. Before mythography individual myths live as *membra disiecta*, although that phrase leaves the misimpression that this stage is preceded by one of organi-city — of mythology. When grappling with such questions, we enter a rugged terrain that will be familiar instantly to anyone who has ever worried over the

---

[30] Aegidius of Paris, *Aurora*, ed. by Beichner, I, 12: 'Mintologi cedant et apud gymnasia uatum | Hec habeant primum precipuumque locum'.

[31] Wiseman, *The Myths of Rome*.

[32] Kirk, *Myth*, p. 251.

relationship between heroic lay and epic — and a landscape that Richard Martin covers ably in his contribution to this volume.[33]

Mythography is the rationalization of myth, and given the conventional tension between reason and religion it has stood on an often shaky divide. Even in much of the Roman era the traditional stories of Greek and Roman myth had ceased to be entrenched in popular culture as belief. Paradoxically, many components of mythology retained their salience as stock elements of elite culture. From the Hellenistic period on, versatility in recognizing the myths became ever more the prerequisite to comprehension of the literature and art that surrounded anyone who frequented the rich and powerful. Myths formed part of what could be styled 'cultural literacy'. From this stage, if not earlier, the collectivity of myths turned into a storehouse of topoi, exempla, images, comparisons, metonymies, metaphors, motifs, and materials that could serve the ends of those in all sorts of arts and crafts. Thus mythology became a so-called 'poetic heuristic' long before the heyday of Johann Gottfried Herder (1744–1803) and German Romanticism.[34]

Despite the increasing prestige attached to them, myths were no longer automatically familiar as they once would have been from the caregivers of early childhood. Acquisition of mythology became a function of elementary schooling, and the didactic element that seems always to be a constituent of mythography loomed even larger. In the Latin tradition myth was intimately connected with writing, since it was purveyed within the confines of grammar. The very name of *grammatica* speaks to the letteredness of this craft, since its key element is *gramma*, the Greek word for a written letter. But where in biblical terms the letter kills, in this instance grammar offers life support or even adrenaline. Viewed from this perspective, the relationship between myth and mythography may be seen as tantamount to that between oral and written epic (primary and secondary).

The focus of schoolmasters on myth can be inferred readily from the amount of mythological and mythographic information provided by commentators, especially Servius. The tendency to concentrate upon myths in commentaries had been memorialized already in Greek literature in scholia to the *Iliad* and *Odyssey*. In the Latin tradition, Virgil exerted a magnetic effect comparable to that of Homer. No single individual would merit the name of *mythographus Vergilianus* as the *mythographus Homericus* has done, although Alan Cameron has made a convincing case for the existence of so-called mythographic companions to Virgil, Ovid, and other learned poets. He even dates in the second or third century the *Argumenta* or *Narrationes fabularum Ovidianarum* that have often cir-

---

[33] See above, pp. 45–66.

[34] Herder, 'Ueber die neuere Deutsche Litteratur', p. 444.

culated under the name of Lactantius Placidus.[35] Servius goes beyond the explication of myth that is the traditional stock in trade of the mythographer, since often
he supplies mythological explanations even when they are not explicit in the text.

The mythographic comparisons and Servian commentaries speak to antiquari-
anism, not to religious belief. Long before the advent of Christianity the power of
myth diminished. Then again, the immediacy of myth as a vehicle for philosophical meaning only increased. Thus Stoics and Epicureans, conceiving of the tales as
similitudes and the gods in them as personifications of natural powers, explained
the myths allegorically.[36] This tendency was complemented by euhemerism, the
practice named after the Greek philosopher Euhemeros (340–260 BC) whereby
the gods in myths were effectively stripped of their divinity and explained away as
heroes who had been upgraded from legendary to mythical.

Probably in the later second century AD, the Roman grammarian Sextus
Pompeius Festus belittled this theory, perhaps implying that it was more far-
fetched than the myths themselves: 'Sus Minervam. A proverb to indicate that
a person claims to teach another what he does not know himself. Varro and
Euhemerus preferred to wrap this proverb in absurd myths rather than merely to
relate it'.[37]

The 'Mythographic Purge'

There is no need to belabour the banality that words are frequently defined in
opposition to others; human minds and language often work in binaries. Myths
that do not belong to the religion of the viewer run the risk of being labelled
as false beliefs, which is the sense in which 'That's just a myth' may be uttered
dismissively. In Greek the antonym of *mythos* was *logos*. Under Christianity
myth came to be branded ever more as fictitious and false, in contrast to the
sacred Christian narratives that were held to be true. The Greco-Roman gods
are literally demonized. The polytheism of the ancient Greek and Roman
world of gods and heroes was understandably resisted initially, as Christian
monotheism endeavoured to take hold. Writers pay lip service to this concep-

[35] Cameron, *Greek Mythography in the Roman World*. On the authorship, see Otis, 'The
Argumenta of the So-Called Lactantius'.

[36] Allen, *Mysteriously Meant*, and Murrin, *The Veil of Allegory*.

[37] Pompeius Festus, *De verborum*, ed. by Lindsay, p. 408, ll. 15–21: '"Sus Minervam" in
proverbio est, ubi quis id docet alterum, cuius ipse inscius est. Quam rem in medio, quod aiunt,
positam Varro et Euhemerus ineptis mythis involvere maluerunt, quam simpliciter referre'.

tion of myth even after Christianity has triumphed decisively over paganism. Thus in the section of the *Etymologies* (early seventh century) devoted to the pagan gods, Isidore of Seville demeans myths as *vanae fabulae* (VIII. 11. 29) and the efforts of pagans to rationalize them as *gentilium fabulosa figmenta* (VIII. 11. 89).[38]

Myth or *fabula* as pagan was at the start at best irrelevant and at worst a threat to Christianity, yet the gods were built into literary, especially poetic, language. We resort without a second thought to adjectives such as jovial, mercurial, martial, and saturnine. We can refer to v.d. (which after all abbreviates venereal disease) without visualizing mighty Aphrodite or her Roman counterpart any more than when speaking of a sexually transmitted disease. We pour milk over cereal without turning our minds to Ceres, just as we can drive a Saturn (while the make is still with us) without having an image of a Roman god flash before our eyes. But this was not the case in early Christianity, when the koine of cultural expression contained much to give a believer pause. Merely to mention the gifts of Bacchus as an expression for wine made a concession to paganism that many believers begrudged making. In the spirit of spurning such formulations and (more importantly) the belief system behind them, the Christian Latin writer Arnobius wrote in rhymed prose his seven-book diatribe against pagans, the *Adversus nationes* (*c.* 303), in which he assembled the immoral episodes in ancient mythology so as to refute polytheism.[39] Yet the language and literature of the gods were too deeply rooted to be abandoned completely. From the need to resolve this fundamental conflict arose the images of the despoiling of the Egyptians (*spoliatio Aegyptiorum*) and the captive slave girl (*captiva gentilis*), formulated respectively by Augustine and Jerome on the basis of episodes in the Bible. Both images embodied the possibility that the appearance of pagan monuments, literary or otherwise, could be retained so long as the content was Christianized. The effect of the imagery was to validate Christian allegorical readings of texts that would have been suspect in the absence of such interpretation. How much time had to pass before Christians in the West became fully comfortable in absorbing Greco-Roman mythology — how long it was before they could live easily with imagery that may have seemed to conflict with their theology — are questions that have still not been answered fully.[40]

---

[38] Macfarlane, *Isidore of Seville*, pp. 17, 32.

[39] Arnobius, *Adversus nationes libri VII*, ed. by Marchesi.

[40] Hugo Rahner made an effort to address such issues in relation to the Greek East: Rahner, *Greek Myths and Christian Mystery*, trans. by Battershaw.

The 'Mythographic Resurgence'

Despite intermittent efforts to jettison the pagan classics, educators throughout the Middle Ages had to surmount the hurdle of justifying the inclusion of Virgil, Ovid, and other pagan poets in whose oeuvre myths were central, since basic education — grammar school — was founded upon them. Once teachers had decided to include the gentiles, they had to figure out how to do so.

Mythography is regarded now most often as a form of literary criticism. In the Middle Ages literary criticism was subsumed under the heading of *grammatica*, which was devoted not only to correct speaking and writing but also to the explication of the poets. The last-mentioned component of grammar encompassed mythography as the interpretation or explanation of myth.

Classical mythographers had sought to explain — or explain away — stories of the gods that caused embarrassment because of their sexuality or scandal. The typical method of explanation was allegorical. In the Middle Ages the myths in question were also first and foremost classical Greco-Roman myth. The mythographers followed many procedures, but in the main they relied on conceptions and principles that had been laid down already in Late Antiquity by Macrobius (*c.* AD 400). According to his neo-Platonic presuppositions, poetry comprises an exterior of *fabula* that as *figura* covers a *philosophia*. When the *fabula* deals with the pagan gods, Macrobius advocates two methods for interpreting them. The 'mythical' explains them on the basis of euhemerism, the 'physical' on the basis of natural allegory that construes the interaction of the gods as relating to the operations of the four elements.[41]

In the case of Virgil's *Aeneid*, we have systematic allegorical interpretations in Fulgentius and (Pseudo-) Bernardus Silvestris (twelfth century). Ovid's *Metamorphoses* filters into the curriculum only at the beginning of the twelfth century. A commentary from that period portrays Ovid as monotheistic and contemptuous of the pagan gods but obliged for political expedience to strike a pose as polytheistic.[42] This commentary detects in the Roman poet basic elements of Platonism. An anonymous mock-sermon from the same period alternates between moralizing the *Metamorphoses* and allegorizing.[43] In this reading the *mystica fabula* of the myths offer good examples to its monastic and clerical readers. This poem anticipates the 'subversion of the twelfth-century project of read-

---

[41] Brinkmann, *Mittelalterliche Hermeneutik*, pp. 184–86, 283–84.

[42] Villa, 'Tra *fabula* e *historia*', pp. 247–48.

[43] Dronke, *Medieval Latin*, I, 232–38, and II, 452–63.

ing classical myth "integumentally" — as a covering — by Jean de Meun in the *Roman de la Rose* (second half of the thirteenth century).[44] Ovid's *Metamorphoses* received its fullest allegorization in the so-called Vulgate Commentary (mid-thirteenth century), in the anonymous *Ovide moralisé*, and in Petrus Berchorius.[45]

In form the medieval tradition of mythography resembles closely the classical. Much is contained in scattershot fashion in the commentary tradition, where words, names, and phrases are explicated in glosses, either interlinear or marginal, with or without lemmata, and in sustained introductions and commentaries that are transmitted sometimes as autonomous works and in other cases chopped up selectively in the guise of longer glosses.

The Mythopoeic Splurge of the Twelfth and Thirteenth Centuries

The convention of demythologizing pagan stories took shape in the late twelfth century in application to Ovid's *Metamorphoses* by Arnulf of Orleans, who is followed closely by John of Garland in the *Integumenta Ovidii* (c. 1234).[46] The tradition extends to the classicizing Oxford friars of the early fourteenth century, John Ridevall and Thomas Walsingham.[47]

The so-called Third Vatican Mythographer wrote a treatise that was ascribed in the Middle Ages to Alexander Neckam but is now often attributed to Alberic of London. The text demythologizes the classical pagan pantheon by taking two tacks. One is to contend euhemeristically that the gods were mortals, while the other is to apply principles of philosophical allegory, whereby they stood for natural elements or stages in life (thus Jupiter and Juno represented respectively upper and lower air, Saturn old age). The Third Vatican Mythographer had a healthy afterlife, being used heavily by Petrus Berchorius and Thomas Walsingham.[48]

An as yet unexplained paradox of the twelfth and thirteenth centuries is that just as Aristotle began taking by storm what would now be called the educational establishment of Western Europe, Plato — despite the restricted circulation of his works — exercised a stronger influence, whether directly or indirectly,

---

[44] *The Middle Ages*, ed. by Minnis and Johnson, p. 131.

[45] *The 'Vulgate' Commentary on Ovid's 'Metamorphoses'*, ed. by Coulson; Coulson, 'A Study of the "Vulgate" Commentary'; *'Ovide moralisé'*, ed. by de Boer, de Boer, and van't Sant; Petrus Berchorius, *De formis figurisque deorum*, ed. by Engels.

[46] John of Garland, *Integumenta Ovidii*, ed. by Ghisalberti.

[47] Smalley, *English Friars and Antiquity*.

[48] Rigg, *A History of Anglo-Latin Literature*, p. 125.

on many poets. Bernard of Chartres, who flourished in the first quarter of the twelfth century, seems to have been the first to use the term *integumentum* to describe not merely the veil of allegory but in addition the techniques necessary to remove the veil. He fused or helped to fuse myth — *fabula* in his terminology — with the effort to explore the relationship of God to the created universe. His acolyte William of Conches, who was particularly active in the mid-twelfth century, carried on his undertaking, especially by employing myth as a resource for Neoplatonic philosophizing.[49] The mid-twelfth-century author of commentaries on the *Aeneid* and on Martianus Capella who is often known as Bernardus Silvestris belongs to the same tradition. To paraphrase a shrewd observation, mythology and cosmology share an uneasy but profitable relationship in the Chartrian reading of classical poetry, which endeavours without wholesale success to reconcile 'violence and adultery among the gods with their roles as symbols of cosmic and psychological order'.[50] Still more impressively Bernardus Silvestris sets in motion a series of competing cosmological epics — a 'Myth Universe Contest'.

The most lasting outcome of Christian Neoplatonism went beyond conventional mythography to achieve the unique mythopoeia of Bernardus Silvestris in his *Cosmographia* or *De mundi universitate*, of Alan of Lille in his *De planctu Naturae* and *Anticlaudianus*, and of Jean de Meun in his *Roman de la Rose*.[51] These texts are remarkable for presenting new myths that centre upon hypostases — upon personification allegory — but that also incorporate in exuberant profusion myths garnered from the full spectrum of mythographic sources. More tellingly for our purposes, they bring to a culmination the inversion of myth and mythography that had been initiated in Late Antiquity. Commentators such as Macrobius and Fulgentius had interpreted the experiences of Aeneas as indicative of the intellectual and spiritual development that a human being undergoes in the course of life. The poets — mythopoets — Bernardus Silvestris, Alan of Lille, and Jean de Meun made this interpretation on the basis of their new myths. Thus mythography, which often thrives only when the object of its study dies or has died, was made myth, and the poems of these authors may be rightly deemed to have reached mythic proportions. In terms of popularity (as can be gauged by numbers of codices) these works attained 'myth congeniality'.

---

[49] *The Middle Ages*, ed. by Minnis and Johnson, pp. 132–33.

[50] Wetherbee, *Platonism and Poetry*, p. 9.

[51] Bernardus Silvestris, *Cosmographia*, ed. by Dronke; Alan of Lille, *De planctu Naturae*, ed. and trans. by Wetherbee; Alan of Lille, *Anticlaudianus*, ed. and trans. by Wetherbee; Jean de Meun, *Roman de la Rose*, ed. by Lecoy.

The Renaissance has been extolled, among many other things, for having freed mythology from a Christian imprisonment.[52] If the greatest freedom is to live, change, and grow, we may wish to give more credit to the twelfth and thirteenth centuries. More than mere coincidence, or the strange proclivities of the editors in choosing contributors to this volume, may be at work in the dates of not only the Latin authors Geoffrey of Monmouth (*c.* 1100–*c.* 1155) and Saxo Grammaticus (1150–1220) but also the Old Icelandic Snorri Sturlson (1179–1241).

---

[52] Wehrli, 'Antike Mythologie im christlichen Mittelalter'.

Works Cited

Primary Sources

Aegidius of Paris, *Aurora: Petri Rigae Biblia versificata; A Verse Commentary on the Bible*, ed. by Paul E. Beichner, Publications in Mediaeval Studies, 19, 2 vols (Notre Dame: University of Notre Dame Press, 1965)

Alan of Lille, *Anticlaudianus*, ed. and trans. by Winthrop Wetherbee (Cambridge, MA: Harvard University Press, 2013)

——, *De planctu Naturae*, ed. and trans. by Winthrop Wetherbee (Cambridge, MA: Harvard University Press, 2013)

Arnobius, *Adversus nationes libri VII*, ed. by Concetto Marchesi, 2nd edn (Torino: Paraviae, 1953)

Arnulf of Orleans, 'Allegoriae super Ovidii Metamorphosin', in *Arnolfo d'Orléans, un cultore di Ovidio nel secolo XII*, ed. by Fausto Ghisalberti, Memorie del Reale Istituto Lombardo di scienze e lettere, 24 (Milano: Hoepli, 1932), pp. 157–234

Augustine, *City of God*, ed. by Bernard Dombart and Alfons Kalb, *Santi Aurelii Augustini episcopi De civitate Dei libri XXII*, 2 vols (Stuttgart: Teubner, 1981)

——, *Soliloquiorum libri duo; De inmortalitate animae; De quantitate animae*, ed. by Wolfgang Hörmann, Corpus scriptorum ecclesiasticorum Latinorum, 89 (Wien: Hoelder-Pichler-Tempsky, 1986)

Bernardus Silvestris, *Cosmographia*, ed. Peter Dronke, Textus minores 53 (Leiden: Brill, 1978)

Bulfinch, Thomas, *The Age of Fable: or, Stories of Gods and Heroes* (Boston, MA: Sanborn, Carter, and Bazin, 1855)

Cassiodorus, *Expositio Psalmorum*, ed. by Marcus Adriaen, in *Magni Aurelii Cassiodori Senatoris opera*, ed. by A. J. Fridh, J. W. Halporn, and Marcus Adriaen, Corpus Christianorum, series latina, 96–98, 3 vols (Turnhout: Brepols, 1958–73), II–III (1958)

Eberhard of Béthune, *Graecismus*, ed. by Johannes Wrobel (Breslau: Koebner, 1887)

Hyginus, *Fables*, ed. and trans. by Jean-Yves Boriaud, Collection des universités de France, 344 (Paris: Belles lettres, 1997)

Jean de Meun, *Roman de la Rose*, ed. by Félix Lecoy, 2 vols, Classiques français du Moyen Âge, 92, 95, 98 (Paris: Champion, 1965–75)

John of Garland, *Integumenta Ovidii: poemetto inedito del secolo XIII*, ed. by Fausto Ghisalberti, Testi e documenti inediti o rari, 2 (Messina: Principato, 1933)

A Late Eighth-Century Latin-Anglo-Saxon Glossary Preserved in the Library of the Leiden University (Ms. Voss. Q° Lat. n°. 69), ed. by John Henry Hessels (Cambridge: University Press, 1906)

Martianus Capella, *De nuptiis Philologiae et Mercurii*, ed. by Adolf Dick, rev. by Jean Préaux (Stuttgart: Teubner, 1969)

——, *The Marriage of Philology and Mercury, in Martianus Capella and the Seven Liberal Arts*, trans. by William Harris Stahl and Richard Johnson with E. L. Burge, Records of Civilization: Sources and Studies, 84, 2 vols (New York: Columbia University Press, 1971–77), II

Orderic Vitalis, *Ecclesiastical History*, ed. by Marjorie Chibnall, 6 vols (Oxford: Clarendon Press, 1969–1980)

Osbern of Gloucester, *Derivazioni*, ed. by Ferruccio Bertini and Vincenzo Ussani, Biblioteca di 'Medioevo Latino', 16 (Spoleto: Centro italiano di studi sull'alto medioevo, 1996)

'Ovide moralisé': Poème du commencement du quatorzième siècle publié d'après tous les manuscrits, ed. by C. de Boer, Martina G. de Boer, and Jeannette Th. M. van't Sant, 5 vols (Amsterdam: Müller, 1915–38)

Petrus Berchorius, *De formis figurisque deorum. Reductorium morale, liber XV: Ovidius moralizatus, cap. i. Textus e codice Brux., Bibl. Reg. 863–9 critice editus*, ed. by J. Engels, Werkmateriaal, 3 (Utrecht: Rijksuniversiteit, Instituut voor Laat Latijn, 1966)

Plato, *Phaedo,* ed. by Laurentius Minio-Paluello, *trans.* by Henry Aristippus, *Corpus Platonicum medii aevii: Plato latinus*, 2 (London: Warburg Institute, 1950)

Pompeius Festus, Sextus, *De verborum significatu quae supersunt cum Pauli epitome*, ed. by Wallace Martin Lindsay (Leipzig: Teubner, 1913)

Ratherius Veronensis, *The Complete Works of Rather of Verona*, trans. by Peter L. D. Reid, Medieval & Renaissance Texts & Studies, 76 (Binghamton: Medieval & Renaissance Texts & Studies, 1991)

——, *Phrenesis*, in *Ratherii Veronensis: Praeloquiorum libri VI, Phrenesis, Dialogus confessionalis, Exhortatio et preces*, ed. by Peter L. D. Reid, Corpus Christianorum, continuatio Mediaevalis, 46 (Turnhout: Brepols, 1984), pp. 206–18

Servius, *Aeneidos librorum VI–XII commentarii*, in *Servii grammatici qui feruntur in Vergilii carmina commentarii*, ed. by Georg Thilo and Hermann Hagen, 3 vols (Leipzig: Teubner, 1881–1902), II (1884)

Theodulus, *Ecloga: il canto della verità e della menzogna*, ed. Francesco Mosetti Casaretto, Per verba, 5 (Florence: SISMEL edizioni del Galluzzo, 1997)

Thesaurus linguae Latinae, ed. by Deutsche Akademie der Wissenschaften zu Berlin and Internationale Thesauruskommission, 10 vols to date (Leipzig: Teubner, 1900–99; München: Saur, 2000–06; Berlin: Gruyter, 2007–)

Uguccione da Pisa, *Derivationes: edizione critica princeps*, ed. by Enzo Cecchini and others, Edizione nazionale dei testi mediolatini, 11; Edizione nazionale dei testi mediolatini, 1st ser., 6, 2 vols (Firenze: SISMEL edizioni del Galluzzo, 2004)

The 'Vulgate' Commentary on Ovid's 'Metamorphoses': The Creation Myth and the Story of Orpheus, ed. by Frank Thomas Coulson, Toronto Medieval Latin Texts, 20 (Toronto: Pontifical Institute of Mediaeval Studies, 1991)

Walahfrid Strabo, *Carmina*, in *Poetae latini aevi Carolini II*, ed. by Ernst Dümmler, in *Monumenta Germaniae Historica: Poetarum latinorum medii aevi*, ed. by Ernst Dümmler and others, 6 vols (Berlin: Weidmann, 1881–1951), II (1884), 267–423

Secondary Studies

Allen, Don Cameron, *Mysteriously Meant: The Rediscovery of Pagan Symbolism and Allegorical Interpretation in the Renaissance* (Baltimore, MD: Johns Hopkins University Press, 1970)

Bies, Werner, 'Mythologie', in *Enzyklopädie des Märchens*, ed. by Kurt Ranke and others, 14 vols to date (Berlin: Gruyter, 1977–), IX (1998), cols 1073–86

Brinkmann, Hennig, *Mittelalterliche Hermeneutik* (Tübingen: Niemeyer, 1980)

Cameron, Alan, *Greek Mythography in the Roman World*, American Classical Studies, 48 (Oxford: Oxford University Press, 2004)

Chance, Jane, *Medieval Mythography*, 2 vols (Gainesville: University Press of Florida, 1994–2000)

Frank Thomas Coulson, 'A Study of the "Vulgate" Commentary on Ovid's *Metamorphoses* and a Critical Edition of the Glosses to Book One" (unpublished PhD thesis, University of Toronto, 1982)

Coupe, Laurence, *Myth*, 2nd edn (London: Routledge, 2009)

Dronke, Peter, *Medieval Latin and the Rise of European Love-Lyric*, 2nd edn, 2 vols (Oxford: Clarendon, 1968)

Goetz, George, ed., *Hermeneumata pseudodositheana*, in *Corpus glossariorum Latinorum*, ed. by George Goetz and others, 7 vols (Leipzig: Teubner: 1888–1923), III (1892)

Gruppe, Otto, 'Geschichte der klassischen Mythologie und Religionsgeschichte während des Mittelalters im Abendland und während der Neuzeit', in Otto Gruppe, *Geschichte der Klassischen Mythologie und Religionsgeschichte* (Leipzig: Teubner, 1921), pp. 1–26; supplement to *Ausführliches Lexikon der griechischen und römischen Mythologie*, ed. by Wilhelm Heinrich Roscher, 6 vols (Leipzig: Teubner, 1884–1937)

Hays, Gregory, 'The Date and Identity of the Mythographer Fulgentius', *Journal of Medieval Latin*, 13 (2003), 163–252

Herder, Johann Gottfried, 'Ueber die neuere Deutsche Litteratur. Fragmente. Eine Beilage zu den Briefen, die neueste Litteratur betreffend', in *Herders sämmtliche Werke*, ed. by Bernhard Suphan, 33 vols (Berlin: Weidmann, 1877–1913), I (1877), 426–49

Herren, Michael, 'The Earliest European Study of Graeco-Roman Mythology AD 600–900', *Acta classica universitatis scientiarum Debreceniensis*, 34–35 (1998–99), 25–49

——, 'Literary and Glossarial Evidence for the Study of Classical Mythology in Ireland AD 600–800', in *Text and Gloss: Studies in Insular Learning and Literature Presented to Joseph Donovan Pheifer*, ed. by Helen Conrad-O'Briain and others (Dublin: Four Courts, 1999), pp. 49–67

——, 'The Transmission and Reception of Graeco-Roman Mythology in Anglo-Saxon England, 670–800', *Anglo-Saxon England*, 27 (1998), 87–103

Kaske, Robert E., *Medieval Christian Literary Imagery: A Guide to Interpretation* (Toronto: University of Toronto Press, 1988)

Kirk, Geoffrey Stephen, *Myth: Its Meaning and Functions in Ancient and Other Cultures*, Sather Classical Lectures, 40 (Berkeley: University of California Press, 1970)

Laistner, Max Ludwig Wolfram, 'Fulgentius in the Carolingian Age', in *The Intellectual Heritage of the Early Middle Ages: Selected Essays*, ed. by Chester G. Starr (Ithaca: Cornell University Press, 1957), pp. 202–15

Latham, Ronald Edward, and David E. Howlett, eds, *Dictionary of Medieval Latin from British Sources*, 14 vols to date (London: Oxford University Press for The British Academy by, 1975–)

Lausberg, Heinrich, *Handbook of Literary Rhetoric: A Foundation for Literary Study*, ed. by David E. Orton and R. Dean Anderson, trans. by Matthew T. Bliss, Annemiek Jansen, and David E. Orton (Leiden: Brill, 1998)

Lehmann, Paul, *Pseudo-antike Literatur des Mittelalters*, Studies of the Warburg Institute, 13 (Leipzig: Teubner, 1927)

Macfarlane, Katherine Nell, *Isidore of Seville on the Pagan Gods (Origines VIII.11)*, Transactions of the American Philosophical Society, 70, pt 3 (Philadelphia: American Philosophical Society, 1980)

Minnis, Alastair, and Ian Johnson, eds, *The Middle Ages*, in *The Cambridge History of Literary Criticism*, ed. by George Alexander Kennedy, 9 vols (Cambridge: Cambridge University Press, 1989–2001), II (2005)

Murrin, Michael, *The Veil of Allegory: Some Notes Toward a Theory of Allegorical Rhetoric in the English Renaissance* (Chicago: University of Chicago Press, 1969)

Otis, Brooks, 'The *Argumenta* of the So-Called Lactantius', *Harvard Studies in Classical Philology*, 47 (1936), 131–63

Rahner, Hugo, *Greek Myths and Christian Mystery*, trans. by Brian Battershaw (New York: Harper & Row: 1963)

Reynolds, Leighton Durham, and others, eds, *Texts and Transmission: A Survey of the Latin Classics* (Oxford: Clarendon Press, 1983)

Rigg, A. G., *A History of Anglo-Latin Literature, 1066–1422* (Cambridge: Cambridge University Press, 1992)

Smalley, Beryl, *English Friars and Antiquity in the Early Fourteenth Century* (Oxford: Blackwell, 1960)

Villa, Claudia, 'Tra *fabula* e *historia*: Manegoldo di Lautenbach e il "maestro di Orazio"', *Aevum*, 70 (1996), 245–56

Wehrli, Max, 'Antike Mythologie im christlichen Mittelalter', *Deutsche Vierteljahrsschrift für Literaturwissenschaft und Geistesgeschichte*, 57 (1983), 18–32

Wetherbee, Winthrop, *Platonism and Poetry in the Twelfth Century: The Literary Influence of the School of Chartres* (Princeton: Princeton University Press, 1972)

Wiseman, Timothy P., *The Myths of Rome* (Exeter: University of Exeter Press, 2004)

Dead Men Don't Wear Plaid:
Celtic Myth and Christian Creed in Medieval Irish Concepts of the Afterlife

Bernhard Maier*

hen in 2003 the *Rheinisches Landesmuseum* (Regional Rhenish Museum) in Bonn was reopened after five years of construction work, all exhibits had been rearranged thematically. Grave goods from the Late Hallstatt-Period, which used to be shown together with contemporaneous non-religious artefacts, had been detached from their cultural context and now served to illustrate a development which visitors were to appreciate under the catchy title *Von den Göttern zu Gott: Religion, Tod, Jenseits* (From the Gods to God: Religion, Death, the Afterlife). Among the scenes which had been reconstructed, using a blend of archaeological findings and scholarly imagination, was the interior of a Late-Hallstatt-Period burial mound dating to the sixth century BC, showing the deceased person wrapped in a blue-and-red plaid, stretched out on a four-wheeled waggon. Having watched Steve Martin's and Carl Reiner's 1982 film *Dead Men Don't Wear Plaid* (then brand-new) as a young student during my first year in Celtic, I may be forgiven for feeling reminded of its title by this scene. On a less personal level, the reconstruction may make us wonder why the museum specialists should have assumed that the pre-Roman Celtic inhabitants of the Rhineland used a kind of Scotch tartan to enshroud their dead.

While textile finds from the pre-Roman Iron Age are on the whole extremely rare, some fairly well preserved samples are known from the shafts of salt mines at

* Bernhard Maier (bernhard.maier@uni-tuebingen.de) is Professor of Comparative Religion at the University of Tübingen. He has authored *Die Religion der Kelten* (München: Beck, 2001), *Die Religion der Germanen* (München: Beck, 2003), and many other works on Celtic and comparative mythological and religious traditions.

Writing Down the Myths, ed. by Joseph Falaky Nagy, CURSOR 17, (Turnhout: Brepols, 2013)
pp. 107–136   BREPOLS PUBLISHERS   10.1484/M.CURSOR-EB.1. 100849

Dürrnberg near Hallein and Hallstatt in Austria. Predominantly made of wool, they were produced on warp-weighted looms in a variety of complex weaving techniques, several blue, green and yellow dyes being used to produce striped and chequered fabrics.[1] Yet although these finds may have contributed to shaping the modern image of pre-Roman Iron Age clothing, it is safe to assume that they did not create it, as most of them are comparatively recent, not widely known and rather unspectacular, at least to the non-specialist eye. The same holds good for their Insular counterparts, the famous yellow-and-brown, check-patterned piece of cloth known as the 'Falkirk Tartan' (presumed to date back to the third century AD) having been discovered as late as 1933.[2] The findings of Celtic philology can hardly have played a significant role either, as Scottish Gaelic *plaide* (originally meaning 'mantle' or 'blanket') has no plausible Indo-European etymology, while English *tartan* is generally supposed to be of Romance origin, neither of the two words being known from the Continental Celtic record. On the other hand, what seems to have played a crucial role in linking Scottish plaids and ancient Celts is a statement of the classical historian Diodorus Siculus, presumably based on the authority of the Stoic philosopher and historian Posidonius:

> The clothing they [the Celts] wear is striking — shirts which have been dyed and embroidered in varied colours, and breeches, which they call in their tongue *bracae*; and they were striped coats, fastened by a buckle on the shoulder, heavy for winter wear and light for summer, in which are set checks, close together and of varied hues.[3]

It hardly needs the translator's note ('Diodorus appears to be trying to describe a kind of Scotch tartan') to help us make the connection. Nor should we assume that this is a recent association, as already an early Victorian historian of costumes referred to the clothing described by Diodorus as 'the undoubted origin of the Scotch plaid or tartan', assuring us that 'a Highland chief in his full costume [...] affords as good an illustration of the appearance of an ancient Briton of distinction as can well be imagined'.[4] In fact, the connection can be traced back to the

---

[1] *The Cambridge History of Western Textiles*, ed. by Jenkins, pp. 67–70. Recent technical studies include Rast-Eicher, *Textilien, Wolle, Schafe der Eisenzeit*; *Hallstatt Textiles*, ed. by Bichler and others; Banck-Burgess, *Die Textilfunde*; Banck-Burgess, *Mittel der Macht*; and von Kurzynski, '*...und ihre Hosen nennen sie bracas*'.

[2] See, for example, Cheape, *Tartan*, p. 7.

[3] Diodorus Siculus, *Library of History*, v. 30. 1. On Diodorus's indebtedness to Posidonius, see, for example, Malitz, *Die Historien des Poseidonios*.

[4] Planché, *History of British Costume*, p. 8.

Scottish humanist George Buchanan (1506–1582) who noted with respect to the inhabitants of the Western Isles, 'Majores sagis versicoloribus plurifariam distinctis utebantur, ut adhuc plærisque mos est' (Their ancestors used to wear coats of many different colours, and some of them still retain this custom), adding, 'Vetere Gallorum sermone paulum mutato utuntur' (They use the ancient language of the Gauls, somewhat modified).[5] Unsurprisingly, in an English translation made in the early nineteenth century, the coats have turned into plaids and the ancient language of the Gauls has become 'the ancient Gaelic language'.[6] Combining the evidence of classical ethnography and modern archaeology, we may be persuaded that among the ancient Celts, dead men *did* wear plaid after all — or, at least, that they might have worn it.

Having established this unbroken thread or rather twill of continuity stretching from the Central European Iron Age to the Insular Celtic present, we may proceed to ask what happened to those other yarns which used to be spun among the ancient Celts, especially those connected with the belief in life after death. Were they cut in the wake of Christianization, or were they merely redyed? For some three hundred years, the attention of scholars has focused on the literature of early medieval Ireland, which even today is widely regarded as a repository of ancient Celtic beliefs, although the extent of the pagan influence and the way in which the native tradition was amalgamated with Latin learning and the Christian religion continue to be hotly disputed. To what extent did the old beliefs and stories continue to be remembered in early medieval Ireland? How do we know that something is genuinely pagan? What were the Christian authors' leading ideas in combining pagan and Christian elements? In what follows, I propose to tackle these questions by a comparative study of one particular text which has the triple advantage of being short, early and replete with notions that can be linked to the belief in life after death.

The text known as *Echtrae Chonnlai* is generally taken to have been composed in the eighth century AD, having come down to us as a more or less complete text in seven manuscripts dating from the late eleventh to the late sixteenth centuries.[7] Taking up just over two pages of the diplomatic edition of *Lebor na hUidre* (the oldest extant codex in Irish), the text may be given in full, adopting the literal English translation of its most recent editor:

---

[5] Buchanan, *Rerum Scoticarum Historia*, pp. 19–20.

[6] Buchanan, *The History of Scotland*, trans. by Aikman, i, 40–41.

[7] *Echtrae Chonnlai*, ed. by McCone, pp. 1–47.

Connlae the Ruddy, son of (lit. to) Conn of the Hundred Battles, when he was at his father's side (lit. on his father's hand) on (lit. in) the summit of Uisnech, he saw the woman in unfamiliar clothing. Connlae said: 'Whence have you come, O woman?'. The woman replied: 'I have come from (the) lands of (the) living, in which there is neither death nor sin nor transgression (/original sin). We consume (ever)lasting feasts without service (/exertion). (There is) harmony with us without strife. (It is) great peace in which we are so that it is from these we are called people of peace'. 'Who are you talking to?' said Conn of the Hundred Battles. No one saw the woman but Connlae alone. The woman replied: 'He is talking to a young, beautiful woman of good family who does not expect death or old age. I have loved Connlae the Ruddy. I summon him to the Plain of Delights in which Bóadag the everlasting is king without grief, without woe in his land since he assumed sovereignty. Come with me, O speckled-necked, candle-red Connlae the Ruddy. The yellow head of hair which is upon you above a purplish face, it will be a distinction of your kingly appearance (/form). If you come with me, the youth (and) beauty of your appearance (/form) will not perish until dream-laden judgement'.

Conn said to his druid, whose name was Coran(n) (lit. Coran[n] his name) when all heard what the woman had said and they did/could not see her: 'I beseech you, O Corann of great song (and) of great art. An excessive demand has come upon me that is beyond my counsel, that is beyond my power, a struggle that has not come upon me since I assumed sovereignty. (It is) a deceitful contest of unseen forms (that) compels me with a view to stealing my exceedingly fair son through evil moves. He is carried (away) from my kingly hand (=side) by women's spells'. Then he intoned over the seat/location of the woman so that no one heard the woman's voice and so that Connlae did not see the woman at that time. When the woman went away (lit. out of it) in response to (lit. before) the druid's chanting she threw an apple to Connlae: Thereafter Connlae was without drink (and) without food until the end of a month and he did not deem any sustenance worth eating (lit. any sustenance was not worthwhile with him for consuming) save his apple. Nothing that he ate took anything away from the apple but it remained (lit. was still) whole. Longing then seized Connlae for the appearance of the woman that he had seen.

The day their month was up (lit. full), the aforesaid Connlae was at his father's side (lit. on his father's hand) in the plain of Arcommin. He saw the woman (coming) up to him, when she said to him: 'Grandly does Connlae sit amidst the short-lived dead awaiting terrible death. The everliving living invite you. You are a champion to the people of the sea, who behold you every day in the assemblies of your fatherland amidst your beloved near ones'. As Conn of the Hundred Battles heard the woman's voice, he said to his people: 'Call the druid to me. I see (that) his tongue has been cast off from her today'. Thereupon the woman said: 'O Conn of the Hundred Battles, do not love druidry. It is in a little while that the Great High King's righteous (and) decent one will reach your judgements with many wondrous followers. His law will soon come to you. He will destroy the spells of the druids of base teaching in front of the black, bewitching Devil'.

Conn thought it strange (lit. it was strange with Conn) (that) Connlae would not give answer to anyone except when (lit. that) the woman should come (i.e. be present). 'Has what the woman said penetrated (lit. gone/got under) your mind, O Connlae?', said Conn. Connlae said. 'It is not easy for me and besides I love my people. Yet longing for the woman has seized me'. The woman said: 'You have — let me free us from requests — your longing towards the sea (and away) from them. In my ship of crystal may we encounter it, if we should reach the peace of Bóadag. There is another land that may not be the nearest to seek. I see (that) the sun is setting. Though it be far, we shall reach (it) before night. It is the land which gladdens the mind of everyone whom it encompasses (lit. The land which gladdens the mind of everyone whom it encompasses is it). There is no race there save only women and maidens'. Thereupon Connlae took a leap from them so that there was escape (to safety) in the pure ship. They saw them (going) from them as far as their vision reached it (lit. as far as their vision could follow it). (It is) a voyage of the sea that they did and they were not seen thereafter. The End.[8]

Looking for the associations of this story with the pre-Christian religion of Ireland, we may start by observing that both the name of the protagonist and the setting of the opening scene locate it neatly in the pagan period, Conn of the Hundred Battles being assumed to have lived in the second century AD, and the Hill of Uisnech in the province of Meath being taken to have been the ritual centre of pre-Christian Ireland. As regards the pagan religion, our text specifically mentions or alludes to four elements which are known from other early sources and thus are susceptible to a comparative study: the mysterious woman from the 'people of peace', the druid, magic produced by 'women's spells' and what for brevity's sake we may call the mythical island.

As pointed out by the editor, the way in which the mysterious woman whom Connlae encounters refers to her own people as the 'people of peace' implies a pun which is based on the homonymy of Old Irish *síd* 'burial mound' and *síd* 'peace'. While it was widely believed in early medieval Ireland that prehistoric burial mounds were the dwelling-places of supernatural beings who were for this reason referred to as *áes síde*, 'the people of the hollow hills', the woman proposes an alternative etymology of this traditional designation, connecting it with 'harmony [...] without strife' ('cáinchomrac [...] cen debuid') and 'great peace' ('síd már'), 'so that it is from these we are called people of peace' ('conid de suidib no-

[8] *Echtrae Chonnlai*, ed. by McCone, pp. 125–99, where the translation is given piecemeal as part of the textual notes which follow McCone's edition. Note that the division into paragraphs is mine and that no attempt has been made to retain the alliterative and metrical character of much of the direct speech.

n:ainmnigther áes síde').[9] The pivotal role which the woman plays in our text
makes it important to know just what the author and his audience might have
believed about the *áes síde*, but this is far from obvious, as contemporary sources
are scarce and do not present a clear picture, based as they are on an amalgamation of pagan Irish, classical Roman, and Latin Christian ideas. In *Fiacc's Hymn*
on Saint Patrick, which is dated to the eighth century, we read 'For tūaith Hérenn
bái temel | tūatha adortais síde | ní creitset in fírdeacht | inna trindōte fíre'.[10]
Translated by the editors as 'On the folk of Ireland there was darkness: the people
used to worship *síde*: they believed not the true Godhead of the true Trinity',
these verses might lead us to suppose that the *áes síde* were no other than the old
pagan gods of Ireland. However, this may be no more than a Christian reinterpretation, the early medieval author assuming with the Fathers of the Church that
the old gods were only demons and that, the *áes síde* being a kind of demons, they
once must have been worshipped as gods by the pagan Irish. Significantly, the
form *sidi* in one of the two manuscripts from which the text was edited is paralleled by the word *ídla* 'idols' in the other.[11] In fact, it may even be asked whether
tūatha should not be taken as a mere calque on Latin *gentes* (= Greek *éthnē*) 'hea-
thens', so that *tūatha adortais síde* would mean no more than 'the pagans worshipped demons'.

Of special interest in this connection is the text known as the *Collectanea* of
Tírechán, in which the word *síde* (genitive plural) is assumed to be glossed by
deorum terrenorum 'of earth-gods'.[12] Once more, however, things are not as clear-
cut as we would wish them to be. Relating the encounter of Patrick and his retinue with two daughters of the pagan king Loíguire, the text describes the reaction of the two sisters as follows:

---

[9] *Echtrae Chonnlai*, ed. by McCone, pp. 56–57; and see Ó Cathasaigh, 'The Semantics of
"*síd*"'; Hamp, 'Varia x'; and Sims-Williams, 'Some Celtic Otherworld Terms'. On the medieval
Irish belief in the *áes síde*, see most recently Borsje, 'Monotheistic to a Certain Extent'.

[10] See *Thesaurus Palaeohibernicus*, ed. by Stokes and Strachan, II, 317.

[11] As pointed out by Borsje, 'Monotheistic to a Certain Extent', p. 59 n. 27. For a comprehensive study of the early Christian equation of pagan gods with idols and demons, see
Woyke, *Götter, 'Götzen', Götterbilder*.

[12] To my knowledge, the first publication in which it is assumed that *deorum terrenorum*
is a mere gloss on *síde*, referring to the chthonic nature of the *síde*, is an account of Irish fairy
beliefs by John O'Donovan, 'Irish Popular Supersitions'; see also the account given under *sídh*
in *An Irish-English Dictionary*, ed. by O'Reilly and O'Donovan. Since then, O'Donovan's view
has been widely adopted, for example by Mac Cana, *Celtic Mythology*, p. 63; Mac Mathúna,
'Paganism and Society in Early Ireland', p. 3; and Nagy, *Conversing with Angels and Ancients*,
p. 101 n. 97.

Et quocumque essent aut quacumque forma aut quacumque plebe aut quacumque regione non cognouerunt, sed illos uiros side aut deorum terrenorum aut fantassiam estimauerunt, et dixerunt filiae illis: 'Ubi uos sitis et unde uenistis'?

(And they did not know whence they were or of what shape or from what people or from what region, but thought they were men of the other world or earth-gods or a phantom; and the maidens said to them: 'Whence are you and whence have you come'?[13])

Obviously, taking *deorum terrenorum* as a mere gloss on the word *síde* presupposes that *aut* 'or' is used to introduce this gloss. However, we would expect *uel* rather than *aut* in this function, and elsewhere in the sentence *aut* is clearly used to introduce new pieces of information rather than explanatory glosses.[14] In addition, it may be asked whether we are justified in taking *terrenus* in the sense of *chthonic*, referring to the burial-mounds as dwelling-places of the *áes síde*. Elsewhere, Tírechán uses *terrenus* in the sense of 'earthen' (referring to the building-material of churches). In other texts it means 'terrestrial' (as opposed to *caelestis* 'celestial'), and there does not seem to be any other text from medieval Ireland in which the *áes síde* are explicitly called *dei terreni*. Moreover, in a later reworking of this episode in the text known as *Vita Auctore Probo*, Loíguire's daughters are said to have taken Patrick and his followers to be 'deorum terrenorum sacerdotes aut phantasiam' (leaving us to guess why the *áes síde* as pagan gods should have been taken to have priests), while in the story *Bricriu's Feast* the expression *día talmaide*, being the Irish equivalent of *deus terrenus*, is used of king Conchobar of Ulster who elsewhere is treated as an ordinary human being.[15] To solve these difficulties, we should perhaps envisage the possibility that all these texts use *deus terrenus* in the ancient Roman sense of 'sovereign ruler', a usage which was in fact revived in the twelfth century when the Christian emperor came to be called *deus terrenus* to distinguish his authority from that of the pope.[16] This usage, incidentally, would also explain why in the late Middle Irish compilation known as the

[13] Text and translation quoted from *The Patrician Texts in the Book of Armagh*, ed. and trans. by Bieler, pp. 142–43.

[14] Rehearsing an earlier discussion of this passage by Maartje Draak, these difficulties are duly pointed out by Borsje, 'Monotheistic to a Certain Extent', pp. 58–70, who nevertheless decides in favour of the traditional interpretation of *deorum terrenorum* as a gloss on *síde*.

[15] See Borsje, 'Monotheistic to a Certain Extent', pp. 61 and 78.

[16] See Kantorowicz, *The King's Two Bodies*, p. 92 n. 16. It may be noted that we also find the expression in the *Getica* of Jordanes, who makes the Gothic king Athanaric exclaim on his arrival at Constantinople on 14 January 381, 'No doubt, the emperor is a god on earth' ('"deus", inquit, "sine dubio terrenus est imperator"'); see North, *Heathen Gods in Old English Literature*, p. 148.

Fitness of Names (*Cóir Anmann*), the supernatural being known by the name of the Dagda is said to have been a 'god of the earth' to his contemporaries 'because of the greatness of his power' (bá día talmhan dóibh é ar mhét a chumachta): Exceptional power rather than any chthonic associations is the criterion which makes a *deus terrenus*, and this is why the epithet is bestowed on the Dagda (as well as on king Conchobar), but not on any other of the *áes síde* that we know by name.[17] In conclusion, it should be stressed that although the persistent association of the *áes síde* with prehistoric burial mounds suggests that the medieval and early modern ideas about them evolved from earlier ideas about the living dead, we do not really know what these ideas looked like in the pre-Christian period. After Christianization, there appears to have been a certain variety of opinions about the *áes síde*, some texts identifying them with demons, some with the old pagan gods, and some with (fallen) angels.[18]

With the appearance of Conn's druid on the scene, we encounter the second element which links our text to the religion of pre-Christian Ireland. First mentioned by Greek ethnographers such as Posidonius, the Continental Celtic druids loom large in Julius Caesar's account of Gaulish society,[19] and soon came to be admired as Barbarian philosophers cum politicians, being widely regarded as precious relics of a bygone Golden Age of mankind. Rediscovered by the Humanists of fifteenth- and sixteenth-century France, the druids have continued to excite the imagination of philosophers, political theorists, historians, Celticists, and comparative religionists ever since, so that the amount of writings which they generated appears almost inversely proportional to the established facts.[20] Known in Ireland as *magus* or — in vernacular writings — *druí* (plural *druíd*, *druíde*, and *druídi*), the pre-Christian priest of the pagan past looms large in both hagiography and pseudo-historical narrative, although it is most difficult to know just how much of what we are told is rooted in native tradition rather than biblical and apocryphal writings or pure imagination. To illustrate the problem, we may well look at the following story from the epic *Táin Bó Cuailnge*, put into the mouth of one of the characters and involving the pagan king Conchobar, the druid Cathbad and the youthful future hero Cú Chulainn:

---

[17] See, however, Borsje, 'Monotheistic to a Certain Extent', pp. 78–79, where it is stated that the Dagda is 'connected with the earth in that he secures the grain and milk'.

[18] See Carey, *A Single Ray of the Sun*, especially pp. 1–38.

[19] Julius Caesar, *The Gallic War*, IV. 13–14.

[20] For recent surveys of our knowledge of the Druids and their role in the history of European scholarship and imagination, see Brunaux, *Les Druides*; Hutton, *Blood and Mistletoe*; and Maier, *Die Druiden*.

Cathbad the druid was with his son Conchobar mac Nessa. There were with him a hundred active men learning the druid's art — that was the number that Cathbad used to instruct. One of his pupils asked him for what that day would be of good omen. Cathbad said that if a warrior took up arms on that day, his name for deeds of valour would be known throughout Ireland and his fame would last forever.

Cú Chulainn heard this. He went to Conchobar to ask for arms. Conchobar asked:

'Who prophesied good fortune for you?'.

'Master Cathbad', said Cú Chulainn.

'We know him indeed', said Conchobar.

He gave him a spear and a shield. [...]

Then Cathbad came to them and asked:

'Is the boy taking up arms?'.

'Yes', said Conchobar.

'That is not lucky for the son of his mother', said he.

'Why, was it not you who instructed him?'.

'It was not I indeed', said Cathbad.

'What use is it for you to deceive me so, you sprite?' said Conchobar to Cú Chulainn.

'O king of the Fían, it is no deceit', said Cú Chulainn. 'He prophesied good fortune for his pupils this morning and I heard him from where I was on the south side of Emain, and then I came to you'.

'It is indeed a day of good omen', said Cathbad. 'It is certain that he who takes up arms today will be famous and renowned, but he will, however, be short-lived'.

'A mighty thing!' said Cú Chulainn. 'Provided I be famous, I am content to be only one day on earth'.[21]

While it is tempting to use this passage as a source for the history of religions, it must be said that, due to our imperfect knowledge of pre-Christian Ireland, interpretations may vary considerably, depending on the preoccupations and the perspective of the interpreter. Starting from classical ethnography, the fact that Conchobar is stated to be the son of a druid might remind us of Caesar's references to the children of the Gaulish druid Diviciacus,[22] making us infer that neither the Gaulish druids nor their Irish colleagues were celibate. Starting from medieval church history, however, we might reflect that nothing else was to be expected, early medieval Christian clerics not being celibate either, and that the story-teller may just have projected the mores of his own times into a distant past. Similarly, Cú Chulainn's insistence that imperishable fame will compensate for

---

[21] Translation quoted from *Táin Bó Cúalnge*, ed. and trans. by O'Rahilly, pp. 142–43.

[22] Julius Caesar, *The Gallic War*, I. 31. 8.

the shortness of his life might make an Indo-Europeanist think of the common origin of Irish *clú*, Greek *kléos* and Sanskrit *śravas*, all meaning 'fame', while a social anthropologist might interpret this parallel in terms of the structural opposition between 'honour' and 'shame', and a literary historian as a borrowing from classical literature. Certainly, the observation of 'lucky' and 'unlucky' days which is presupposed in the above-quoted episode may well have been a feature of the pre-Christian Irish world-view. On the other hand, such ideas are so widespread that we do not need to assume some kind of continuity to account for its presence in our text. In fact, even Christianity turned out to be ambiguous on this point, with Church Fathers such as Augustine and Ambrose holding the observation of lucky and unlucky days to be superstitious but conceding that God might well use the stars and their courses to give mankind an indication of future events.[23] Could it be that the anonymous Irish story-teller knew the custom from his own experience and projected it back into the distant past just because it was a topic much discussed in his own day?

Turning from the *Táin Bó Cuailnge* to early medieval hagiography, we encounter the same kind of problems. Thus we read in the oldest Irish Life of St Brigit that at the time of her birth a druid who was watching the stars saw a fiery column above the house in which she was born.[24] Mindful of classical references to the druids as astronomers,[25] we might be inclined to credit the Irish druids with an interest in astronomy similar to that of their Continental Celtic colleagues.[26] On the other hand, it can hardly be denied that the story of the fiery column marking Brigit's birth-place is heavily indebted both to the fiery column leading the Israelites out of Egypt (Exodus 13. 21–22) and to the star indicating to the magi the place where Jesus is born (Matthew 2. 9–11), so that the hagiographer's view of the druids as astronomers may be no more than a fanciful inference drawn from their equation with the magi of classical and biblical literature. Significantly, already the hagiographer Muirchú modelled his account of the confrontation between Patrick and the druids of the pagan king Loíguire on the biblical stories of the conflict between Moses and the magicians of Pharaoh (Exodus 7) and between the apostle Peter and the pagan sorcerer Simon Magus (Acts 8. 9–25), while an Old Irish gloss on II Timothy 3. 8 (referring to Exodus 7. 11) calls the

---

[23] See, for example, Hartinger, *Religion und Brauch*, pp. 18–19.

[24] *Bethu Brigte*, ed. and trans. by Ó hAodha, pp. 1 (text) and 20 (translation).

[25] See for example Julius Caesar, *The Gallic War*, VI. 14. 6, and Pomponius Mela, *Chorographie*, ed. by Silberman, III. 2. 18.

[26] Thus Kelly, *A Guide to Early Irish Law*, p. 60.

magicians of Pharaoh without more ado 'two Egyptian druids who quarrelled with Moses' ('da druith ægeptacdi robatar ocimbresun frimmoysi').[27] In conclusion, it may be said that although medieval Irish writers invariably regarded the druids as the representatives of Irish paganism, it is by no means clear how much reliable information on them they still had.

Moving on to the next pagan element in our story, namely the expression 'by women's spells' ('brechtaib ban'), we may note that this is neatly paralleled by a passage in an Old Irish Hymn ascribed to Saint Patrick, in which divine help is invoked not only 'against black laws of heathenry' and 'against false laws of heretics', but also 'against spells of women and smiths and druids' ('fri brichtu ban 7 gobann 7 druad'), the text presumably enumerating those three groups of people in early Christian Ireland who were particularly notorious for their skills in magic.[28] As regards the first of these groups, the Irish expression is closely paralleled by the words *bnanom bricto[m]*, presumably meaning 'magic of women', which is to be found in a Gaulish inscription discovered in August 1983 at the Gallo-Roman cemetery of l'Hospitalet-du-Larzac near La Graufesenque, Gaulish *brictom* being cognate with both Irish *bricht* and the second part of the Welsh compound *lled(f)rith*, which in the second of the *Four Branches of the Mabinogi* is coupled with *hud* 'magic' and must have had a similar meaning.[29] Nevertheless, the almost identical wording need not be taken to imply a particular cultural proximity or even the continuity of formulaic speech. As magic tends to be regarded as a domain of women in many cultures, both the Gaulish expression and its Irish counterpart may just as well be seen as illustrations of a general tendency in the history of religions. On the other hand, it should be noted that the ascription of magic to the druids does not necessarily reflect the reality of pre-Christian Ireland, but may just as well be due to the medieval Christian tendency to conflate pagan magic and religion even in those cases where the pagans themselves kept them neatly apart. In fact, the translation of *druí* as 'wizard' by the editors of *Thesaurus Palaeohibernicus* reminds us that in speaking of contemporary druids, the early medieval authors need not have thought of pagan priests at all, but may have used the term in a rather loose and unspecific way, meaning no more than 'soothsayers' or 'magicians'.

[27] See *The Patrician Texts in the Book of Armagh*, ed. and trans. by Bieler, pp. 74–99, and *Thesaurus Palaeohibernicus*, ed. by Stokes and Strachan, I, 695.

[28] See *Thesaurus Palaeohibernicus*, ed. by Stokes and Strachan, II, 357.

[29] See Lambert, *La Langue gauloise*, pp. 166–72. For Welsh *lledfrith*, see *Pedeir Keinc*, ed. by Williams, pp. 63 and 247.

Apart from the explicit references to the pagan period so far discussed, *Echtrae Chonnlai* may be assumed to contain yet another, rather implicit reference to pagan mythology in its allusion to an overseas otherworld. This may be connected not only with later Irish stories about mysterious regions encountered after adventurous sea-voyages, but also with classical references to the religious and ritual significance of offshore islands among the ancient Celts. 'Then there is an island abounding in grass and sacred to Saturn' ('post pelagia est insula | herbarum abundans ad<que> Saturno sacra'), we read in the *Ora maritima*,[30] a versified description of the sea-coast between Brittany and the Black Sea which was written in the second half of the fourth century AD by the Latin poet Rufus Festus Avienus. As it is widely assumed that Avienus reproduces much earlier geographic sources, some of which may go back to the fifth century BC, this item is perhaps the earliest reference of its kind, leaving us to wonder not only about the meaning of *pelagia* (which would be important to know if we were to attempt to locate the island), but also about the indigenous name of the god here designated Saturn and the possible mythological significance of the abundance of grass with which the mysterious island is credited.[31] More specifically, the geographer Strabo tells us on the authority of the historian Artemidorus of Ephesus 'that there is an island off the shore of Britain on which there is a cult similar to that of Demeter and Kore in Samothrake'.[32] Interestingly, this piece of information is preceded by another report according to which there was an island off the estuary of the Loire on which a group of women were devoted to the cult of Dionysus.[33] Although it is generally assumed that Strabo gleaned this story from Posidonius, its ultimate source is widely taken to have been once more Artemidorus, whose lost *Geography* is assumed to have been based on extensive travels undertaken around 100 BC.[34]

From the Roman Imperial period, three more references to the religious significance of offshore islands among the Celts are due to the geographer Pomponius Mela and the historian Plutarch. Writing shortly before the middle of the first century AD, Pomponius Mela maintains that there was an island by the name of Sena off the coast of Brittany, on which nine virginal priestesses

[30] Avienus, *Ora maritima*, ed. by Mangas and Plácido, pp. 164–65.

[31] See text, German translation and commentary in Hofeneder, *Die Religion der Kelten*, I, 20–22.

[32] Strabo, *Geography*, IV. 4. 6; Hofeneder, *Die Religion der Kelten*, I, 109–11.

[33] Strabo, *Geography*, IV. 4. 6.

[34] Hofeneder, *Die Religion der Kelten*, I, 132–36.

tended a celebrated oracular sanctuary.[35] While this story is unparalleled in classical literature, it has been taken to anticipate both the nine virgins tending the supernatural cauldron of the Middle Welsh poem *Preiddeu Annwfn* and the nine healing sisters on the isle of Avallon who are mentioned in the *Vita Merlini* of Geoffrey of Monmouth.[36] Writing presumably at the beginning of the second century AD, Plutarch in *De defectu oraculorum* has the scholar Demetrius of Tarsus state that many of the islands off the shore of Britain were isolated and uninhabited and that some of them were named after demigods and heroes.[37] According to Demetrius, there also was there an island on which Cronus lay asleep, watched over by Briareus.[38] The latter story is repeated and slightly elaborated in Plutarch's *De facie in orbe lunae*, presumably written around the same time as *De defectu oraculorum*.[39]

Looking for points of comparison in medieval Irish literature, we may think first of all of the mythical figure known as Donn, 'the Dark One', who appears to have been envisaged as an ancestor figure and lord of the dead residing on an island off the coast of Kerry known as 'Donn's House' (*Tech nDuinn*).[40] Turning to medieval Welsh tradition, we may note the texts related to the shadowy figure of Gweir who is mentioned in the *Welsh Triads* as one of the 'Three Exalted Prisoners of the Island of Britain' and also figures as a prisoner in the poem *Preiddeu Annwfn*, the name Ynys Weir ('Gweir's Island' or 'Grass Island') being used of both the Isle of Wight and Lundy Island.[41] While it is impossible to know just how many individual pieces of information from classical antiquity and the Middle Ages may be linked to each other, there can be little doubt that offshore islands did play a major part in the mythology of pre-Christian Ireland and that they were related to beliefs about fertility and the realm of the dead.

Having surveyed the evidence for references to pagan Irish mythology in *Echtrae Chonnlai*, we may now proceed to study its allusions to Christian ideas about Paradise. Before we do so, however, it may be useful to outline the back-

---

[35] Pomponius Mela, *Chorographie*, ed. by Silberman, III. 48.

[36] See Hofeneder, *Die Religion der Kelten*, II, 272–74.

[37] Plutarch, *The Obsolescence of Oracles*, 18, p. 419E–420A.

[38] See Hofeneder, *Die Religion der Kelten*, II, 532–35.

[39] Plutarch, *Concerning the Face Which Appears in the Orb of the Moon*, 26, p. 940F–941B. See Hofeneder, *Die Religion der Kelten*, II, 536–40.

[40] See Ó hÓgáin, *Myth, Legend and Romance*, pp. 165–67, and literature there cited.

[41] See *Trioedd Ynys Prydein*, ed. and trans. by Bromwich, pp. 140–42, and see Maier, *Die Religion der Kelten*, pp. 94–99.

ground against which such allusions need to be viewed. Confining ourselves to those features of the tradition which are immediately relevant to an understanding of our text, we may note that in the Early Middle Ages Paradise was widely taken to refer to the blissful state enjoyed by a few exceptional characters such as prophets, apostles and martyrs, who after their deaths were granted a foretaste of Heaven, which was assumed to be enjoyed by all the righteous at the end of time after the Resurrection. In their attempts to visualize and describe this interim state of bliss, Christian writers fell back on the New Testament allusions to Heaven, but also on the Old Testament references to the primordial state of bliss enjoyed by Adam and Eve in the Garden of Eden. Moreover, they would draw upon the visions of Paradise enshrined in apocryphal writings such as the *Apocalypse of Peter* and the *Apocalypse of Paul*, similar visionary reports in the acts of martyrs, and theological speculations by the Church Fathers.[42]

In our text, the first explicit reference to the Christian Paradise is to be found in the very first words spoken by the mysterious woman. Telling Connlae that she has come 'from (the) lands of (the) living', she obviously alludes to the Christian interpretation of Psalms 27 (26). 13, 142 (141). 6 and 116 (114). 9, in which the Hebrew expression *æræs hayyim*, rendered in the Vulgate by *terra viventium* and *regio vivorum*, is taken to refer not to this world of living beings, but rather to a future state of heavenly bliss. This eschatological interpretation is reinforced by the woman's insistence on the absence of sin (Old Irish *peccad* from Latin *peccatum*) in the lands of the living, echoing Paul's dictum that 'sin's pay is death, but God's free gift is eternal life' (Romans 6. 23). This neatly squares with the ruler's name Boadag, which is presumably a variant of the adjective *buadach* 'victorious', reminding us of the Pauline view that Christ has overcome death (Romans 5. 12–21).[43]

---

[42] For reasons of space, only some classic studies and a sample of the most recent scholarly literature can be quoted. For the development of ideas about the Garden of Eden, Paradise and Heaven from the Old Testament to the New Testament, see Bremmer, 'Paradise'; Noort, 'Gan-Eden'; Hultgård, 'Das Paradies'; and Di Pede and Wénin, 'Aux origins du Jardin d'Éden'. For the development of these ideas in the early church, see Stuiber, *Refrigerium interim*; Grimm, *Paradisus Coelestis*; Benjamins, 'Paradisiacal Life'; and Bregni, '"Paradisus, locus amoenus"'. For studies of the ancient and medieval visionary accounts of Paradise, see especially Amat, *Songes et visions*; Himmelfarb, *Ascent to Heaven*; Carozzi, *Le Voyage de l'âme dans l'au-delà*; Bauckham, *The Fate of the Dead*; Kabir, *Paradise, Death and Doomsday*; and Gooder, *Only the Third Heaven?*. For anthologies of relevant texts, see *Visioni dell'aldilà in occidente*, ed. by Ciccarese, and *Visions of Heaven and Hell*, ed. by Gardiner.

[43] *Echtrae Chonnlai*, ed. by McCone, pp. 94–95 for the use of *buadach* in Christian contexts.

Less obviously Christian and sometimes still taken to be of pagan Irish origin, the 'Plain of Delights' to which Connlae is summoned may also be related to biblical and apocryphal texts. Translating Genesis 2. 8, the Septuagint had taken עדן to be a place-name and had understood the following adverbial phrase מקדם not in a temporal, but in a spatial sense: 'Kai ephyteusen kyrios ho theos paradeison en Edem kata anatolas' (And the Lord God planted a garden eastward in Eden). The Vulgate, however, opted for an alternative interpretation of the text, taking עדן to be a homonymous generic noun meaning 'delight' and understanding the phrase מקדם not in a spatial, but in a temporal sense: 'Plantaverat autem Dominus Deus paradisum voluptatis a principio' (And the Lord God planted a garden of delight from the beginning). For those who assumed that there was a Paradise on this earth rather than in any of the celestial regions, this rendering opened the possibility to look for it not only in the east, but in any direction, possibly enabling early medieval Irish writers to identify or at least associate pagan stories about fabulous islands to the west of Ireland with Christian references to Paradise.[44] Moreover, the Vulgate translation of עדן as *voluptas* created a widespread association of Paradise with words expressing 'delight', reinforcing an interpretation which had in fact begun with the Septuagint rendering of עדן as *tryphē* 'delight' in Genesis 3. 23 and elsewhere.

As regards the replacement of 'garden' or 'paradise' by words meaning 'meadow', 'field' or 'plain', this has to be seen in the light of an early Christian conflation between paradise and the ideal landscape (*locus amoenus*) of classical literature. An early witness to this development is the apocryphal *Apocalypse of Peter* which is thought to have been written around AD 135 and has come down to us in a Greek and an Ethiopic version diverging considerably from each other.[45] Discovered in 1886 at the desert necropolis of Akhmim in Upper Egypt, the Greek version was studied as a *nekyia* or journey through the abode of the dead by the classical philologist and historian of religions Albrecht Dieterich (1866–1908), who postulated a Hellenistic or more specifically Orphic influence which is immediately apparent in the description of Paradise:

> And the Lord showed me a widely extensive place outside this world, all gleaming with light, and the air there flooded by the rays of the sun, and the earth itself budding with flowers which fade not, and full of spices and plants which blossom gloriously and fade not and bear blessed fruit. So great was the fragrance of the flowers that it was borne thence even unto us. The inhabitants of that place were

[44] For a survey of the attempts to locate and map Paradise, see Scafi, *Mapping Paradise*.

[45] See Bauckham, *The Fate of the Dead*, pp. 160–258, and *The Apocalypse of Peter*, ed. by Bremmer and Czachesz.

clad with the shining raiment of angels and their raiment was suitable to their place of habitation.[46]

Greek influence is also evident in the Ethiopic version of the *Apocalypse of Peter*, which uses Christian adaptations of the netherworld names *Acherōn* and *Ēlysion*, making Christ promise his followers:

> And then I will give my elect, my righteous, the baptism and salvation which they requested of me. In the field of Akerosya which is called Aneslasleya a portion of the righteous have flowered, and I will go there now. I will rejoice with them. I will lead the peoples into my eternal kingdom and I will make for them what I have promised them, that which is eternal, I and my heavenly father.[47]

Interestingly, the first of these two Greek terms is also found in the apocryphal *Apocalypse of Paul* relating the ascent to heaven of the apostle Paul. Presumably written in the fifth century and soon translated from Greek into Latin, this was meant to expand on the visionary experience related in II Corinthians 12. 1–10, proving to be one of the most popular texts of its kind during the whole of the Middle Ages.[48] Like *Echtrae Chonnlai*, the *Apocalypse of Paul* also knows of a boat made of precious material in which a human being and his angelic guide are taken across an expanse of water from this world towards Paradise:

> The angel answered and said to me: 'Follow me and I will bring you into the city of Christ'. He stood by Lake Acherusa and set me in a golden ship. Angels, three thousand it seemed, sang a hymn before me until I came to the city of Christ. Those who dwelt in the City of Christ rejoiced greatly over me as I came to them, and I entered and saw the City of Christ.[49]

Following the composition of the earliest apocryphal texts, visionary accounts of Paradise are also to be found in the acts of martyrs such as those of saints Perpetua and Felicitas:

> Then I saw an immense garden, and in it a grey-haired man sat in shepherd's garb; tall he was, and milking sheep. And standing around him were many thousands of

[46] Translation quoted from Adamik, 'The Description of Paradise', p. 79. See also Dieterich, *Nekyia*.

[47] Adamik, 'The Description of Paradise', p. 79.

[48] See *The Visio Pauli*, ed. by Bremmer. For the significance of the Acherusian Lake, see Copeland, 'Sinners and Post-Mortem "Baptism"', pp. 91–101, and Kraus, 'Acherousia und Elysion'. For the influence of the classical *locus amoenus*, see Aitken, 'The Landscape of Promise', and for later vernacular retellings, Jiroušková, *Die Visio Pauli*.

[49] Translation in *Visions of Heaven and Hell*, ed. by Gardiner, p. 30.

people clad in white garments. He raised his head, looked at me, and said: 'I am glad you have come, my child'.[50]

Or again in the retelling of a visionary experience in the Martyrdom of Saints Montanus and Lucius:

'I saw some centurions come to us', he said, 'and when they had conducted us a long distance, we came to a huge field, where we were joined by Cyprian and Leucius. Next we arrived at a very bright spot, and our garments began to glow, and our bodies became even more brilliant than our bright clothing'.[51]

While the bucolic nature of the Paradise depicted in these texts clearly betrays the influence of the classical *locus amoenus*, it may also be linked to *Echtrae Chonnlai*'s references to 'harmony without strife' and 'great peace', expressions which would have reminded the early medieval audience of the numerous references to eternal *quies, pax,* and *tranquilitas* to be found in the writings of the Church Fathers and in early Christian prayers for the dead.[52] In these texts we also encounter copious references to the dead being made welcome in Paradise by the saints. This squares neatly not only with the above-quoted passage from the *Apocalypse of Paul*, but also with Connlae being invited by all the 'everliving living', the joys of Paradise being always depicted as communal in Christian visionary texts.[53] In this context it may be worth noting the woman's remark to Connlae that the everliving living 'behold you every day in the assemblies of your fatherland amidst your beloved near ones'. While it is difficult to see how they could do so from an overseas realm, the image makes perfect sense if we assume that this idea was taken over from a text in which the dead were supposed to look down on the living from a celestial paradise such as we find it in Cicero's story of *Somnium Scipionis*. Interestingly, in this story Scipio's dead grandfather Africanus predicts his grandson's future just as in *Echtrae Chonnlai* the mysterious woman predicts the Christianization of Ireland, while the mysterious woman's insistence that Connlae sits 'amidst the short-lived dead' recalls Africanus's dictum that 'they live who have soared away from the bonds of the body as from a prison; but your so-called life is really death'.[54] While Cicero's idea that what we call life may really be death was taken

---

[50] See *The Acts of the Christian Martyrs*, ed. by Musurillo, pp. 106–31 (p. 111).

[51] See *The Acts of the Christian Martyrs*, ed. by Musurillo, pp. 214–39 (p. 223).

[52] See Ntedika, *L'Évocation de l'au-delà*, pp. 200–20.

[53] See Ntedika, *L'Évocation de l'au-delà*, pp. 220–25.

[54] Cicero, *On the Republic*, VI. 14. 14.

up by both Lactantius and Augustine,[55] the most far-reaching influence emanated no doubt from its elaboration by Macrobius in his widely read commentary on *Somnium Scipionis*.

Another feature of the woman's description which needs to be discussed in this context is her insistence that the inhabitants of the lands of the living 'consume everlasting feasts *cen frithgnam*'. Presumably based on the New Testament usage of describing heavenly joy as a feast (Revelation 19. 9), we find the image of Paradise as a feast already in the acts of martyrs, as may be seen from the following account of the death of Bishop Fructuosus:

> Many out of brotherly affection offered him a cup of drugged wine to drink, but he said: 'It is not yet the time for breaking the fast'. For it was still in the fourth hour, and in gaol they duly observed the stational fast on Wednesdays. And so on Friday he was hastening joyfully and confidently to break his fast with the martyrs and prophets in heaven, which the Lord has prepared for those who love Him.[56]

But what does *cen frithgnam* mean? While the most recent editor of *Echtrae Chonnlai* was wavering between 'without service' and 'without exertion', I would argue that 'exertion' does not really make good sense, since anybody who is invited to a feast is not supposed to exert himself. Opting for 'service', on the other hand, can hardly imply that the author thought of a celestial set buffet where prophets, patriarchs and martyrs take a plate and join the queue. However, it may well be taken to refer to the supernatural origin of the food, heavenly nourishment being sometimes identified with the biblical manna which was also known as the 'bread of angels'.[57] Elsewhere in the early Christian tradition, we find the notion of supernatural food in Paradise expressed by the pagan Greek concept of *ambrosia*, as in the *Hamartigenia* by the late Latin poet Prudentius:

> Then as the exiled soul returns to be reinstated in her heavenly country, hoary Faith receives her in her bosom and comforts her nursling with tender fondness while with plaintive voice she tells over the many toils she has endured since she took up her lodging in the flesh. There, stretched on a shining couch, she enjoys the scents that breathe from unfading flowers and drinks the ambrosial dew from her bed of roses.[58]

---

[55] Lactantius, *Divinarum institutionum*, ed. by Heck and Wlosok, VI. 19; Augustine, *City of God*, XIII. 10.

[56] See *The Acts of the Christian Martyrs*, ed. by Musurillo, pp. 176–85 (pp. 179–81).

[57] See Exodus 16. 4; Psalm 78. 24–25; and Revelation 2. 17.

[58] Prudentius, *Origin of Sin*, in *Prudentius*, ed. by Thomson, I, 265.

Noting once more the close proximity between classical and Christian imagery, it should be observed that these similarities did of course not escape the attention of the Church Fathers either. One way of dealing with them was to assume some kind of diffusion, assuming that pagan writers had borrowed or stolen biblical truths, so that Christian authors like Tertullian could maintain that the Greek notion of the Elysian Field anticipated the Christian idea of Paradise.[59] Needless to say, a similar stance might have been taken by any early medieval Irish author with regard to the native Irish tradition. Another way of dealing with such similarities was typological exegesis, assuming that paganism and Christianity stood in the same relation to each other as the Old and the New Testament, following a providential scheme of promise and fulfilment. In any case, a wide range of possible interpretations was opened by assuming a fourfold sense of scripture, so that any given word or passage could be interpreted literally (using the nearest possible historical reference), allegorically (taking it to refer to the Church), tropologically (assuming it to have an ethical meaning) or anagogically (taking it to have an eschatological meaning). The method may be illustrated by applying it to the *Song of Solomon* 2. 3: 'As the apple-tree among the trees of the woods, so is my beloved among the sons. I sat down under his shadow with great delight, and his fruit was sweet to my taste'. Assuming a fourfold sense of scripture, the speaker might be assumed to be either one of Solomon's loves, or the Church, or the human soul, or the Heavenly Jerusalem. Interpreting the apple-tree typologically as corresponding to the cross, its fruit could easily be taken to signify Christ.

Returning from the principles of patristic exegesis to *Echtrae Chonnlai*, it will be noted that the apple which Connlae is given may be interpreted as a symbol of Paradise, but also as a specimen of heavenly nourishment, used as a foretaste of heavenly bliss to whet Connlae's appetite and make it easier for him to sever his bonds with this world. This motif is found already in the acts of the saints Montanus and Lucius, in which the imprisoned Christian woman Quartillosa, whose husband and son had suffered martyrdom three days before, is made to say:

> I saw my son that has suffered come to the prison. He sat down at the rim of the water-trough and said: 'God has seen your pain and tribulation'. After him there entered a young man of remarkable stature carrying in each of his hands two drinking-cups full of milk. And he said: 'Be of good heart. God has been mindful of you'. And he gave everyone to drink from the cups which he carried, and they were never empty.

[59] Tertullian, *Apology*, chap. 47.

Suddenly the stone which divided the window into two sections was removed and the window became bright and allowed us to have an unimpeded view of the heavens. The young man put down the cups he was carrying, one on his right, and the other on his left, and he said: 'Look, you are filled and there is still more: still a third cup will be left over for you'. Then he went away.[60]

In this connection, it is worth looking once more at the original text of our story. When Connlae tells his father that 'longing for the woman has seized' him, we naturally think of erotic attraction. Nevertheless, of all the words that would have been possible to express longing, the author chose *eólchaire*, which is normally used to express homesickness or longing for home, suggesting that the author thought of the Christian notion of Paradise as the true home of the soul.

At this point of our investigation, it may be noted that most of the post-biblical Christian texts which have been used for the purpose of comparison are visionary accounts, purporting to be based on the personal experience of saints or martyrs who were given a glimpse of Paradise and yet came back to talk about their experience. However, as Connlae is not said to have ever returned, his story really reads rather like a Jewish or Christian assumption narrative, reminiscent of the stories about Enoch or Elijah who were believed to have been taken away from this world before their natural deaths to live on in Paradise.[61] Significantly, the author's final remark that Connlae and the mysterious woman 'were not seen thereafter' recalls the biblical statement that when Elijah was taken away, his son Elisha 'saw him no more' (II Kings 2. 12), confirming the observation that 'assumption narratives are normally reported from the perspective of those who are left behind, not the one taken away'.[62] Interestingly, the king's complaint to his druid that the mysterious woman is intent on 'stealing' his son recalls the Greek verb *harpázo* 'steal away', which is not used in the biblical accounts, but character-istic of apocryphal assumption narratives.[63]

Despite all these similarities, at the very end of the woman's speech we encounter what is perhaps the most baffling feature of her description: 'There is another land that may not be the nearest to seek. [...] Though it be far, we shall reach (it) before night. [...] There is no race there save only women and maidens'.

---

[60] *The Acts of the Christian Martyrs*, ed. by Musurillo, p. 221.

[61] On the Old Testament origin of this idea, see Schmitt, 'Zum Thema "Entrückung" im Alten Testament'. On the patristic views of Enoch and Elijah, see Felber, 'Die Henochgestalt in der Patristik'; Landesmann, *Die Himmelfahrt des Elija*; and Wright, 'Whither Elija?'.

[62] Smith, 'The Assumption of the Righteous Dead', p. 288.

[63] See Smith, 'The Assumption of the Righteous Dead', pp. 290–92.

Obviously, any interpretation of these lines must take into account a very similar passage which in the roughly contemporaneous story of *Immram Brain* is put into the mouth of Manannán mac Lir: 'Steadily then let Bran row, | Not far to the Land of Women, | Emne with many hues of hospitality | Thou wilt reach before the setting of the sun'.[64] Both of these passages form the last utterances made by the two otherworld characters in *Echtrae Chonnlai* and *Immram Brain* respectively, but while *Echtrae Chonnlai* only tells us that Connlae subsequently leapt into the boat and was seen no more, *Immram Brain* goes on to tell us what happened when Bran and his companions actually reached the Land of Women: 'Thereupon they went into a large house, in which was a bed for every couple, even thrice nine beds.'[65]

In the history of scholarship, the close similarity of the two above-quoted passages and the existence of further verbal and structural parallels between *Echtrae Connlai* and *Immram Brain* have been interpreted in different ways by different scholars.[66] While Alfred Nutt in 1895 assumed that the two stories might 'possibly [...] be due to the same writer' or should be 'looked upon as products of one school' (two possibilities also favoured by James Carney in 1955 and 1976, respectively), John Carey in 1995 suggested that *Echtrae Chonnlai* was one of several texts on which the author of *Immram Brain* drew, while Kim McCone in 2000 argued that even if *Echtrae Chonnlai* came first, *Immram Brain* is likely to have been composed shortly afterwards and that, 'on grounds of form as well as content', the last lines spoken by the mysterious woman might have been inserted into the finished text at a very early stage as an afterthought under the influence of *Immram Brain*.

If McCone's suggestion is correct, the expression 'the Land of Women' may well have originated with the author of *Immram Brain*, and there is no way of knowing whether the brief allusion at the End of *Echtrae Chonnlai* is a mere echo of *Immram Brain* or whether it reflects ideas more widely current at the time in which the two texts were composed.[67] In any case, we should be wary of assuming

---

[64] Translation quoted from *The Voyage of Bran*, ed. by Meyer and Nutt, I, 28. For a more recent edition and translation, see *Immram Brain*, ed. and trans. by Mac Mathúna, supplemented by the critical remarks of Breatnach, 'Review of S. Mac Mathúna, *Immram Brain*'. See also Ó hAodha, 'Some Remarks on the Happy Otherworld', and literature there cited.

[65] See *The Voyage of Bran*, ed. by Meyer and Nutt, I, 30.

[66] See the summary in *Echtrae Chonnlai*, ed. by McCone, pp. 106–19.

[67] To illustrate my warning against mistaking literary invention for oral tradition by a more recent example, I quote Raymond Chandler's remarks to his fellow detective writer Cleve Adams in a letter dated 4 September 1948: 'Throughout the play *The Iceman Cometh* O'Neill

that this is a relic of the pagan past. Referring to a partial translation of *Immram Brain* which Heinrich Zimmer had published in the *Zeitschrift für deutsches Alterthum*, Kuno Meyer remarked that although his colleague had rendered the word *lánamain* by 'married couple' (*ehepaar*), he preferred to do without the 'married', noting that there was 'no reason for being so particular'.[68] Nevertheless, the explicit reference to 'a bed for every couple, even thrice nine beds' clearly suggests that what the author of *Immram Brain* had in mind was neither an orgy nor sexual promiscuity or polygamy, but rather a series of twenty-seven monogamous relationships. On the one hand, this presents a striking contrast to early medieval Irish society, in which polygyny was opposed by the Church but nevertheless 'permitted, and probably widespread'.[69] On the other hand, it squares nicely with early medieval ideas about the state of affairs in the Garden of Eden, a poet like Avitus stressing the sacred nature of monogamous sexuality and telling his readers that Eve rose from the rib of Adam sleeping, just as the Church arose from the side of Christ sleeping in his tomb in order to be His Bride.[70] While I would argue that the handling of sexuality in *Immram Brain* is fully in line with the attitude of men like Avitus, we may well wonder whether the confirmed polygynists of pagan Ireland would indeed have taken a 'Land of Women' to be the source of consummate pleasure envisaged by some modern academics. Does such an assumption not presuppose a much more rigorous view of human sexuality than that which can be shown to have prevailed in early Christian Ireland? Looking for a possible origin of the expression 'Land of Women', I would rather point to apocryphal Christian literature, the Ethiopic *Liber Requiei* telling us about the reception of the apostles in Paradise:

> And the soul of Abraham was there, and the soul of Isaac, and the soul of Jacob, along with many others [whom] the Saviour had brought from death to life by his resurrection and placed in the Paradise of the living. David was there with his harp, making music, and Elizabeth was there with them, although there was another place for women.[71]

uses the expression "the big sleep" as a synonym for death. He is apparently under the impression that this is a current underworld or half world usage, whereas it is a pure invention on my part. If I am remembered long enough, I shall probably be accused of stealing the phrase from O'Neill, since he is a big shot'. See Chandler, *Selected Letters*, ed. by MacShane, pp. 126–27.

[68] *The Voyage of Bran*, ed. by Meyer and Nutt, i, 30 n. 2.

[69] See Kelly, *A Guide to Early Irish Law*, pp. 70–71.

[70] See Avitus, *The Poems*, ed. and trans. by Shea, pp. 17–18, and see Grimm, 'Die Paradiesesehe', and literature there cited.

[71] Shoemaker, *Ancient Traditions of the Virgin Mary's Dormition*, p. 346.

Commenting on the somewhat cryptic ending of this passage, the translator noted:

> No further explanation is given as to what this 'other place' might be, but it seems
> clear that this narrative imagined some sort of gender separation in the heavenly
> realms. It may be that the Garden of Paradise was thought to be reserved for men
> alone, the souls of women being assigned to some other corner of heaven. Alter-
> natively, the text may envision a divided Paradise, in which the souls of men and
> women were separated from one another inside the Garden.[72]

Rather than assuming a pre-Christian origin for the 'Land of Women', I would
suggest that either *Echtrae Chonnlai* or *Immram Brain* or both drew on and
developed an apocryphal Christian tradition which just happens not to have survived elsewhere in early medieval Ireland.[73] In this context, we should perhaps
consider the possibility of yet another intertextual relationship. As was noted
by H. P. A. Oskamp, *Immram Brain*'s depiction of Manannán as a charioteer
driving a chariot over the waves is strikingly reminiscent of a letter written by
St Columbanus to Pope Boniface IV in 613, presenting Christ in the image of
a charioteer riding over the sea of nations even to Ireland. Commenting on this
observation, Kim McCone noted that although on straightforward chronological grounds Columbanus could not possibly have drawn this image from *Immram
Brain*, there was 'no obvious reason why the member of a northern monastery
(perhaps Druim Snechtai) responsible for *Immram Brain* should not have been
acquainted with works by Columbanus'.[74] Elsewhere, Columbanus envisages
human life in the striking and by no means common image of a single day's journey.[75] Could it be that this image is at the back of *Echtrae Chonnlai*'s and *Immram
Brain*'s insistence that Paradise will be reached before sunset?

Having surveyed both the pagan and the Christian allusions of *Echtrae
Chonnlai* at length and in some detail, we may appropriately conclude our investigation by asking what the unknown author may have intended by combining
these heterogeneous elements in the way he did. Here we may start by observing
that the pagan and the Christian pans of the scale seem hardly of equal weight,

---

[72] Shoemaker, *Ancient Traditions of the Virgin Mary's Dormition*, p. 191.

[73] According to Bauckham, *The Fate of the Dead*, p. 344, the above-quoted passage is
lacking in the Irish version that has come down to us, but is probably original. As noted by
Sims-Williams, *Religion and Literature in Western England*, p. 248, 'visions of heaven and hell
[...] were widely reported in Western Europe in the sixth and seventh centuries, for stories about
them circulated at a sub-literary level among ascetic circles'.

[74] See Oskamp, *The Voyage of Máel Dúin*, pp. 80–81, and see *Echtrae Chonnlai*, ed. by
McCone, p. 112.

[75] See Dinzelbacher, 'Die Mittelalterliche Allegorie der Lebensreise', p. 71.

for the Christian elements are not only more numerous and more specific, but also more coherent. In fact, if we ignore the narrative setting for a moment and merely look at the description of the other world to which Connlae is invited, it might be argued that there is nothing pagan at all in those lines within inverted commas, the description which the mysterious woman gives squaring neatly with other early medieval texts dealing with life after death, all of them drawing their inspiration from the Bible, Jewish and Christian Apocrypha, the visions of monks and martyrs, and the writings of the Church Fathers. Why, then, did our author choose to put this description into the mouth of a woman from the *áes síde*? At first glance, we might be tempted to think that he meant to reconcile paganism and Christianity or even present a syncretistic world-view. However, there do not seem to be any genuine pagan Irish elements in his description of Paradise, and the woman effectively denounces druidry as a 'base teaching', engineered by 'the black, bewitching devil' and destined to be destroyed on the arrival of Christianity. Obviously, the author meant his audience to take her point of view, as they would know from hindsight that in reality Christianity triumphed over paganism just as in the story the mysterious woman triumphed over Conn's druid. But if the author meant to convey a thoroughly Christian message and held such a negative view of paganism, why did he bring in the *áes síde* at all? And why is the narrative framework of *Echtrae Chonnlai* so very different from those Christian texts in which we find the closest correspondences to individual motifs?

To solve this conundrum, I would like to go back once more to the title of my paper. Written by Carl Reiner and Steve Martin, the 1982 film *Dead Men Don't Wear Plaid* may be said to be both a parody of and an homage to the pulp detective movies of the 1940s and 1950s. To achieve a maximum of (artificial) film noir patina, the film-makers devised a fantastic mystery plot set in the late 1940s, narrated in voice-over technique, shot in black and white, and involving an assortment of traditional film noir characters such as a hard-boiled private eye, a mysterious female client, an unworldly scientist and a bunch of vengeful Nazis greedy for world domination. Moreover, they imitated the lighting and camera techniques of the 1940s and enlisted the help of experienced veterans such as costume designer Edith Head (1897–1981) and composer Miklós Rózsa (1907–1995). To crown it all, they interweaved newly shot scenes featuring Steve Martin, Rachel Ward, Carl Reiner and Reni Santoni with old black and white movie clips from films such as *This Gun For Hire*, *Double Indemnity*, and *The Big Sleep*, making the modern comedians interact with stars like Alan Ladd, Barbara Stanwyck, Humphrey Bogart, and Fred MacMurray. Needless to say, the sum total is not another film noir, but a hilarious comedy in which the expectations of the audience are constantly thwarted by tongue-in-cheek twists and turns, making us realize every once in a while that times have changed indeed.

Returning from the film to our story, I would like to suggest that *Echtrae Chonnlai* is fundamentally similar to *Dead Men Don't Wear Plaid*. This similarity results first and foremost from the fact that both the film and the story employ a cut-and-paste technique which makes the final product look extremely artificial. If we concede that no modern cinemagoer would assume that Steve Martin might actually have talked with Alan Ladd, Humphrey Bogart, and Barbara Stanwyck, why should an eighth-century Irishman have been prepared to take at face value a story in which an angel from Paradise behaves like a fairy-lover? And why should he have believed that the son of a pagan king was actually taken away from this world into Paradise when he knew from the Church Fathers that this was a fate reserved for some righteous few like Enoch and Elijah?

Granting that neither the film nor our story were meant to be realistic, it will be noted that the comical effect of *Dead Men Don't Were Plaid* largely depends on the different stylistic conventions and the lapse of time that separate film noir and modern comedy. Turning to *Echtrae Chonnlai*, I would argue that much of its effect depends on the contrast between the conventions of traditional fairy-stories and those of Christian devotional literature, and on the lapse of time which separates the pagan world of Conn Cétchathach and his druid from that of our monastic author and his audience. Like Carl Reiner and Steve Martin, the author of *Echtrae Chonnlai* may have aimed at entertainment and amusement. Presumably he also pursued the more serious aim of extolling the new religion at the expense of the old by making the pagan king and his druid look like fools, reminding his audience that for their conduct of this earthly life the Christian teaching was sufficient and that on their dying day they might rest assured of one thing: Dead men don't wear plaid.

Works Cited

Primary Sources

The Acts of the Christian Martyrs, ed. by Herbert Musurillo (Oxford: Clarendon Press, 1972)

Avienus, Rufus Festus, *Ora maritima, Descriptio orbis terrae, Phaenomena*, ed. by Julio Mangas and Domingo Plácido, Testimonia Hispaniae Antiqua, 1 (Madrid: Ediciones Historia, 2000)

Alcimus Ecdicius Avitus, *The Poems of Alcimus Ecdicius Avitus*, ed. and trans. by George W. Shea (Tempe: Medieval and Renaissance Texts and Studies, 1997)

Bethu Brigte, ed. and trans. by Donncha Ó hAodha (Dublin: Dublin Institute for Advanced Studies, 1978)

Buchanan, George, *The History of Scotland*, trans. by James Aikman, 4 vols (Glasgow: Blackie, Fullarton, 1827)

——, *Rerum Scoticarum Historia* (Aberdeen: Chalmers, 1762)

Chandler, Raymond, *Selected Letters of Raymond Chandler*, ed. by Frank MacShane (London: Cape, 1981)

Echtrae Chonnlai and the Beginnings of Vernacular Narrative Writing in Ireland: A Critical Edition with Introduction, Notes, Bibliography and Vocabulary, ed. by Kim McCone (Maynooth: National University of Ireland, 2000)

Immram Brain: Bran's Journey to the Land of the Women , ed. and trans. by Séamus Mac Mathúna (Tübingen: Niemeyer, 1985)

Lactantius, L. Caelius Firmianus, *Divinarum institutionum libri septem*, ed. by Eberhard Heck and Antonie Wlosok, 4 vols (München: Gruyter, 2005–11)

The Patrician Texts in the Book of Armagh, ed. and trans. by Ludwig Bieler, Scriptores Latini Hiberniae, 10 (Dublin: Dublin Institute for Advanced Studies, 1979)

Pedeir Keinc y Mabinogi allan o Lyfr Gwyn Rhydderch, ed. by Ifor Williams, 2nd edn (Caerdydd: Gwasg Prifysgol Cymru, 1951)

Pomponius Mela, *Chorographie*, ed. by A. Silberman (Paris: Belles Lettres, 1988)

Prudentius, with an English Translation, ed. by H. J. Thomson, 2 vols (London: Heinemann, 1949)

Táin Bó Cúailnge: Recension I, ed. and trans. by Cecile O'Rahilly (Dublin: Dublin Institute for Advanced Studies, 1976)

Thesaurus Palaeohibernicus: A Collection of Old-Irish Glosses, Scholia, Prose, and Verse, ed. by Whitley Stokes and John Strachan, 2 vols (Cambridge: Cambridge University Press, 1901–03)

Trioedd Ynys Prydein: The Welsh Triads, ed. and trans. by Rachel Bromwich, 2nd edn (Cardiff: University of Wales Press, 1978)

The Visio Pauli and the Gnostic Apocalypse of Paul, ed. by Jan N. Bremmer and István Czachesz (Leuven: Peeters, 2007)

Visioni dell'aldilà in occidente: fonti, modelli, testi, ed. by Maria Pia Ciccarese, Biblioteca Patristica, 8 (Firenze: Nardini, 1987)

Visions of Heaven and Hell before Dante, ed. by Eileen Gardiner (New York: Italica, 1989)
The Voyage of Bran Son of Febal to the Land of the Living, ed. and trans. by Kuno Meyer and Alfred Nutt, 2 vols (London: Nutt, 1895)

Secondary Studies

Adamik, Tamás, 'The Description of Paradise in the Apocalypse of Peter', in *The Apocalypse of Peter*, ed. by Jan N. Bremmer and István Czachesz (Leuven: Peeters, 2003), pp. 78–90

Aitken, Ellen Bradshaw, 'The Landscape of Promise in the *Apocalypse of Paul*', in *Walk in the Ways of Wisdom: Essays in Honor of Elisabeth Schüssler Fiorenza*, ed. by Shelly Matthews, Cynthia Briggs Kittredge, and Melanie Johnson-DeBaufre (Harrisburg: Trinity, 2003), pp. 153–65

Amat, Jacqueline, *Songes et visions: l'au-delà dans la literature latine tardive* (Paris: Études Augustiniennes, 1985)

Banck-Burgess, Johanna, *Die Textilfunde aus dem späthallstattzeitlichen Fürstengrab von Eberdingen-Hochdorf (Kreis Ludwigsburg) und weitere Grabtextilien aus hallstatt- und latènezeitlichen Kulturgruppen*, Hochdorf, 4 (Stuttgart: Theiss, 1999)

—— , *Mittel der Macht: Textilien bei den Kelten* (Stuttgart: Theiss, 2012)

Bauckham, Richard, *The Fate of the Dead: Studies on the Jewish and Christian Apocalypses*, Supplements to Novum Testamentum, 93 (Leiden: Brill, 1998)

Benjamins, Hendrik S., 'Paradisiacal Life: The Story of Paradise in the Early Church', in *Paradise Interpreted: Representations of Biblical Paradise in Judaism and Christianity*, ed. by Gerard P. Luttikhuizen, Themes in Biblical Narrative, 2 (Leiden: Brill, 1999), pp. 153–67

Bichler, Peter, and others, eds, *Hallstatt Textiles: Technical Analysis, Scientific Investigation and Experiment on Iron Age Textiles* (Oxford: Archaeopress, 2005)

Borsje, Jacqueline, 'Monotheistic to a Certain Extent: The "Good Neighbours" of God in Ireland', in *The Boundaries of Monotheism: Interdisciplinary Explorations into the Foundations of Western Monotheism*, ed. by Anne-Marie Korte and Maaike de Haardt, Studies in Theology and Religion, 13 (Leiden: Brill, 2009), pp. 53–81

Breatnach, Liam, 'Review of S. Mac Mathúna, *Immram Brain* (Tübingen 1985)', *Celtica*, 20 (1988), 177–92

Bregni, Simone, '"Paradisus, locus amoenus": immagini del paradiso nei primi cinque secoli dell'era cristiana', *Rivista di storia e letteratura religiosa*, 41 (2005), 297–328

Bremmer, Jan N., 'Paradise: From Persia, via Greece, into the Septuagint', in *Paradise Interpreted: Representations of Biblical Paradise in Judaism and Christianity*, ed. by Gerard P. Luttikhuizen, Themes in Biblical Narrative, 2 (Leiden: Brill, 1999), pp. 1–20

Bremmer, Jan N., and István Czachesz, eds, *The Apocalypse of Peter* (Leuven: Peeters, 2003)

Brunaux, Jean-Louis, *Les Druides: des philosophes chez les Barbares* (Paris: Seuil, 2006)

Carey, John, *A Single Ray of the Sun: Religious Speculation in Early Ireland; Three Essays* (Andover: Celtic Studies Publications, 1999)

Carozzi, Claude, *Le Voyage de l'âme dans l'au-delà d'après la littérature latine (V^e–XIIIe siècle)*, Collection de l'École française de Rome, 189 (Roma: École française de Rome, 1994)

Cheape, Hugh, *Tartan: The Highland Habit* (Edinburgh: National Museums of Scotland, 2006)

Copeland, Kirsti B., 'Sinners and Post-Mortem "Baptism" in the Acherusian Lake', in *The Apocalypse of Peter*, ed. by Jan N. Bremmer and István Czachesz (Leuven: Peeters, 2003), pp. 91–107

Di Pede, Elena, and André Wénin, 'Aux origins du Jardin d'Éden: de la Genèse à Ézéchiel', *Graphè*, 17 (2008), 19–42

Dieterich, Albrecht, *Nekyia: Beiträge zur Erklärung der neuentdeckten Petrusapokalypse* (Leipzig: Teubner, 1893)

Dinzelbacher, Peter, 'Die mittelalterliche Allegorie der Lebensreise', in *Monsters, Marvels and Miracles: Imaginary Journeys and Landscapes in the Middle Ages*, ed. by Leif Søndergaard and Rasmus Thorning Hansen (Odense: University Press of Southern Denmark, 2005), pp. 65–112

Felber, Anneliese, 'Die Henochgestalt in der Patristik', *Protokolle zur Bibel*, 11 (2002), 21–32

Gooder, Paula R., *Only the Third Heaven? 2 Corinthians 12. 1–10 and Heavenly Ascent* (London: Clark, 2006)

Grimm, Reinhold R., 'Die Paradiesesehe: Eine erotische Utopie des Mittelalters', in *'Getempert und gemischet' für Wolfgang Mohr zum 65. Geburtstag*, ed. by Franz Hundsnurscher and Ulrich Müller (Göppingen: Kümmerle, 1972), pp. 1–25

——, *Paradisus Coelestis—Paradisus Terrestris: Zur Auslegungsgeschichte des Paradieses im Abendland bis um 1200* (München: Fink, 1977)

Hamp, Eric, 'Varia X: Irish *síd* "tumulus" and Irish *síd* "peace"', *Études celtiques*, 19 (1982), 141

Hartinger, Walter, *Religion und Brauch* (Darmstadt: Wissenschaftliche Buchgesellschaft, 1992)

Himmelfarb, Martha, *Ascent to Heaven in Jewish and Christian Apocalypses* (Oxford: Oxford University Press, 1993)

Hofeneder, Andreas, *Die Religion der Kelten in den antiken literarischen Zeugnissen, 3 vols* (Wien: Österreichischen Akademie der Wissenschaften, 2005–11)

Hultgård, Andrers, 'Das Paradies: vom Park des Perserkönigs zum Ort der Seligen', in *La cité de Dieu die Stadt Gottes*, ed. by Martin Hengel, Siegfried Mittmann, and Anna Maria Schwemer, Wissenschaftliche Untersuchungen zum Neuen Testament, 129 (Tübingen: Mohr Siebeck, 2000), pp. 1–43

Hutton, Ronald, *Blood and Mistletoe: The History of the Druids in Britain* (New Haven: Yale University Press, 2009)

'Irish Popular Superstitions, Chapter III: Medical Superstitions, Fairy Lore, and Enchantment', *The Dublin University Magazine*, 33 (1849), 707–18

Jenkins, David, ed., *The Cambridge History of Western Textiles* (Cambridge: Cambridge University Press, 2003)

Jiroušková, Lenka, *Die Visio Pauli: Wege und Wandlungen einer orientalischen Apokryphe im lateinischen Mittelalter unter Einschluss der alttschechischen und deutschsprachigen Textzeugen*, Mittellateinishe Studien und Texte, 34 (Leiden: Brill, 2006)

Kabir, Ananya Jahanara, *Paradise, Death and Doomsday in Anglo-Saxon Literature* (Cambridge: Cambridge University Press, 2001)

Kantorowicz, Ernst H., *The King's Two Bodies: A Study in Mediaeval Political Theology* (Princeton: Princeton University Press, 1957)

Kelly, Fergus, *A Guide to Early Irish Law* (Dublin: Dublin Institute for Advanced Studies, 1988)

Kraus, T. J., 'Acherousia und Elysion: Anmerkungen im Hinblick auf deren Verwendung auch im christlichen Kontext', *Menemosyne*, 56 (2003), 145–64

Kurzynski, Katharina von, '...und ihre Hosen nennen sie bracas': Textilfunde und Textiltechnologie der Hallstatt- und Latènezeit und ihr Kontext* (Espelkamp: Leidorf, 1996)

Lambert, Pierre-Yves, *La Langue gauloise: description linguistique, commentaire d'inscriptions choisies*, pref. by Michel Lejeune (Paris: Errance, 1994)

Landesmann, Peter, *Die Himmelfahrt des Elija: Entstehen und Weiterleben einer Legende sowie ihre Darstellung in der frühchristlichen Kunst* (Wien: Böhlau, 2004)

Mac Cana, Proinsias, *Celtic Mythology*, new rev. ed. (New York: Bedrick Books, 1983)

Mac Mathún, Seamus, 'Paganism and Society in Early Ireland', in *Irish Writers and Religion*, ed. by Robert Welch (Gerrards Cross: Smythe, 1992), pp. 1–14

Maier, Bernhard, *Die Druiden* (München: Beck, 2009)

——, *Die Religion der Kelten: Götter, Mythen, Weltbild* (München: Beck, 2001)

Malitz, Jürgen, *Die Historien des Poseidonios* (München: Beck, 1983)

Nagy, Joseph Falaky, *Conversing with Angels and Ancients: Literary Myths of Medieval Ireland* (Dublin: Four Courts, 1997)

Noort, Edward, 'Gan-Eden in the Context of the Mythology of the Hebrew Bible', in *Paradise Interpreted: Representations of Biblical Paradise in Judaism and Christianity*, ed. by Gerard P. Luttikhuizen, Themes in Biblical Narrative, 2 (Leiden: Brill, 1999), pp. 21–36

North, Richard, *Heathen Gods in Old English Literature*, Cambridge Studies in Anglo-Saxon England, 22 (Cambridge: Cambridge University Press, 1997)

Ntedika, Joseph, *L'Évocation de l'au-delà dans la prière pour les morts: étude de patristique et de liturgie latines (IVe—VIIIe S.)* (Louvain: Éditions Nauwelaerts, 1971)

Ó Cathasaigh, Tomás, 'The Semantics of "síd"', *Éigse*, 17 (1977–79), 137–55

Ó hAodha, Donncha, 'Some Remarks on the Happy Otherworld of the "Voyage of Bran"', in *Apocalyptic and Eschatological Heritage: The Middle East and Celtic Realms*, ed. by Martin McNamara (Dublin: Four Courts, 2003), pp. 137–43

Ó hÓgáin, Dáithí, *Myth, Legend and Romance: An Encyclopaedia of the Irish Folk Tradition* (New York: Prentice Hall, 1991)

O'Reilly, Edward, and John O'Donovan, eds, *An Irish-English Dictionary, with Copious Quotations from the Most Esteemed Writers: With a Supplement* (Dublin: Duffy, 1864)

Oskamp, Hans Pieter Atze, *The Voyage of Máel Dúin: A Study in Early Irish Voyage Literature* (Groningen: Wolters-Noordhoff, 1970)

Planché, James Robinson, *History of British Costume* (London: Knight, 1834)

Rast-Eicher, Antoinette, *Textilien, Wolle, Schafe der Eisenzeit in der Schweiz* (Basel: Archäologie Schweiz, 2008)

Scafi, Alessandro, *Mapping Paradise: A History of Heaven on Earth* (Chicago: Chicago University Press, 2006)

Schmitt, Armin, 'Zum Thema "Entrückung" im Alten Testament', *Biblische Zeitschrift*, 26 (1982), 34–49

Shoemaker, Stephen J., *Ancient Traditions of the Virgin Mary's Dormition and Assumption* (Oxford: Oxford University Press, 2002)

Sims-Williams, Patrick, *Religion and Literature in Western England, 600–800*, Cambridge Studies in Anglo-Saxon England, 3 (Cambridge: Cambridge University Press, 1990)

——, 'Some Celtic Otherworld Terms', in *Celtic Language, Celtic Culture: A Festschrift for Eric P. Hamp*, ed. by A. T. E. Matonis and Daniel F. Melia (Van Nuys: Ford and Bailie, 1990), pp. 57–81

Smith, Daniel A., 'The Assumption of the Righteous Dead in the Wisdom of Solomon and the Sayings of Gospel Q', *Studies in Religion*, 29 (2000), 287–99

Stuiber, Alfred, *Refrigerium interim: die Vorstellungen vom Zwischenzustand und die früh-christliche Grabeskunst* (Bonn: Hanstein, 1957)

Woyke, Johannes, *Götter, 'Götzen', Götterbilder: Aspekte einer paulinischen 'Theologie der Religionen'* (Berlin: Gruyter, 2005)

Wright, J. Edward, 'Whither Elija? The Ascension of Elijah in Biblical and Extrabiblical Traditions', in *Things Revealed: Studies in Early Jewish and Christian Literature in Honor of Michael E. Stone*, ed. by Ester G. Chazon, David Satran, and Ruth A. Clements (Leiden: Brill, 2004), pp. 123–38

VESSELS OF MYTH

Kimberly Ball[*]

The late eleventh-/early twelfth-century Irish manuscript *Lebor na hUidre* (*Book of the Dun Cow*) contains a text bearing the title *Síaburcharpat Con Culaind* (*The Phantom Chariot of Cú Chulainn*), which relates how Saint Patrick once summoned the long-dead Ulster hero Cú Chulainn from Hell to help convince the high king of Ireland, Lóegaire, to convert to Christianity.[1] Lóegaire, so the story goes, specifically asks the saint to produce Cú Chulainn 'fó míadamla feib adfíadar i scélaib' (with the glory that is told of in stories) before he will consent to believe in the powers of Patrick or his God.[2] Patrick obliges, and a suitably glorious Cú Chulainn arrives in his chariot pulled by his horses the Liath Macha and Dub Sainglend and driven by his charioteer Lóeg, all appearing as advertised in the Ulster Cycle. Lóegaire, however, remains unconvinced for, as he tells Patrick, 'Mása é Cu Culaind atconnarc is garit limsa ro boí ic comaccallaim' (If it is Cú Chulainn I have seen, I think his conversation with me was short).[3]

---

[*] Kimberly Ball (kimberlyball@charter.net) finished her PhD dissertation in Comparative Literature at the University of California, Irvine, in 2009. This paper is based in part on a section from her dissertation, Ball, 'The Otherworld Vessel'.

[1] Besides the version in *Lebor na hUidre*, *Síaburcharpat* is found in two later manuscripts, BL, MS Egerton 88 and BL, MS Additional 33993, which represent a different, shorter recension of the story. The basic plot is the same in both recensions, with the exception that it is only in the *Lebor na hUidre* version that Lóegaire is said to convert to Christianity at the story's end.

[2] The Irish text of *Síaburcharpat Con Culaind* reproduced here is from the semi-diplomatic edition, *Lebor na hUidre*, ed. by Best and Bergin, p. 278, ll. 9225–26. The translation throughout is based on 'Siabur-Charpat Con Culaind', ed. and trans. by Crowe. The translation of the Tír Scáith poem is based, in addition, on 'Die Sage von Curoi', ed. and trans. by Thurneysen, pp. 196–98.

[3] *Lebor na hUidre*, ed. by Best and Bergin, p. 279, ll. 9282–83.

Writing Down the Myths, ed. by Joseph Falaky Nagy, CURSOR 17, (Turnhout: Brepols, 2013)
pp. 137–155   BREPOLS 🖳 PUBLISHERS   10.1484/M.CURSOR-EB.1. 100850

Indeed, the text mentions no talk between Cú Chulainn and Lóegaire on this first visit, but Cú Chulainn returns, words are exchanged, and finally Lóegaire believes. As it turns out, Lóegaire requires not only to behold the hero of stories but also to hear stories from the hero's mouth, for on this second visit he requests that Cú Chulainn recount his 'márgnímaib' (great deeds) and objects when the first few exploits Cú Chulainn relates are not sufficiently impressive, intimating that the *real* Cú would have better tales to tell.[4] Accordingly, Cú Chulainn utters a poem more to Lóegaire's liking in which he describes two of his otherworld adventures: one in Lochlainn, a Scandinavian locale inhabited by giants, and one in Tír Scáith, the 'Land of Shadow':

Tairred dochuadusa a Lóegairi	A journey I went, O Lóegaire,
día lád hi tír Scaith.	For plunder to the Land of Shadow.
dún Scáith and cona glassaib íarn	The Fortress of Shadow there with its iron locks,
forurmius láim fair.	I laid hand on it.
Uii. múir imón cathraig sin	Seven walls around that city
ba etig a dend.	Ugly was its aspect.
Sonnach íarn for cach múr	An iron palisade on each wall,
forsin bátár nóe cend.	On which were nine heads.
Dorse iarn for cach slis	Doors of iron on each side,
frimna niro chosnoda.	Against us no great defence.
atacomcussa com láu	I struck with my foot,
condarrala i mbrosnacha.	Made them into fragments.
Buí cuithe isin dún	There was a pit in that fortress,
lasin ríg adfét.	Belonging to the king, it is said.
.x. nathraig doróemdatar	Ten snakes burst
dara or ba bét.	Over its edge — what a deed!
Iar sin atarethusa	After that I attacked,
cíar adbol a ndrong.	Though vast the throng.
co ndernus a n-ordnecha	Until I crushed them to fragments
eter mo dá dornd.	Between my two fists.
Tech lán do loscannaib	A house full of toads
dofarlaicthe dún.	Were loosed on us.
míla géra gulbnecha	Sharp-beaked animals,
ro leltar im srúb.	They stuck in my snout.
Bíastai granni dracondai	Horrible draconic monsters,
cucund dofutitis.	To us they were falling.

---

[4] *Lebor na hUidre*, ed. by Best and Bergin, p. 280, l. 9317.

tréna a n-amainsi	Strong their witchery
echdíli cíadcutís.	Who obtained such waterhorses.[5]
Iar sin atarrethusa	After that I attacked,
in tan bá fóm rois.	When there was a rush on me.
cotamfoltsa comtar menbacha	I ground them to fragments,
eter mo dí bois.	Between my two palms
Baí coire isin dún sin	There was a cauldron in that fortress,
lóeg na teóra mbó.	Calf of the three cows.[6]
.xxx. aige ina chroes	Thirty joints of meat in its maw
nirbo luchtlach dó.	Were not enough to fill it.
Taithigtis in cairi sin	They used to frequent that cauldron,
bá mellach in bág.	Delightful was the contest.
ní théigtis úad for nách leth	They used not to go from it on any side
co fácbaitis lán.	Until they left it full.
Baí mór di ór 7 argut and	There was much gold and silver in it,
bá hamrae in fríth.	Wondrous was the find.
dobirt in cori sin	I carried off that cauldron
la ingin ind ríg.	with the daughter of the king.
Na téora bai dobertamár	The three cows we carried off,
ro snaidet a muir.	They strong-swam the sea.
ba here desi di ór	There was a double load of gold
la cách fora muin.[7]	Carried by each on his shoulder.

Síaburcharpat depicts a pivotal moment in Ireland's transition from paganism to Christianity — hence from a primary oral culture to one in which writing would play an increasingly important role — when the possibility, desirability, and proper methodology of carrying stories of the pagan past into the future would have come into question.[8] It has been suggested that texts like *Síaburcharpat*,

---

[5] My rendering of this line is mere speculation. Crowe has 'Horse-tribe though [they] explained them' ('Siabur-Charpat Con Culaind', ed. and trans. by Crowe, p. 387), and Thurneysen declares that he cannot translate it ('Die Sage von Curoi', ed. and trans. by Thurneysen, p. 197).

[6] In *Aided Conrói* (*The Death of Cú Roí*), it is explained that the cauldron was known as the cows' *lóeg* (calf) because they used to fill it with their milk (Best, 'The Tragic Death of Cúrói mac Dári', p. 20).

[7] *Lebor na hUidre*, ed. by Best and Bergin, pp. 282–83, ll. 9378–425.

[8] The earliest evidence of writing in Ireland consists of inscriptions on stones, dated to the fifth century or possibly earlier, made in the native Ogam script based on the Latin alphabet. Jane Stevenson argues that this evidence reflects a pre-Christian literacy acquired through contacts with the Roman Empire and beginning 'in the fourth century at the latest' (Stevenson,

wherein Irish saints make miraculous contact with pagan ancients, played a validating role within the context of this transition. Robin Flower saw such tales as
designed to lend greater credence to the oral tradition on which, lacking a written record, Christian scribes had to base their accounts of Ireland's past: information from an 'eyewitness' would be more reliable than hearsay, and, as such
pre-Christian eyewitnesses could not be expected to write down their own 'testimony', saints would provide the most unassailable 'warrants' for the resulting
texts.[9] Joseph Nagy, on the other hand, makes the case that the underlying story
pattern (replacing saint with poet or druid) most likely originated in the pre-
Christian oral tradition itself, where such stories would have served to increase
the authority of particular oral narratives and narrators.[10] According to Nagy,
the saint was especially well-suited to replace the poet or druid as interlocutor
with the past's representative because, as a liminal figure traversing the boundary between human and divine, the saint is a natural mediator between different realms — whether these be this world and the otherworld (and, like Cú
Chulainn, ancients in these tales tend to tell of otherworld exploits), pagan past
and Christian future, or the oral tradition and its translation into written texts.[11]
In a text like *Acallam na Senórach* (*Dialogue of the Ancients*), where Saint Patrick
sees to it that the tales told by his pagan informants are written down, the saint
plays an overtly validating role by sanctioning the recording of pre-Christian oral
narrative for Christian/literate posterity.[12] In *Síaburcharpat* no mention is made

'The Beginnings of Literacy in Ireland', pp. 138–39, 144–45, 165. In part, Stevenson bases this
conclusion on Ireland's rapid development of an abundant vernacular literature soon after the
entry of the first Christian missionaries in the fifth century, with the earliest vernacular texts
going at least as far back as the sixth century (pp. 127–28, 158, 165). But even if literacy
preceded Christianity in Ireland, the Christian Church was doubtless the driving force behind
Ireland's early literary abundance.

[9] Flower, *The Irish Tradition*, pp. 6–9.

[10] Nagy, 'Close Encounters', pp. 136–37. Joseph Szövérffy also claims a validating role for
Síaburcharpat, arguing that the text's purpose was to 'rehabilitate Cú Chulainn in the eyes of the
Irish of the tenth century' by Christianizing him (Szövérffy, 'Siaburcharpat Conculainn', p. 73).

[11] Nagy, 'Close Encounters', pp. 148–49; Nagy, *Conversing with Angels and Ancients*,
pp. vii–viii. See Nagy, *Conversing with Angels and Ancients*, pp. 265–78, for a detailed reading of
Síaburcharpat along these lines.

[12] *Acallam na Senórach* has manuscript witnesses from the fifteenth century (Oxford, Bodl.
Lib., MS Laud 610; Chatsworth, The Book of Lismore; and Oxford, Bodl. Lib., MS Rawl.
B. 487), the sixteenth century (Dublin, UC, Franc. MS (Killiney) A 4), and the seventeenth
century (Dublin, UC, Franc. MS (Killiney) A 20). It has been dated to the end of the twelfth
or the beginning of the thirteenth centuries (*Tales of the Elders of Ireland*, trans. by Dooley and
Roe, p. viii).

of writing down Cú Chulainn's stories, but by summoning, using, and ultimately saving the hero of the Ulster Cycle from damnation, Saint Patrick implicitly gives his blessing to the preservation of the pagan narrative tradition at a time of transition when the future of this 'past' is uncertain.[13]

Elva Johnston points out that the time of *Síaburcharpat*'s composition, dated to a period extending from the eighth century into the eleventh,[14] was transitional in another respect, in that political power was being consolidated in Ireland resulting in competition among various elite groups for control.[15] According to Johnston, *Síaburcharpat* is specifically concerned with the question, 'Who should control access to knowledge in early Ireland?', to which its answer is the Church, understood as a textual community in Brian Stock's sense of a group led by an individual interpreter of texts, represented in *Síaburcharpat* by Saint Patrick.[16] One implication of *Síaburcharpat*, as Johnston reads it, is that if control falls into the right hands then society will be saved, just as Patrick saves Lóegaire (and by extension all Ireland) by exerting control over the pagan past (and knowledge of that past) in the person of Cú Chulainn.[17] Kim McCone likewise regards Patrick as the controlling force in *Síaburcharpat*, observing that the saint maintains 'virtually complete control over the hero's image and message' throughout the text, while Nagy describes the phantom chariot and its chief occupant as 'completely under the control of Patrick', who drives the titular chariot 'as it were, by remote control'.[18] Indeed, it is as if Cú Chulainn were merely Patrick's tool in this text, for upon arrival the hero pauses only briefly to beg the

---

[13] Although the earliest written records of the Ulster Cycle are found in manuscripts produced in Christian Ireland, the tales are set in Ireland's pre-Christian past and are thought by many to have roots in a pre-existing oral tradition. See, for example: Murphy, *Saga and Myth in Ancient Ireland*; Jackson, *The Oldest Irish Tradition*; *Táin Bó Cúalnge*, ed. and trans. by O'Rahilly, pp. ix–xiv; Dillon, *Celts and Aryans*. For discussion of the debate as to the extent of oral-traditional influence on early Irish literature, see Ó Coileáin, 'Oral or Literary?', and Nagy, 'Orality in Medieval Irish Narrative'.

[14] *Síaburcharpat*'s composition has been dated variously to the eighth century ('Siabur-Charpat Con Culaind', ed. and trans. by Crowe, p. 373), the ninth or tenth century (Zimmer, 'Keltische Beiträge I', p. 256), the late tenth century (Thurneysen, *Die irische Helden- und Königsage*, I, 567–71), and the eleventh century (Murphy, *The Ossianic Lore*, p. 21).

[15] Johnston, 'The Salvation of the Individual', pp. 111–14.

[16] Stock, *The Implications of Literacy*; Johnston, 'The Salvation of the Individual', pp. 112–13, 125.

[17] Johnston, 'The Salvation of the Individual', pp. 114, 116.

[18] McCone, *Pagan Past and Christian Present*, p. 201; Nagy, *Conversing with Angels and Ancients*, p. 265.

saint for salvation before beginning to proselytize King Lóegaire, and everything Cú Chulainn says or does thereafter occurs within this proselytizing framework. But the attempt to exert control over the past and its messages is in general a problematic undertaking, and I suggest that in *Síaburcharpat* the control exerted by Patrick (and by extension the Christianizing/'mythographing' project he represents) is less than total. One aspect of the text that complicates the idea that Christian/literary control can be exerted over pagan/oral tradition, or that the present can simply use the past to its own ends, is the part played in this story by otherworld vessels, such as the cauldron Cú Chulainn plunders from the Land of Shadow, upon whose description the hero lingers for three stanzas of his narrative display, or the phantom chariot that carries Cú Chulainn out of Hell, which takes top billing in the text's title.

At one point Cú Chulainn says of the chariot, 'is Patraic ro cruthaigestar' (It is Patrick who formed it), providing yet another indication of the saint's control over the hero, whom he has contained in a vehicle of his own device.[19] A clue that this control may be incomplete, however, is given in the designation of Cú Chulainn's vehicle and the text that tells of it as *síabur-*. The *síabur-* component of *síaburcharpat* relates to the noun *síabair/síabrae*, which may refer to 'a spectre, phantom, [or] supernatural being'.[20] While the use of a spectral modifier seems well-suited, given that this is the vehicle that brings the long-dead Cú Chulainn back to the world of the living, the *síabur-* designation may also refer to 'witchery, enchantment [or] delusion'.[21] Cú Chulainn himself seems to reference the dubiousness of things *síabur-* in this sense when he repeatedly attempts to gain Lóegaire's trust and thereby effect his conversion with the reassurance that 'ní síabrae rodatánic is Cú Chulaind mac Sóalta' (it is not a *síabrae* that has come to you; it is Cú Chulainn, son of Soalta).[22] Nagy points out that, despite the hero's protestations, Cú Chulainn is undeniably a *síabrae* in a third sense of the word, in that the noun *síabair* and verb *síabraid* are elsewhere used with reference to the 'distortion' and 'transformation' of Cú in his battle fury, which involves a sort of supernatural shapeshifting.[23] Adding yet another strand to *síaburcharpat*'s semantic web, *síabur-* is reminiscent, visually and acoustically, of the *síde*,

---

[19] *Lebor na hUidre*, ed. by Best and Bergin, p. 286, l. 9510.

[20] *Dictionary of the Irish Language*, ed. by Marstrander and others, under *síabair*.

[21] *Dictionary of the Irish Language*, ed. by Marstrander and others, under *síabrad*.

[22] *Lebor na hUidre*, ed. by Best and Bergin, p. 280, l. 9302; also see p. 287, l. 9538.

[23] *Dictionary of the Irish Language*, ed. by Marstrander and others, under *síabraid*; Nagy, *Conversing with Angels and Ancients*, p. 264.

hills and ancient tumuli on the Irish landscape supposed to be entrances to an otherworld not readily assimilable to Christian theology. After all, Lóegaire first encounters Cú Chulainn's *síaburcharpat* when he is going to 'Cnuc Síde in Broga' (the Hill of the *Síd* of the *Brug*) — in a possible reference to the Neolithic grave complex at Brug na Bóinne — and a 'tromchíach' (heavy fog) suddenly descends, a traditional sign in Irish narrative that one is crossing over into the otherworld.[24] It is explicitly stated in the text that Cú Chulainn rides forth from Hell, a more Christianized location, but Hell is akin to the *síde* in that both are subterranean otherworlds associated with Ireland's pagan past: Hell is the purported home to the deceased Irish prior to Patrick (with a few notable exceptions), and many of the *síde* are ancient gravesites, said to be inhabited by the Tuatha Dé Danann (People of the Goddess Danu), sometimes identified as gods of a pagan Irish pantheon. Making a more explicit connection between *síabur-* and Ireland's pagan past, an eleventh-century text entitled *Senchas na Relec* (*Lore of the Cemeteries*) gives the following alternative version of King Cormac's death: 'No siabhra ro h-ort .i. Tuatha de Danainn, áir ic friu atberta siabra, i.e.' (Or else the *síabhra* [plural] killed him, that is, the Tuatha Dé Danann, for they were called *síabhra*).[25]

At play in the semantics of *síabair/síabraid* are meanings related to the supernatural ranging from the ghostly to the delusory to shapeshifting to the pagan divine. By invoking this play of meaning, *síabur-* marks both chariot and text with associations seemingly at odds with their role as Christian vehicles constructed for the containment, conveyance, and control of pagan content. The designation of the chariot Patrick constructs as *síabur-* calls attention to the saint's supernatural abilities along with the troubling idea that such abilities can be used to deceive, for the kinds of delusion termed *síabrad* tend to be supernaturally induced, as through glamour or enchantment. At the same time, the text explicitly and implicitly brings the supernatural that Patrick represents into relation with the pre-Christian supernatural of the *síde*, while ghostly connotations suggest that this past may come forth from its burial mounds to haunt the Christian present. *Síabur-* also introduces a sense of instability, inherent to the shapeshifting strand of meaning but also implicit in the tension between the otherwise inseparable pair of chariot and hero: the one proclaimed in the text's very title to be *síabur-*, and the other repeatedly denying that he is a *síabrae*, though the narrative tradition might lead one to disbelieve this claim. With his repeated denials

---

[24] *Lebor na hUidre*, ed. by Best and Bergin, p. 278, ll. 9238–39, 9244.

[25] From the version of the *Senchas* in Dublin, TC, MS 1336 (H. 3. 17), a sixteenth-century manuscript, as it is cited in Petrie, 'The Ecclesiastical Architecture of Ireland', p. 98, note 'd'. On the death of Cormac, see Ó Cathasaigh, *The Heroic Biography of Cormac mac Airt*, pp. 68–72.

Cú Chulainn implies that if he *had* been a *síabrae* Lóegaire would have been within his rights to reject his testimony and the Christianity he advocates, yet Patrick constructs a chariot that is unabashedly *síabur-*, which, if Cú Chulainn's insinuation is correct, raises doubts as to its trustworthiness and its fitness for use as a tool of conversion.

If the *síaburcharpat* is a problematic vessel, Cú Chulainn, *síabrae* or not, constitutes dangerous content difficult to contain. Marie-Louise Sjoestedt designates Cú Chulainn 'the hero of the tribe', contrasting him with the hero of an altogether different narrative cycle, Finn Mac Cumaill, whom she dubs a 'hero outside the tribe'.[26] As has been frequently observed, the hero within the tribe may sometimes present a threat to the society that attempts to keep such a powerful force within its bounds.[27] In the *Macgnímrada Con Culaind* (*Boyhood Deeds of Cú Chulainn*) as recounted in the earliest recension of the *Táin Bó Cúailnge* (*Cattle Raid of Cooley*), likewise found in *Lebor na hUidre*, several episodes portray the difficulties undergone by Cú Chulainn's community in order to contain the young hero.[28] When he arrives at court, Cú Chulainn is so violent and powerful that the resident boy-troop, comprising three fifties of Cú Chulainn's peers, cannot manage to surround the hero in order to throw him in a wrestling match.[29] On the occasion of one of Cú Chulainn's first battle frenzies, the Ulster warriors must seize him and immerse him successively in three tubs of cold water, the first of which bursts and the second of which boils over, before he is rendered fit for society.[30] Cú Chulainn sleeps with his head and feet against pillar stones, which he shatters when too suddenly awakened.[31] And when he asks the Ulster king, Conchobar, to give him a chariot, the first twelve offered by the king explode when Cú Chulainn touches them; only when Conchobar offers his own chariot does the hero find himself suitably contained.[32] Like the hound he replaces, Cú is a force to be unleashed only with caution and only within circumscribed boundaries, which he always threatens to transgress.[33]

---

[26] Sjoestedt, *Gods and Heroes of the Celts*, trans. by Dillon, pp. 73–110.

[27] McCone, 'Aided Cheltchair Maic Uthechair'; Nagy, 'Heroic Destinies in the Macgnímrada'; Lowe, 'Kicking over the Traces'.

[28] *Táin Bó Cúailnge: Recension 1*, ed. and trans. by O'Rahilly, pp. 13–26, ll. 398–824.

[29] *Táin Bó Cúailnge: Recension 1*, ed. and trans. by O'Rahilly, p. 18, ll. 556–58.

[30] *Táin Bó Cúailnge: Recension 1*, ed. and trans. by O'Rahilly, p. 25, ll. 814–18.

[31] *Táin Bó Cúailnge: Recension 1*, ed. and trans. by O'Rahilly, pp. 15–16, ll. 462–26, 485–86.

[32] *Táin Bó Cúailnge: Recension 1*, ed. and trans. by O'Rahilly, p. 20, ll. 649–52.

[33] It is reported in the *Macgnímrada Con Culaind* that Cú Chulainn received his name in the following manner: Arriving late to a feast hosted by the smith Culann, the hero (then known

Although Cú Chulainn is pre-Christian content in need of containment and control, he may also be regarded as a container in his own right. In *Síaburcharpat* the hero reminisces to Lóegaire about his life with the Ulstermen, saying: 'Ro boí tan a Lóegairi bá messe immátheged immatimchellad immidamthellech' (It was I who used to go among them, who used to go around them, who used to keep them together).[34] Here Cú Chulainn refers to his role as warrior-hero, as one charged with defending the perimeter of his community from attack, providing protective containment (and perhaps *esprit de corps*). He also describes himself as 'chomrar cacha runi do andrib Ulad' (a casket for every secret of the Ulster maidens), and in the story of the raid on the Land of Shadow he recounts to Lóegaire how in escaping from the island fort a storm struck at sea, after which he had to act as a vessel for his men:

Iar sin immórousa	After that I floated them,
gíarba gábud grind.	Though it was a clear danger.
nonbur cechtar mo dá lám	Nine on each of my two hands
xxx. for mo chind.	Thirty on my head.
Ochtur form díb slíastaib	Eight upon my two thighs
rom leltar dim churp.	They clung to my body.
sbá samlaid sain ro snausa in farrci	It was in that manner I swam the ocean
co mboí isin phurt.[35]	Until I was in the harbour.

In *Síaburcharpat*, Cú Chulainn acts as a vessel within a vessel. What he contained and conveyed in the past were his people and their secrets, keeping them safe and allowing them to survive. In a sense he continues to do this after death, for what Cú Chulainn transports with him to the Patrician fifth century and beyond via the *síaburcharpat* are stories, which provide a kind of continued existence for people and knowledge of the past. One of these stories features yet another vessel, a 'wondrous' cauldron of remarkable capacity which Cú Chulainn describes at some length.

The cauldron from the Land of Shadow lies at the heart of *Síaburcharpat*, both in its central position in the story within the story, and in its pivotal role,

---

as Sétanta) was attacked by a ferocious hound, which had been unleashed from three chains held by three men to patrol the enclosed grounds of Culann's fort. After killing the hound, the hero received his name, which means 'Hound of Culann', when he offered to take over the canine's job as guardian of Culann's property until a suitable replacement could be found (*Táin Bó Cúailnge: Recension I*, ed. and trans. by O'Rahilly, pp. 17–19, ll. 540–607).

[34] *Lebor na hUidre*, ed. by Best and Bergin, p. 280, l. 9309.

[35] *Lebor na hUidre*, ed. by Best and Bergin, p. 281, ll. 9335–36, p. 284, 9430–37.

for it is only when Cú Chulainn relates the tale of the cauldron's acquisition that Lóegaire accepts his identity and judges Patrick's end of the conversion bargain fulfilled. In *Síaburcharpat*, the Land of Shadow narrative and the cauldron it contains are used as tools of conversion, but in referencing them Cú Chulainn invokes a narrative complex which in some ways challenges the proselytizing programme that is underway. This narrative complex revolves around the relationship between Cú Chulainn and another important Cú in the Ulster Cycle, Cú Roí.[36]

A more elaborate account of the raid in which the cauldron is acquired occurs in the narrative *Aided Conrói* (*The Death of Cú Roí*).[37] The Yellow Book of Lecan version, thought to have been composed sometime between the tenth and twelfth centuries, begins with the question: 'Cīssī tucaid ar romarbsad Ulaid Coinrāi mac Dáiri?' (What reason did the men of Ulster have to kill Cú Roí son of Dáire?).[38] The text replies that it was because of certain items taken in the siege on the Land of Shadow, to wit: Blathnait (daughter of Menn, ruler of the Land of Shadow), the three red-spotted cows of Iuchna, three birds that used to sit on the cows' ears and sing to them, and the cauldron known as the cows' '*lóeg*' (calf) because they used to fill it with their milk.[39]

Cú Roí, dressed in an identity-concealing cloak, goes with the Ulstermen and participates in the attack on the Land of Shadow to the extent that when King Conchobar asks each warrior who emerges from the fort with a head taken from one of the enemy, 'Cīa romarb in fer sin?' (Who killed that man?), the warrior replies, 'Misi 7 fear in broit lachtna' (I, and the man in the cream-coloured

---

[36] Lóegaire's insistence, shortly after Cú Chulainn begins to narrate his exploits, that: 'Níptar gníma con' (These were not the deeds of a cú), and Cú Chulainn's response, as he attempts to define just what kind of *cú* (hound) he is, may be taken as a reminder that other *coin* exist in this narrative tradition (*Lebor na hUidre*, ed. by Best and Bergin, p. 280, l. 9324).

[37] Early versions of *Aided Conrói* are found in three manuscripts: Dublin, TC, MS 1318 (fourteenth century); Oxford, Bodl. Lib., MS Laud 610 (fifteenth century); and BL, MS Egerton 88 (sixteenth century).

[38] For the dating of the Dublin, TC, MS 1318 version, see Best, 'The Tragic Death of Cúrói mac Dári', p. 18; Thurneysen, *Die irische Helden- und Königsage*, I, 440; and *Two Death Tales from the Ulster Cycle*, trans. by Tymoczko, p. 16. The Irish text of *Aided Conrói* is taken from Richard Irvine Best's edition of the Dublin, TC, MS 1318 version (Best, 'The Tragic Death of Cúrói mac Dári', p. 20). The translation is from *Two Death Tales from the Ulster Cycle*, trans. by Tymoczko, pp. 23–35. Following the convention of each text, page numbers are given rather than line numbers.

[39] Best, 'The Tragic Death of Cúrói mac Dári', p. 20; *Two Death Tales from the Ulster Cycle*, trans. by Tymoczko, p. 23.

cloak).[40] The Ulstermen, however, in an act lacking '*cert*' (justice), refuse to share the spoils with Cú Roí, who in retaliation for this treatment seizes the girl, the cows, the birds, and the cauldron.[41] Cú Chulainn attempts to stop him, but is shamefully unsuccessful:

> Ní roacht neach do Ultaib comacallaim fair acht Cúchulaind a óenur. Imsói friside contarad isin talmain conici a dā ascaill 7 co roberr māil fair cosin chloduib, 7 co rochomail cacc ina mbō inna chend 7 luid ūaidib īarsein co rānic a thech.[42]

> (None of the Ulstermen managed to speak to him but Cú Chulainn alone. Cú Roí turned on him and pushed him into the earth up to his armpits. He sheared him bald with his sword and dumped the cows' dung on his head. Cú Roí went from them then and reached his house.[43])

Afterwards, Cú Chulainn secludes himself from the men of Ulster for a year. One day during his seclusion, a flock of ravens leads him to the hill fort of Cú Roí, whereupon he realizes that Cú Roí must be the man in the cream-coloured cloak. Blathnait, the kidnapped daughter, plots with Cú Chulainn to overthrow Cú Roí. She convinces Cú Roí to send his men away from the fort and Cú Chulainn attacks with the Ulstermen. In the midst of battle, Cú Chulainn beheads Cú Roí, whose grief-stricken poet, Ferchertne, grabs Blathnait and jumps off a cliff. No further mention is made of the cows, the birds, or the cauldron.

The Cú Roí of this tale is the same Cú Roí who provides challenges to determine who among the Ulstermen deserves the hero's portion in *Fled Bricrend* (*Bricriu's Feast*), another tale from the cycle of stories centred on Ulster and Cú Chulainn in particular.[44] Just as Cú Roí deprives the Ulstermen of their glory in *Aided Conrói*, by over-participating in their raid and by dishonouring their chief hero, Cú Roí bestows glory on Cú Chulainn, and by extension the Ulstermen, in

---

[40] Best, 'The Tragic Death of Cúrói mac Dári', p. 20; *Two Death Tales from the Ulster Cycle*, trans. by Tymoczko, p. 24.

[41] Best, 'The Tragic Death of Cúrói mac Dári', p. 20; *Two Death Tales from the Ulster Cycle*, trans. by Tymoczko, p. 24.

[42] Best, 'The Tragic Death of Cúrói mac Dári', p. 22.

[43] *Two Death Tales from the Ulster Cycle*, trans. by Tymoczko, p. 24.

[44] Portions of *Fled Bricrend* are found in several manuscripts, including *Lebor na hUidre*, which contains all but the final episode of the story. The ending is only found complete in Edinburgh, NLS, MS Ed. XL, pp. 69–76, where it is entitled: *Cennach ind ruanada*. George Henderson dates *Cennach ind ruanada* to the sixteenth century, but opines that the text was copied from an older manuscript, now lost (*Fled Bricrend, Bricriu's Feast*, ed. and trans. by Henderson, pp. xxix–xxx).

Fled Bricrend. The final challenge Cú Roí presents in *Fled Bricrend* is a decapitation contest in which he has a distinct advantage, for, like the Green Knight, Cú Roí can replace his own head on his body after it has been chopped off.[45] Cú Chulainn is the only one brave enough to submit to a compensatory decapitation (which Cú Roí spares him), and thus wins the hero's portion:

> 'Attfraid suas, a Cúchulaind [...] sbies do lataiph gaoile ufer n-Ulad nó Erenn beth ar a menmain beth im coipeis frit do ghoil na gaisged no firinde. Rige laech n-Eirenn duit on tratso 7 in curadmir gen chosnum.'[46]

> ('Rise, Cú Chulainn!' [Cú Roí said]. 'Of all the warriors of Ulster and Ireland, whatever their merit, none is your equal for courage and skill and honour. You are the supreme warrior of Ireland, and the champion's portion is yours, without contest.'[47])

In his role as bestower or remover of glory, Cú Roí stands in a similar relationship to the Ulstermen and their hero as the narrative tradition: he rewards heroic behaviour with fame and honour, and unheroic behaviour with shame and dishonour.[48] In contrast to the events of *Fled Bricrend*, Cú Chulainn's beheading of Cú Roí is fatal in *Aided Conrói*, but even here Cú Roí exhibits a kind of immortality that allows him to win the decapitation contest once more, for his son will ultimately avenge his death by in turn beheading Cú Chulainn in *Aided Con Culainn* (*The Death of Cú Chulainn*), in an action that bespeaks the survival of the narrative tradition through transmission and reproduction.[49] Cú Roí is ultimately responsible for Cú Chulainn's death, in that his shaming of Cú Chulainn obliges the hero to slay him, an act that in turn obliges Cú Roí's vengeful son to slay Cú Chulainn, and if we take Cú Roí to be a representative of the nar-

---

[45] For a discussion of the connections between these two tales, see Jacobs, '*Fled Bricrenn*'.

[46] The Irish text is from Edinburgh, NLS, MS Ed. xl, as reproduced in *Fled Bricrend, Bricriu's Feast*, ed. and trans. by Henderson, p. 128, ll. 4–8.

[47] The translation (with minor changes) is from *Early Irish Myths and Sagas*, ed. and trans. by Gantz, p. 255.

[48] Petra S. Hellmuth observes that characters in early Irish literature who, like Cú Roí, shape-shift between 'splendid human' and 'monstrous' forms tend to possess 'a poetic dimension' (Hellmuth, 'The Role of Cú Roí', pp. 61–64). Hellmuth also notes that in *Fled Bricrend*, when Cú Roí enters the hall where the beheading contest will take place, he stands in a spot that may have been traditionally reserved for a poet (Hellmuth, 'The Role of Cú Roí', p. 60).

[49] Maria Tymoczko identifies the oldest extant version of the account of Cú Chulainn's death, *Aided Con Culainn* in the Book of Leinster, as the ancestor to all other known versions (*Two Death Tales from the Ulster Cycle*, trans. by Tymoczko, p. 14). Julius Pokorny dates the story to no later than the mid-eighth century (Pokorny, 'Germanisch-Irisches', p. 123).

rative tradition it is fitting that this be so. In the *Macgnímrada Con Culaind*, it is related that Cú Chulainn chose to receive his first grown-up weapons on a day when it was prophesied: 'Is glé bid airdairc 7 bid animgnaid intí gebas gaisced and acht bid duthain nammá' (It is certain that he who takes up arms today will be famous and renowned, but he will, however, be short-lived).[50] It is Cú Chulainn's choice of fame, a valuing of life in the narrative tradition over physical life, that seals the hero's fate.[51]

In *Síaburcharpat* it is apt that Cú Chulainn should recount the raid on the Land of Shadow as part of his proselytizing of Lóegaire and that he should dwell on the cauldron, for, as part of the contested plunder that ignites the Cú Chulainn/Cú Roí dispute, it could be regarded as a cause of events leading to Cú Chulainn's death and subsequent removal to Hell. Immediately after finishing the story Cú Chulainn briefly alludes to his demise at Lugaid's hands, adding that afterwards 'Roucsat demna m'anmain/isin richis rúaid' (Demons carried my soul/Into the red charcoal), thereby warning Lóegaire of what awaits if he will not heed Patrick and convert.[52] Yet despite its overtly proselytizing purpose, the narrative complex called up by the cauldron seems in some ways out of place within *Síaburcharpat*'s context of Christian conversion, wherein the saint and the Christianity he represents wield the sole power to save figures of the pagan past from eternal damnation. Taken together, *Fled Bricrend* and the death tales of Cú Roí and Cú Chulainn portray the pre-Christian narrative tradition, figured in Cú Roí, as a powerful force in its own right, which, though unable to grant heroes life eternal either in heaven or in manuscripts, can impart a certain immortality of fame. Cú Roí's status as a pagan figure whose death-defying powers rival those of Patrick reflects the reality that oral traditions, and narrative traditions more generally, have lives of their own which cannot be contained within any particular text, or controlled by the leader of any particular textual community. A narrative tradition's ultimate uncontrollability is especially evident when 'content' becomes a container in its own right — as when Cú Chulainn tells tales, or the cauldron conveys meanings from beyond the text at hand via its associations with other narratives. The cauldron resonates with the *síaburcharpat* as another otherworld vessel with the capacity for conveying into new contexts what might be thought

---

[50] *Táin Bó Cúailnge: Recension I*, ed. and trans. by O'Rahilly, p. 20, ll. 638–39.

[51] Patrick K. Ford cites this episode from the *Táin* as an example of the importance in early Irish literature of the kind of fame attained specifically through having one's exploits recounted in oral narrative (Ford, 'The Idea of Everlasting Fame').

[52] *Lebor na hUidre*, ed. by Best and Bergin, p. 284, ll. 9443–46.

not to belong there. The cauldron also resonates with the text *Síaburcharpat*, which itself serves as a kind of vessel insofar as it is a frame narrative.[53]

Written representations of myth, epic, and traditional narrative in general often use more or less elaborate framing devices to contain the stories they convey. The *Odyssey*, the *Aeneid*, Ovid's *Metamorphoses*, *The Golden Ass*, Snorri's *Edda*, and the *Panchatantra*, to name just a few, all embed tales within tales. John Barth even suggests that the invocations to the Muses which open various works of Greek and Roman mythography constitute a kind of framing device, and Maria Tymoczko makes a similar claim for the questions that traditionally open works of early Irish literature, like the one that begins *Aided Conrói*, 'Císsí tucaid ar romarbsad Ulaid Coinrāi mac Dáiri?' (What reason did the men of Ulster have to kill Cú Roí son of Dáire?).[54] Tymoczko points out that such openings 'simulate the beginning of an oral performance of the tale', as if the narrative were given in response to an audience member's request for information, implying a storytelling frame outside the tale at hand.[55] As seen in Irish opening questions and classical invocations to the Muses (who are typically called upon to sing, or inspire singing), the most common means for framing one tale within another is through the portrayal of oral performance. Accordingly, Walter Ong characterizes literary framing as a transitional device employed to bridge the gap between orality and literacy.[56] Noting that the literary frame tale achieved its greatest prominence in Europe in the Late Middle Ages, which he characterizes as a time of 'audience readjustment', Ong suggests that the purpose of such framing was to provide a familiar (if fictional) context into which both writers and readers could imagine themselves as tellers of or listeners to oral stories.[57] Bonnie Irwin observes, moreover, that it is not just oral narrative, but traditional oral narrative that is most frequently presented within medieval literary frames, leading her to regard the device used in this context as primarily 'a means of textualizing the oral tradition'.[58]

---

[53] Some would restrict the term 'frame narrative' to tales that serve primarily to introduce other tales (Clawson, 'The Framework of the Canterbury Tales'; Gittes, *Framing the Canterbury Tales*; Irwin, 'What's in a Frame?'). I use the term more loosely here, without any implied judgement as to what *Síaburcharpat*'s 'main purpose' may be.

[54] Barth, 'Tales within Tales within Tales', p. 49. *Two Death Tales from the Ulster Cycle*, trans. by Tymoczko, p. 87 n. 1.

[55] *Two Death Tales from the Ulster Cycle*, trans. by Tymoczko, p. 87 n. 1.

[56] Ong, 'The Writer's Audience', p. 16.

[57] Ong, 'The Writer's Audience', p. 16.

[58] Irwin, 'What's in a Frame?', pp. 32, 35.

The narrative frame is, however, not an exclusively literary device, and framing serves other purposes beyond providing a ready way to textualize the oral.[59] Stories that contain other stories, whether written or spoken, are always to some extent narratives about narration, and narration tends to be the telling of past events, or at least the telling of events as if they were past. Given that the framing narrative is itself usually set in the past, framed tales depict a past doubly removed from the now of the audience, thus providing not just a representation of the past, but a representation of a representation of the past, which allows such representation to be contemplated on a *meta*-level. Stories that employ framing are about bringing the past into the present via representation, and what happens as a result. When framed tales are myth, set *in illo tempore*, framing presents a confrontation with a past that is not part of a temporal continuum but an absolute from which one is always equally distant wherever one stands in time, for this 'past' is identical with its representation and therefore may be invoked directly, like Cú Chulainn. Tzvetan Todorov coined the term 'narrative man' to describe the device whereby one story is embedded in another through the entry of a new character, who introduces the story of himself, but Cú Chulainn takes this designation to new levels.[60] As a figure from a narrative tradition who tells his own narratives, Cú Chulainn's narration of the past is coincident with the arrival of that 'past' in the present, in a vehicle, no less, that is synonymous with a text.

Síaburcharpat, on the levels of both story and form, communicates a message about the simultaneous appropriability and uncontrollability of traditional narrative. The traditional tale within the tale is like the cauldron wrested from the Land of Shadow or like Cú Chulainn summoned from Hell (or the *síd*): each is made to serve new purposes elsewhere, yet carries associations from a world beyond. This Chinese Box or Trojan Horse aspect of traditional narrative, well portrayed in the figure of the vessel, is akin to what Albert Lord terms 'suprameaning' with respect to oral epic. Lord explains the concept thus: 'Each theme, small or large — one might even say, each formula — has around it an aura of meaning which has been put there by all the contexts in which it has occurred

---

[59] Irwin notes that frametales do exist in the oral tradition, as documented by Linda Dégh in her study of Hungarian folktales (Dégh, 'Adatok a mesekeret jelentöségéhez'; Dégh, *Folktales and Society*, trans. by Schossberger, pp. 85, 363 n. 134; Irwin, 'What's in a Frame?', p. 36). As to uses of narrative framing, Geraldine Parsons, for example, suggests that framing in *Acallam na Senórach* serves to enhance and complicate the audience's understanding of particular issues by presenting sets of narratives constituting 'variations on a theme' (Parsons, 'The Structure of *Acallam na Senórach*', p. 20).

[60] Todorov, 'Narrative Men', p. 70.

in the past'.[61] John Miles Foley describes something similar in his explanation of traditional narrative's 'depth of signification', where he states that 'each occurrence [of a traditional element] summons to a present reality the ongoing traditional meaning reflected in the innumerable other uses of the phrase or scene'.[62] According to Lord and Foley, elements of the oral tradition accrue meaning over time as they are repeatedly recontextualized. If these observations are transferable to the remediation of the oral tradition into writing (and I think they are), then rather than being contained and controlled, this wealth of meaning is transmitted and expanded when myths are 'written down'.

In *Síaburcharpat*, Patrick is victorious and Ireland's future is decided. Lóegaire converts, and Ireland will follow. But Lóegaire's condition, that Cú Chulainn be summoned and made to tell stories, transforms the narrative of Ireland's conversion into a frametale, effectively requiring that a space be made for the past within the present (and the future). J. R. R. Tolkien once suggested that certain muchused motifs ('step-mothers, enchanted bears and bulls, cannibal witches, taboos on names, and the like') may be retained for the very reason that they are ancient and carry with them a sense of the past's great depth.[63] As such, 'they open a door on Other Time, and if we pass through, though only for a moment, we stand outside our own time, outside Time itself, maybe'.[64] The otherworld vessel is itself such a motif, and it is the emblem of such motifs and the narratives that contain them. The otherworld vessel serves to represent traditional narrative's capacity to convey meaning from other times, other tales, and other media into new contexts, and its ability to combat the tyranny of the here and now by transporting us into the realm of the 'other', whatever that may signify.

---

[61] Lord, *The Singer of Tales*, p. 97.

[62] Foley, *The Theory of Oral Composition*, p. 111.

[63] Tolkien, 'On Fairy-Stories', p. 31.

[64] Tolkien, 'On Fairy-Stories', p. 31.

Works Cited

Manuscripts and Archival Documents

Dublin, Trinity College, MS 1336 (H. 3. 17)

Chatsworth, Derbyshire, The Book of Lismore

Dublin, Trinity College, MS 1318 (H. 2. 16)

Dublin, University College, Franciscan MS (Killiney) A 4

Dublin, University College, Franciscan MS (Killiney) A 20

Edinburgh, National Library of Scotland, MS Ed. XL

London, British Library, MS Egerton 88

London, British Library, MS Additional 33993

Oxford, Bodleian Library, MS Laud 610

Oxford, Bodleian Library, MS Rawlinson B. 487

Primary Sources

Early Irish Myths and Sagas, ed. and trans. by Jeffrey Gantz (New York: Dorset, 1981)

Fled Bricrend, Bricriu's Feast: An Early Gaelic Saga Transcribed from Older MSS into the Book of the Dun Cow, ed. and trans. by George Henderson, Irish Texts Society, 2 (London: Irish Texts Society, 1899)

Lebor na hUidre: Book of the Dun Cow, ed. by Richard Irvine Best and Osborn Bergin (Dublin: Royal Irish Academy, 1929)

Pañcatantra: The Book of India's Folk Wisdom, ed. by Patrick Olivelle (Oxford: Oxford University Press, 1997)

'Die Sage von Curoi', ed. and trans. by Rudolf Thurneysen, *Zeitschrift für Celtische Philologie*, 9 (1913), 189–234

'Siabur-Charpat Con Culaind: From "Lebor na hUidre" (Fol. 37, et Seqq.), a Manuscript of the Royal Irish Academy', ed. and trans. by John O'Beirne Crowe, *Journal of the Royal Historical and Archæological Association of Ireland*, 1 (1870–71), 371–448

Snorri Sturluson, *Edda*, ed. and trans. by Anthony Faulkes (London: Dent, 1987)

Táin Bó Cúailnge: Recension I, ed. and trans. by Cecile O'Rahilly (Dublin: Dublin Institute for Advanced Studies, 1976)

Táin Bó Cúalnge from the Book of Leinster, ed. and trans. by Cecile O'Rahilly (Dublin: Institute for Advanced Studies, 1967)

Tales of the Elders of Ireland: A New Translation of 'Acallam na Senórach', trans. by Ann Dooley and Harry Roe (Oxford: Oxford University Press, 1999)

Two Death Tales from the Ulster Cycle: The Death of Cu Roi and the Death of Cu Chulainn, trans. by Maria Tymoczko (Dublin: Dolmen, 1981)

Secondary Studies

Ball, Kimberly, 'The Otherworld Vessel as Metatraditional Motif in Northern European Literature and Folk Narrative' (unpublished doctoral dissertation, University of California, Irvine, 2009)

Barth, John, 'Tales Within Tales Within Tales', *Antæus*, 43 (1981), 45–63

Best, Richard Irvine, 'The Tragic Death of Cúrói mac Dári', *Ériu*, 2 (1905), 18–35

Clawson, W. H., 'The Framework of the Canterbury Tales', *University of Toronto Quarterly*, 20 (1951), 137–54

Dégh, Linda, 'Adatok a mesekeret jelentöségéhez' ['Contributions to the Meaning of the Folktale Frame'], *Ethnographia*, 55 (1944), 130–39

——, *Folktales and Society: Story-Telling in a Hungarian Peasant Community*, trans. by Emily M. Schossberger (Bloomington: Indiana University Press, 1969)

Dillon, Myles, *Celts and Aryans: Survivals of Indo-European Speech and Society* (Simla: Indian Institute of Advanced Study, 1975)

Flower, Robin, *The Irish Tradition* (Oxford: Oxford University Press, 1947)

Foley, John Miles, *The Theory of Oral Composition: History and Methodology* (Bloomington: Indiana University Press, 1988)

Ford, Patrick K., 'The Idea of Everlasting Fame in the *Táin*', in *Ulidia: Proceedings of the First International Conference on the Ulster Cycle of Tales, Belfast and Emain Macha, 8–12 April 1994*, ed. by J. P. Mallory and Gerard Stockman (Belfast: December, 1994), pp. 255–61

Gittes, Katharine S., *Framing the Canterbury Tales: Chaucer and the Medieval Frame Narrative Tradition* (New York: Greenwood, 1991)

Hellmuth, Petra S., 'The Role of Cú Roí in *Fled Bricrenn*', in *Fled Bricrenn: Reassessments*, ed. by Pádraig Ó Riain, Irish Texts Society, 10 (Dublin: Irish Texts Society, 2000), pp. 56–69

Irwin, Bonnie D., 'What's in a Frame? The Medieval Textualization of Traditional Story-telling', *Oral Tradition*, 10 (1995), 27–53

Jackson, Kenneth Hurlstone, *The Oldest Irish Tradition: A Window on the Iron Age* (Cambridge: Cambridge University Press, 1964)

Jacobs, Nicholas, '*Fled Bricrenn* and *Sir Gawain and the Green Knight*', in *Fled Bricrenn: Reassessments*, ed. by Pádraig Ó Riain, Irish Texts Society, 10 (Dublin: Irish Texts Society, 2000), pp. 40–55

Johnston, Elva, 'The Salvation of the Individual and the Salvation of Society in *Síabur-charpat Con Culaind*', in *The Individual in Celtic Literatures*, ed. by Joseph Falaky Nagy, Celtic Studies Association of North America Yearbook, 1 (Dublin: Four Courts, 2001), pp. 100–25

Lord, Albert Bates, *The Singer of Tales*, Harvard Studies in Comparative Literature, 24 (Cambridge, MA: Harvard University Press, 1960)

Lowe, Jeremy, 'Kicking over the Traces: The Instability of Cú Chulainn', *Studia Celtica*, 34 (2000), 119–30

Marstrander, Carl J. S., and others, eds, *Dictionary of the Irish Language: Based Mainly on Old and Middle Irish Materials*, 16 vols (Dublin: Royal Irish Academy, 1913–76)

McCone, Kim, '*Aided Cheltchair Maic Uthechair*: Hounds, Heroes and Hospitallers in Early Irish Myth and Story', *Ériu*, 35 (1984), 1–30

——, *Pagan Past and Christian Present in Early Irish Literature*, Maynooth Monographs, 3 (Maynooth: Sagart, 1990)

Murphy, Gerard, *The Ossianic Lore and Romantic Tales of Medieval Ireland* (Dublin: O Lochlainn, 1955)

——, *Saga and Myth in Ancient Ireland* (Dublin: O Lochlainn, 1961)

Nagy, Joseph Falaky, 'Close Encounters of the Traditional Kind in Medieval Irish Literature', in *Celtic Folklore and Christianity: Studies in Memory of William W. Heist*, ed. by Patrick K. Ford (Santa Barbara: McNally and Loftin, 1983), pp. 129–49

——, *Conversing with Angels and Ancients: Literary Myths of Medieval Ireland* (Ithaca: Cornell University Press, 1997)

——, 'Heroic Destinies in the *Macgnímrada* of Finn and Cú Chulainn', *Zeitschrift für celtische Philologie*, 40 (1984), 23–39

——, 'Orality in Medieval Irish Narrative: An Overview', *Oral Tradition*, 1 (1986), 272–301

Ó Cathasaigh, Tomás, *The Heroic Biography of Cormac mac Airt* (Dublin: Dublin Institute for Advanced Studies, 1977)

Ó Coileáin, Seán, 'Oral or Literary? Some Strands of the Argument', *Studia Hibernica*, 17–18 (1977–78), 7–35

Ong, Walter J., 'The Writer's Audience Is Always a Fiction', *PMLA*, 90 (1975), 9–21

Parsons, Geraldine, 'The Structure of *Acallam na Senórach*', *Cambrian Medieval Celtic Studies*, 55 (2008), 11–39

Petrie, George, 'The Ecclesiastical Architecture of Ireland Anterior to the Anglo-Norman Invasion; Comprising an Essay on the Origin and Uses of the Round Towers of Ireland' (= *Transactions of the Royal Irish Academy*, 20 (1845))

Pokorny, Julius, 'Germanisch-Irisches', *Zeitschrift für celtische Philologie*, 13 (1919), 111–29

Sjoestedt, Marie-Louise, *Gods and Heroes of the Celts*, trans. by Myles Dillon (London: Methuen, 1949)

Stevenson, Jane, 'The Beginnings of Literacy in Ireland', *Proceedings of the Royal Irish Academy*, Section C, 89 (1989), 127–165

Stock, Brian, *The Implications of Literacy: Written Language and Models of Interpretation in the Eleventh and Twelfth Centuries* (Princeton: Princeton University Press, 1983)

Szövérffy, Joseph, 'Siaburcharpat Conculainn, the Cadoc-Legend, and the Finding of the Táin', *Bulletin of the Board of Celtic Studies*, 17 (1957), 69–77

Thurneysen, Rudolf, *Die irische Helden- und Königsage bis zum siebzehnten Jahrhundert*, 2 vols (Halle: Niemeyer, 1921)

Todorov, Tzvetan, 'Narrative Men', in Tzvetan Todorov, *The Poetics of Prose*, trans. by Richard Howard (Ithaca: Cornell University Press, 1977), pp. 66–79

Tolkien, J. R. R., 'On Fairy-Stories', in J. R. R. Tolkien, *Tree and Leaf* (Boston: Houghton Mifflin, 1965), pp. 3–84

Zimmer, Heinrich, 'Keltische Beiträge i', *Zeitschrift für deutsches Alterthum*, 32 (1888), 196–334

'VENERABLE RELICS'?
RE-VISITING THE *MABINOGI*

Sioned Davies*

Introduction

In 1821, Sir Richard Hoare published an account in the *Cambro-Briton*: 'An Account of the Discovery, in 1813, of an Urn, in which there is every reason to suppose, the ashes of *Bronwen* (White-Bosom), the daughter of Llyr, and aunt to the great Caractacus, were deposited'.[1] According to the account, the funeral urn was discovered by a local farmer on the banks of the river Alaw, in Anglesey, in a spot called Ynys Bronwen; inside were ashes and half-calcined fragments of bone. Hoare continues:

> The report of this discovery soon went abroad, and came to the ears of the parson of the parish, and another neighbouring clergyman, both fond of, and conversant in, Welsh antiquities, who were immediately reminded of a passage in one of the early Welsh romances, called the *Mabinogion* .... 'Bedd petrual a wnaed i Fronwen ferch Lyr ar lan Alaw, ac yno y claddwyd hi,' — A square grave was made for Bronwen, the daughter of Llyr, on the banks of the Alaw, and there she was buried.[2]

He adds that the spot is still called the Islet of Bronwen — 'a remarkable confirmation of the genuineness of this discovery'. Angharad Llwyd, an antiquarian of the period, takes the discovery a step further: 'The discovery of this urn was a most fortunate event, as it serves to give authenticity to our ancient British

* Sioned Davies (DaviesSM@cardiff.ac.uk) is holder of the Chair of Welsh at Cardiff University, the translator of *The Mabinogion* (Oxford: Oxford University Press, 2007), and the author of many studies of Welsh oral tradition, medieval and modern.

[1] Hoare, 'Tomb of Branwen', p. 72.

[2] This is an attempt to explain the Bronze Age burial mound by the river Alaw known traditionally as Bedd Bronwen.

Writing Down the Myths, ed. by Joseph Falaky Nagy, CURSOR 17, (Turnhout: Brepols, 2013)
pp. 157–179   BREPOLS PUBLISHERS   10.1484/M.CURSOR-EB.1. 100851

documents, the Mabinogion [...]'.[3] Cause for celebration indeed! This 'venerable relic' was not only proof of Bronwen's existence but also authenticated the tales themselves.[4]

In the course of this essay I will examine these 'ancient British documents'. What are they? Why were they produced? What are the modern scholarly takes on what is, in essence, a packaging of 'mythological' tradition? And how would the tales have been received by a medieval audience? At the outset, it should be emphasized that *Mabinogion* is an umbrella term that describes eleven medieval Welsh tales found mainly in two manuscripts, namely the White Book of Rhydderch (Aberystwyth, LGC/NLW, MS Peniarth 4–5), dated *c.* 1350, and the Red Book of Hergest (Oxford, Jesus College, MS 111), dated 1382 x *c.* 1410.[5] The title is testimony to the far-reaching effects of translation, having been popularized in the nineteenth century with the first ever translation of the tales into English by Lady Charlotte Guest (between 1838 and 1849). The term is in fact a scribal error for *mabinogi*, probably derived from the Welsh word *mab* meaning 'son, boy'. Guest interpreted *mabinogion* as the plural form of *mabinogi* — the suffix -*(i)on* is a common plural ending in Welsh — and saw the term as an ideal title for her 'collection'. It should be emphasized that the term *Mabinogion* is no more than a label, and a modern-day one at that: despite many common themes, they were never conceived as an organic group, and are certainly not the work of a single author.

Of the eleven tales, it is clear that four of them form a distinct group, generally known as 'The Four Branches of the Mabinogi'. These are the *Mabinogi* proper, as it were, so called because each one ends with the same formula in both the White and Red Books: 'and so ends this branch of the Mabinogi'. They are the only tales in the corpus that refer to themselves as *mabinogi*, divided into 'branches' (*ceinciau*), a term used in medieval French narrative also to denote a textual division.[6]

---

[3] Llwyd, *A History of the Island of Mona*, p. 46. For a discussion of her contribution, see Davies, 'Syw ddynes wiw ddoniol'.

[4] The term 'venerable relic(s)' is used by Charlotte Guest in the dedication at the beginning of her translation of the *Mabinogion* which appeared in seven parts between 1838 and 1849 (*The Mabinogion*, trans. by Guest (1838–49)). These were then published in three splendid volumes in 1849 (*The Mabinogion*, trans. by Guest (1849)). A second edition was published in 1877, in one volume (*The Mabinogion*, trans. by Guest (2nd edn)). All quotations will be from the 1877 edition.

[5] For a discussion of the dates, see Huws, *Medieval Welsh Manuscripts*.

[6] Some scholars have argued that a *mabinogi* was a tale for boys, or perhaps a tale told by young or apprentice storytellers; however, the general consensus is that its original meaning was 'youth' or 'story of youth', confirmed by the appearance of the term as a translation of the

Even so, the link between them is fairly tenuous; the only hero to appear in all four is Pryderi — he is born in the First Branch, is merely named in the Second as one of the seven who return from Ireland, is imprisoned in the Third, and is killed in the Fourth.[7] Although they have survived in written form, it is clear that these four tales draw heavily on oral tradition and on the narrative techniques of the medieval storyteller.[8] Of course, they are not merely written versions of oral narratives, but rather, as I will argue, the work of an author using and shaping traditional material for his own purposes. However, unlike the poetry of the period, the tales are not attributed to an identified author, suggesting that there was no sense of 'ownership' as such, and that the texts were perhaps viewed as part of the collective memory. Indeed, on several occasions the author draws attention to his sources, but in so doing he distances himself from those sources and sets himself up as merely the mouthpiece of tradition, for example: 'A herwyd y dyweit y kyuarwydyt, ef a uu arglwyd wedy hynny ar Wyned' (And according to the tale, he was lord over Gwynedd after that).[9] This was a common medieval authorial position, where a literary work was not judged by its originality but by how the author shaped and reshaped tradition.

Defining and dating that 'tradition', on the other hand, is no easy matter. What were the author's sources? From where did he get his material? And how old is this material? Indeed, how old are the tales themselves? They are set in a non-Christian milieu, with references to baptizing 'in the way it was done at that time'.[10] Even so, characters swear oaths to God, and a cleric, a priest, and a bishop each makes a cameo appearance. Many scholars have attempted to show that resonances of 'Celtic mythology' are apparent throughout these four tales, as mortals come into contact with characters who possess supernatural powers, from Gwydion the

Latin *infantia*, and that finally it meant no more than 'tale' or 'story'. For a discussion of *ceinc* ('branch'), see Lloyd-Morgan, 'The Branching Tree of Medieval Narrative'.

[7] This led Erich P. Hamp to argue that the term *Mabinogi* refers to a collection of material pertaining to the god Maponos or Mabon, a character who is stolen from the bed of his mother Modron in the tale of 'How Culhwch won Olwen'; this material, he further argues, is the debris of an ancient oral narrative tradition. Hamp takes his lead from earlier scholarship in identifying Mabon and Modron with the mother and son of the first branch, namely Rhiannon and Pryderi, and suggests that the original hero of all Four Branches may perhaps have been Pryderi, the only character to appear in all four tales. See Hamp, 'Mabinogi'.

[8] For a discussion of these techniques, see Davies, *Crefft y Cyfarwydd*.

[9] *Pedeir Keinc y Mabinogi*, ed. by Williams, p. 92; *The Mabinogion*, trans. by Davies, p. 64. Henceforth, all translations will be from *The Mabinogion*, trans. by Davies, and the original Welsh text will be from *Pedeir Keinc y Mabinogi*, ed. by Williams.

[10] *The Mabinogion*, trans. by Davies, p. 18.

shape-shifter who can create a woman out of flowers, to Bendigeidfran the giant, who lies across the river as a bridge for his men to cross; from Math the magician whose feet must lie in the lap of a virgin, to the beautiful Rhiannon whose magical white horse is impossible to catch. Indeed, characters such as Lleu, Teyrnon and Rhiannon may well derive from Celtic deities while many of the events, such as the Otherworld visit, may draw on forgotten 'mythologies'.[11] However, despite drawing sometimes on what is much older material — how much older we do not know — I would argue that the author of the *Four Branches* attempts to make the tales relevant to his own time, and indeed to any period.

Modern scholarship has not always approached the tales in this way. As noted earlier, the *Mabinogion* corpus first gained international recognition with their translation into English in the nineteenth century by Lady Charlotte Guest. She translated very much in the spirit of the Romantic Revival, which saw medieval texts reinvented, through Victorian eyes. Writers — and artists too — projected their own ideals and values onto the legendary characters and events so that the chivalric past became a vehicle for educating the present, as reflected in the works of Walter Scott and Tennyson. Romances were seen as a pattern for behaviour. King Arthur became a symbol of chivalry and of monarchy; English gentlemen saw themselves as medieval knights; 'medieval' balls were held and portraits in costume and in armour became the vogue; chivalry, honour, and bravery were promoted as an ideal for manhood.[12] Indeed, Guest presents her translation to two of her sons, hoping they will become 'imbued with [a] chivalric and exalted sense of honour, and [the] fervent patriotism'.[13] But she was also anxious to reveal to the English speaking world the supremacy of the 'ancient' Celtic literature, of the 'venerable relics of ancient lore':

> My dear Children,
> Infants as you yet are, I feel that I cannot dedicate more fitly than to you these venerable relics of ancient lore, and I do so in the hope of inciting you to cultivate the Literature of 'Gwyllt Walia', in whose beautiful language you are being initiated, and amongst whose free mountains you were born.[14]

In her opinion, Welsh literature had an intrinsic worth, and the tales of the *Mabinogion* deserved a place on the European stage; indeed, she went so far as to

---

[11] See, for example, Mac Cana, *Celtic Mythology*, pp. 72–81 and 122–31.

[12] For a discussion of Guest's translation, see Davies, 'A Charming Guest'.

[13] Dedication in *The Mabinogion*, trans. by Guest (2nd edn).

[14] Dedication in *The Mabinogion*, trans. by Guest (2nd edn).

argue that 'the Cymric nation [...] has strong claims to be considered the cradle of European Romance'. She argues further:

> Why should we disregard our own traditions [...] because they have not been handed down in Greek or Latin? For my own part, I love the old Legends and Romances as they teach us so naturally the manners and opinions of those who were, in fact, much more nearly connected with *us* of the present day than were any of the heroes of Rome.[15]

Similar views are expressed by nineteenth-century translators, translating from Irish into English, as outlined by Michael Cronin, where he argues that 'translation relationships between minority and majority languages are rarely divorced from issues of power and identity'. He continues:

> The differing perceptions of the translator, as a field-worker in the scholarly dig of antiquarianism or as the champion of an imperilled culture, have profound implications for the political appropriation of translated literature in the nineteenth century.[16]

Indeed, in Wales, as in Ireland, associations emerged to promote scholarship in the language — ancient texts were resurrected from manuscripts and translated to show the 'colonizers' that the 'colonized' were civilized and in possession of a noble literary heritage.

Charlotte Guest's agenda was therefore, in part, political. However, although she emphasizes time and time again the 'antiquity' of the texts, she makes no reference to 'mythology' nor to gods and goddesses in her argument. Perhaps this is not surprising — the notion of the pagan Celtic world was developed in the latter part of the nineteenth century, typified by James Frazer in his highly influential work *The Golden Bough* (1890).[17] To Guest, the antiquity of the tales is derived from the place- names mentioned — they often allude to a character in the story, or commemorate a specific event, for example Llyn y Morwynion (Lake of the Maidens/Virgins) in the Fourth Branch.[18] She claims:

> But as these names could not have preceded the events to which they refer, the events themselves must be not unfrequently as old as the early settlement in the country.

---

[15] Quoted from Charlotte Guest's diary in *Lady Charlotte Guest*, ed. by Guest and John, p. 103.

[16] Cronin, *Translating Ireland*, p. 4.

[17] Frazer, *The Golden Bough*.

[18] *The Mabinogion*, trans. by Davies, p. 63.

And as some of these events and fictions are the subjects of, and are explained by, existing Welsh legends, it follows that the legends must be, in some shape or other, of very remote antiquity.[19]

This is why she placed such importance on the discovery of Branwen's grave, for it 'authenticated' the tale. Indeed, the event made such an impression on her that she gave the title 'Branwen daughter of Llŷr' to the Second Branch and included a sketch of the funeral urn in her notes.[20]

As a result of Charlotte Guest's translation, the Four Branches were placed on a European stage, and became the focus of scholarly interest for the first time ever. Since then, the interpretive ideas put forward by critics may be broadly classified into four main models: the 'peasant hut', the 'magpie's hoard', the 'twisted braid', and the 'moral mirror'.[21] The first model owes its title to a much-quoted paragraph by Matthew Arnold in his *On the Study of Celtic Literature*:

> The very first thing that strikes one, in reading the *Mabinogion*, is how evidently the mediaeval story-teller is pillaging an antiquity of which he does not have the secret; he is like a peasant building his hut on the site of Halicarnassus or Ephesus; he builds, but what he builds is full of materials of which he knows not the history, or knows by a glimmering tradition merely — stones 'not of this building', but of an older architecture, greater, cunninger, more majestical.[22]

This Grimmian approach had far-reaching effects; it set the scene for *Mabinogi* scholarship until fairly recently, allowing for wild speculation with the Four Branches viewed as the survival of a pagan past.[23] Exponents included John Rhŷs who in his *Lectures on the Origin and Growth of Religion* in 1888 saw the remnants of ancient gods in the so-called 'culture hero' Gwydion and the 'solar hero' Lleu.[24] One of his pupils, Sir Edward Anwyl, attempted to reconstruct the original narrative behind the decayed grandeur, arguing that the four tales represented

---

[19] *The Mabinogion*, trans. by Guest (2nd edn), p. xvii.

[20] For a discussion of the title, see Davies, 'A Charming Guest'. A sketch of the urn is reproduced in *The Mabinogion*, trans. by Guest (2nd edn), p. 389.

[21] I have followed the convenient and visually tantalizing headings adopted by Davies, 'The Moral Structure of *Pedeir Keinc*', p. 19. The 'critical heritage' of the text is discussed by her at length (pp. 16–63) together with case studies for each critical model. For a selection of essays reflecting the major critical approaches to the Four Branches, see *The Mabinogi*, ed. by Sullivan.

[22] Arnold, *On the Study of Celtic Literature*, p. 54.

[23] Breeze, 'Some Critics of the Four Branches', p. 158.

[24] Rhŷs, *Lectures on the Origin and Growth of Religion*.

a fragmented version of the life story of the young hero Pryderi.[25] This theory was further developed by another of Rhŷs's pupils, W. J. Gruffydd, who praised the medieval author for attempting to make sense out of a contaminated mythology.[26] To Gruffydd, as to Arnold, the extant text is merely a ruin, a relic of the past, and the redactor, although a literary artist,[27] is flawed and does not fully understand his sources. Gruffydd himself admits that part of his highly elaborate reconstruction is based on 'intuition';[28] most scholars today would agree that his approach does not further our understanding of the text as it stands and as it was viewed by a medieval audience.

The second model embraces the eclectic theory, namely that the tales have grown by the slow accretion of assorted story elements:

> The author of the extant text strove with considerable skill to weld these assorted elements into a cohesive consecutive narrative, and, if he was not wholly successful, this was probably due to the innate intractability of his materials and to the fact that he was attempting an ordered conflation of discrete elements such as was not — and for that matter still may not be — congenial to the Celtic artistic genius.[29]

The author is thus a compiler, sorting through debris and attempting to restore the story elements to their original condition. The focus here is on the nature and origins of folk traditions, reflecting the Finnish or historic-geographic method. Its greatest exponent is Kenneth Jackson in his *The International Popular Tale and Early Welsh Tradition* (1961).[30] But, as emphasized by R. M. M. Davies, this method is flawed — 'it is assumed that there can be a normative form of any story, a right shape which can then be deformed'.[31] Juliette Wood and Andrew Welsh develop Jackson's theory, arguing that the author's use of folklore sources is rather a creative and controlled activity. The author, they claim, used folklore traditions but reworked them, developing dramatic possibilities and characterization — see, for example, Wood's discussion of the Calumniated

---

[25] Anwyl, 'The Four Branches of the Mabinogi (I, II)'; Anwyl, 'The Four Branches of the Mabinogi, Chapter III'; Anwyl, 'The Four Branches of the Mabinogi, Chapter IV'.

[26] Gruffydd, *Math Vab Mathonwy*, and Gruffydd, *Rhiannon*. He defines 'myth' as 'a tale dealing with an other-world personage' in Gruffydd, 'Mabon vab Modron', pp. 130–31.

[27] Gruffydd, *Rhiannon*, p. 2.

[28] Gruffydd, 'Mabon vab Modron', p. 146.

[29] Mac Cana, *The Mabinogi*, p. 31.

[30] Jackson, *The International Popular Tale*.

[31] Davies, 'The Moral Structure of *Pedeir Keinc*', p. 36.

Wife motif.[32] Moreover, folklore sources are not the only elements found in the 'magpie's hoard': other scholars have argued for the existence of Irish literary material,[33] onomastics,[34] and echoes of history.[35]

With the third model, the focus moves to form and structure rather than content. Here critics have borrowed Eugène Vinaver's model of the 'twisted braid' or 'interlace', developed to read Arthurian romance in particular.[36] Structural echoes come to the fore, which in turn draw attention to significant events. John K. Bollard shows how three 'themes' or incidents are in evidence, namely friendship, marriage, and feud,[37] while Jeffrey Gantz analyses the repeated patterns of action within the text, arguing that themes develop out of the sequences of parallels and contrasts.[38] Brynley F. Roberts uses 'theme' in the sense of 'ideological pattern' and sees the Four Branches as being structured by the exploration of certain concepts, each with their own key words — insult, friendship, shame.[39] These revisionist approaches emphasized, for the first time, the coherence of the four tales.

Roberts's analysis leads us to the final model — 'the moral mirror' — which explores the significance of the tales to their contemporary audience. As early as 1996, Pennar Davies argued that a positive use was being made of the debris of ancient tradition, with old beliefs turning into eloquent symbols.[40] Roberta L. Valente, in her examination of the thematic structure of the tales, argues that the branches 'illustrate in some way the codes which must be obeyed to maintain the social order, as well as the kinds of reparation which are owed if a charac-

---

[32] Wood, 'The Calumniated Wife'. She considers the relationship between this particular international folktale motif and its literary context, showing how it reveals something about the nature of the connection between the Four Branches and their cultural context, 'which can help to clarify the meaning and significance of these works for the modern reader' (p. 38).

[33] See Mac Cana, *Celtic Mythology*; Mac Cana, *The Mabinogi*; and Mac Cana, *Branwen Daughter of Llŷr*.

[34] Hunter, 'Onomastic Lore'.

[35] Koch, 'A Welsh Window on the Iron Age'; Koch, 'Brân, Brennos'. He suggests that Brân and Manwydan are historical characters and maps historical events of *c.* 54 BC onto events in the Third Branch. Furthermore, he equates Manawydan with the traitor Mandubracios and Brân with Brennos who led a Celtic tribe in a raid on Delphi in the third century BC.

[36] Vinaver, *Form and Meaning in Medieval Romance*.

[37] Bollard, 'The Structure of the Four Branches'.

[38] Gantz, 'Thematic Structure in the Four Branches'.

[39] Roberts, 'From Traditional Tale to Literary Story'. See also Roberts, *Studies on Middle Welsh Literature*.

[40] Davies, *Rhwng Chwedl a Chredo*, p. 102.

ter wilfully goes against the rules of society';[41] she concludes that the successful social group is the one that respects both male and female power and knowledge. Glenys Goetinck, on the other hand, argues that the author sees women as the source of all trouble and that the overall aim was to teach Christian virtues.[42] Whatever our reading of the 'moral mirror', this final model is a far cry from the 'peasant hut', projecting a view of an author who is in control of his material and whose personal voice is clearly audible: the tales are imbued with the author's own ideals and values as he projects a moral code of conduct that is essential for a society to survive.[43] In the first three branches, the nature of insult, compensation, and friendship are explored, and acts of revenge shown to be totally destructive — legal settlement and hard bargaining are to be preferred. In the Fourth Branch, however, further considerations are raised. Math, king of Gwynedd, is not only insulted, but also dishonoured — his virgin foot-holder is raped, and his dignity as a person is attacked. The offenders, his own nephews, are transformed into animals — male and female — and are shamed by having offspring from one another. However, once their punishment is complete, Math forgives them in the spirit of reconciliation. As noted by Brynley Roberts, 'Legal justice is necessary for the smooth working of society, but without the graces of forgetting and forgiving, human pride will render the best systems unworkable.'[44] Throughout the Four Branches, therefore, the author conveys a scale of values which he commends to contemporary society, doing so by implication rather than by any direct commentary. The listeners are left to draw their own conclusions, and to realize that the image of a man alone, at the end of the Fourth Branch, with no wife and no heir, does not make for a promising future.[45]

In this, the Four Branches are very different from the other tales in the *Mabinogion* corpus — thematic threads knit them together, lifting the whole 'into the realm of cultural myth',[46] where 'myth' may be defined not as a 'sacred text' or 'the legend of the gods' but rather as a 'code of good conduct [...] grounded in pragmatic, realistic encounters with others and with important aspects of the natural and cultural worlds in which we dwell'.[47] Mythical accounts more often

[41] Valente, 'Gwydion and Aranrhod', p. 1.

[42] Goetinck, 'Pedair Cainc y Mabinogi'.

[43] See *The Four Branches of the Mabinogi*, ed. and trans. by Davies.

[44] Roberts, 'From Traditional Tale to Literary Story', p. 228.

[45] Valente, 'Gwydion and Aranrhod', p. 9.

[46] Bollard, 'The Role of Myth and Tradition', p. 86.

[47] Doty, *Myth*, p. 30. For an in-depth survey of definitions of myth from the eighteenth century onwards, see Von Hendy, *The Modern Construction of Myth*.

than not embody ideas of 'order replacing chaos' — they 'coalesce social values that have been found worthy of repetition' and are 'guiding models for modes of attitudes and behaviours'.[48] As argued by Malinowski, instead of being trivial stories, they represent 'founding charters' for society, embodying important socio-cultural notions. They have an authority about them, because they are told and retold; hence mythmaking can be seen as 'the ongoing process of constructing, authorizing and reconstructing social identities or social formations'.[49] Burton Mack's comment is particularly relevant here in the context of the *Mabinogi*: 'Social formation and mythmaking are group activities that go together, each stimulating the other in a kind of dynamic feedback system. Both speed up when new groups form in times of social disintegration and cultural change'.[50]

In what historical and social context therefore was the *Mabinogi* first written down, and what was the agenda for their production? A complete version of the four tales appears in the White Book of Rhydderch (dated *c.* 1350)[51] and the Red Book of Hergest (dated between 1382 and *c.* 1410),[52] while fragments of the second and third branches occur in NLW Peniarth MS 6, dated to the second half of the thirteenth century.[53] Based on circumstantial evidence, scholars have argued for various dates of composition, ranging between the eleventh and thirteenth centuries but, as emphasized by Simon Rodway, none are conclusive.[54] What is certain, however, is that this was a period of social disintegration in Wales. During these centuries the Welsh struggled to retain their independence in the face of the Anglo-Norman conquest which ultimately transformed the society, economy, and church of Wales. The country was divided into four major kingdoms — Gwynedd in the north-west, Powys which stretched from the borders of Mercia into central Wales, Deheubarth in the south-west, and Morgannwg or Glamorgan in the south-east. These were further divided into smaller units ruled by independent princes who vied with each other for supremacy. There was, therefore, no central unity, largely due to the difficulties imposed by physical geography, so that Wales did not develop into a single kingdom or kingship. With

---

[48] Doty, *Mythography*, p. 60.

[49] McCutcheon, 'Myth', p. 202. See also Von Hendy, *The Modern Construction of Myth*, pp. 204–12.

[50] Mack, *Who Wrote the New Testament?*, p. 203.

[51] Aberystwyth, LGC/NLW, MS Peniarth 4–5.

[52] Oxford, Jesus College, MS 111.

[53] Aberystwyth, LGC/NLW, MS Peniarth 6.

[54] Rodway, 'The Where, Who, When and Why of Medieval Welsh Prose', p. 59.

the erosion of Welsh authority in the south of the country, together with the establishment of the rule of the Anglo-Norman barons along the Welsh-English border, there was an attempt to create a single Welsh principality under the leadership of the native princes of Gwynedd, figures such as Llywelyn son of Iorwerth (otherwise known as Llywelyn the Great who was married to Joan, illegitimate daughter of King John), and Llywelyn ap Gruffudd, whose death at the hands of the English in 1282 brought any hopes of Welsh independence to an end. It is no surprise that R. M. M. Davies,[55] and more recently Helen Fulton,[56] view the Four Branches as a mirror for *princes* in particular, typifying the *speculum principum* tradition which was widespread among medieval European cultures. As in the works of John of Salisbury and Giraldus Cambrensis, the nature of kingship and rulership is probed, the tales exemplifying both good and bad government.

Central to Mack's thesis regarding social formation and mythmaking is the fact that these are group activities, which is a crucial point. Myths dramatize and make abstractions concrete; they are mostly narrative and performative. In other words, we must respect 'the ideal context in which they are *spoken or enacted* in rituals'.[57] As I have argued elsewhere,[58] the Four Branches draw heavily on the narrative techniques of oral storytelling. Performance features are an integral part of their fabric, partly because the author inherited preliterary modes of narrating, and partly because the tales were composed for oral delivery, so that their reception and dissemination continued to have an influence on both style and structure. A silent reading certainly does not do them justice — they call for a voiced performance. Unfortunately, we know relatively little of the performance arena in which medieval Welsh tales would have been narrated; in fact, we should probably be thinking in terms of a continuum, from 'festive' events to 'ordinary' moments, and from recitation from memory to public reading. Plenty is known, on the other hand, about the performance of poetry. According to the Welsh laws, there were three types of poet — the *pencerdd* (chief poet), the *bardd teulu* (household bard), and the *cerddor* (*joculator*), a generic term for poets and musicians, rather than the more specific 'jester' or 'buffoon'.[59] No reference at all is made to storytelling or to public reading, implying perhaps that it was

---

[55] Davies, 'The Moral Structure of *Pedeir Keinc*', pp. 183–210.

[56] Fulton, 'The *Mabinogi* and the Education of Princes'.

[57] Doty, *Myth*, p. 8.

[58] See, for example, Davies, '"He was the best teller of tales in the world"'.

[59] See Edwards, 'Popular Entertainers in Medieval Wales'. Also Ford, 'Agweddau ar Berfformio'.

given much less priority than elegy and eulogy, the poet's major sphere of activity. The situation, therefore, was not only a complex, but surely a dynamic one: despite the hierarchical structure, one could expect a certain degree of interaction between the various professional 'performers' as they entertained at courtly feasts and gatherings.

In such performance arenas, the social 'usefulness' of the Four Branches as 'charters' becomes apparent. Victor Turner's observations are relevant in this context:

> By means of such genres as theatre, including puppetry and shadow theatre, dance drama, and professional story-telling, performances are presented which probe a community's weaknesses, call its leaders to account, desacralize its most cherished values and beliefs, portray its characteristic conflicts and suggest remedies for them, and generally take stock of its current situation in the known 'world'.[60]

The *Mabinogi* does exactly this, not through any authorial comment on events and situations; rather, the author cleverly highlights the *choices* that his characters have to make. The listeners witness the results of the choices made, and are invited to judge for themselves, as individuals and as a group, whether the right decision was taken. In this way, ethical dilemmas are posed concerning moral, political and legal issues. A close reading of the text shows that most of the decision-making in the Four Branches is made when characters find themselves in a liminal state, physically separated from the rest of society.[61] This is a time of upheaval and disorder; but such disruption can be innovative and lead to regenerative possibilities. In this way, the author sets up a dialogue with the audience, and moral education takes place; as argued by R. M. M. Davies, no authorial comment is needed, for the consequences will highlight the ethical validity of any decision.[62]

A few examples will suffice to illustrate the point. The First Branch of the Mabinogi opens with Pwyll, prince of Dyfed, hunting with his hounds in Glyn

---

[60] Turner, *From Ritual to Theatre*, p. 11.

[61] See Turner's model of liminality as reflected, for example, in Turner, *The Forest of Symbols*, and Turner, *From Ritual to Theatre*. Turner builds on the pioneering work of Arnold van Gennep, (Van Gennep, *The Rites of Passage*, trans. by Vizedom and Caffee; Van Gennep, *Les Rites de passage*), who draws attention to the three phases in a rite of passage: separation, transition and incorporation. Joseph Falaky Nagy explores liminality in the Irish context in Nagy, 'Liminality and Knowledge in Irish Tradition', where he focuses in particular on the figure of the poet. R. M. M. Davies applies Turner's model of liminality to the Four Branches in Davies, 'The Moral Structure of *Pedeir Keinc*', pp. 146–181, and I draw on her discussion here.

[62] Davies, 'The Moral Structure of *Pedeir Keinc*', p. 158.

Cuch. He comes across a second pack of hounds — 'they were a gleaming shining white, and their ears were red'[63] — who bring a stag they are chasing to the ground. Pwyll moves from the familiar to an unfamiliar world, a world of doubt and uncertainty. He is in a forest, yet not in a forest — 'And he could see a clearing in the forest, a level field'.[64] He is in a liminal zone, a no man's land, neither of this world nor of the other world, where anything may happen. Pwyll has to make a decision: he drives the strangely coloured pack away, and feeds his own hounds on the dead stag, so insulting the owner of the pack, namely Arawn, king of Annwfn, the Otherworld. He has not lived up to his name — Pwyll (meaning 'wisdom'). As shown by R. M. M. Davies, there are several boundaries tied up in this episode — the Cuch valley where Pwyll is hunting formed a boundary separating two commots; there is also a thin line in the legal texts as to which principle in the Welsh law might apply to Pwyll's actions here.[65] Pwyll compensates Arawn for his discourtesy by agreeing to change places with him and so goes to live in Annwfn for a year and a day, in the shape and form of Arawn. The latter has explicitly stated that Pwyll shall have 'the most beautiful woman you have ever seen to sleep with you every night'.[66] But the situation creates for Pwyll a complex ethical problem. What is he to do? This time he makes the right decision — 'As soon as they got into bed, he turned his face to the edge of the bed, and his back to her'.[67] At the end of the year, Pwyll keeps his word and fights Hafgan on behalf of Arawn as part of the bargain — they meet at the ford, another liminal zone. Pwyll has been warned:

> '[...] And you must give him only one blow — he will not survive it. And although he may ask you to give him another, you must not, however much he begs you. Because no matter how many more blows I gave him, the next day he was fighting against me as well as before.'[68]

Again, Pwyll acts wisely, dealing Hafgan only one single blow as instructed. The initial meeting in the clearing thus leads to a lasting friendship between the two characters, and a profitable relationship between the lands of Annwfn and Dyfed. It is clear, therefore, that margins are dangerous places. As argued by Mary

---

[63] *The Mabinogion*, trans. by Davies, p. 3.

[64] *The Mabinogion*, trans. by Davies, p. 3.

[65] Davies, 'The Moral Structure of *Pedeir Keinc*', p. 161.

[66] *The Mabinogion*, trans. by Davies, p. 4

[67] *The Mabinogion*, trans. by Davies, p. 5.

[68] *The Mabinogion*, trans. by Davies, p. 4.

Douglas, 'If they are pulled this way or that the shape of fundamental experience is altered. Any structure of ideas is vulnerable at its margins'.[69]

Pwyll finds himself in another liminal zone in the next section of the tale — Gorsedd Arberth — the mound at Arberth: '[...] The strange thing about the mound is that whatever nobleman sits on it will not leave there without one of two things happening: either he will be wounded or injured, or else he will see something wonderful'.[70] There are two faces to the supernatural — the friendly and the threatening. But Pwyll is not to know which face he will encounter. He accepts the challenge, and voluntarily places himself in a situation of doubt and uncertainty by sitting on the mound. He sees a woman on a pale-white horse and sends men after her — he chooses to 'hunt' her rather than talk to her directly, and does so for three consecutive days. Eventually he asks her to stop upon which request she answers: 'I will wait gladly', she said, 'and it would have been better for the horse if you had asked that a while ago!'.[71] She is Rhiannon, an otherworld figure whom Pwyll eventually marries. In the Third Branch, Gorsedd Arberth reveals the threatening aspect of the supernatural — a mist descends on Dyfed as Rhiannon and her second husband Manawydan, and Rhiannon's son Pryderi and his wife, Cigfa, sit on the mound. The land of Dyfed itself now becomes the liminal zone — a wasteland. How can the four inhabit the place when all its people and livestock have vanished? They choose to travel to England to make their fortune, but are forced to return to Dyfed on account of the envy of the local craftsmen. Then, one morning, Pryderi and Manawydan go and hunt — a signal that a supernatural event is about to take place. And, indeed, they see a 'gleaming-white wild boar'.[72] Both are led to a 'huge, towering fort, newly built, in a place where they had never before seen either stone or building'.[73] Pryderi ignores the signs, just like his father Pwyll in the First Branch, and follows his hounds into the fort where he sees a golden bowl suspended by chains that reach up to the sky. He is immediately enraptured by the beauty of the gold and grabs the bowl — 'But as soon as he grabs the bowl, his hands stick to it and his feet stick to the slab on which he was standing, and the power of speech is taken from him so that

---

[69] Douglas, *Purity and Danger*, p. 122.

[70] *The Mabinogion*, trans. by Davies, p. 8. Offshore islands also act as liminal zones: compare the role of the otherworld feast on the island of Gwales (Grassholm) in the Second Branch, where a choice has to be made regarding the opening of the third door.

[71] *The Mabinogion*, trans. by Davies, p. 10.

[72] *The Mabinogion*, trans. by Davies, p. 39.

[73] *The Mabinogion*, trans. by Davies, p. 39.

he could not utter a single word':[74] he has entered into some kind of a semi-life. His mother, Rhiannon, follows him and in turn she too undergoes the same fate before the fort disappears, taking them both. In the face of these supernatural events, Manawydan is forced to make choices: he travels to England again, but returns to Dyfed this time with a load of wheat which he sows. However, his crops are destroyed by mice. He manages to catch one of the mice — a pregnant one — and decides to punish it in accordance with the law, namely to hang it. And there on Gorsedd Arberth he succeeds in securing Rhiannon and Pryderi's release, the restoring of Dyfed and ensuring that no vengeance will ever be taken. It is small wonder that to many, Manawydan is the ultimate pragmatist and peace-maker. Indeed, the choices made by Manawydan have been interpreted as reflecting a changing cultural worldview, and a metaphor for a new way of life.[75]

In the Four Branches, liminal situations can occur in certain geographical zones; they can also occur at certain times in the Celtic calendar, namely the eve of the first of November (the beginning of winter) and the eve of the first of May (the beginning of summer). In Irish tradition, too, we see a special significance attached to these dates — they are junctures between two distinct periods where the barriers between the mortal world and the otherworld are suspended.[76] Events that happen on May eve in the First Branch test the relationship of both Pwyll and Rhiannon, and Teyrnon and his wife. Rhiannon and Pwyll's son disappears the night he is born, and Rhiannon is accused of destroying him. Pwyll adheres to the letter of the law: 'I know that she has a child, and I will not divorce her. If she has done wrong, let her be punished for it'.[77] Pwyll's actions finally reflect the true meaning of his name. Rhiannon accepts her punishment, stoically playing the role of the 'calumniated wife', an international theme linked with the wife's liminal position as a member of her husband's family and yet an outsider who is seen as a threat. Teyrnon and his wife unknowingly find the child — he is delivered to them by some monster claw — and they rear him until he is eventually restored to his rightful parents. A conflation of three widely used motifs is found here: the Calumniated Wife (Rhiannon is accused of barrenness and then of killing her child), the Monster Hand, and the Congenital Animal. Jackson, drawing on comparative folklore study, argues that the text as it stands shows how the tale has been contaminated;[78] I would agree with Wood, however, who argues that we see here

---

[74] *The Mabinogion*, trans. by Davies, p. 40.

[75] Welsh, 'Manawydan fab Llŷr'.

[76] Mac Cana, *Celtic Mythology*, p. 127.

[77] *The Mabinogion*, trans. by Davies, p. 17.

[78] Jackson, *The International Popular Tale*, pp. 86–95.

a skilled narrator, deliberately rearranging and adapting.[79] The author is not concerned with the identity of the monster, but with the characters and the choices they make. A medieval audience would surely recognize the sign — May eve — and expect the unexpected. What is significant is the reaction and the choices made by the two couples to the supernatural events during this liminal period.

A further example of a calumniated wife appears in the Second Branch, which focuses on two countries — Ireland and Wales — practically destroying each other. Good advice and bad advice is given, highlighting the complex relationship between a king and his country. It is exemplified in the way the king of Ireland and the king of Wales each in turn deal with a family of giants. Matholwch, king of Ireland, makes an unwise choice as he is hunting on a mound: he sees the giant and his pregnant wife climb out of a lake, carrying the Cauldron of Rebirth, and welcomes them, but then keeps the family marginalized; he is unable to rule them and finally is forced by his men to attempt to burn them alive in an iron house. They flee to Wales, however, where Bendigeidfran, King of the Island of the Mighty (namely Britain), reacts to them differently — he takes advantage of their strength and succeeds in harnessing their skills. As noted by Bollard, this is a tale

> [...] which probes a very crucial aspect of the structure of the social machinery available in that culture to prevent war and as such it is a mythic paradigm of that all-important facet of society. The fact that the story ends in disaster heightens the mythic function of the tale, for it provides the audience with an archetypal example of a kind of cultural failure which must have seemed endemic.[80]

It is little wonder that a Manawydan was called for in the next branch, to question the ways of the old regime. 'A uo penn bit pont' (He who is a leader, let him be a bridge) are Bendigeidfran's words as he lies across the Liffey so that his men can cross the river in pursuit of the Irish.[81] The author reminds us that these words are still used as a proverb: a leader who is not a bridge, that is who does not socialize the marginal, will never truly succeed.

And this is the problem explored in the Fourth Branch. Math is Lord of Gwynedd; however, 'he could not live unless his feet were in the lap of a virgin, except when the turmoil of war prevented him.'[82] He is in an unusual social position — normally, of course, it is the female who is (legally) dependent on her male kin. This 'house-bound' lord is ineffective as a leader, and it is his nephew,

---

[79] Wood, 'The Calumniated Wife'.

[80] Bollard, 'The Role of Myth and Tradition', p. 86.

[81] *The Mabinogion*, trans. by Davies, p. 30.

[82] *The Mabinogion*, trans. by Davies, p. 47.

Gwydion, who drives the action of the story.[83] He and his brother Gilfaethwy commit a sexual offence — they rape Lord Math's foot-holder on whose virginity his life depends, and are transformed by Math into animals as punishment. Math therefore inflicts liminality upon them, transforming them into a stag and a hind, then a wild boar and wild sow, and finally a wolf and she-wolf; one of them gives birth each year, and they produce three sons. They are thus not only humiliated, as was Goewin the foot-holder, but are also marginalized as they live out this liminal existence as men yet not men, animals yet not animals, and emasculated as they become, in turn, the female of the species and give birth. As noted by Valente, 'It is as though the Lord of Gwynedd has chosen this punishment to teach them the vulnerability of the female role when men are unconcerned with the codes that protect women.'[84] Indeed, this sets the tone for the remainder of the branch as both men and women challenge social conventions and rules, culminating in Blodeuedd's condemnation to marginality for ever as she is transformed into an owl for her infidelity.[85] She is no longer a woman, but neither is she one of the birds — she is a bird of the night, confined to the margins of society for all eternity. She loses her name Blodeuedd (flowers) and is given a new name to suit her new appearance — Blodeuwedd (flower face). She thus returns to nature, having never been born into the human race; rather, she was created from flowers (hence her original name) specifically to break the taboo of Aranrhod who swore a destiny on her son, Lleu, that he would 'never have a wife from the race that is on this earth'.[86]

The Four Branches of the Mabinogi are clearly located in a pre-Christian past, but these so-called 'venerable relics' are invested with a new meaning, relevant to a medieval audience — they are grounded firmly in the Welsh landscape and deal with real problems regarding human behaviour. The tales may well point to gods and goddesses, but it is impossible to 'peel away a veneer' and 'see the myths and rituals of ancient Celts beneath';[87] neither is the traditional religious definition of myth as sacred text very useful. Rather, I have argued the Four Branches are

---

[83] Fulton, 'The *Mabinogi* and the Education of Princes', p. 245.

[84] Valente, 'Gwydion and Aranrhod', p. 6.

[85] The liminal features again in the elaborate killing of Lleu who cannot be destroyed while in any firm category: '"I cannot be killed indoors", he said, "nor out of doors; I cannot be killed on horseback, nor on foot"' (p. 60). This is a well-known international theme — the riddling tasks. Blodeuedd takes a lover, and they both attempt to kill Lleu; however, he is transformed into an eagle and enters into some sort of semi-life before he is rescued by his uncle, Gwydion.

[86] *The Mabinogion*, trans. by Davies, p. 58.

[87] Wood, 'Celtic Goddesses', p. 121.

mythical accounts in that they represent 'founding charters' for society: they are a code of good conduct in which the mythological tradition is packaged for a contemporary audience, raising — and answering — the questions that would have faced medieval society.[88] This is done in the main through exploring the liminal condition which gives the characters choices, so opening up a dialogue with the audience and forcing upon them the possibility of other scenarios. Indeed, many of the questions evoked by the tales are still pertinent today, and continue to inspire writers and poets alike,[89] so, ironically, reinvesting the *Mabinogi* with that 'sacred' quality that may once have been part of their fabric.

Postscript

What happened to the remains of Branwen? In a letter written by Angharad Llwyd to Dr Owen Pughe in 1825, she tells us:

> I was not at home when her resurrection happened — in a few weeks afterwards the Rev Mr T. E. Owen [...] called at my lodgings at Beaumaris — a friend of long date — and Bronwen and the disturbing of her was told by him — When I first heard of it said he I went to Glan Alaw and was surprised when told that the urn was in the garden, Mrs Thomas the tenant's wife having declared that she should not sleep in the house — if she was not taken out on this ejectment. Mr Owen set out for Trefeilir, the abode of Mr Hugh Evans his relative and the proprietor of Glan Alaw — who not having anything of the antique in his composition immediately resigned to him the old Dame in perpetuity [...] sometime afterwards Mr O finding his health declining removed to Beaumaris with his family — where on my calling some time after his death on Mrs Owen, she asked me to accept of the urn and its contents for said she 'its being in this house is a profound secret for if it was known I could not prevail on a servant to stay with me on any terms' — I did accept receipt of it and here it is waiting your consignement of it [...] It is impossible to tell how highly Sir Richard Hoare enjoys the exhumation of Bronwen in its furnishing a date as to the mode and time of urn burial [...]. It has also done much in confirming and attaching credibility to our too much neglected manuscripts.[90]

---

[88] Note that *cyfarwyddyd*, the Welsh word for story, also means 'guidance, instruction'.

[89] See, for example, Welsh language writers Saunders Lewis and Gareth Miles. For a general discussion, see Sullivan, *Welsh Celtic Myth in Modern Fantasy*. A recent development has been the commissioning of a series of novels by Seren Publishers entitled 'New Stories from the Mabinogion', where leading authors 'rework the ancient myths of the Mabinogion'. According to Seren, 'each author reinvents a story in their own way: creating fresh, contemporary tales that speak to us as much of our own world as of events long gone' (Seren, 'New Stories from the Mabinogion').

[90] Aberystwyth, LGC/NLW, MS 13263, p. 645.

Recently a set of radiocarbon dates were undertaken on key cremated burials from Bedd Branwen. They were found to span the period 2140–1730 BC, at 95.4% probability (or 2040–1750 BC at 68.2% probability), that is the middle part of the Early Bronze Age, this period now spanning 2200–1500 BC.[91] Angharad Llwyd and Matthew Arnold would be delighted!

---

[91] Personal communication with Frances Lynch. See also Lynch, *Prehistoric Anglesey*, and Lynch, 'Report on the Re-Excavation'.

Works Cited

Manuscripts and Archival Documents

Aberystwyth, Llyfrgell Genedlaethol Cymru/National Library of Wales, MS 13263
——, MS Peniarth 4–5
——, MS Peniarth 6
Oxford, Jesus College, MS 111

Primary Sources

The Mabinogion, trans. by Sioned Davies (Oxford: Oxford University Press, 2007)
The Mabinogion: From the Llyfr Coch o Hergest, and Other Ancient Welsh Manuscripts: with an English Translation and Notes, trans. by Lady Charlotte Guest, 3 vols in 7 pts (London: Longman, 1838–49)
The Mabinogion: From the Llyfr Coch o Hergest, and Other Ancient Welsh Manuscripts: with an English Translation and Notes, trans. by Lady Charlotte Guest, 3 vols (London: Longman, 1849)
The Mabinogion From the Llyfr Coch o Hergest, and Other Ancient Welsh Manuscripts with an English Translation and Notes, trans. by Lady Charlotte Guest, 2nd edn (London: Quaritch, 1877)
Pedeir Keinc y Mabinogi, ed. by Ifor Williams (Cardiff: University of Wales Press, 1930)

Secondary Studies

Anwyl, Edward, 'The Four Branches of the Mabinogi (I, II)', *Zeitschrift für celtische Philologie*, 1 (1897), 277–93
——, 'The Four Branches of the Mabinogi, Chapter III', *Zeitschrift für celtische Philologie*, 2 (1899), 124–33
——, 'The Four Branches of the Mabinogi, Chapter IV', *Zeitschrift für celtische Philologie*, 3 (1901), 123–43
Arnold, Matthew, *On the Study of Celtic Literature* (London: Everyman, 1910; orig. publ. London: Smith, Elder, 1867)
Bollard, John K., 'The Role of Myth and Tradition in the *Four Branches of the Mabinogi*', *Cambridge Medieval Celtic Studies*, 6 (1983), 67–86
——, 'The Structure of the Four Branches of the Mabinogi', *Transactions of the Honourable Society of Cymmrodorion* (1974–77), 250–76
Breeze, Andrew, 'Some Critics of the *Four Branches of the Mabinogi*', in *Constructing Nations, Reconstructing Myth: Essays in Honour of T. A. Shippey*, ed. by Andrew Wawn, Graham Johnson, and John Walter, Making the Middle Ages, 9 (Turnhout: Brepols, 2007), pp. 155–66
Cronin, Michael, *Translating Ireland: Translation, Languages, Cultures* (Cork: Cork University Press, 1996)

Davies, Rhiannon M. M., 'The Moral Structure of *Pedeir Keinc y Mabinogi*' (unpublished doctoral thesis, University of Wales, Cardiff, 1993)

Davies, Sioned, 'A Charming Guest: Translating the *Mabinogion*', *Studia Celtica*, 38 (2004), 157–78

——, *Crefft y Cyfarwydd: Astudiaeth o Dechnegau Naratif yn Y Mabinogion* (Cardiff: University of Wales Press, 1995)

——, The Four Branches of the Mabinogi (Llandysul: Gomer, 1993)

——, '"He was the best teller of tales in the world": Performing Medieval Welsh Narrative', in *Performing Medieval Narrative*, ed. by Evelyn Birge Vitz, Nancy Freeman Regalado, and Marilyn Lawrence (Cambridge: Brewer, 2005), pp. 15–26

——, 'Syw ddynes wiw ddoniol', in *Yr Angen am Furiau*, ed. by Tegid Roberts (Llanrwst: Gwasg Carreg Gwalch, 2009), pp. 43–63

Davies, William Thomas Pennar, *Rhwng Chwedl a Chredo: Datblygiad meddwl crefyddol Cymru yn yr oesoedd cynnar a chanol* (Cardiff: University of Wales Press, 1966)

Doty, William G., *Myth: A Handbook* (Westport: Greenwood, 2004)

——, *Mythography: The Study of Myths and Rituals*, 2nd rev. edn (Tuscaloosa: University of Alabama Press, 2000)

Douglas, Mary, *Purity and Danger: An Analysis of the Concepts of Pollution and Taboo* (London: Routledge, 1966)

Edwards, Huw M., 'Popular Entertainers in Medieval Wales', in Huw M. Edwards, *Dafydd ap Gwilym: Influences and Analogues* (Oxford: Clarendon Press, 1996), pp. 1–37

Ford, Patrick K., 'Agweddau ar Berfformio ym Marddoniaeth yr Oesoedd Canol', in *Cyfoeth y Testun: Ysgrifau ar Lenyddiaeth Gymraeg yr Oesoedd Canol*, ed. by R. Iestyn Daniel and others (Cardiff: University of Wales Press, 2003), pp. 77–108

Frazer, Sir James George, *The Golden Bough: A Study in Magic and Religion*, 2 vols (London: Macmillan, 1890)

Fulton, Helen, 'The *Mabinogi* and the Education of Princes in Medieval Wales', in *Medieval Celtic Literature and Society*, ed. by Helen Fulton (Dublin: Four Courts, 2005), pp. 230–47

Gantz, Jeffrey, 'Thematic Structure in the Four Branches of the Mabinogi', *Medium Aevum*, 47 (1978), 247–54

Gennep, Arnold van, *Les Rites de passage: étude systématique des rites* (Paris: Librairie Critique, 1909)

——, *The Rites of Passage*, trans. by Monika B. Vizedom and Gabrielle L. Caffee, intro. by Solon T. Kimball (London: Routledge and Kegan Paul, 1960)

Goetinck, Glenys, 'Pedair Cainc y Mabinogi: Yr Awdur a'i Bwrpas', *Llên Cymru*, 15 (1988), 249–69

Gruffydd, W. J., 'Mabon vab Modron', *Y Cymmrodor*, 42 (1931), 129–47

——, *Math Vab Mathonwy: An Inquiry into the Origins and Development of the Fourth Branch of the Mabinogi with the Text and a Translation* (Cardiff: University of Wales Press, 1928)

——, *Rhiannon: An Inquiry into the Origins of the First and Third Branches of the Mabinogi* (Cardiff, University of Wales Press, 1953)

Guest, Revel, and Angela V. John, eds, *Lady Charlotte Guest: An Extraordinary Life* (London: Weidenfeld and Nicholson, 1989; repr., Stroud: Tempus, 2007)

Hamp, Erich P., 'Mabinogi', *Transactions of the Honourable Society of Cymmrodorion* (1974–75), 243–49

Hoare, R. C., 'Tomb of Branwen', *Cambro-Briton*, 2 (1821), 71–73

Hunter, T. Gerald, 'Onomastic Lore in the Native Middle Welsh Prose Tales' (unpublished masters thesis, University of Wales, Aberystwyth, 1988)

Huws, Daniel, *Medieval Welsh Manuscripts* (Aberystwyth: University of Wales Press and The National Library of Wales, 2000)

Jackson, Kenneth Hurlstone, *The International Popular Tale and Early Welsh Tradition* (Cardiff: University of Wales Press, 1961)

Koch, John T., 'Brân, Brennos: An Instance of Early Gallo-Brittonic History and Mythology', *Cambridge Medieval Celtic Studies*, 20 (1990), 1–20

——, 'A Welsh Window on the Iron Age: Manawydan, Mandubracios', *Cambridge Medieval Celtic Studies*, 14 (1987), 17–52

Lloyd-Morgan, Ceridwen, 'The Branching Tree of Medieval Narrative: Welsh *cainc* and French *branche*', in *Romance Reading on the Book: Essays on Medieval Narrative Presented to Maldwyn Mills*, ed. by Jennifer Fellows and others (Cardiff: University of Wales Press, 1996), pp. 36–49

Llwyd, Angharad, *A History of the Island of Mona, or Anglesey* (Ruthin: Jones, 1833; repr. Llansadwrn: Magma, 2007)

Lynch, Frances, *Prehistoric Anglesey*, 2nd edn (Llangefni: Anglesey Antiquarian Society, 1991)

——, 'Report on the Re-Excavation of Two Bronze Age Cairns in Anglesey: Bedd Branwen and Treiorwerth', *Archaeologia Cambrensis*, 120 (1971), 11–83

Mac Cana, Proinsias, *Branwen Daughter of Llŷr: A Study of the Irish Affinities and of the Composition of the Second Branch of the Mabinogi* (Cardiff: University of Wales Press, 1958)

——, *Celtic Mythology* (London: Newnes, 1968)

——, *The Mabinogi*, 2nd edn (Cardiff: University of Wales Press, 1992)

Mack, Burton L., *Who Wrote the New Testament? The Making of the Christian Myth* (San Francisco: Harper, 1995)

McCutcheon, Russell T., 'Myth', in *Guide to the Study of Religion*, ed. by Willi Braun and Russell T. McCutcheon (London: Cassell, 2000), pp. 190–208

Nagy, Joseph Falaky, 'Liminality and Knowledge in Irish Tradition', *Studia Celtica*, 16–17 (1981–82), 135–43

Rhŷs, John, *Lectures on the Origin and Growth of Religion as Illustrated by Celtic Heathendom* (London: Williams and Norgate, 1888)

Roberts, Brynley F., 'From Traditional Tale to Literary Story: Middle Welsh Prose Narratives', in *The Craft of Fiction: Essays in Medieval Poetics*, ed. by Leigh A. Arrathoon (Rochester: Solaris, 1984), pp. 226–28

——, *Studies on Middle Welsh Literature* (Lampeter: Mellen, 1992)

Rodway, Simon, 'The Where, Who, When and Why of Medieval Welsh Prose Texts: Some Methodological Considerations', *Studia Celtica*, 41 (2007), 47–89

Seren, 'New Stories from the Mabinogion', <http://www.serenbooks.com/books/mabinogion-stories> [accessed 4 March 2013]

Sullivan, Charles William III, ed., *The Mabinogi: A Book of Essays* (New York: Garland, 1996)

——, *Welsh Celtic Myth in Modern Fantasy* (New York: Greenwood, 1989)

Turner, Victor, *The Forest of Symbols: Aspects of Ndembu Ritual* (Ithaca: Cornell University Press, 1967)

——, *From Ritual to Theatre: The Human Seriousness of Play*, Performance Study Series, 1 (New York: Performing Arts Journal, 1982)

Valente, Roberta L., 'Gwydion and Aranrhod: Crossing the Borders of Gender in *Math*', *Bulletin of the Board of Celtic Studies*, 35 (1988), 1–9

Vinaver, Eugène, *Form and Meaning in Medieval Romance* (Leeds: Modern Humanities Research Association, 1966)

Von Hendy, Andrew, *The Modern Construction of Myth* (Bloomington: Indiana University Press, 2002)

Welsh, Andrew, '*Manawydan fab Llŷr*: Wales, England, and the "New Man"', in *Celtic Languages and Celtic Peoples: Proceedings of the Second North American Congress of Celtic Studies*, ed. by Cyril J. Byrne, Margaret Harry, and Pádraig ó Siadhail (Halifax, NS: St Mary's University, 1992), pp. 369–82

Wood, Juliette, 'The Calumniated Wife in Medieval Literature', *Cambridge Medieval Celtic Studies*, 10 (1985), 25–38

——, 'Celtic Goddesses: Myth and Mythology', in *The Feminist Companion to Mythology*, ed. by Carolyne Larrington (London: Pandora, 1992), pp. 118–36

CAESAR'S SWORD, PROUD BRITONS, AND GALFRIDIAN MYTHS OF DISCONTINUITY

Katherine McLoone*

Geoffrey of Monmouth's *Historia regum Brittaniae* continues the myth of the *Aeneid* when the Trojan Brutus, descendant of Aeneas, founds a new nation on the island of Britain. In so continuing the story of the foundation of Rome, Geoffrey also transforms it. In this paper I will trace Geoffrey's transformation of the genealogical myth of Rome into the foundation narrative of a new, spatially-conceived British nation. I will argue that Geoffrey uses the genealogical tropes of the Roman myth to dismiss the relevance of those tropes for his own history; in so doing, he also frames his text as a revision to the myth of Rome. Furthermore, in establishing the failure of a genealogical model for understanding the British nation, Geoffrey replaces that model with a spatial conception of nationhood.

Geoffrey's *Historia* is a mythographic construct derived primarily from Virgil's *Aeneid*, embellished with native British traditions, and emended considerably with Geoffrey's own invention. Geoffrey consolidates these disparate myths (or commonly-held stories of cultural origins) to create a uniquely British story that itself becomes a myth of great cultural and national importance. In so transforming the myth of Rome, Geoffrey is engaging in *translatio*. *Translatio*, obviously related to our modern English *translation*, had in the Middle Ages the sense of movement, transfer, metaphor, and translation: a middleman was a *translator*, relics were 'translated' when they were moved from site to site.[1] *Translatio imperii et studii*, the translation of power (or dominion) and knowledge is, reductively

* Katherine McLoone (katherine.mcloone@gmail.com) completed her PhD dissertation in Comparative Literature at the University of California, Los Angeles, in 2012.

[1] See Geary, *Furta Sacra*.

Writing Down the Myths, ed. by Joseph Falaky Nagy, CURSOR 17, (Turnhout: Brepols, 2013)
pp. 181–200   BREPOLS ⬚ PUBLISHERS   10.1484/M.CURSOR-EB.1. 100852

put, the movement from ancient Greece to ancient Rome to France, Britain, and Italy — the movement westward and through time into the medieval era. It is a scholastic term, used in the universities and in learned texts, and it is also evident in vernacular popular literature, such as romances.

Geoffrey crafts a brief allegory of *translatio* in his *Historia*. As Julius Caesar, who succeeds in making Britain a tributary of Rome, battles the Britons:

> Et cum mixtim ictus ingeminarent, dedit casus aditum Nennio congressum cum Iulio faciendi. Irruens ergo in liium Nennius ultra modum laetatur se posse uel solum ictum tanto uiro ingerere.[2]

> (When they met, the dense formation of the Britons almost scattered the emperor's cohort. While they traded blows in the melee, Nennius got the chance of attacking Caesar. As he rushed at him, Nennius congratulated himself on being able to exchange even a single blow with so famous a man.)

When Caesar strikes Nennius a fierce blow to the helmet, his sword sticks, and Nennius is able to disarm the emperor:

> Nennius ergo, gladium Caesaris praedicto modod adeptus, abeiecit suum quem tenuerat et abstracto altero in hostes irruere festnat. Quemcumque cum ipso percutiebat, uel ei caput amputabat uel ipsum sauciatum praeteribat ita ut nulla spes uiuendi in eo manerat [...]. Denique, plurima parte diei emensa, irruentibus Britonibus strictis turmis et audaces impetus facientibus uictoria fauente Deo prouenit, et Caesar sese infra castra et naues lacerates Romais recepit.[3]

> (Having got Caesar's sword in this way, Nennius cast aside the one he was holding, freed the other, and hastened to attack the enemy. Once he struck anybody with it, he either cut off his head or left him too badly wounded to hope for recovery [...]. After most of the day had passed, victory went with God's help to the Britons, who attacked in formation and charged boldly, whilst Caesar and the shattered Romans retreated to their camps and ships.)

Nennius succumbs to the wound Caesar dealt him shortly after the battle. Caesar's sword is extraordinarily powerful: it kills anyone it touches and yet seems, oddly, to keep Nennius alive as long as he holds it, even though he is injured by it. The sword, wrested from the classical authority, wields power even against that authority, and helps the Britons to win their battle — although not

---

[2] Geoffrey of Monmouth, *The History of the Kings of Britain*, ed. by Reeve, IV. 56–58 (pp. 70–71). All translations will be from this text.

[3] Geoffrey of Monmouth, *The History of the Kings of Britain*, ed. by Reeve, IV. 64–68, 70–72. (pp. 70–71).

the larger war — against the Romans. Thus it acts as an illustration in miniature of Geoffrey's use of the Roman foundational myth: a co-opting of classical sources that can be redirected and repurposed. Furthermore, Nennius' name is a nod to the eighth-century Welsh historian, alleged writer of the *Historia Brittonum*, one of Geoffrey's main sources. Caesar's weapon sustains Nennius while nearly killing him; the Roman inadvertently gives the Britons a weapon that can be turned against those Romans. In this pithy scene, Geoffrey tells us how to read his use of *translatio*: he may use the authoritative myth of Rome, but in so doing he will be establishing British dominion. The dominant theme from the *Aeneid* that Geoffrey uses and repurposes is that of genealogy.

But how does Geoffrey use his classical authority (the *Aeneid*) against one of the primary tropes of that authority? There are undeniably numerous families — mostly represented by fathers, brothers, sons, and nephews — in the *Historia*, and many scholars have argued that Geoffrey is, in fact, arguing *for* a genealogical understanding of the British nation, in line with Virgil's articulation of a genealogical model of Rome.[4]

Francis Ingledew, one of the most eloquent defenders of this reading, places the rise of the genealogical trope squarely on the shoulders of the historiographers, Geoffrey prominent among them. He argues that 'The Book of Troy', which is to say, the collective representation of Trojans during the War and after,

> [...] Emerges as a concept expressing a new historical consciousness, intimately associated with an aristocratic and lay cultural environment and at odds with the biblically oriented Augustinian-Orosian paradigm, which instead of claiming birth in Troy, confessed birth in the Fall.

> (While this new textual production of Troy must bear the marks of the Christian cultural history that succeeded the pagan Roman Empire, it represents in an effectual manner a return of Virgil: in it reappears several defining features of the Virgilian philosophy of history, namely, the genealogical, the prophetic, and the erotic [...]. When the medieval Book of Troy quite distinctively reawakens the issues of genealogy, prophecy, and eros, it thus opens up the question of history, and it does so according to a broadly Virgilian scheme, even when it does not resolve those issues in a Virgilian manner.[5])

---

[4] Raluca L. Radulescu and Edward Donald Kennedy, drawing on Francis Ingledew's and Gabrielle Spiegel's works, have noted that 'Historical writing in England, Scotland, and France incorporated myth and legend in an effort to trace back the glorious ancestors of the various nations. [...] These works thus gave strength and stability to that past and justified a certain assessment of the present'. Radulescu and Kennedy, 'Introduction', p. 6. See Spiegel, *The Past as Text*.

[5] Ingledew, 'The Book of Troy', pp. 666–67. In her introduction to Wace's translation of

Ingledew notes that the Virgilian model of prophecy and genealogy is one of continuity, and he sees that continuity 'reawakened' in twelfth-century historiography, particularly in Geoffrey. These genealogies (both in roll format and narrativized form) perform the work of representational labour necessary to create a nation, a space constituted 'as home, as inalienable and permanent public and private territory'.[6] Raluca Radulescu continues this argument in her discussion of insular genealogies:

> Literary productions of the post-Conquest period, and in particular Geoffrey's *Historia*, contain attempts to present a continuous line of British kings, despite evident problems in connecting not only the foundation myths of Troy to the Roman Brutus and the British Isles, but also the more recent lineages of the Anglo-Saxon kings and the Welsh with the newly arrived Anglo-Norman rulers.[7]

Radulescu contrasts the Orosian and Virgilian models of history as two possible strategies for reading Geoffrey's use of Virgilian motifs in the manner Ingledew mentions: the Orosian tradition emphasizes a 'divinely ordained sequence of earthly rulers', whereas the Virgilian model contains a 'smooth succession of historical (and pseudo-historical) events'.[8] I will argue, rather, that Geoffrey uses the myth of Rome (what Ingledew calls the 'Book of Troy'; both terms here denote a commonly-held myth of cultural origin) and the increasingly-fictionalized Romans to articulate discontinuities of lineage, and of the texts that describe those lineages.

Because of — or perhaps, despite — the fact that Geoffrey's articulation of British nationhood seems quite early, much of the current Galfridian scholarship has responded, at least implicitly, to Benedict Anderson's *Imagined Communities*. While Anderson argues that nationalism began during the Enlightenment, many medievalists have begun to argue that, particularly in England, nationalism began much sooner. Thorlac Turville-Petre's *England the Nation* is one of the texts that

---

the *Historia*, Judith Weiss notes that Geoffrey — and Wace — see 'domestic treachery as the frequent cause of disaster' (Wace, *Roman de Brut*, trans. by Weiss, p. xix).

[6] Ingledew, 'The Book of Troy', p. 669.

[7] Radulescu, 'Genealogy in Insular Romance', p. 9. On the question of the comparability of the genres of historiography and romance, see Field, 'Romance as History, History as Romance'.

[8] Radulescu, 'Genealogy in Insular Romance', p. 9. Radulescu is here also drawing on Michelle Warren's similar view of the lineage model in medieval England — see Warren, *History on the Edge*. Warren and Radulescu see the predominant tension in these histories as stemming from the use of a lineage model to negotiate contemporaneous politics, such as Geoffrey's attempt simultaneously to please the Anglo-Normans and defend the Britons.

seems firmly to situate the birth of English nationalism in the early fourteenth century, in the run-up to the Hundred Years War.[9] Yet in one of his later essays he steps back, declaring that he was perhaps 'overconcerned' to identify nationalism within the specific era he is treating, and reminds us that 'the concept of national-ism waits in the wings, waiting to be called forward' at numerous points in English and British history.[10] Turville-Petre's revision of his own argument reveals the rather protean nature of current studies in medieval English nationalism: other literary critics and historians have identified English nationalism as appearing briefly in the twelfth century, a generation after Geoffrey of Monmouth, with Henry of Huntingdon.[11] Adrian Hastings has even noticed signs of national-ism as early as Bede, although many scholars, myself among them, concur with Davies's assessment that while Bede may seem to be articulating nationalism and the nation of Britain, he is really describing the *gens Anglorum*.[12]

In Anderson's definition of the 'imagined political community', the nation is sovereign because it is distinct from other nations and demarcated by (occasion-ally fluid) boundaries.[13] No one, Anderson later claims, ever envisions a nation that encompasses the entire world.[14] Rather, a nation requires spatial boundaries to define itself. It is also worthwhile to observe that the nationalism that Anderson is discussing (and the nationalism treated in this chapter) is not a nationalism in favour of the nation: it is not the nationalism of the nineteenth century.[15]

[9] Turville-Petre, *England the Nation*. See also Turville-Petre, '*Havelock* and the History of the Nation', and Speed, 'The Construction of the Nation'.

[10] See Turville-Petre, 'The Brutus Prologue'.

[11] See Gillingham, 'Henry of Huntingdon'. Olivier de Laborderie does not make definite pronouncements about medieval nationalism, but he does dissect genealogy rolls from the fourteenth century in search of a nascent nationalism, in de Laborderie, 'A New Pattern for English History'.

[12] Hastings, *The Construction of Nationhood*. See also Davies, *The First English Empire*, esp. pp. 4–30.

[13] Anderson's landmark book is at its strongest when focusing on post-Enlightenment socie-ties, but his definition of nationalism is nonetheless useful for thinking through Geoffrey's radical departure from Virgilian models of genealogy and his arrival at a spatial definition of the British nation. Anderson defines the nation as follows: 'It is an imaged political community — and imag-ined as both inherently limited and sovereign. It is imagined because the members of even the smallest nation will never know most of their fellow-members, meet them, or even hear of them, yet in the minds of each lives the image of their communion', Anderson, *Imagined Communities*, p. 6.

[14] See Tomasch, 'Introduction: Medieval Geographical Desire'.

[15] For a cogent dissection of the use of 'myths' about medieval nations in the nineteenth century, see Geary, *The Myth of Nations*.

Lesley Johnson clarifies this distinction in her theory of nationalism. Whereas nineteenth-century nationalism defined the nation as a supreme and natural construct, the nationalism at work in the Middle Ages is more fluid — it is constructed, but how it is constructed varies from place to place, year to year, and author to author. As Johnson argues, 'The nation is a construct which requires *representational labour*, is produced in and by representational work of some kind because this notion of community must be larger than any individual could experience directly.'[16] This 'representational labour' may be directed at any facet of the construction of a national identity, whether the spatial (the nationalism that Anderson defines) or the genealogical, which was an increasingly common representation of the nation in the twelfth century and later.

How, then, did Geoffrey represent the nation? His representation uses the language and tropes of the myth of Rome to replace the genealogical model of that myth. Geoffrey begins the work of substitution in one of the early scenes of the *Historia*, where he relates the moment of the linguistic foundation of the nation of Britain:

> Denique Brutus de nomine suo insulam Britanniam appelellat sociosque suos Britones. Volebat enim ex diriuatione nominis memoriam habere perpetuam. Unde postmodum loquela gentis, quae prius Troiana siue curuum Graecum nuncupabatur, dicta fuit Britannica.[17]

> (Brutus named the island Britain after himself and called his followers Britons. He wanted to be remembered forever for giving them his name. For this reason the language of this people, previously known as Trojan or 'crooked Greek', was henceforth called British.)

Here, Geoffrey is describing the moment at which Brutus, descendant of the Trojan Aeneas and exile from his people, takes possession of the isle through naming. Geoffrey's etymology is a story told backwards, from the nearest past (naming the island) to the most remote ('previously known as Trojan'). Re-ordered into a chronological sequence, it would read: there was a language called Greek, which was made 'crooked' by a group of Trojans who, after a massive relocation, renamed themselves Britons, speakers of British, inhabitants of Britain.[18]

---

[16] Johnson, 'Imagining Communities', p. 6. Italics mine.

[17] Geoffrey of Monmouth, *The History of the Kings of Britain*, ed. by Reeve, I. 459–62 (pp. 28–29).

[18] It is quite likely that Geoffrey was also making a rather ingenious pun. Welsh *cam* means 'crooked' or 'bent', while 'Greek' in Welsh is *Groeg*, and so the Welsh word *Cymraeg* meaning

The etymology, which is to say the linguistic genealogy, of the Britons' naming is a story of revisions and discontinuities. There appears to be a connection between Trojan and Greek, but it is one of crookedness: a piebald line and a story told in reverse. This apparent connection, however, is erased in an act of self-reinvention and mandated memorialization by Brutus. His role as pioneer effaces the significance of the link to the classical world, and creates a new British myth that begins with him. Brutus founds the British nation through language, and we see the complexity at work in the relationship between *translatio* and genealogy: Brutus (and Geoffrey) recalls the myth of the *Aeneid*, but in that recollection, erases it to emphasize Brutus's present circumstances. Writ large, the act of recollection connects Geoffrey's text with Virgil's, thus creating a literary genealogy in which the second text destroys the first, much as Brutus murdered his father. Contention with the myth of the *Aeneid* (that is, *translatio*) and genealogy combine to create a complex representation of the British nation.[19]

Brutus's creation, through language, of the British people and the nation of Britain is a striking example of the complex subversion of the genealogical model. But it does not stand alone in the text. Of the ninety-nine kings addressed in the *Historia*, nearly twenty have difficulty with direct succession: often a brother or nephew inherits, although in a few cases the throne is usurped. Perhaps the most notable cases of problematic nepotism is that of Arthur, whose nephew and adopted heir Modred attempts to take the throne while Arthur is fighting the Romans abroad. On the face of it, Modred's treachery is unjustified. But there is a point to be made for it: Modred's treachery is only that if we consider Arthur as king, but if we consider the position of king and its relationship to the queen,

'Welsh' (language) is being read as *Cam (G)roeg*. I am indebted to Dr Antone Minard, who drew my attention to this pun (noted by many Welsh scholars in the past) and had the kindness to explain it in great detail in private correspondence.

[19] Matthew Fisher addresses similar concerns in later chronicles and their relationship to practical questions of inheritance: 'The wave of historiography that combines Galfridian and Bedan history does not merely rewrite the past. These texts recontextualize the genealogical foundations of the island, forcing a reinterpretation of the past. The legendary foundations [...] established genealogical lines that necessarily come to an end. These figures not only decouple ethnicity from the island's foundational narratives, but revise historiography's model of providential history. If regnal continuity is no longer a function of divine providence, then discontinuity is not evidence of divine condemnation. Legally, interrupted genealogies were resolved by simply legislating their exclusion, establishing interruption as the legal grounds for the loss of *seisin* or franchise. Insular historiography embraced and exploited those gaps both to rewrite its own textual genealogy and to make new arguments for the present and the future' (Fisher, 'Genealogy Rewritten', p. 141). It is precisely those exploited 'gaps' and their relationship to *translatio* and the increasingly fictionalized Romans that I seek to address here.

Modred's adulterous relationship with Guinevere positions him as king and high-lights Arthur's weakness once displaced in Guinevere's favour.[20]

Arthur's and Modred's battle for succession came at the end of one of the sequences of fraternal succession. Constantinus II has three sons, all kings: Constans, who rules briefly and dies quickly; Aurelius, the next to rule; and Uther, later Pendragon. Arthur's adoption of Modred is a savvy political move that attempts to reconsolidate the aberrant succession while preventing the disaster that could result from the king dying childless. The true disaster, of course, comes from Modred's unwillingness to wait for what will be his and his attempt to seize the throne before his time. Arthur, like Uther, is a dynastic aberration, uneasily grafted onto the genealogical tree of British kings.[21] Their success and popularity (both are 'elected') is undeniable; their rights to the throne, less so. Uther's kingship, particularly, is not inherited but rather derived from oaths and from fraternal, not paternal, relation.[22]

Arthur, as the only son (illegitimately conceived with the aid of Merlin) of the fourth son of a king is, to speak plainly, a long-shot for the throne. Modred, too, has uneasy claims: both he and Arthur are nephews to previous kings (Constans and Aurelius), and Modred's claim derives from his mother. Radulescu sees Merlin's complicity in Arthur's siring as an insertion of the 'erotic' into the genealogical tree: an intervention that, as mentioned above, has a distinctively feminine valence.[23] Whether one reads Merlin as feminine, as Radulescu seems to, or Uther's lust for Igerna as the erotic, the driving force behind Arthur's birth and eventual succession seems not to be patrilinearity, but a feminized rupture. Modred's claim, on the other hand, derives from his mother, the unnamed sister of Aurelius who married Loth of Scotland. Interestingly, it is as Aurelius's sister — not Uther's — that Modred's mother is identified: 'Loth autem, qui tempore Aurelii Ambrosii sororem ipsius duxerat, ex qua Gualguainum et Modredum genuerat [...]' (Loth, who in the reign of Aurelius Ambrosius had married the king's sister and fathered Gawain and Modred [...]).[24] Geoffrey's phrasing ('sororem ipsius') recalls again the possibility that relative position can be a

---

[20] While Wright and Reeve (Geoffrey of Monmouth, *The History of the Kings of Britain*, ed. by Reeve) give Arthur's wife's name as *Ganhumara*, I will use *Guinevere* for consistency's sake.

[21] For a historical reading of Arthur's paternity, see Parry, 'Geoffrey of Monmouth and the Paternity of Arthur'. See also Guerin, 'The King's Sin', for erotic parallels.

[22] See Stahuljak, *Bloodless Genealogies of the French Middle Ages*.

[23] Radulescu, 'Genealogy in Insular Romance', p. 9.

[24] Geoffrey of Monmouth, *The History of the Kings of Britain*, ed. by Reeve, IX. 205–07 (p. 205).

marker of legitimacy: 'sister of the previously mentioned' lacks the personal quality of 'sister of Aurelius'.[25]

This lateral transmission from brother to brother, as from Constans to Aurelius to Uther, occurs numerous times in the *Historia*: approximately every ten kings there is a break in the paternal transmission and a recursion to fraternal or nepotal inheritance. While fraternity is undeniable still a kinship link, it is not the pure kinship-based transmission requisite of a simple genealogical model that Ingledew sees as Geoffrey's inheritance from Virgil. Rather, fraternal transmission functions as a series of horizontal shifts in the vertical line of transmission as the genealogy turns momentarily askew from its downward movement and becomes a crooked line of descent. These are not the horizontal and vertical matrices of R. Howard Bloch's conception of genealogical epistemology in the twelfth century (which depend on a conception of the land as a horizontal marker and patrilineage as the vertical), but rather the series of jagged edges caused by the incursion of fraternal transmission into the realm of the vertical and patrilineal.[26]

Of the nine instances of fraternal transmission in the *Historia* (many of which involve a sequence of two or more kings, as in the above example), over half are accompanied by some element of interaction with the Romans: the brothers Belinus and Brennius conquer the Italian peninsula; Cassibellaunus (brother of Lud, founder of London) wages war against Julius Caesar for control over Britain; half-brothers Bassianus and Geta fight for the throne — a fight dependent on degrees of Roman and Briton blood; and Constantine, half-Roman himself on his father's side, conquers Rome in a passage highly evocative of Brutus's sortie into the Greek camp at the outset of the *Historia*. Arthur, himself the product of fraternal transmission and intermeshed in the related problem of nepotism, vividly battles the Romans to assert British independence and dominance. Taken together, the episodes of fraternal transmission and related Roman troubles spell a tale of British conquest, Roman retaliation, uneasy compromise (fixedly symbolized by Bassianus and Geta's mixed heritages), and a subversion of patrilineal loyalty in the person of Constantine. The dialectic mode of the first two stages of Briton-Roman interactions (conquest and retaliation) refuses to resolve neatly into a third term: the third and fourth stages of uneasy compromise and *patrilin-*

---

[25] Although Modred is apparently Arthur's cousin, he is referred to in the *Historia* as his nephew ('Modredo nepoti', x. 14 (pp. 222–23); see Geoffrey of Monmouth, *The History of the Kings of Britain*, trans. by Thorpe, p. 349). There is no hint of the incestuous connection between Arthur and his sister that occurs in later tellings of the Arthur story.

[26] See Bloch, *Etymologies and Genealogies*, esp. pp. 65–80. See also Ingledew, 'The Book of Troy', esp. pp. 670–80.

eal subversion depend on the insolubility of Roman blood and, in Constantine's case, the textual refutation of the genealogical imperative in the face of British loyalty.[27] Arthur's last-gasp attempt to finalize Briton-Roman relations concludes by offering no conclusion: the two nations must stand opposed.

Arthur offers numerous justifications for responding as he does to Roman requests for fealty and tributes. He articulates the immorality of conquest:

> Dicit [Lucius] enim ipsum sibi dari debere quia Iulio Caesari ceterisque succes-soribus suis redditum fuerit, qui discidio ueterum nostrorum inuitati cum armata manu applicuerunt atque patriam domesticus motibus uacillantem suae potestati ui et uiolentia summiserunt. Quia igitur eam hoc modo adepti fuerunt, uectigal ex illa iniuste ceperunt. Nichil enim quod ui et uiolentia acquiritur iuste ab ullo pos-sidetur qui uiolentiam intulit.[28]

> ([Lucius] claims that he ought to receive [the tribute] on the grounds that it was paid to Julius Caesar and his successors, who landed with an army after being called in because of dissent on our ancestors' part, and who by force of arms subjected our country to their power, when it was weakened by internal strife. Because they obtained it by these means, the tribute they exacted from us was unjust. What is obtained by force of arms is never the rightful possession of the aggressor.)

Arthur's justification depends on an inherited sense of wrongdoing — inherited not from his ancestors, as the translation has it, but from a communal under-standing of the wrongs done to the nation, the *patria* (nation) and the *veteres* (ancients). He continues in the same speech: 'Ego censeo quod Roma michi tributum dare debet, quia *antecessores* mei eam antiquitus optinuerunt' (I [...] judge that Rome owes tribute to me, because my *predecessors* once captured her).[29] Despite obvious etymological connections to modern English 'ancestors', *antecessores* refers to antecedents and 'predecessors in office' more than genealogi-cal forebears.[30] As Arthur co-opts the Roman justification for war and attempts

---

[27] This nepotal genealogy may have biblical analogues; as Karin R. Andriolo has noted, the younger brothers are typically the heroes in Genesis. See Andriolo, 'A Structural Analysis of Genealogy', esp. p. 1661. I am indebted to the anonymous reader who suggested this tantalizing parallel.

[28] Geoffrey of Monmouth, *The History of the Kings of Britain*, ed. by Reeve, IX. 456–62 (pp. 216–17); italics mine.

[29] Geoffrey of Monmouth, *The History of the Kings of Britain*, ed. by Reeve, IX. 468–69 (pp. 218–19); italics mine.

[30] *A Latin Dictionary*, ed. by Lewis and Short, under *antecessor*; *Dictionary of Medieval Latin*, ed. by Latham and Howlett, under *antecessor* ('ancestor' is given as the fourth definition of *antecessor*, although none of the examples predate 1200).

to turn it back on the foreign aggressors, he is also articulating a model of vertical comradeship: in his self-positioning, Arthur is not the most recent of a long line of related kings, but one occupying a position held by other functionaries of the state. Auguselus of Scotland is the only one of the lords who, in this scene, articulates that 'mors dulcet erit dum eam in uindicando patres nostros' (death [...] will be sweet, as long as I die avenging our forefathers).[31] This line, of course, also has a textual antecedent in Horace's *Odes* — a pithy nod to the *translatio* at work in the project of historiography.[32] Once on the continent, Arthur's speech to his 'commilitones' (comrades) lacks any mention of past defeats or victories, and instead focuses on the possible future of victory.[33]

Geoffrey refuses to portray genealogy as a continuous lineage both by presenting numerous instances of horizontal (fraternal) transmission, and by inserting the feminine — via Modred or Arthur — into key moments of transmission. Arthur's speech, in particular, emphasizes the relationships of kinship and kingship: he has predecessors in office, not ancestors. The problematic fraternal transmission preceding Arthur's reign, of which we will see more below, is frequently occasioned by Roman incursions. These are, of course, the same Romans who can also trace their ancestry back to Aeneas and the myth of Rome, just as Geoffrey does with for Brutus in the opening of the *Historia*. This deeply ironic strategy toys with the conception of *translatio*, as well: they both ignore the past that Arthur and the Romans have in common, which is grounded in the *Aeneid*, although the reader cannot.

This readerly awareness is the key to Geoffrey's transformation of the myth of Rome. When Brutus founded the nation of Britons with a pun (in Latin) on the twelfth-century name for those Britons, Geoffrey mobilized the language and tropes of the myth of Rome to articulate a new nation. Nennius's use of Caesar's sword functions in a similar vein: a Roman weapon, once co-opted, gives might to the Britons. Arthur, by contrast, refuses to engage the Roman past and instead articulates a break from the mythic underpinnings of the British nation: he does not have forebears, but predecessors. Geoffrey, at the same time, is moving his text away from a dependence on the myth of Rome, and towards a new conceptualization of the nation and the project of representational labour that is not genealogically connected to that myth. In using his heroes' battles to represent the new myth that he is creating, and in opposing the new myth to the Roman

---

[31] Geoffrey of Monmouth, *The History of the Kings of Britain*, ed. by Reeve, IX. 514–15 (pp. 220–21).

[32] Horace, *Odes and Epodes*, III. 2. 13.

[33] Geoffrey of Monmouth, *The History of the Kings of Britain*, ed. by Reeve, X. 226 (pp. 236–37).

myth he is dismissing, Geoffrey is also arguing against a genealogical model of history and a genealogical model of mythic transmission, or *translatio*.

Geoffrey does provide us with an alternative method of conceiving of the British nation, and again makes use of Roman incursions to do so. Specifically, he supplants the genealogical with the geopolitical. Both Arthur and Lucius, the Roman consul, are described in terms of the geopolitical units they command: Arthur dominates Northern and Western Europe, and Lucius Eastern Europe, Spain, and Africa. Arthur's journey is particularly highlighted, as Geoffrey details his departure from Portus Hamonis (Southampton), his arrival in Barba (Barfleur), and the famous episode of his defeat of the monster of Mont-Saint-Michel. Arthur's victory in his French territories is commemorated with a funerary church dedicated to Hoel's niece, killed by the monster, and one of only seven named funerary monuments mentioned in the text. From his arrival, therefore, Arthur quite literally marks his territory with his conquests and victories. From a more global perspective, the split world of Romans and Britons, in which each is given nearly equal territory and strength, reifies the boundaries implicit in a geopolitical conception of the nation. Arthur and Lucius both have their sides of the world, and the question of tribute is a question of whether or not those boundaries can be fluid enough to have a nation that does cover the whole world.

Arthur's battle with, and victory over, the Romans, as well as the binary division of the world into two spheres of influence, west and east, delineates a static moment in the map of the world that Geoffrey presents. Indeed, at the beginning of his text, Geoffrey defines the boundaries of Britain more circumspectly:

> Britannia, insularum optima, in occidentali occeano inter Galliam et Hiberniam sita [...]. Postremo quinque inhabitatur populis, Normannis uidelicet atque Britannis, Saxonibus, Pictis, et Scotis; ex quibus Britones olim ante ceteros *a mari usque ad mare* insederunt donce ultione diuina propter ipsorum superbiam suerueniente Pictis et Saxonibus cesserunt.[34]

> (Britain, the best of islands, lies in the western ocean between France and Ireland [...]. It is finally inhabited by five peoples, the Normans, the Britons, the Saxons, the Picts, and the Scots; of these the Britons once occupied it from shore to shore before the others, until their pride brought down divine retribution upon them and they gave way to the Picts and the Saxons.)

Bede's introduction, one of Geoffrey's most important historiographical sources, offers an alternate conceptualization of space:

---

[34] Geoffrey of Monmouth, *The History of the Kings of Britain*, ed. by Reeve, I. 24–25, 42–44 (pp. 6–7); italics mine.

Brittania Oceani insula, cui quondam Ambion nomen fuit, inter septentrionem et occidentem locata est, Germaniae Gallieae Hispaniae, maximis Europae partibus, multo intervallo adversa.[35]

(Britain, once called Albion, is an island of the ocean and lies to the north-west, being opposite Germany, Gaul, and Spain, which form the greater part of Europe, though at a considerable distance from them.)

Bede's introduction situates Britain in the middle of an ocean, as though its island status divorces it from political boundaries. His perspective is pointedly European (Britain is only north-west if one is on the Continent), and the location of Britain is quickly subsumed into its comparison with the three countries that form the greater part of Europe. Geoffrey, by contrast, again situates Britain in the middle of an ocean, but his ocean functions not as a nebulous unclaimed space, but a physical boundary between two rival geopolitical groups (France and Ireland). Whereas Bede's focus quickly pans east to the continental powers, Geoffrey focuses on the peoples of the island and, notably, the dominion from *mare ad mari* (shore to shore). This shift in focus, from an island bounded by rival nations to an island fully inhabited by its people, mark the two levels of Geoffrey's spatial nationalism: one, dependent on the boundaries that define the nation (as we saw with Arthur and the Romans dividing the world between them) and a second, dependent on the construction of a national space on the island itself.[36]

When Belinus, who also conquered Rome and the Italian peninsula, ratifies his father's law codes, he builds a national road system, and constructs Kaerleon, later Arthur's favoured court:

Rex [...] omne ambiguum legi suae auferre uolens, conuocauit omnes operarios totius insulae iussitque uiam ex caemento et lapidibus fabricari quae insulam in longitudinem a Cornubico mari usque ad Katanesium litus secaret et ad ciuitates quae infra errant recto limite duceret. Iussit etiam aliam fieri in latitudinem regni quae a Meneuia urbe, quae super Demeticum mare sita est, usque ad Portum Ham-

---

[35] Bede, *Ecclesiastical History*, ed. by Colgrave and Mynors, p. 4.

[36] Ingledew notes this new conception of space and the nation at work in Geoffrey: 'What Geoffrey does in the *Historia* is to provide the most thorough statement thus far of the basis of 'nation' — king, aristocracy, people — in the compounding of territory and time' (Ingledew, 'The Book of Troy', p. 686). Ingledew's argument differs from mine both in his emphasis on Geoffrey's use of genealogy, and, more significantly, in his lack of attention to precisely how Geoffrey defines the nation spatially — it is not the goal of his argument, which is to situate Geoffrey in the historiographic and historical modes.

onis extensa ad urbes infra positas ductum ostenderet, alias quoque duas ab obliquo insulae quae ad ceteras ciuitates ducatum praestarent. Deinde sanciuit eas omni honore omnique dignitate iurisque sui esse praecepit quod de illata super eas uiolentia uindicta sumeretur.[37]

(The king, wishing to eliminate all uncertainty from his laws, summoned all the workmen from the whole island. He ordered them to make a road of cement and stone which would traverse the length of the island from the Cornish sea to the shore at Caithness and lead directly to the cities on the way. He commanded that another road be built across the width of the island from the city of St David's on the coast of Demetia to Southampton, to lead to the cities there, as well as two more roads diagonally across the island, leading to all the remaining cities. He inaugurated them with all honour and dignity, proclaiming that it would be his own responsibility to take retribution for any act of violence committed upon them.)

Geoffrey here correlates Belinus's public works projects with his codifications of a national law. Indeed, the national law determines the safety of those travelling on the roads that crisscross the island, but they also serve as a medium for the laws' transmission from shore to shore. These roads both provide easy passages of people and goods, and demarcate the island itself: the roads divide the island, but in doing so, unite it as all connected to one road. The workers, even, are pan-British: the roads are built by all Britons to establish a demarcated island. The ambiguity of the Latin, which is apparent in the English translation, also makes it unclear if the punishments that Belinus codified applies to violence done to people on the roads, or violence to the roads themselves. This significant ambiguity points to the importance of these roads as something far more than passages, something beginning to approximate a strong nationalistic sense of space as defined by both the ruler (Belinus) and the representational labour of all participants within the nation.

The roads, then, stand for the creation of a national law code. With this metonymic move, Geoffrey also develops the twinned conceptions of a body politic inhabiting a body of land: a space of nationalism. This space of nationalism itself requires translation, as Geoffrey refers us to useful secondary sources:

Siquis autem scire uoluerit omnia quae de ipsis statuerit, legat Molmutinas leges, quas Gildas hystoricus de Britannico in Latinum, rex uero Aluredus de Latino in Anglicum sermonem transtulit.[38]

[37] Geoffrey of Monmouth, *The History of the Kings of Britain*, ed. by Reeve, III. 80–89 (pp. 52–53).

[38] Geoffrey of Monmouth, *The History of the Kings of Britain*, ed. by Reeve, III. 89–91 (pp. 52–53).

(If anyone wishes to discover all his edicts concerning the roads, they should read the Molmutine laws, which the historian Gildas translated from British into Latin, and King Alfred from Latin into English.)

Geoffrey's reckoning with the historical past includes a cheeky awareness of the constant necessity of translation — not the translation of Latin sources such as the *Aeneid* into a British context, but the translation of the materials of British nationalism into the universal language of Latin and the regional language (in Geoffrey's time) of English. (This sequence of translation from British to Latin to English mirrors the shift in insular power from the Britons to the Romans to the Saxons.) The need for translated materials of earlier law-codes emphasizes the *past-ness* of Geoffrey's topic: it is so antiquated as to be unintelligible without authorial aids, and it must be brought into (*transtulit*) the twelfth century. Read in this light, Geoffrey's emphasis on the bisecting and island-spanning roads has the distinct air of a critical commentary on previous source texts, a vibrant ekphrastic illustration of the spatial consequences of what came before. Notably, in defining this aspect of national space, Geoffrey does not advert to the *Aeneid* or the myth of Rome. Rather, he depends on native sources, because the work of creating a national space is an outright rejection of the genealogical myth of Rome.

This spatialized representational labour of British nation-building and myth-making is soon troubled by a Roman incursion. When Maximianus is given the throne on the grounds of maternal transmission (prefiguring the problem of feminine incursions into Arthur's and Modred's genealogies), he is quickly dispatched by Gratianus's friends:

> Gratianus Municeps, cum de nece Maximiani audiuisset, cepit diadema regni et sese in regem promouit. Exin tantam tyrannidem in populum exercuit ita ut cateruis factis irruerunt in illum plebani et interfecerunt [...]. Ob hanc infestationem ac dirissimam oppressionmen legati Romam cum epistulis mittuntur, militarem manum ad se uindicandam lacrmosis postulationibus poscentes et subiectionem sui in perpetuum uouentres si hostis longuis arceretur [...]. Ad quos iussit construere murum inter Albiniam et Deiram *a mari usque ad mare* ut esset arcendis hostibus a turba instructus terrori, ciuibus uero tutamini [...]. Collecto igitur priuato et public sumptu, incumbent indigenae operi et murum perficiunt.
>
> Romani ergo, patriae denuntiantes nequaquam se tam laboriosis expeditionibus posse frequentius uexari et ob imbelles et erraticos latrunculos Romana stegmata, tantum talemque exercitum, terra ac mari fatigari, sed ut pocius solis consuescendo armis ac uiriliter dimicando terram, substantiam, coniuges, liberos, et quod his maius est liberatatem uitamque totis uiribus defenderent.[39]

[39] Geoffrey of Monmouth, *The History of the Kings of Britain*, ed. by Reeve, VI. 1–3, 6–9, 13–15, 17–24 (pp. 110–13); italics mine.

(When Gratianus Municeps heard of Maximianus's murder, he seized the crown and made himself king. So tyrannically did he treat the people that a crowd of commoners attacked and killed him [...]. On account of a resultant attack [by the Irish, Norwegians, and Danes] and the direst oppression, envoys were sent to Rome with letters, requesting with tearful entreaties an armed force to avenge them and pledging their submission forever, if the foe could be warded off [...]. They ordered the people to build a wall from coast to coast between Scotland and Deira, which, when garrisoned by the crowd, would overawe such enemies as needed to be kept away [...]. The Britons set to work and built the wall, using both private and public funds.

The Romans then proclaimed to the British that it was out of the question for them to be troubled further by such demanding expeditions or for Rome's standards and her mighty army to be worn down by land and sea on account of weak, wandering bands of robbers; rather, the Britons should get used to defending themselves and, by fighting bravely, protect with their strength, their country, possessions, wives, children, and, above all, their freedom and their lives.)

The murder of the tyrannical usurper occasions a momentary loss of pride for the Britons: forced to ask for assistance from their disinterested overlords, the Britons are condescendingly instructed to take care of their own problems — but not before the Romans make use of the power vacuum to insert a wedge (a wall built by Britons at Roman command) into the body of the island. This bisection of the island literally begins a new chapter for the *Historia*, one that derives from the strife of mixed-blood rulers, competing overlords, and confused vassalage. The Roman assertion of a boundary into the island divides the previous geopolitical unit that had spanned, in an echo of the opening lines of the text, from shore to shore (*a mari [...] ad mare*).

This division also prefigures one of Geoffrey's most eloquent passages, occasioned by post-Arthurian strife in the wake of Modred's betrayal:

> Age ergo, age ciuile discidium, parum intelligens euangelicum illud 'omne regnum in se ipsusm diuisum desolabitur, et domus supra domum cadet'. Quia ergo regnum tuum in se diuisum fuit [...] .[40]

> (Go on, wage your civil war, unmindful that in the gospel it says: 'every kingdom divided against itself shall be laid waste, and house fall on house'. Your kingdom is divided against itself [...].)

Forced into the untenable position of attempting to inhabit a nation that has been divided in two, the British populace attempt to defend themselves against

---

[40] Geoffrey of Monmouth, *The History of the Kings of Britain*, ed. by Reeve, XI. 146–147 (pp. 256–57).

incursions, and it is only the arrival of a second Constantinus, from Brittany, that saves the divided nation. Earlier, the Roman general Lucius (a different Lucius from the one who summons Arthur)[41] was made a British king, and it is he that brought a tentative Christianity to Britain, and divided it into dioceses. Geoffrey's reading of this division is positive, particularly as it emphasizes the religious might of Rome instead of its political power. But it is also, as above, a scene that requires reference:

> Eorum nomina et actus in libro reperiuntur quem Gildas de uictoria Aurelii Ambrosii inscripsit. Quod autem ipse tam lucido tractatu perarauerat nullantenus opus fuit ut inferiori stilo renouaretur.[42]

> ([The priests'] names and acts can be found in the book which Gildas wrote about the victory of Aurelius Ambrosius. I saw no need to repeat in my inferior style what he had narrated in so distinguished a work.)

The division of Britain into units of spiritual dominion does not have the tragic consequences of the Roman partition of the island, but its details go unmentioned, and the reader is invited to break from the text to refer to a second text — one that relates, as Geoffrey emphasizes, precisely the break in paternal transmission that leads to Arthur's ascension. Again here, Geoffrey relies on native historiography to build a spatialized myth of the nation, just as he relied on the language of genealogy, derived from the *Aeneid*, to dismiss the myth of Rome's relevance. The Romans here undeniably evoke the Roman past that Geoffrey is refashioning, but they are out of place. Although the Romans here represent a grave threat to the spatially-conceived nation, at least that spatial conception is not based on Roman texts.

In the *Historia*, Geoffrey both depends on and dismisses the Virgilian myth of the foundation of Rome; he pointedly uses that myth to perform the representational labour of creating a British nation. After Brutus's punning foundation, Geoffrey stages a series of encounters between the Britons and a Roman Empire that grows increasingly distant, and increasingly ahistorical. Arthur's battle with the Romans, and Arthur's own emphasis — as related by Geoffrey, of course — on the break between Briton and Roman marks the culmination of Geoffrey's

---

[41] Parry, 'Geoffrey of Monmouth and Josephus', argues that Lucius's name may be derived from a Latin translation of Josephus's Greek account of one Longos (or Longinus), a Roman soldier who killed himself instead of surrendering to the Jewish army.

[42] Geoffrey of Monmouth, *The History of the Kings of Britain*, ed. by Reeve, IV. 431–433 (pp. 88–89).

reframing of the myth of Rome (and its genealogical models) into a new myth that defines Britain and its inhabitants, and the development of a spatial model of nationhood. Like Nennius with Caesar's sword, however, Geoffrey, returning to the strength of his predecessors, relies on Roman incursions to define this new narrative of cultural understanding, which is to say, to define this new British myth.

Works Cited

Primary Sources

Bede, *Bede's Ecclesiastical History of the English People*, ed. and trans. by Bertram Colgrave and R. A. B. Mynors (Oxford: Clarendon Press, 1969)

Geoffrey of Monmouth, *The History of the Kings of Britain*, trans. by Lewis Thorpe (New York: Penguin, 1966)

——, *The History of the Kings of Britain: An Edition and Translation of the 'De gestis Britonum' (Historia Regum Britanniae)*, ed. by Michael D. Reeve, trans. by Neil Wright, Arthurian Studies, 69 (Woodbridge: Boydell, 2007)

Wace, *Wace's Roman de Brut: A History of the British, Text and Translation*, trans. by Judith Weiss (Exeter: University of Exeter Press, 1999)

Secondary Studies

Anderson, Benedict, *Imagined Communities*, rev. ed. (London: Verso, 2006)

Andriolo, Karin R., 'A Structural Analysis of Genealogy and Worldview in the Old Testament', *American Anthropologist*, n.s., 75 (1973), 1657–69

Bloch, R. Howard, *Etymologies and Genealogies: A Literary Anthropology of the French Middle Ages* (Chicago: University of Chicago Press, 1983)

Davies, Robert Rees, *The First English Empire: Power and Identities in the British Isles, 1093–1343* (Oxford: Oxford University Press, 2002)

Field, Rosalind, 'Romance as History, History as Romance', in *Romance in Medieval England*, ed. by Maldwyn Mills, Jennifer Fellows, and Carol Meale (Cambridge: Brewer, 1991), pp. 163–74

Fisher, Matthew, 'Genealogy Rewritten: Inheriting the Legendary in Insular Historiography', in *Broken Lines: Genealogical Literature in Medieval Britain and France*, ed. by Raluca L. Radulescu and Edward Donald Kennedy, Medieval Texts and Cultures of Northern Europe, 16 (Turnhout: Brepols, 2008), pp. 123–41

Geary, Patrick J., *Furta Sacra: Thefts of Relics in the Central Middle Ages* (Princeton: Princeton University Press, 1978)

——, *The Myth of Nations: The Medieval Origins of Europe* (Princeton: Princeton University Press, 2002)

Gillingham, John, 'Henry of Huntingdon and the Twelfth-Century Revival of the English Nation', in John Gillingham, *The English in the Twelfth Century: Imperialism, National Identity, and Political Values* (Woodbridge: Boydell, 2000), pp. 123–44

Guerin, M. Victoria, 'The King's Sin: The Origins of the David-Arthur Parallel', in *The Passing of Arthur: New Essays in Arthurian Tradition*, ed. by Christopher Baswell and William Sharpe (New York: Garland, 1988), pp. 15–30

Hastings, Adrian, *The Construction of Nationhood: Ethnicity, Religion and Nationalism* (Cambridge: Cambridge University Press, 1997)

Ingledew, Francis, 'The Book of Troy and the Genealogical Construction of History: The Case of Geoffrey of Monmouth's Historia regum Britanniae', *Speculum*, 69 (1994), 665–704

Johnson, 'Imagining Communities: Medieval and Modern', in *Concepts of National Identity in the Middle Ages*, ed. by Simon Forde, Lesley Johnson, and Alan V. Murray, Leeds Texts and Monographs, 14 (Leeds: School of English, University of Leeds, 1995), p. 1–19

Laborderie, Olivier de, 'A New Pattern for English History: The First Genealogical Rolls of the Kings of England', in *Broken Lines: Genealogical Literature in Medieval Britain and France*, ed. by Raluca L. Radulescu and Edward Donald Kennedy, Medieval Texts and Cultures of Northern Europe, 16 (Turnhout: Brepols, 2008), pp. 45–62

Latham, Ronald Edward, and David E. Howlett, eds, *Dictionary of Medieval Latin from British Sources*, 14 vols to date (London: Oxford University Press for The British Academy by, 1975–)

Lewis, Charlton T., and Charles Short, eds, *A Latin Dictionary: Founded on Andrews' Edition of 'Freund's Latin Dictionary'*, rev. edn (Oxford: Clarendon Press, 1879)

Parry, John J., 'Geoffrey of Monmouth and Josephus', *Speculum*, 2 (1927), 446–47

——, 'Geoffrey of Monmouth and the Paternity of Arthur', *Speculum*, 13 (1938), 271–77

Radulescu, Raluca L., 'Genealogy in Insular Romance', in *Broken Lines: Genealogical Literature in Medieval Britain and France*, ed. by Raluca L. Radulescu and Edward Donald Kennedy, Medieval Texts and Cultures of Northern Europe, 16 (Turnhout: Brepols, 2008), pp. 7–25

Radulescu, Raluca L., and Edward Donald Kennedy, 'Introduction', in *Broken Lines: Genealogical Literature in Medieval Britain and France*, ed. by Raluca L. Radulescu and Edward Donald Kennedy, Medieval Texts and Cultures of Northern Europe, 16 (Turnhout: Brepols, 2008), pp. 1–5

Speed, Diane, 'The Construction of the Nation in Medieval English Romance', in *Readings in Medieval English Romance*, ed. by Carol M. Meale (Cambridge: Brewer, 1994), pp. 135–57

Spiegel, Gabrielle M., *The Past as Text: The Theory and Practice of Medieval Historiography* (Baltimore: Johns Hopkins University Press, 1997)

Stahuljak, Zrinka, *Bloodless Genealogies of the French Middle Ages: Translatio, Kinship, and Metaphor* (Gainesville: University Press of Florida, 2005)

Tomasch, Sylvia, 'Introduction: Medieval Geographical Desire', in *Text and Territory: Geographical Imagination in the European Middle Ages*, ed. by Sylvia Tomasch and Sealy Gilles (Philadelphia: University of Pennsylvania Press, 1998), pp. 1–14

Turville-Petre, Thorlac, 'The Brutus Prologue to *Sir Gawain and the Green Knight*', in *Imagining a Medieval English Nation*, ed. by Kathy Lavezzo, Medieval Cultures, 37 (Minneapolis: University of Minnesota Press, 2004), pp. 340–46

——, *England the Nation: Language, Literature, and National Identity, 1290–1340* (Oxford: Clarendon Press, 1999)

——, '*Havelock* and the History of the Nation', in *Readings in Medieval English Romance*, ed. by Carol M. Meale (Cambridge: Brewer, 1994), pp. 121–34

Warren, Michelle R., *History on the Edge: Excalibur and the Borders of Britain, 1100–1300* (Minneapolis: University of Minnesota Press, 2000)

SNORRI STURLUSON AND THE CONSTRUCTION OF NORSE MYTHOGRAPHY

Margaret Clunies Ross[*]

The purpose of this essay is to place the mythography of the Icelandic writer Snorri Sturluson (1179–1241) in its medieval context, to establish the nature of its originality and the possible debts it might have to indigenous Norse and non-Norse sources, and to discuss its reception both in Iceland in the Late Middle Ages and in Iceland and beyond after the medieval period.

It is generally assumed that Snorri composed his *Edda*, probably a term meaning 'Poetics',[1] in the first half of the 1220s. Current thinking is that the part that usually appears last in modern editions, *Háttatal* 'List of Verse-Forms', was the first to have been composed, following Snorri's first visit to Norway in 1218–20. *Háttatal* is a *clavis metrica*, a key to a variety of Old Norse verse-forms presented within an encomium in praise of Jarl Skúli Bárðarson, regent of Norway at the time, and the young Norwegian king Hákon Hákonarson. Anthony Faulkes has suggested that Snorri sent the poem to Norway in written form rather than delivering it orally, as was traditional with skaldic praise-poems.[2] Neither *Háttatal*, nor what is now regarded as the third part of the *Edda*, *Skáldskaparmál* (The Language of Poetry), is primarily a mythographical work, though *Skáldskaparmál* contains sections of mythic narrative, ostensibly to explain the nature of some

* Margaret Clunies Ross (margaret.cluniesross@sydney.edu.au) is Emeritus Professor of English and Honorary Professor, Medieval and Early Modern Centre, University of Sydney, and the author of *Prolonged Echoes: Old Norse Myths in Medieval Northern Society, 1: The Myths*, and *2: The Reception of Norse Myths in Medieval Iceland* (Odense: Odense University Press, 1994 and 1998); she is one of the major figures in the study of Eddic and skaldic poetry, and Snorri Sturluson.

[1] For discussion of the meaning of the term *edda*, see Faulkes, 'Edda'.

[2] Snorri Sturluson, *Edda: Háttatal*, ed. by Faulkes, p. ix.

Writing Down the Myths, ed. by Joseph Falaky Nagy, CURSOR 17, (Turnhout: Brepols, 2013) pp. 201–221　BREPOLS　PUBLISHERS　10.1484/M.CURSOR-EB.1. 100853

types of skaldic diction, particularly of the kind we call (after Snorri) kennings, but in fact *Skáldskaparmál*'s mythic narratives go well beyond what would have been required to simply explain kennings with mythological subjects. Working backwards, the second part of the *Edda*, *Gylfaginning* (The tricking of Gylfi),[3] is almost wholly mythographical in nature, and comprises a systematic account of the creation of the cosmos, the nature and diversity of the supernatural beings that inhabit it, high points in their lives, and the final battle between them, at Ragnarøkr 'Twilight of the powers' (as Snorri calls it), that will bring their world to an end. It is this second part of the *Edda* that has been a major influence on the world outside Iceland and brought Old Norse myth into Western consciousness from the early seventeenth century up to the present time. In the *Edda*'s four major manuscripts, *Gylfaginning* is preceded by an untitled Prologue, which places the mythological content of the *Edda* in a context acceptable to thirteenth-century Christians. It explains pre-Christian Norse beliefs both as an example of a natural religion and by way of the teachings of euhemerism, namely that the belief in pagan gods was to be understood as a deification of the lives and deeds of famous men and women of an earlier age. Thus the framing theoretical tendency of the *Edda* is both historical and theological, and, as we shall see, is based firmly in traditional Norse poetics.

The standard modern view of the genesis of Snorri's *Edda* is that it was formed around a nucleus comprising an exposition of the metrics and diction of skaldic poetry, a kind of elaborate, largely encomiastic verse that began, as far as we have evidence, at the courts of Norwegian rulers in the ninth century. This implies that Snorri's primary model and his primary inspiration was grammatical literature which, in the Middle Ages, included metrics and some account of the tropes and colours of rhetoric, in Snorri's case applied to vernacular poetry. He already had an indigenous model for *Háttatal*, namely *Háttalykill* (Key to the verse-forms), a mid-twelfth-century poetic *clavis metrica* composed by an Icelander, Hallr Þórarinsson, and the Orkney Earl Rǫgnvaldr Kali Kolsson. There is no evidence, however, that the largely systematic, theorized exposition of the diction of skaldic poetry that is found in part in *Háttatal* and more expansively in *Skáldskaparmál* had ever been attempted before in Iceland or indeed in any other part of Scandinavia or Western Europe. Scholars have assumed that Snorri must have developed this part

---

[3] Gylfi was the name of a legendary Swedish king, who had been subjected to trickery by the Æsir (the Icelandic name for the Old Norse gods), immigrants from Troy to Scandinavia, according to the *Edda*. He was determined to find out the secrets of their power. To this end he disguised himself as a wayfarer and made his way to their hall, where he questioned them on their beliefs. Such is the frame narrative of *Gylfaginning*.

of the *Edda* with Latin grammars as his model, though no specific model has been identified and opinion is sharply divided on whether Snorri, the first known lay author of an Icelandic text, could read and understand Latin or whether he knew concepts derived from Latin works at second hand, from educated friends or from vernacular preaching.[4] My own view is that, given the subject and substance of the *Edda* as a whole, it is improbable that Snorri was unacquainted with at least the rudiments of Latin, which he could have learnt during his youth at the farm Oddi, owned by his foster-father, Jón Loptsson, the grandson of the first known Icelandic historian, Sæmundr fróði 'the Learned' Sigfússon.

The evidence of the medieval manuscript compilations in which Snorri's *Edda* has been preserved in whole or in part leaves little doubt that its medieval audience regarded its status as indigenous *grammatica* as primary. While it is difficult to determine exactly how widely known the work was in the century or so after it was composed, the surviving manuscripts point to a transmission and appreciation mainly within educational circles, probably in schools attached to religious foundations. Guðrún Nordal has argued that skaldic poetry may have been taught in Icelandic schools alongside Latin from about the middle of the twelfth century to illustrate the figures of *grammatica*.[5] If so, Snorri's initiative in creating a vernacular *grammatica* is understandable in such a context. Although Guðrún's theory cannot be proved conclusively, the circumstantial evidence provided by the manuscripts discussed here lends it considerable support. There is also evidence of a negative kind from the fourteenth century to show that Snorri's *Edda* was still influential then among the educated classes. This comes from several mid-fourteenth-century religious poems in which their clerical composers repudiate what they consider to be the excessive obscurity and unnatural syntax advocated in what the poet of *Lilja* (The Lily) calls *eigi glögg regla eddu* (the obscuring rule of the Edda) (stanza 97, l. 7), undoubtedly a reference to Snorri's work. Almost certainly, these poets' motivation was religious: the word of Christianity needed to be expressed in terms of light and clarity, not in a poetic idiom that delighted in obscurity.[6]

---

[4] Anthony Faulkes is on record in a number of his publications, most recently Faulkes, 'Snorri Sturluson', p. 311, as claiming that Snorri is unlikely to have known Latin ('There is no trace in Snorri's writings of any knowledge of Latin; he almost never uses Latin words and never quotes Latin works'). This position has been supported recently, though for different reasons, by Wanner, *Snorri Sturluson and the Edda*, pp. 67, 116–17.

[5] Nordal, *Tools of Literacy*, pp. 19–72.

[6] See the new edition, *Lilja*, ed. by Chase, pp. 554–677, and especially notes to stanzas 97–98 on pp. 672–75.

The other chief point of circulation of Snorri's *Edda* was within his own family. Two of his nephews, Óláfr and Sturla Þórðarson, both poets and scholars in their own right, seem to have been particularly closely influenced by his work.[7] This is evident from their own poetry, in which they imitate some of their uncle's prescriptions, and, in the case of Óláfr, in his treatise on poetics, the so-called *Third Grammatical Treatise* (*c.* 1250), which shows direct influence of technical terminology from the *Edda*, although Óláfr, unlike Snorri, follows the structure and terminology of Latin grammars in his analysis of skaldic diction.[8] Influence from both Snorri and Óláfr is perceptible in the anonymous fourteenth-century *Fourth Grammmatical Treatise*, preserved only in the Codex Wormianus. Four manuscripts, three medieval and one early modern copy of a medieval witness, contain all four parts of Snorri's *Edda*, although the parts are not always complete. These are, in chronological order, U, the Codex Upsaliensis of *c.* 1300; R, the Codex Regius of *c.* 1325–50; W, the Codex Wormianus of *c.* 1350; and T, the paper Codex Trajectinus of *c.* 1595.[9] There are in addition three significant medieval manuscripts that contain parts of *Skáldskaparmál*,[10] together with *þulur*, that is, verse lists of poetic synonyms, which are also found in some of the main manuscripts but are probably not Snorri's work. Most of these manuscripts contain various additional items: poetry, grammatical treatises, additional lists of kennings, and a genealogy of the Sturlung family. R also contains the texts of two poems at the end, *Jómsvíkingadrápa* and *Málsháttakvæði*, both probably composed by Bishop Bjarni Kolbeinsson of the Orkneys, while W includes, beside the text of the *Edda*, four grammatical treatises and several poems.[11] It is clear from the nature of these compilations, whether they preserve the whole of Snorri's *Edda* or part of it, that they are primarily collections of texts whose focus is on poetry and

---

[7] For succinct information on Snorri's nephews and their work, see Nordal, *Tools of Literacy*, pp. 181–84 and 191–93 and references given there.

[8] See Clunies Ross, *A History of Old Norse Poetry*, pp. 186–202.

[9] Uppsala, Uppsala UL, De la Gardie 11; Reykjavík, Stofnun Árna Magnússonar í íslenzkum fræðum, MS GKS 2367 4°; København, Arnamagnaean, MS AM 242 fol; Utrecht, Utrecht UL, Traj 1374.

[10] These are Reykjavík, Stofnun Árna Magnússonar í íslenzkum fræðum, MS AM 748 I b 4° (hereafter A) of *c.* 1325; Reykjavík, Stofnun Árna Magnússonar í íslenzkum fræðum, MS AM 757 a 4° (hereafter B) of *c.* 1400; and Reykjavík, Stofnun Árna Magnússonar í íslenzkum fræðum, MS AM 748 II 4° (hereafter C) of *c.* 1400. All these manuscripts were formerly housed in the Arnamagnæan Collection at the University of Copenhagen.

[11] See the extensive codicological discussion in Johansson, *Studier i Codex Wormianus*, and the table of MS W's contents on p. 29.

poetic theory, not mythology. Further, the medieval witnesses reveal that interest in Iceland in the later Middle Ages revolved around *Skáldskaparmál*, and to a lesser extent, *Háttatal*, and not so much around *Gylfaginning* and the Prologue.[12]

This focus of attention persisted in Iceland into the Renaissance and beyond. There are many post-medieval manuscripts of Snorri's *Edda*, mostly derived from the surviving medieval witnesses, but in some instances containing material that has been lost from them, like the beginning of the Prologue in R and additional material on poetic diction from the W text.[13] A number of early modern texts of the *Edda* offer expanded versions, almost always adding material to the treatment of poetry and poetic diction, with extended discussions of the minutiae of poetic language. There is little evidence in Icelandic manuscripts, where copying by hand continued into the nineteenth and even sometimes the twentieth century, that such post-medieval copies were made by persons primarily interested in the synthesis of Norse myth to be had in *Gylfaginning*, nor in the theorizing of that mythology to be found in the Prologue and in a few other parts of the *Edda*. Indeed, the Prologue has until recent decades been regarded as spurious by many scholars and translators, not on codicological grounds but because they have believed that Snorri could not have authored a work that had such obvious connections with medieval Christian learning. A few scholars still appear to adhere to this view.[14]

The only clear authorial direction that may indicate Snorri's own view of the nature of his creation comes from a passage in the early part of *Skáldskaparmál* where the narrator's voice addresses itself directly to its audience, represented here as 'young poets', immediately after it has been asserted that there are two basic categories of poetic language, diction and verse-forms:

En þetta er nú at segja ungum skáldum þeim er girnask at nema mál skáldskapar ok heyja sér orðfjǫlða með fornum heitum eða girnask þeir at kunna skilja þat er hulit er kveðit: þá skili hann þessa bók til fróðleiks ok skemtunar. En ekki er at gleyma eða ósanna svá þessar sǫgur at taka ór skáldskapinum fornar kenningar þær er hǫfuðskáld hafa sér líka látit. En eigi skulu kristnir menn trúa á heiðin goð ok

---

[12] There is one medieval manuscript fragment, Reykjavík, Stofnun Árna Magnússonar í íslenzkum fræðum, MS AM 756 4° of the fifteenth century, which contains parts of both *Gylfaginning* and *Skáldskaparmál*, in a text derived from W.

[13] See Snorri Sturluson, *Two Versions of Snorra Edda*, ed. by Faulkes, and Snorri Sturluson, *Edda: Prologue and Gylfaginning*, ed. by Faulkes, p. xxix.

[14] This opinion has been strong in the German-speaking world, beginning with Andreas Heusler's seminal study of the learned background to the Prologue in Heusler, *Die gelehrte Urgeschichte*.

eigi á sannyndi þessar sagnar annan veg en svá sem hér finnask í upphafi bókar er
sagt er frá atburðum þeim er mannfólkit viltisk frá réttri trú.

(But these things have now to be told to young poets who desire to learn the language
of poetry and to furnish themselves with a wide vocabulary using traditional terms;
or else they desire to be able to understand what is expressed obscurely. Then
let such a one take this book as scholarly inquiry and entertainment. But these
stories are not to be consigned to oblivion or demonstrated to be false, so as to
deprive poetry of ancient kennings which major poets have been happy to use. Yet
Christian people must not believe in heathen gods, nor in the truth of this account
in any other way than that in which it is presented at the beginning of this book,
where it is told what happened when mankind went astray from the true faith.[15])

This passage is revealing and is likely to represent the authorial voice. In the first
place, it confirms the *Edda*'s educational purpose, and its focus on poetry within
education. Whether that poetic education was thought of as formal or informal
it is not possible to say, but it is noticeable that Snorri employs the standard medieval schoolroom formula that literature should be both entertaining and educational. Secondly, it confirms that, in Snorri's mind, it was primarily the practice
of poetry rather than a delight in mythological stories that required young poets
to understand traditional and sometimes obscure terms. Thirdly, it implies that
to Snorri the stories (*sǫgur*) that underpinned Norse poetic diction had value in
themselves and not just as the sources of exemplary poetic figures. At this point
we are able to see how the nexus between poetics and mythography came into
being and developed beyond an embryonic narrative notation, where it could
have remained. The impetus to record myths is expressed here through the negative injunctions 'not to forget' (*ekki at gleyma*) and 'not to declare untrue' (*ekki
at ósanna*), with a glance over the shoulder at conventional Christian attitudes
to pagan myths as satanic illusions. The negative is balanced out, however, by the
implicit positive of preserving cultural memory, as sanctioned by the chief traditional cultural authorities, the major Norwegian and Icelandic poets (*hǫfuðskáld*,
'chief poets'). Thus it is still the high-status Norse arts of poetry and poetics that
drive Snorri's mythography here and make the recording of pagan narratives
about the pre-Christian gods permissible for Christians, in terms articulated in
the Prologue, to which this passage indubitably refers.[16]

---

[15] The Icelandic text is taken from Snorri Sturluson, *Edda: Skáldskaparmál*, ed. by
Faulkes, I, 5 and the English translation from Snorri Sturluson, *Edda*, ed. and trans. by Faulkes,
pp. 64–65. This passage appears in slightly different forms in other manuscripts, but is present
in R, T, W, U, and B.

[16] See Snorri Sturluson, *Edda: Skáldskaparmál*, ed. by Faulkes, I, 154, note to p. 5, ll. 32–35.

By contrast with the codicological evidence we can use to establish both medieval and post-medieval Icelandic interest in Snorri's *Edda* as a treatise on poetry, there is little material evidence to indicate how contemporaries regarded its mythological parts. However, a comparison of how the various medieval manuscript witnesses handle the mythographic sections of the *Edda* may lead us to some tentative conclusions on that score and may also help us to understand how Snorri and his later redactors constructed a mythography alongside and partly within a poetic treatise. First, however, it is necessary to chart how the text of Snorri's *Edda* has become known to the modern world, because the nature and arrangement of the text in the various manuscripts are different enough for the editorial choice of a base manuscript to have had a significant influence on the text that has been available over the years to scholars and the reading public. This is particularly true of the mythographical parts, as we shall see.

The mythographic parts of the *Edda* comprise the Prologue, the whole of *Gylfaginning* and parts of *Skáldskaparmál*. The first part of *Skáldskaparmál*, incorporating two major myths, the narrative of the giant Þjazi's theft of the goddess Iðunn and her apples, along with its sequel, and the myth of the origin of the mead of poetry and how Óðinn acquired it for the gods and men, was treated by most earlier editors as part of *Gylfaginning*, and the chapter numbers were run on from there.[17] In the Icelandic tradition the first part of *Skáldskaparmál* was referred to as *Bragaræður* (Bragi's speeches), alluding to the fact that this section of the text uses the device of a dialogue frame in which the myths were told by Bragi, god of poetry, to Ægir, a sea-deity who is said to have held a feast for the gods. In the R and W manuscripts, but not in U, the first section of *Skáldskaparmál* is rounded off with a passage suggesting that the myths of the Norse gods and their deeds at Ragnarøkr can be understood as versions of the classical story of the Trojan War and the heroes who fought it. It used to be common for scholars to regard this passage as a learned interpolation, one that could not possibly be original to Snorri, but it matches a similar interpretation in the Prologue and at the end of *Gylfaginning*, and there is no reason to doubt its authenticity. It is thought that a version of *Trójumanna saga* (The Saga of the Troy-men), based on the *De excidio Troiae historia* by 'Dares Phrygius' and a number of other medieval sources, already existed in Iceland by the early thirteenth century.[18] Further, there

---

[17] The great nineteenth-century Arnamagnæan edition, Snorri Sturluson, *Edda* (1848–87), does this and its numbering is usually indicated in modern editions, even if they do not follow it themselves. See Snorri Sturluson, *Edda: Skáldskaparmál*, ed. by Faulkes, I, pp. viii–x.

[18] See Eldevik, 'Trójumanna saga'.

is substantial evidence in Icelandic historical works from the twelfth century that the Troy story was known quite widely well before Snorri's time.[19]

The uncertainty of earlier modern editors about where to draw the line between *Gylfaginning* and *Skáldskaparmál* echoes the practice of the redactor of the U manuscript. Whereas the scribes of R and W each begin *Skáldskaparmál* with a very large, decorated initial letter on a new page (in R it is fol. 18[r]; in W, p. 40) and clearly designate a new section of the text, U's rubricator runs the text of *Gylfaginning* on with the much abbreviated opening section of *Skáldskaparmál*, distinguishing it from what went before only with the rubric *Frá heimbóði Ása með Ægi* (About Ægir's invitation to the gods to visit [him]), followed by a normal-sized capital letter.

Even though U is the oldest surviving manuscript of the *Edda* and seems to have had connections with Snorri's family, the Sturlungar,[20] it has not normally been used as the basis of modern editions of the work since the early nineteenth century, for several reasons. First, it is much shorter than the two other 'complete' medieval witnesses, R and W, and, although R and W diverge in some places, they are much more like each other than they are like U, in terms of length, text division and sequencing of material. U also rearranges some of the material in the *Edda*, in comparison with R and W, in ways that have been considered illogical by some modern editors.[21] A new project, undertaken by a team of scholars from the Department of Scandinavian Languages at Uppsala University, aims to discover the relationship between the R, T, W, and U versions by in-depth examination of the U manuscript's codicology, lexicology, and palaeography, and their study may indicate whether the U redactor worked from an exemplar closely related to that of R, T, and W, or from a different text.[22]

All modern critical editions of the *Edda* now use the R version of Snorri's text as their base, but before Rasmus Rask's 1818 edition,[23] as far as I know, all printed editions had based themselves on other manuscripts. This made a considerable difference to the product presented to the reader. Rask used R as his main text, but included readings from the other manuscripts, sometimes preferring U

[19] On this, see Faulkes, 'The Genealogies and Regnal Lists'; and Stefán Karlsson, 'Ættbogi Noregskonunga'.

[20] It includes a genealogy of the Sturlungar and a list of Icelandic law-speakers, ending with Snorri himself.

[21] See Snorri Sturluson, *Edda: Prologue and Gylfaginning*, ed. by Faulkes, p. xxx.

[22] See Heimir Pálsson, 'A Short Report'. A new edition of the U version of the *Edda* has recently been published as Snorri Sturluson, *The Uppsala Edda*, ed. by Pálsson.

[23] Snorri Sturluson, *Snorra-Edda*, ed. by Rask.

for substantial passages. Peder Hansen Resen's edition of 1665,[24] which became the vehicle through which many European readers and commentators accessed Snorri's *Edda* in the seventeenth and eighteenth centuries, was based largely on the slightly earlier edition by the Icelander Magnús Ólafsson, the so-called *Laufás Edda*,[25] which in turn was based on sources most similar to W, though with additional material not found in any surviving medieval manuscript. It was the Latin translation by the Danish historian Stephanius in Resen's tri-lingual Icelandic-Danish-Latin edition that shaped the early modern reception of Snorri's *Edda* outside Iceland, especially after it had been incorporated into Paul-Henri Mallet's influential *Monumens de la mythologie et de la poésie des Celtes* [*sic*], first published in 1756.[26]

Another influential early edition that helped to shape the modern reception history of Snorri's *Edda* was the Swede Johan Göransson's 1746 edition of the Prologue and *Gylfaginning* parts only of the U manuscript. Because U had been obtained by the Swedish nobleman Count Magnus Gabriel de la Gardie in 1650 and presented to Uppsala University Library in 1662, it was easily accessible to Göransson as the basis of his edition and its Latin translation. The U-text achieved further influence in the English-speaking world when Thomas Percy included the Latin translation from Göransson in both the first (1770) and second (1809) editions of his extremely popular *Northern Antiquities*.[27] It was only in that book's third edition (1847), revised by I. A. Blackwell, that a heavily edited English translation of Rask's edition of *Gylfaginning* and the *Bragarœður*, minus the Prologue, which Blackwell deemed absurd,[28] was available for the general reader and scholar alike.

It is difficult to tell whether the amalgamation of a number of the extended mythic narratives of *Skáldskaparmál* with the mythography of *Gylfaginning*, which we see in U, was an earlier arrangement from which R and W diverged or whether it was the work of a redactor seeking to rearrange Snorri's text in a differ-

---

[24] Snorri Sturluson, *Two Versions of Snorra Edda*, ed. by Faulkes, II: *Edda Islandorum*.

[25] Snorri Sturluson, *Two Versions of Snorra Edda*, ed. by Faulkes, I: *Edda Magnúsar Ólafssonar*.

[26] Mallet, *Monumens de la mythologie*. The second edition included Mallet's earlier volume, Mallet, *Introduction à l'histoire de Dannemarc*, and was published in six volumes in Geneva in 1763 (Mallet, *Histoire de Dannemarc*).

[27] Thomas Percy, *Northern Antiquities* (1770); followed by a second edition, Thomas Percy, *Northern Antiquities* (1809); and the amply revised third edition of 1847: Thomas Percy, *Northern Antiquities* (1847), rev. by Blackwell.

[28] [Thomas Percy], *Northern Antiquities*, rev. by Blackwell, p. 397.

ent way. We do not of course have Snorri's text, which, as Faulkes surmises,[29] may have existed on loose sheets of vellum that different redactors arranged as seemed best to them. However, the fact that the redactor of U intersperses considerable amounts of non-Snorronian material in his version of the *Edda* may suggest that for him the textual and thematic unity of Snorri's work in a modern sense were not very important criteria.[30] Moreover, the opening rubric of the Uppsala *Edda*, which seems to be in the same hand as that of the main text,[31] indicates an uncertainty about how to categorize the mythographical sections, which may suggest that this redactor did not fully understand the basis for the separation of the *Gylfaginning* material from that in *Skáldskaparmál*, if that was indeed the original arrangement, as the combined codicological evidence of R, W, and the lost medieval prototype of T seems to indicate.[32]

The opening rubric of U reads:

> Bók þessi heitir Edda. Hana hefir saman setta Snorri Sturluson eptir þeim hætti sem hér er skipat. Er fyrst frá Ásum ok Ymi, þar næst Skáldskaparmál ok heiti margra hluta, síðast Háttatal er Snorri hefir ort um Hákon konung ok Skúla hertuga.

> (This book is called *Edda*. It was compiled by Snorri Sturluson in the manner in which it is arranged here. There is told first about the Æsir and Ymir, then *Skáldskaparmál* [the language of poetry] and terms for many things, finally *Háttatal* [list of verse-forms] which Snorri has composed about King Hakon and Duke Skuli.[33])

There are two points to note about this rubric in the context of the present discussion. The first is that it asserts that the manner in which the material is arranged (*er skipat*) is the way in which Snorri arranged it, which if true goes against the weight of codicological evidence I have just presented and suggests that the more

---

[29] Snorri Sturluson, *Edda: Skáldskaparmál*, ed. by Faulkes, I, p. xlvi; Snorri Sturluson, *Edda: Prologue and Gylfaginning*, ed. by Faulkes, p. xxx.

[30] He includes *Skáldatal* 'List of Skalds', a genealogy of the Sturlungar, a list of law-speakers down to Snorri, the *Second Grammatical Treatise*, and an incomplete version of *Háttatal*, which is separated from rest of the *Edda* text.

[31] Thorell, 'Inledning', p. x.

[32] It seems clear that the U redactor considered that the *Skáldskaparmál* proper began after the full-page illustration of Gylfi questioning the trinity of deities about their beliefs on fol. 26^v, because at the top of the next page (fol. 27^r) he begins the text with the rubric *Hér hefr skáldskapar mál ok heiti margra hluta* (Here begins the language of poetry and the names of many things).

[33] A normalized text is taken from Snorri Sturluson, *Edda: Prologue and Gylfaginning*, ed. by Faulkes, p. xiii, and the English translation from Snorri Sturluson, *Edda*, ed. and trans. by Faulkes, p. xxvi.

extended and better integrated narratives of R and W were the work, not of Snorri, but of later redactors. The second point is that, whereas whoever wrote the rubric had a name for the parts both he and we call *Skáldskaparmál* and *Háttatal*, he had no general term he could apply to the mythographical parts of the *Edda*, even though he, and only he of all the medieval redactors, records the name *Gylfaginning*, which we nowadays apply to that section of the *Edda*. It is in a rubric right at the end of the Prologue.[34] Alongside the codicological evidence presented earlier for the *Edda* being regarded primarily as a work of poetics in medieval Iceland, the U rubricator's inability to find a name for its mythological parts may suggest that the concept of a sustained account of the pre-Christian beliefs of his ancestors, and that of Icelanders generally, was something he was unfamiliar with.

There is also evidence from manuscripts A, B, and C, which contain parts of *Skáldskaparmál*, but no other sections of the *Edda* as witnessed by R, T, W, and U, together with a number of other texts, that various combinations of mythographical and poetic-pedagogical material were being experimented with by thirteenth-century Icelandic writers. Of particular interest here are a short account of the mythic wolf Fenrir in A and B, and the short text known in modern times as *Litla Skálda* 'Little Poetics' which precedes it in both these manuscripts. Judith Jesch has recently drawn attention to the interweaving of mythographical material with lists of kenning referents in *Litla Skálda* in a fashion different from the presentation of both kinds of material within versions of Snorri's *Edda*, and has suggested that *Litla Skálda* may represent a different compiler's use of mythographic and poetic material available both to himself and independently to Snorri Sturluson.[35] If so, the crucial breakthrough in the development of a systematic Old Norse mythography may have come when someone, presumably Snorri, began to isolate the mythographical material needed to understand Norse poetics and to treat it as a subject important in its own right, though still linked to the exposition of skaldic poetics and the kenning system.

In fact, the evidence of all *Edda* manuscripts supports the hypothesis that Snorri's originality was perhaps greater but less recognized by contemporaries in the area of mythography than in the field of poetics, especially when it came

---

[34] It reads (my normalized text of U, see Snorri Sturluson, *Snorre Sturlassons Edda Uppsala-Handskriften DG 11*, ed. by Grape and others, II, 3, ll. 18–20): 'Hér hefr Gylfaginning frá því er Gylfi sótti heim Alfǫðr í Ásgarð með fjǫlkyngi, ok frá villu ása ok frá spurningu Gylfa' (Here begins *Gylfaginning* concerning Gylfi's visit to the All-father in Ásgarðr by means of magic, and about the error [or 'delusion'] of the gods and Gylfi's questioning).

[35] Jesch, 'The Sea-Kings of *Litla Skálda*'.

to extended mythic narratives. The manuscripts in their present form also suggest that Snorri may not have fully worked out how to present his mythography. His use of a narrative frame to motivate the telling of myths and so keep him, the Christian puppet-master, at arm's length, is sporadic and not fully integrated with the rest of his subject-matter, especially in *Skáldskaparmál*. There are also differences between the manuscripts, particularly in *Skáldskaparmál*, in whether or not they back up the mythic narratives in prose with verse quotation. Again, U stands out as different from the other main witnesses, because it does not include citations of large blocks of several important mythological narrative poems which clearly formed the basis of some of the prose narratives. The prose narratives stand on their own, but the redactors of R, T, and W included the poetry as well, a gesture appropriate to a treatise on poetics, perhaps less so to one on myth. The inclusion of the poetry as well as the prose may have been something that evolved gradually in the *Edda*'s transmission history, and there are some signs that the poetry might not have been originally included in the exemplars of some manuscripts. For example, the mid-fourteenth-century copyist of W seems not to have known, or had to hand, a full text of the poem *Haustlǫng* (Autumn Long) by the late ninth-century Norwegian poet Þjóðólfr of Hvinir, because he does not include several stanzas, though he leaves a gap for them, presumably because he knew of their existence and wanted to include them, but had to find a text of them first (whether written or oral) or get someone else to add them.[36]

A pointer to the equivocal status of *Skáldskaparmál*, from a modern perspective, as a work pulled in the direction of mythography as well as of poetics, is the positioning in R, T, and W of the thirteen stanzas of *Haustlǫng* relating the myth of the giant Þjazi's abduction of the goddess Iðunn immediately after a list of typical kennings for this goddess rather than after the extended prose telling of the myth right at the beginning of *Skáldskaparmál*, where it would seem more satisfactorily placed to a modern reader, for whom narrative cohesion is an important criterion, and where it is located in manuscript U in shortened form. But there is a logic to its manuscript placement in R, T, W, from the perspective of poetic theory, as the stanzas certainly illustrate kennings for Iðunn.

Considered from several different perspectives, Snorri (and/or his later redactors)[37] had good reason to separate the myths narrated in *Gylfaginning* from

---

[36] Missing are stanza 11, l. 6–stanza 13, l. 8, and the location is p. 56. The question of whether specialist verse copyists were sometimes used for entering poetry in Icelandic manuscripts is outside the scope of this chapter, but it looks as though that might have been the case, at least sometimes.

[37] From this point in the chapter I will refer to Snorri alone as the originator of the changes

those told in *Skáldskaparmál*, as they are placed in R, T, and W. In the first place the myths of *Gylfaginning* are myths of cosmology, cosmogony and eschatology, while those told in *Skáldskaparmál* either concern the dealings of gods with giants, especially the combats of the god Þórr with various giants, or they narrate a number of heroic legends, predominantly in later sections, where Snorri appears to have had access to a source of Danish legendary history similar to the now-lost *Skjǫldunga saga* (Saga of the Skjǫldungar [Danish dynasty]). From the perspective of modern structural analysis, the developed myths of *Skáldskaparmál* largely belong on the horizontal axis of the Old Norse mythological world and encode a steady state of divine-giant interaction,[38] while the myths of *Gylfaginning* largely involve the vertical axis that treats of life, death, fate, and the hereafter. It is as if Snorri had an intuitive or an explicit awareness of this fundamental mythographical division.

He was certainly attuned to a less abstract divide between *Gylfaginning* and *Skáldskaparmál* which doubtless articulated a traditional chronological sense that *Gylfaginning* provided a witness to ancient times, whereas skaldic poetry reported the events of Norse myth obliquely, often through kennings. He expressed this divide in poetic terms: almost all the poetry quoted in *Gylfaginning* in support of the myths told there is in the Old Norse version of the anonymous, older, common Germanic alliterative verse-form, and is often placed in the mouths of supernatural beings as their speech. Most of the poetry in *Skáldskaparmál*, on the other hand, is in the metres of the skalds, poets of the ninth to the mid-twelfth centuries, many of whom were known to Snorri by name. The myths narrated there are primarily chosen to illustrate points of skaldic diction, particularly to explain obscure kennings, yet every now and then the mythographical temper, as it were, gets the better of the pedagogic, and an extended mythic narrative is created.

Snorri's mythography is grounded in native poetry throughout, except in the learned, mainly historically-based interpretations of the pre-Christian myths of Scandinavia he offers in the Prologue and parts of *Gylfaginning* and *Skáldskaparmál*. The whole structure of *Gylfaginning* depends on three poems of the so-called Poetic Edda, that is, mythological poems recorded in a late thirteenth-century collection of poetry in the older Germanic verse-form. These

that created an Old Norse mythography as well as a treatise on poetics, while admitting that whoever produced the exemplar of R, T, W (manuscripts that are very likely to have had a common source) may possibly have played a part in the developments that differentiate R, T, W from U and A, B, C.

[38] A distinction first enunciated in Meletinskij, 'Scandinavian Mythology as a System, ı', and Meletinskij, 'Scandinavian Mythology as a System, ıı'.

three poems are *Vǫluspá* (The Prophecy of the Sybil), *Vafþrúðnismál* (The Speech of Vafþrúðnir [a giant]) and *Grímnismál* (The Speech of Grímnir [a name of the god Óðinn])'. Other poems of this collection also influenced the form and content of *Gylfaginning*; for example, the opening scene where Gylfi, disguised as a traveller, enters the Æsir's hall, is partly based on the beginning of the poem *Hávamál* (Speech of the High One [Óðinn]), where it is the god Óðinn who speaks of how the traveller must be on his guard when entering strange halls. The delicious irony of this situation is lost on the obtuse Gylfi but would not have been lost on an audience literate in Norse poetry, whether oral or written. Moreover, the narrative incorporates a Christian perspective, which has been signalled in the Prologue, in such a way that the admittedly distorted outlines of a Christian theology are apparent through the detail of Norse myth, just as, in the Prologue, the theory of natural religions claimed that they should be.

Even when his poetic sources for a particular myth in *Gylfaginning* are as much skaldic as eddic, Snorri suppresses the skaldic material to make his narrative conform with the unspoken classificatory and chronological rules he must have set himself. The account of the death and funeral of the god Baldr, which occupies a key place in *Gylfaginning* and leads on directly to the events of Ragnarøkr, illustrates his practice. His main poetic sources were probably four: first *Vǫluspá*; second, an unknown poem in eddic form from which he quotes one stanza; third, the poem *Baldrs Draumar* (The Dreams of Baldr), an eddic poem extant only in a fragmentary manuscript of the *Edda* (A), which he does not quote but partly paraphrases; and fourth, the skaldic poem *Húsdrápa* (Poem with a refrain about a House) by the late tenth-century Icelander Úlfr Uggason, which he quotes in individual stanzas in several parts of *Skáldskaparmál* but not at all in *Gylfaginning*.[39]

Both eddic and skaldic poetry must have served Snorri as models for his extended prose mythic narratives, although more often than not, like much oral narrative, they tend to allude to myths rather than recount them in full Aristotelian mode, from beginning to end. As John Lindow has observed, there are other linguistic, stylistic and syntactic characteristics of skaldic poetry that get in the way of their telling a good story incorporating an initial situation, with developed characterization, action towards a climax, and resolution.[40] By contrast, Snorri's mythic narratives have all these characteristics and are often humorous to boot. In *Skáldskaparmál*, one of the motivating forces behind the creation

---

[39] For a fuller analysis, see Clunies Ross, 'Snorri's *Edda* as Medieval Religionsgeschichte'.

[40] Lindow, 'Narrative and the Nature of Skaldic Poetry'.

of extended mythic narratives is his expressed desire to explain the obscurities of skaldic language, and particularly kennings, to 'young poets', but the fully formed narratives that result go far beyond the merely pedagogical unpacking of kennings, which typically express an unnamed referent by means of a genitival yoking of two nouns, whose relationship is often only explicable in terms of a myth. Thus, to give an example, *Fróða mjǫl* (Fróði's meal) is a kenning for gold, because the legendary Danish king Fróði engaged a pair of giantesses to grind gold instead of flour from a magical mill. In *Gylfaginning*, on the other hand, the pedagogical motive is more general and diffused, and the mythography that results has a greater independence of its poetic sources, though in most cases they can be traced. *Gylfaginning* also offers a truly synthetic view of Norse myth, and this can be seen in numerous places where Snorri successfully reconciles conflicting sources or blends material he has obtained from more than one poetic source.

We do not know whether Snorri had any predecessors in the creation of a Norse mythography in prose, based largely on indigenous sources, mainly poetry, although short works like *Litla Skálda* may suggest that others experimented with the task. There is a fragment in a fourteenth-century manuscript, AM 162 M fol,[41] which clearly reflects some passages from *Gylfaginning*, possibly from memory, along with other learned material similar to what is in the Prologue to the *Edda*. However, in framing his indigenous mythography as an extended example of a natural religion and as applied euhemerism, Snorri was not alone, either within the Old Norse cultural milieu or in medieval Europe more generally. The conclusion to the *Íslendingabók* (Book of the Icelanders) by the early twelfth-century Icelandic historian Ari Þorgilsson shows that the linking of euhemerized Scandinavian dynasties with the Troy legend (or the Turks, as appears both here and in Snorri's text) was already in play nearly a century before Snorri,[42] and, as has already been mentioned, several versions of the popular medieval *Matter of Troy* seem to have been known in Iceland before the early thirteenth century. The substance of this euhemerized view of the Old Norse gods as immigrants into Scandinavia from Troy is much expanded in the legendary history of the kings of Norway, *Ynglinga saga*, which acts as the introduction to *Heimskringla* (Circle of the World), a historical work usually ascribed to Snorri and considered to have been written a little later than the *Edda*.

---

[41] The text was printed in Snorri Sturluson, *Edda* (1848–87), ii, 635–36, and in part by Stefán Karlsson, 'Ættbogi Noregskonunga', pp. 683–85.

[42] Ari Þorgilsson, *Íslendingabók*, ed. by Jakob Benediktsson, i, 27–28.

Snorri's Prologue was also influenced by another historicizing mode: the regnal list, the use of which was widespread in early medieval historiography.[43] Faulkes has shown that many of the names in the list of the euhemerized Óðinn's ancestors are of Old English origin, and the Prologue itself indicates that they are foreign but have Old Norse equivalents, as between Voden and Óðinn and Scialdun and Skjǫldr.[44] Snorri's Prologue follows closely an Icelandic regnal list whose closest counterpart is an English list in an Anglo-Saxon manuscript, Cotton Tiberius B v, fols 22–23, 'probably written at Christ Church Canterbury in the second quarter of the eleventh century'.[45] The Icelandic list exists now only in a post-medieval copy, but probably goes back to an exemplar that antedates Snorri's *Edda*. However, Snorri did not follow this list slavishly, but blended information in it with other genealogical and historical information available to him from works such as the now lost *Skjǫldunga saga*.

The presentation of Norse myth and beliefs in pagan gods as a natural religion, by means of which adherents grasp the essentials of Christianity without being possessed of spiritual wisdom, is also present in some medieval Icelandic sources, though never as fully developed as it is in Snorri's *Edda*. The Arnamagnaean manuscript AM 162 M fol, mentioned above, includes a brief passage on pagan religions as nature worship, which seems to be indebted to a passage on the lives of the Desert Fathers of the Christian Church.[46] There are numerous sagas and other texts that represent good men of the pre-Christian age as understanding that the world was created by a single deity, and anticipating the Christian virtues in their daily lives.[47] Some scholars have pointed to parallels between the *Edda* and medieval mythographers writing in Latin, like Fulgentius and the Second and Third Vatican Mythographers, while Dronke and Dronke suggested similarities between Snorri's non-polemical and non-moralistic attitude to his subject-matter and the stance of many Neoplatonist writers of the School of Chartres like William of Conches.[48] Undoubtedly, there are similarities with these Latin works, but no specific sources have been traced.

---

[43] For comparative Anglo-Saxon examples, see Fulk, 'Myth in Historical Perspective'.

[44] Faulkes, 'The Genealogies and Regnal Lists'.

[45] Faulkes, 'The Genealogies and Regnal Lists', p. 177.

[46] Stefán Karlsson, 'Ættbogi Noregskonunga', p. 679 n. 6, and references cited there.

[47] The classic treatment of the subject of the 'noble heathen' in Old Norse texts is Lönnroth, 'The Noble Heathen'.

[48] See Heusler, *Die gelehrte Urgeschichte*; Dronke and Dronke, 'The Prologue of the Prose *Edda*'; and Faulkes, 'Pagan Sympathy'.

A final ingredient in the learned perspective that Snorri offers on his *Edda* mythography comes from the medieval encyclopedic tradition, which was the major vehicle for the transmission of classical learning about the natural world and geographical lore in the Middle Ages. Some years ago I showed that, beginning with the section of the Prologue describing how the world was divided into three continents, there are many passages distributed throughout the *Edda*, particularly in *Gylfaginning*, that employ the medieval discourse of natural science to present aspects of the Norse myths Snorri was expounding.[49] Such a perspective is in accord with a view that saw men who had lost the name of God, as the Prologue has it, using their five senses to understand the nature of the cosmos. As a subject that included geography, the encyclopedic mode led easily into the euhemeristic account of the migration of the Norse Æsir out of Asia and into Europe.

I will conclude by situating Snorri's achievement in writing a systematic Norse mythology in the general context of Icelandic literary activity of the early thirteenth century, because only such a consideration allows one to understand how he was able to create extended and explicit prose narratives from what one must presume to have been his extensive knowledge of traditional Norse poetry and his understanding of its meaning, which required a knowledge of myths that may only rarely have been told in full, and perhaps had never previously achieved written form. If we are to believe literary historians, the late twelfth and early thirteenth centuries, Snorri's formative years, were times of intense literary creativity in Iceland which saw the development of the saga genre. The saga, like Snorri's *Edda*, was a prose form that incorporated poetry, but unlike the *Edda*, which was a predominantly didactic and educational work, sagas were largely for entertainment. They also told stories, and in some cases, like the *fornaldarsögur* (sagas of ancient time), turned narratives that were previously transmitted mainly in the form of eddic poetry, into prose. Snorri can be seen to be doing for Norse myth what the writers of the *fornaldarsögur* were doing for old heroic legends, like the story of the Danish king Hrólfr kraki 'Pole-ladder' (also known to the poet of *Beowulf*) or the legends of Sigurðr Fáfnisbani (Killer of Fáfnir), which were known throughout the Germanic world. Indeed, Snorri incorporates knowledge of both these and other heroic legends into the latter part of *Skáldskaparmál*.

The literary structures that appear in Snorri's mythic narratives are also reminiscent of some of the narrative structures of the Icelandic saga, including his skilful, externalized characterization of supernatural beings and his use of dialogue as well as third-person narrative. A distinctive feature of his narratives is his wry sense of humour, which sometimes descends to knockabout farce when the sub-

---

[49] Clunies Ross, *Skáldskaparmál*, pp. 151–73.

ject calls for it. Such a comic or ironic presentation of the Norse gods and their
giant adversaries is also to be found in both eddic and skaldic poetry, and was
probably a traditional Norse attitude. The fact that many of Snorri's mythic narratives, especially those in *Skáldskaparmál*, conform to Proppian folktale structures may suggest a common cultural substrate from which Old Norse myths and
later Scandinavian and other European folktales were generated.[50] It is indeed
possible that, when people in early Iceland and other parts of the Nordic world
did narrate myths in an oral non-poetic medium, they used what we call folktale
structures to do so.

Snorri's *Edda* is one of the most original works of the European Middle Ages,
as far as one can judge. It was original in its production of a coherent account of
Norse poetic practice, and that had an undoubted influence in Iceland during
and well beyond the Middle Ages. The *Edda*'s influence as a treatise on poetics outside Iceland has largely been felt from the nineteenth century onwards
and it continues to grow. It is mainly confined to scholars interested in medieval
poetry and literary theory and its terminology has been appropriated, rightly or
wrongly, by most scholars working on Germanic poetry in other languages like
Old English and Old and Middle High German, as it is the only such medieval
treatise in existence. Snorri's *Edda* as a work of mythography, by contrast, seems
not to have been particularly highly valued by his contemporaries, to judge by
the codicological evidence, but its importance began to be recognized as soon as
the mythographical parts were translated into Latin and disseminated to the educated world of Europe in the seventeenth century. It was not until the nineteenth
century, however, that a reliable text of the R manuscript appeared, and it was
not until the twentieth century that reliable, unbowdlerized and complete translations into key European vernaculars became available. Alongside these, many
partial translations, works of fantasy and so on have appeared in contest with or
in dialogue with Snorri's *Edda*, depending on one's point of view. Snorri's *Edda*
as mythography in all its guises and reinterpretations continues to grow and prosper. The full history of the reception of this remarkable Icelandic text has yet to
be written, and recently — and perhaps foolhardily — I have undertaken to write
it, with the help of other scholars.[51]

---

[50] See Clunies Ross and Martin, 'Narrative structures and Intertextuality'.

[51] The history of research into Snorri's *Edda* and its reception from the Middle Ages until
the present day will form part of a large project under the direction of the Snorrastofa, Reykholt,
Iceland, to re-evaluate the pre-Christian religions of the north.

Works Cited

Manuscript and Archival Documents

København, Arnamagnaean Collection, AM 242 fol (W, Codex Wormianus)
Reykjavík, Stofnun Árna Magnússonar í íslenzkum fræðum, AM 162 M fol
——, AM 748 I b 4° (A)
——, AM 748 II 4° (C)
——, AM 756 4°
——, AM 757 a 4° (B)
——, GKS 2367 4° (R, Codex Regius)
Uppsala, Uppsala University Library, De la Gardie 11 (U, Codex Upsaliensis)
Utrecht, Utrecht University Library, Traj 1374 (T, Codex Trajectinus)

Primary Sources

Ari Þorgilsson, *Íslendingabók*, ed. by Jakob Benediktsson, Íslenzk Fornritafélag, 1, 2 pts (Reykjavík: Hið íslenzka fornritafélag, 1968)
Lilja, ed. by Martin Chase, in *Poetry on Christian Subjects*, ed. by Margaret Clunies Ross, Skaldic Poetry of the Scandinavian Middle Ages, 7 (Turnhout: Brepols, 2008), pp. 554–677
Snorri Sturluson, *Edda*, ed. and trans. by Anthony Faulkes (London: Dent, 1987)
——, *Edda: Háttatal*, ed. by Anthony Faulkes (London: Viking Society for Northern Research, 1999)
——, *Edda: Prologue and Gylfaginning*, ed. by Anthony Faulkes, 2nd edn (London: Viking Society for Northern Research, 2005)
——, *Edda: Skáldskaparmál*, ed. by Anthony Faulkes, 2 vols (London: Viking Society for Northern Research, 1998)
——, *Edda Snorra Sturlusonar: Edda Snorronis Sturlæi*, 3 vols (Osnabrück: Zeller, 1966; orig. publ. København: Sumptibus Legati Arnamagnæani, 1848–87)
——, *Snorra-Edda: Ásamt Skáldu og þarmeð fylgjandi Ritgjörðum*, ed. by Rasmus Kr. Rask (Stockholm: Elménska prentsmiðja, 1818)
——, *Snorre Sturlassons Edda Uppsala-Handskriften DG 11*, ed. by Anders Grape and others, 2 vols (Uppsala: Almqvist och Wiksell International, 1977)
——, *The Uppsala Edda*, ed. by Heimir Pálsson (London: Viking Society for Northern Research, 2012)
——, *Two Versions of Snorra Edda from the 17th Century*, ed. by Anthony Faulkes, 2 vols (Reykjavík: Stofnun Árna Magnússonar, 1977–79)
[Thomas Percy], *Northern Antiquities: Or, a Description of the Manners, Customs, Religion and Laws of the Ancient Danes, and Other Northern Nations: Including Those of Our Own Saxon Ancestors. With a Translation of the Edda, or System of Runic Mythology, and Other Pieces from the Ancient Islandic Tongue*, 2 vols (London: Carnan, 1770)

——, *Northern Antiquities: Or, a Description of the Manners, Customs, Religion and Laws of the Ancient Danes, and Other Northern Nations: Including Those of Our Own Saxon Ancestors. With a Translation of the Edda, or System of Runic Mythology, and Other Pieces from the Ancient Islandic Tongue*, 2nd edn, 2 vols (Edinburgh: Stewart, 1809)

——, *Northern Antiquities: Or, a Description of the Manners, Customs, Religion and Laws of the Ancient Danes, and Other Northern Nations: Including Those of Our Own Saxon Ancestors. With a Translation of the Edda, or System of Runic Mythology, and Other Pieces from the Ancient Islandic Tongue*, rev. by I. A. Blackwell, 3rd edn, 2 vols (London: Bohn, 1847)

Secondary Studies

Clunies Ross, Margaret, *A History of Old Norse Poetry and Poetics* (Cambridge: Brewer, 2005)

——, *Skáldskaparmál: Snorri Sturluson's Ars Poetica and Medieval Theories of Language* (Odense: Odense University Press, 1987)

——, 'Snorri's *Edda* as Medieval *Religionsgeschichte*', in *Germanische Religionsgeschichte: Quellen und Quellenprobleme*, ed. by Heinrich Beck, Detlev Ellmers, and Kurt Schier (Berlin: Gruyter, 1992), pp. 633–55

Clunies Ross, Margaret, and B. K. Martin, 'Narrative Structures and Intertextuality in *Snorra Edda*: The Example of Þórr's Encounter with Geirrøðr', in *Structure and Meaning in Old Norse Literature: New Approaches to Textual Analysis and Literary Criticism*, ed. by John Lindow, Lars Lönnroth, and Gerd Wolfgang Weber (Odense: Odense University Press, 1986), pp. 56–72

Dronke, Ursula, and Peter Dronke, 'The Prologue of the Prose *Edda*: Explorations of a Latin Background', in *Sjötíu Ritgerðir: Helgaðar Jakobi Benediktssyni 20. Júlí 1977*, ed. by Einar G. Pétursson and Jónas Kristjánsson, Stofnun Árna Magnússonar á Íslandi, 12, 2 vols (Reykjavík: Stofnun Árna Magnússonar, 1977), I, 153–76

Eldevik, Randi, 'Trójumanna saga', in *Medieval Scandinavia: An Encyclopedia*, ed. by Phillip Pulsiano and others (New York: Garland, 1993), pp. 658–59

Faulkes, Anthony, 'Edda', *Gripla*, 2 (1977), 32–39

——, 'The Genealogies and Regnal Lists in a Manuscript in Resen's Library', in *Sjötíu Ritgerðir: Helgaðar Jakobi Benediktssyni 20. Júlí 1977*, ed. by Einar G. Pétursson and Jónas Kristjánsson, Stofnun Árna Magnússonar á Íslandi, 12, 2 vols (Reykjavík: Stofnun Árna Magnússonar, 1977), I, 177–90

——, 'Pagan Sympathy: Attitudes to Heathendom in the Prologue to *Snorra Edda*', in *Edda: A Collection of Essays*, ed. by Robert J. Glendinning and Haraldur Bessason, University of Manitoba Icelandic Studies, 4 (Winnipeg: University of Manitoba Press, 1983), pp. 283–314

——, 'Snorri Sturluson: His Life and Work', in *The Viking World*, ed. by Stefan Brink and Neil Price (London: Routledge, 2008), pp. 311–14

Fulk, R. D., 'Myth in Historical Perspective: The Case of Pagan Deities in the Anglo-Saxon Royal Genealogies', in *Myth: A New Symposium*, ed. by Gregory Schrempp and William Hansen (Bloomington: Indiana University Press, 2002), pp. 225–39

Heimir Pálsson, 'A Short Report from the Project on *Codex Upsaliensis* of *Snorra Edda*', in *Á austrvega: Saga and East Scandinavia: Preprint Papers of the 14th International Saga Conference Uppsala 9th–15th August 2009*, ed. by Agneta Ney and others, Institutionen för humaniora och samhällsvetenskaps skriftserie, 14, 2 vols (Gävle: Gävle University Press, 2009), I, 369–72

Heusler, Andreas, *Die gelehrte Urgeschichte im altisländischen Schrifttum* (Berlin: Abhandlungen der Königlichen Preussischen Akademie der Wissenschaften, 1908)

Jesch, Judith, 'The Sea-Kings of *Litla Skálda*', in *Á austrvega: Saga and East Scandinavia; Preprint Papers of the 14th International Saga Conference Uppsala 9th–15th August 2009*, ed. by Agneta Ney and others, Institutionen för humaniora och samhällsvetenskaps skriftserie, 14, 2 vols (Gävle: Gävle University Press, 2009), I, 443–51

Johansson, Karl G., *Studier i Codex Wormianus: skrifttradition och avskriftsversamhet vid ett isländskt skriptorium under 1300-talet*, Nordistica Gothoburgensia, 20 (Göteborg: Acta Universitatis Gothoburgensis, 1997)

Lindow, John, 'Narrative and the Nature of Skaldic Poetry', *Arkiv för nordisk filologi*, 97 (1982), 94–121

Lönnroth, Lars, 'The Noble Heathen: A Theme in the Sagas', *Scandinavian Studies*, 41 (1969), 1–29

Mallet, Paul-Henri, *Histoire de Dannemarc*, 2nd edn, 6 vols (Genève: [n. pub.], 1763)

——, *Introduction à l'histoire de Dannemarc, or l'on traite de la religion, des loix, des moeurs et des usages de anciens Danois* (København: [n. pub.], 1755)

——, *Monumens de la mythologie et de la poésie des Celtes et particulierement des anciens Scandinaves* (København: [n. pub.], 1756)

Meletinskij, Eleazar, 'Scandinavian Mythology as a System, I', *Journal of Symbolic Anthropology*, 1 (1973), 43–58

——, 'Scandinavian Mythology as a System, II', *Journal of Symbolic Anthropology*, 2 (1974), 57–78

Nordal, Guðrún, *Tools of Literacy: The Role of Skaldic Verse in Icelandic Textual Culture of the Twelfth and Thirteenth Centuries* (Toronto: University of Toronto Press, 2001)

Stefán Karlsson, 'Ættbogi Noregskonunga', in *Sjötíu Ritgerðir: Helgaðar Jakobi Benediktssyni 20. Júlí 1977*, ed. by Einar G. Pétursson and Jónas Kristjánsson, Stofnun Árna Magnússonar á Íslandi, 12, 2 vols (Reykjavík: Stofnun Árna Magnússonar, 1977), II, 677–704

Thorell, Olof, 'Inledning', in *Snorre Sturlassons Edda Uppsala-Handskriften DG 11*, ed. by Anders Grape and others, 2 vols (Uppsala: Almqvist och Wiksell International, 1977), II, pp. ix–xxi

Wanner, Kevin J., *Snorri Sturluson and the Edda: The Conversion of Cultural Capital in Medieval Scandinavia* (Toronto: University of Toronto Press, 2008)

Thor and the Midgard Serpent: Whom Should We Read, Snorri or Finnur?

Gísli Sigurðsson[*]

O
ne of the besetting problems of the study of ancient texts that tell of supernatural beings is the question of whether and to what extent these texts reflect traditional knowledge and belief and/or represent creative speculation on the part of a writer who may or may not have had 'genuine sources' to build on. We as scholars tend to exaggerate the distinction between the 'genuine and authentic tradition' and the 'distorted' sources we have to work with. The original, pristine oral 'golden age' lies beyond our reach, and we have no option but to make do with the written remains that have come down to us and which may, to a greater or lesser extent, reflect whatever went before them. But this involves a presupposition: what if the tradition never was 'original, authentic, and genuine', but was constantly changing and fluctuating, depending on the individuals who were part of it? The idea of a lost 'golden age' of 'authentic tradition' imperfectly reflected in subsequent texts may be beguiling. But is it justified? Perhaps the written sources should be treated as authentic reflections of the tradition in their own right, with their own 'authenticity' and to be treated on an equal footing with anything that might have been recorded a hundred, or two hundred, or three hundred years earlier. Tradition is, after all and by definition, never stable and thus constantly subject to change, interpretation and creativity.

* Gísli Sigurðsson (gislisi@hi.is) is Research Professor of Folklore at the Árni Magnússon Institute, University of Iceland, and the author of *The Medieval Icelandic Saga and Oral Tradition: A Discourse on Method*, trans. by Nicholas Jones (Cambridge, MA: Milman Parry Collection of Oral Literature, 2004), and many other works on Icelandic literature and Northern European cultural connections. Sincere thanks go to my friend Nicholas Jones who was kind enough to read this article in draft form and suggest a number of helpful improvements.

Writing Down the Myths, ed. by Joseph Falaky Nagy, CURSOR 17, (Turnhout: Brepols, 2013)
pp. 223–240   BREPOLS PUBLISHERS   10.1484/M.CURSOR-EB.1. 100854

In recent decades we have become increasingly aware of how deeply our knowledge and ideas about the past have been shaped by different ideologies and scholarly methods. This has led to re-evaluations in many fields, questioning the very foundations of our knowledge about the past and about the written sources that tell us about the past. Rather than acting as neutral gateways to the past, scholarly editions of ancient texts have often served as a barrier between us as modern readers and the sources they present, a barrier that is now being dismantled under the attack of scholars equipped with methods and ideas going back to the work of the New Philologists and sometimes revealing a very different picture of what the sources have to tell us from what had previously been assumed.

To take a striking example, all our thinking about one of the better known Old Norse mythological narratives — the story of Thor's fishing expedition with the giant Hymir — has been deeply coloured by Finnur Jónsson's edition of the corpus of extent skaldic poetry in his *Skjaldedigtning* and the way he presented and interpreted the various verses that refer to, or purport to refer to, this story.[1] In his edition, Finnur takes a number of verses, mostly preserved in a single place in Snorri Sturluson's *Edda*, and, based on Snorri's attribution of these verses to different named poets, rearranges them and ascribes them to different poems from different centuries. In some cases, Finnur 'reconstructs' longer poems of whose very existence we have no independent evidence. This rearrangement presupposes that we know the poetical remains of these skalds sufficiently well to interpret them as independent works of art. It also presupposes that Snorri knew whole poems from which he selected single stanzas or fragments to act as 'sources' for his prose narratives and as examples for his discussion of metrics and poetic diction.

The Hymir myth, if such we can call it, is attested in a range of sources: pictorial material on memorial stones and Eddic and skaldic poetry, as well as Snorri Sturluson's prose account in *Gylfaginning* (The Tricking of Gylfi), the first main section of the *Edda*. I have discussed these representations of the myth elsewhere and came to the conclusion that Snorri's account in *Gylfaginning* must have been based on a knowledge of the story that derived from both poetry and 'self-contained' oral prose narratives, and that these oral prose narratives must have had a long background in the tradition. Crucially, Snorri's account contains a significant detail that must be old — it is attested on a Viking-Age picture stone from Sweden — but which is not found in any of the extant verse, namely Thor's foot/feet breaking through the bottom of his boat.[2]

---

[1] *Den norsk-islandske skjaldedigtning*, ed. by Finnur Jónsson. Page references are to these two volumes, with textual citations from the normalized version in B1.

[2] Gísli Sigurðsson, *The Medieval Icelandic Saga*, trans. by Jones, pp. 6–17. On p. 10 the

While such considerations perhaps allow us to feel a degree of greater confidence in our sources, we need always to bear in mind how our ideas about these sources have been formed. To what extent are they based on the sources themselves? And to what extent on the interpretation of scholars and editors of later times? As a starting point, we need to ask ourselves whether we are justified in basing our conclusions on the way that the skaldic verses referring to Thor's fishing expedition are presented by Finnur Jónsson in *Skjaldedigtning* — as has been standard procedure among just about all scholars who have discussed this myth. Research based on Finnur's suppositions will naturally revolve around identifying different versions of the myth and arranging them chronologically to elicit various interpretations of its development. Analysis of this kind has tended to accept *a priori* Finnur's editorial presentation of the different poems, citing Finnur's reconstructions and even his verse numbers as if his texts were genuinely authentic primary sources, and therefore to ignore the only ancient source in which the verses actually appear, namely, Snorri's *Edda*. This approach needs questioning: in the case of Thor's fishing expedition, most of the verses that are generally cited as evidence of the regional and temporal distribution of the myth are found only in one place, in Chapter 12 of *Skáldskaparmál*,[3] the second main section of the *Edda*, where their primary function is to act as examples of 'Thor kennings'.[4] Relying on Finnur Jónsson's assignment of these verses to specific poems involves an act of faith in both Snorri and Finnur.

There can be no doubt that most of the verses cited in *Skáldskaparmál*, Chapter 12 do indeed refer to Thor's encounter with the Midgard Serpent,[5] a

---

story is summarized as follows: 'In this tale, Þórr uses a bull's head as bait for the world serpent Miðgarðsormr, which he catches and pulls up as far as the gunwales of the boat; but when god and serpent meet eye to eye and he raises his hammer to strike, Hymir cuts through the line and the serpent sinks back into the sea.' For an annotated edition of *Hymiskviða* with an introduction, see *Eddukvæði*, ed. by Gísli Sigurðsson, pp. 108–18.

[3] The chapter numbering follows the standard scholarly edition, Snorri Sturluson, *Edda*, ed. by Finnur Jónsson.

[4] Kennings are conventional metaphorical periphrases, for example, 'steed/horse/charger of the sea/ocean/waves' for 'ship', and are a central element of Old Norse poetic diction. The *Edda* is a handbook for poets and much of *Skáldskaparmál* consists of chapters illustrating how to 'kenna' different referents, for example, king, woman, the gods, horse, the sea.

[5] Old Norse *Miðgarðsormr*. *Miðgarðr* (Middle Earth) is the world of men, as opposed to, for instance, *Ásgarðr*, the world of the gods. *Ormr* is serpent (worm). The serpent also appears in Old Norse texts under the name of *Jǫrmungandr* and in English translations as 'the World Serpent', 'the World Snake', and so on. With a few conventional exceptions (Thor for Þórr, Midgard for Miðgarðr, etc.), names and quotations are given in standardized Old Norse orthography, other

story recounted earlier in the *Edda*, in *Gylfaginning*. It should be noted, however, that the verses are not preserved anywhere else. Their rearrangement and assignment to specific named poems outside their shared context in Snorri's *Edda* is entirely the work of modern scholars. This imposes an order and coherence on what are, in fact, a group of disparate verses found together in a single place and ostensibly with a different function. The modern editions present us with a possibly spurious picture of several different poets treating the same story at different times independent of each other. And this in turn has been used as the basis for research into the versions and dissemination of the myth in Old Norse society.

It therefore makes sense to look at the verses in their original and only medieval context before considering them independently or as fragments of longer poems reconstructed by modern editors. Focusing our attention on the *Edda* itself, and in particular on how the verses are presented in *Skáldskaparmál*, Chapter 12, we can start by asking if their order here is of any significance for their overall interpretation. In this, we might consider the formal or structural information that the verses have to convey about Thor kennings, and then go on to ask if their content is significant in any way — whether, for example, they form some kind of continuous narrative. If we look beyond this single chapter — that is, if we take in all the verses preserved in the *Edda* that are believed to refer to Thor's fishing expedition — we find that there are indeed a number of other verses that might have been included in Chapter 12 as containing examples of Thor kennings, but were presumably not cited there because they merely repeat information already found in Chapter 12, such as further examples of Thor being called 'enemy of giants', and thus add nothing to what Snorri has already said on the subject. If we suppose that there may be some kind of coherent structure to the way the verse fragments are presented in *Skáldskaparmál*, Chapter 12, we then need to account for any verses there that have hitherto been generally interpreted as referring to events other than the fishing expedition. We can ask whether these fragments too might in fact have some connection with the story, allowing for its many different variants — variants that genuinely existed, as we can see from the Eddic poem *Hymiskviða*. This line of questioning may lead ultimately to a hypothesis about an independent version of the myth reflected in the verses in *Skáldskaparmál*, Chapter 12, a version that at times runs counter to the prose narrative in *Gylfaginning* but may be complimented by other representations of the myth.

If we are justified in viewing Snorri as telling a continuous story through the verses he cites as examples of Thor kennings, then many of our received ideas

---

than that *þ* is transliterated *th* in the translations.

about his usage of 'sources' in *Gylfaginning* need to be questioned. Hitherto the general assumption has been that Snorri's prose account was entirely his own creation, constructed exclusively on his interpretation of the varied and often highly ambiguous verses to which he had access, as if all the verses came to him unsupported by additional knowledge in the form of stories and explanations. But we need always to bear in mind that this is an assumption and therefore open to question: Is it generally likely that the prose narratives of *Gylfaginning* originated in such interpretation of poetic 'sources'? Or might Snorri and some of his learned contemporaries have been able to tell (and/or dictate) their myths independently, without relying on poems as their 'sources'? Could they have told these stories 'by ear', so to speak, as opposed to telling them 'by heart'? Whether Snorri had access to such independent knowledge or not, it is of course beyond dispute that he often cites ancient poems to back up and support what he had to tell. The problem is that we have no way of going beyond Snorri and reconstructing poems that we know only from his fragmentary quotations of them.

The left-hand column below gives the opening of *Skáldskaparmál*, Chapter 12. It starts in the customary manner of many of the chapters of *Skáldskaparmál*, with the question: How do you make a kenning for Thor? The answers offered are italicized where they are supported by real examples in the verses that follow. The actual kennings themselves are set out in the right-hand column in order of appearance. In one case the kenning is marked '[?]' since it is open to question whether it really does exemplify one of the kenning types listed by Snorri in the introductory prose.[6] The English version is from the translation of Anthony Faulkes.[7]

Hvernig skal kenna Þór? Svá at kalla hann *son Óðins ok Jarðar; faðir Magna* ok Móða ok *Þrúðar, ver Sifjar, stjúpfaðir Ullar,* *stýrandi* ok eigandi Mjǫllnis ok megingjarða, Bilskirnis, verjandi Ásgarðs, Miðgarðs, *dólgr* ok *bani jǫtna ok trollkvinna, vegandi* Hrungnis, Geirrøðar, *Þrívalda,* drottinn Þjálfa ok Rǫskvu, dólgr Miðgarðsorms, fóstri Vingnis ok Hlóru.

'Viðris arfi', 'sonr Jarðar', 'faðir Magna', 'faðir Þrúðar', 'Sifjar rúni', 'Ulls mágr', 'œgir Qflugbǫrðu', 'gramr Bilskirnis', 'haussprengir Hrungnis', 'sundrkljúfr níu hǫfða Þrívalda', 'þrǫngvir kunnleggs kveldrunninna kvinna', 'hafra njótr' [?], 'fellir fjall-Gauts'.

How shall Thor be referred to? By calling him *son of Óðinn and Iord, father of Magni* and Modi and *Thrud, husband of Sif,*

'Vidrir's [Odinn's] heir', 'Iord's son', 'Magni's father', 'Thrud's father', 'Sif's beloved', 'Ull's relative',

---

[6] The prose text of Snorri's *Edda* used here is based on Snorri Sturluson, *Edda*, ed. by Heimir Pálsson. In this edition, my 'chap. 12' is numbered 11.

[7] Snorri Sturluson, *Edda*, ed. and trans. by Faulkes, p. 72.

stepfather of Ull, ruler and owner of Miollnir [the hammer] and the girdle of might, *of Bilskirnir,* defender of Asgard, Midgard, *enemy and slayer of giants and troll-wives, killer of Hrungnir,* Geirrod, *Thrivaldi,* lord of Thialfi and Roskva, enemy of the Midgard Serpent, foster-son of Vingnir and Hlora. (72) 'Oflugbardi's terrifier', 'Bilskirnir's lord', 'Hrungnir's skull-splitter', 'cleaver apart of Thrivaldi's nine heads', 'oppressor of the kinfolk [trolls] of evening-faring women [troll-wives]', 'goat possessor' [?], 'fell-Gaut's [giant's] feller'.

The first obvious indication of systematization is that Snorri tries to arrange the poetic examples so as to match the order of the kenning types listed in the prose introduction. But this does not explain everything. First, more than one kenning is cited in which Thor is described as the enemy and slayer of giants and troll women. The reference to Thor's hall, Bilskirnir, appears to be placed earlier in the prose than in the exemplary verses that follow — unless the apparent discrepancy can be explained by some unknown story associated with the hammer Mjǫllnir (mentioned in the prose before Bilskirnir) and the name Qflugbarði (which occurs elsewhere only in the feminine, Qflugbarða, as the name of a troll woman). Second, the prose introduction makes no mention of the possibility of referring to Thor as the 'possessor of goats', although a verse is included where he is called precisely this.

Another obviously systematic feature is that Snorri starts with kennings based on Thor's family and relationships to other beings before going on to kennings based on his deeds and accomplishments, most notably his hostility to the giants — again with some indeterminacy surrounding the reference to Bilskirnir.

From these initial observations it seems fair to conclude that Snorri was deliberately attempting to systematize his presentation of the kenning types and the order of his verse examples. He has attempted to set his knowledge within some kind of defined framework rather than citing stanzas that refer to Thor at random as they came into his mind. Such planning is perhaps not surprising but it provides grounds for continuing the questioning and asking ourselves whether, while arranging the poems in this order, Snorri perhaps also gave thought to the content of the verses. Snorri probably had no difficulty understanding the verses, or, at least, far less than modern readers. So it is not straining credibility to imagine that he might also have given consideration to what the verses actually said when selecting suitable examples for quotation. We can ask ourselves, are the verses thematically connected and perhaps arranged to form a narrative of their own? Or is their content irrelevant?

With this possibility in mind it is worth looking more closely at the verse fragments cited by Snorri in his chapter on Thor kennings in *Skáldskaparmál*. All these verses are found in all the manuscripts, with some minor variations that need not concern us here. The text is as follows, with footnotes summarizing Finnur Jónsson's comments in *Skjaldedigtning* on the provenance of the individual verses and skalds.

Svá kvað Bragi skáld:[8] Vaðr lá Viðris arfa | vilgi slakr, es rakðisk, | á Eynæfis ǫndri, | Jǫrmungandr at sandi.

Svá kvað Ǫlvir hnúfa:[9] Œstisk allra landa | umbgjǫrð ok sonr Jarðar.

Svá kvað Eilífr:[10] Vreiðr stóð Vrǫsku bróðir, | vá gagn faðir Magna; | skelfra Þórs né Þjálfa | þróttar steinn við ótta.

Ok sem kvað Eysteinn Valdason:[11] Leit á brattrar brautar | baug hvassligum augum, | œstisk áðr at flausti | ǫggs búð, faðir Þrúðar.

Enn kvað Eysteinn:[12] Sín bjó Sifjar rúni | snarla, framm, með karli, | hornstraum getum Hrímnis | hrœra, veiðarfœri.

Ok enn kvað hann:[13] Svá brá viðr, at (sýjur), | seiðr (rendu framm breiðar) | jarðar, út at borði | Ulls mágs hnefar skullu.

Svá kvað Bragi:[14] Hamri fórsk í hœgri | hǫnd, þás allra landa, | œgir ǫflugbarða, | endiseiðs of kendi.

Svá kvað Gamli:[15] Þás gramr, hinns svik samðit, | snart Bilskirnis, hjarta, | grundar fisk með grandi | gljúfrskeljungs nam rjúfa.

Svá kvað Þorbjǫrn dísarskáld:[16] Þórr hefr Yggs með árum | Ásgarð af þrek varðan.

---

[8] Norwegian, *c.* 800–850: *Den norsk-islandske skjaldedigtning*, ed. by Finnur Jónsson, p. 1, *Ragnarsdrápa*, stanza 16.

[9] Norwegian, ninth century: *Den norsk-islandske skjaldedigtning*, ed. by Finnur Jónsson, p. 6.

[10] Eilífr Goðrúnarson, Icelandic, *c.* 1000: *Den norsk-islandske skjaldedigtning*, ed. by Finnur Jónsson, pp. 144–52.

[11] Icelandic, *c.* 1000: *Den norsk-islandske skjaldedigtning*, ed. by Finnur Jónsson, pp. 131–40. Finnur places this stanza after the next one by Eysteinn.

[12] Stanza 1 in *Den norsk-islandske skjaldedigtning*, ed. by Finnur Jónsson, pp. 131–40. Finnur justifies his reordering of the two verses ascribed to Eysteinn on the grounds that Thor would have prepared his fishing tackle before coming face to face with the serpent. This is possible but by no means certain: fishermen commonly set their line only when they have good reason to believe that there is something to be caught.

[13] Stanza 3 in *Den norsk-islandske skjaldedigtning*, ed. by Finnur Jónsson, pp. 131–40. The verse describes the moment when the serpent takes the bait, referred to by fishermen as a 'strike'.

[14] *Den norsk-islandske skjaldedigtning*, ed. by Finnur Jónsson, p. 3, *Ragnarsdrápa*, stanza 15, placed immediately before 'Vaðr lá Viðris arfa...' (see above, n. 8).

[15] Gamli 'gnævaðarskáld', Icelandic, tenth century: *Den norsk-islandske skjaldedigtning*, ed. by Finnur Jónsson, pp. 132–40.

[16] Icelandic, late tenth century: *Den norsk-islandske skjaldedigtning*, ed. by Finnur Jónsson, pp. 135–40. Most editors do not interpret this stanza in connection with the fishing expedition, but in view of the present hypothesis it might be read as a general reiteration of Thor's role as defender of the gods.

Svá kvað Bragi:[17] Ok borðróins barða | brautar þvengr enn ljóti | á haussprengi Hrungnis | harðgeðr neðan starði.

Enn kvað Bragi:[18] Vel hafið yðrum eykjum | aptr, Þrívalda, haldit | simbli sumbls of mærum, | sundrkljúfr níu hǫfða.

Svá kvað Eilífr:[19] Þrøngvir gein við þungum | þangs rauðbita tangar | kveldrunninna kvinna | kunnleggs alinmunni.

Svá kvað Bragi:[20] Þjokkvaxinn kvezk þykkja | þiklingr firinmikla | hafra njóts at hǫfgum | hætting megindrætti.

Svá kvað Úlfr:[21] Fullǫflugr lét fellir | fjall-Gauts hnefa skjalla | (ramt mein vas þat) reyni | reyrar leggs við eyra;

Enn kvað Úlfr: Víðgymnir laust Vimrar | vaðs af fránum naðri | hlusta grunn við hrǫnnum. | Hlaut innan svá minnum.[22]

(The poet Bragi said this: Vidrir's [Odin's] heir's [Thor's] line lay by no means slack on Eynæfir's ski [boat] when Iormungand uncoiled on the sand.

Olvir Hnúfa said this: The encircler of all lands [Midgard Serpent] and Iord's son became violent.

Eilif said this: Roskva's brother [Thialfi] stood enraged, Magni's father struck a victorious blow. Neither Thor nor Thialfi's power-stone [heart] shakes with terror.

---

[17] *Ragnarsdrápa*, stanza 17 in *Den norsk-islandske skjaldedigtning*, ed. by Finnur Jónsson, following 'Vaðr lá Viðris arfa'. See above, nn. 8 and 14.

[18] Categorized in *Den norsk-islandske skjaldedigtning*, ed. by Finnur Jónsson, among uncertain verses (ubestemmelige vers). Finnur is unable to provide a satisfactory explanation for the (presumed) kenning 'of mœrum simbli sumbls' (notorious giant-feast drinker). It may be possible to see here a reference to the kettle that Thor is supposed to be fetching in the version of the story in *Hymiskviða*.

[19] Finnur Jónsson assigns this verse to *Þórsdrápa* as stanza 16 in the belief that it refers to the moment when Thor catches a piece of glowing iron on his visit to Geirrøðr. Anthony Faulkes accepts this interpretation in his translation.

[20] The Uppsala manuscript of the *Edda* ascribes this verse to Úlfr Uggason (Uppsala, Uppsala UL, De la Gardie 11). This is followed in *Den norsk-islandske skjaldedigtning*, ed. by Finnur Jónsson, pp. 128–37, where it is assigned as *Húsdrápa*, stanza 3.

[21] *Den norsk-islandske skjaldedigtning*, ed. by Finnur Jónsson, pp. 128–37, *Húsdrápa*, stanza 6, interpreted by Finnur Jónsson as describing how Thor strikes first Hymir and then the Midgard Serpent.

[22] After this final quatrain Snorri adds that 'Víðgymnir of Vimr's ford' is a kenning for Thor. Snorri's note is perhaps motivated by the fact that it does not match any of the kenning types listed in the introductory prose.

And as Eystein Valdason said: Thrud's father looked with piercing eyes on steep-way's [land's] ring [Midgard Serpent] until the red-fish's dwelling [sea] surged over the boat.

Eystein also said: Sif's beloved quickly brought out his fishing gear with the old fellow. We can stir Hrimnir's [giant's] horn-flow [mead].

And he also said: The coal-fish of the earth [Midgard serpent] responded thus, that Ull's relative's [Thor's] fists banged out on the gunwale; broad planks pushed forward.

Bragi said this: Oflugbardi's terrifier [Thor] lifted his hammer in his right hand when he recognized the coal-fish that bounds all lands [the Midgard serpent].

Gamli said this: While Bilskirnir's lord, who never nursed treachery in his heart, did quickly destroy the sea-bed-fish [Midgard serpent] with gorge-whale's [giant's] bane [the hammer Miollnir].

Thorbiorn Disarskald said this: Thor has with Ygg's [Odin's] angels [the Æsir] defended Asgard with might.

Bragi said this: And the ugly ring [serpent] of the side-oared ship's road [sea] stared up spitefully at Hrungnir's skull-splitter.

Bragi also said: Well have you, cleaver apart of Thrivaldi's nine heads, held back your steeds with notorious giant-feast drinker [Thrym = thunder].

Eilif said this: The oppressor [Thor] of the kinfolk [trolls] of evening-faring women [troll-wives] yawned with his arm's mouth [fist] over the heavy red lump of tong-weed [iron].

Bragi said this: The stockily built stumpy one [Hymir] is said to have thought tremendous danger in the goat-possessor's [Thor's] enormous heavy haul.

Ulf said this: The most mighty fell-Gaut's [giant's] feller made his fist crash on the reed-bed-bone [rock] frequenter's [giant's] ear. A mighty hurt was that.)

Ulf also said: Vidgymnir of Vimur's ford struck the ear-bed [head] from the shining snake by the waves. Within [on the walls of the house] have appeared these motifs.[23])

At this point Snorri ends his catalogue of the kennings used to refer to Thor and the verse fragments cited to exemplify them.

Elsewhere in the *Edda* Snorri quotes five other verse fragments that have also been interpreted as referring to Thor's fishing expedition, two ascribed to Úlfr Uggason and three to Bragi the Old. The first of Úlfr's stanzas is in fact cited twice: in *Skáldskaparmál*, Chapter 71 as an example of *frón* as a synonym for Jǫrð (Earth), and in Chapter 59 as an example of the construction of man kennings with tree names as their 'head word': in Snorri's words, a man can be called 'reynir vápna eða víga, ferða ok athafnar, skipa ok alls þess er hann ræðr ok reynir' (rowan

---

[23] Snorri Sturluson, *Edda*, ed. and trans. by Faulkes, pp. 72–74.

(*reynir*) of weapons or battles, of expeditions and activities, of ships, and of everything he has in his power or puts to the test (*reynir*)). Finnur Jónsson assigns this verse to *Húsdrápa* as stanza 5: 'En stirðþinull starði | storðar leggs fyr borði | fróns á folka reyni | fránleitr ok blés eitri' (But the sharp-looking stiff earthrope [Midgard serpent] stared over the gunwale at country-bone-[rock-]folk's [giants'] tester/rowan [Thor] and blew poison).[24] The second 'Hymir-myth' verse outside *Skáldskaparmál*, Chapter 12 ascribed to Úlfr is found in only one manuscript, the Codex Wormianus, where it is presented as an example of how the head and eyes can be referred to in terms of the sky and heavenly bodies.[25] Finnur assigns this verse to *Húsdrápa* as stanza 4:

> Innmáni skein ennis | ǫndótts vinar banda; | áss skaut œgigeislum | orðsæll á men storðar.

> (The in-laid moon of the forehead [eye] of the terrifying friend of the gods [Thor] shone; the well-known god shot frightening rays on the ground's lace [serpent] (my translation).)

The verse that Finnur assigns as stanza 19 of Bragi the Old's *Ragnarsdrápa* is lacking in the Uppsala manuscript of Snorri's *Edda*. In Chapter 77 of *Skáldskaparmál* it is cited following a list of the daughters of the sea deities Rán and Ægir which gradually changes into a list of marine features such as *vágr* (bay):

> Vildit vrǫngum ofra | vágs hyrsendir ægi, | hinn's mætygil máva | mœrar skar fyr Þóri.

> (Breeze-sender [giant, Hymir], who cut the thin string [fishing-line] of gulls' Møre [the sea] for Thor, did not want to lift the twisted bay-menacer [Midgard serpent].[26])

The verse placed by Finnur as stanza 18 of *Ragnarsdrápa* is also lacking in the Uppsala manuscript. In Chapter 52 of *Skáldskaparmál* in the other manuscripts it is cited to illustrate a kenning for 'poison' as the 'drink of the Volsungs' (Sigmundr Vǫlsungsson could drink poison without being harmed):

> Þás forns Litar flotna | á fangboða ǫngli | hrøkkviáll of hrokkinn | hekk Vǫlsunga drekku.

> (When on the hook of the old Lit's men's [giants'] fight-challenger [Thor] hung the coiling eel [Midgard serpent] of the Volsungs' drink [poison] coiled.[27])

---

[24] Snorri Sturluson, *Edda*, ed. and trans. by Faulkes, p. 116.

[25] See Snorri Sturluson, *Edda* (1848–87), ii, 499.

[26] Snorri Sturluson, *Edda*, ed. and trans. by Faulkes, p. 142.

[27] Snorri Sturluson, *Edda*, ed. and trans. by Faulkes, p. 106.

The first verse in the *Edda* that refers to the fishing expedition occurs in Chapter 10 of *Skáldskaparmál*, shortly before the main section on Thor kennings, where it is used to exemplify one of the well-known names (*heiti*)[28] for Óðinn, namely *Aldafǫðr* (Father of Mankind). Snorri's rubric ascribes it to Bragi, and Finnur places it as *Ragnarsdrápa*, stanza 14:

> Þat erum sýnt, at snimma | sonr Aldafǫðrs vildi | afls við úri þœfðan | jarðar reist of freista.

> (It is conveyed to me that the son [Thor] of the father of mankind [Odin] was determined soon to test his strength against the water-soaked earth-band [Midgard serpent].[29])

So, if there is anything to the idea that in Chapter 12 of *Skáldskaparmál* Snorri is recounting the story of Thor and the Midgard Serpent through a coherent set of poetic examples, why are these five fragments not included there? Two possible explanations suggest themselves: first, the verses in question do not contain kennings referring to Thor and are therefore redundant to the primary function of the chapter; and, second, the content of these five fragments is covered in the fragments that are included in Chapter 12 and might therefore have been omitted as having nothing new to add to the story.

In both the fragments attributed to Úlfr ('En stirðþinull starði' and 'Innmáni skein ennis') we find Thor kennings formed in a traditional way. (Note that the first of these is used twice in *Skáldskaparmál* to illustrate both a *heiti* and a kenning, so Snorri may have felt that he had already made full use this stanza.) Both these verses refer to the moment when Thor and the serpent come face to face and look into each other's eyes. This topos is already well illustrated by the verses included in Chapter 12, and further exemplification by the two Úlfr fragments would therefore be superfluous.

In the Bragi verse that Finnur Jónsson makes *Ragnarsdrápa*, stanza 19 ('Vildit vrǫngum ofra'), Thor is mentioned directly by name, so the stanza is irrelevant to Snorri's discussion of Thor kennings. Stanza 18 ('Þás forns Litar flotna') is another matter. At first sight this stanza fits in well with the examples cited in Chapter 12, if we are justified in taking *fangboði flotna forns Litar* as a kenning referring to Thor.[30] From the point of view of content, however, it adds little to the informa-

---

[28] *Heiti* are poetic synonyms along the lines of 'charger', 'steed' for horse.

[29] Snorri Sturluson, *Edda*, ed. and trans. by Faulkes, p. 69.

[30] Aage Kabell, 'Der Fischfang Þórs', points out that *litr* appears as a *heiti* for 'ox' in the *þulur* (metrical lists) recorded in Snorri's *Edda*. This may thus suggest a connection with the Midgard Serpent story here, since Thor's bait on his fishing expedition consisted of an ox's head.

tion given by the verses in Chapter 12 ascribed to Eysteinn and Bragi ('Svá brá viðr, at (sýjur)' and 'Hamri fórsk í hœgri'). The reader has in effect already been told: 'When the serpent was coiled on Thor's hook the fists hit the gunwale and/ or Thor raised his hammer'. There is no need to say it again.

What then of the Bragi stanza ('Þat erum sýnt, at snimma') that Finnur assigns to *Ragnarsdrápa*, stanza 14, setting it as an introductory verse to the entire episode? Why is this not included in Chapter 12? To all appearances — in line with Finnur's analysis — this stanza might serve rather well as an opening statement if Snorri's intention here is indeed, at least in part, to present an independent narrative. It would also mirror neatly the final stanza cited by Snorri in Chapter 12: both Bragi's 'Þat erum sýnt, at snimma' and Úlfr's 'Hlaut innan svá minnum' come from poems alluding to visual representations of ancient stories — in Bragi's case a pictorial shield, in Úlfr's, carvings in interior panelling. Contextually, therefore, Bragi's stanza would be fully appropriate as the first example in Chapter 12, and we can only speculate as to why Snorri chose not to cite it here: possibly because the lines had been used earlier to exemplify the Óðinn name Aldafǫðr; possibly because Chapter 12 already contains an example of a kenning for Thor as Óðinn's son in the first verse cited ('Vaðr lá Viðris arfa'). This would have left Snorri with the option of either giving two examples of the same type of kenning or else omitting 'Vaðr lá Viðris arfa' in favour of a fragment that he had already used in another context, something he may have been reluctant to do.

The next question we need to ask ourselves concerns the verses quoted in *Skáldskaparmál*, Chapter 12, that editors have generally interpreted as referring to stories other than Thor's fishing expedition. Is there any way they can be read to fit in with this story? And if so, how do we explain the discrepancies between the version that can be read out of the verse examples in *Skáldskaparmál* and Snorri's prose account of the story in *Gylfaginning*? Of the verse fragments quoted in *Skáldskaparmál*, Chapter 12, three have been almost unanimously interpreted in terms of other tales and myths, two ascribed to Eilífr, and one to Bragi. (The verse 'Þórr hefr Yggs með árum' ascribed to Thorbjǫrn dísarskáld is not generally interpreted in the context of the Midgard Serpent story — calling Thor the defender of the gods is so general that it could have been applied to any of his adventures.)

[Svá kvað Eilífr:] Vreiðr stóð Vrǫsku bróðir, | vá gagn faðir Magna; | skelfra Þórs né Þjálfa | þróttar steinn við ótta.

(Roskva's brother [Thialfi] stood enraged, Magni's father struck a victorious blow. Neither Thor nor Thialfi's powerstone [heart] shakes with terror.[31])

---

[31] Snorri Sturluson, *Edda*, ed. and trans. by Faulkes, p. 72.

[Enn kvað Bragi:] Vel hafið yðrum eykjum | aptr, Þrívalda, haldit | simbli sumbls of mærum, | sundrkljúfr níu hǫfða.

(Well have you, cleaver-apart of Thrivaldi's nine heads, held back your steeds with notorious giant-feast drinker [Thrym = thunder].[32])

[Svá kvað Eilífr:] Þrøngvir gein við þungum | þangs rauðbita tangar | kveldrunninna kvinna | kunnleggs alinmunni.

(The oppressor [Thor] of the kinfolk [trolls] of evening-faring women [troll-wives] yawned with his arm's mouth [fist] over the heavy red lump of tong-weed [iron].[33])

The first verse ascribed to Eilífr is Snorri's third exemplary verse in *Skáldskaparmál*, Chapter 12. It is generally read as belonging to his poem *Þórsdrápa*, which tells the story of Thor's journey with the boy Þjálfi to the home of the giant Geirrøðr. The stanza does not however appear in the long, continuous quotation from *Þórsdrápa* (19 stanzas) found in *Skáldskaparmál*, Chapter 26, in three of the four vellum manuscripts of the *Edda*. It is interesting that the final two lines ('skelfra Þórs né Þjálfa | þróttar steinn við ótta') are essentially identical to the final lines of stanza 10 in the long quotation in Chapter 26: 'Skalfa Þórs né Þjálfa | þróttar steinn við ótta'. In his reconstruction Finnur includes the verse from Chapter 12 as the concluding stanza to the entire poem, which is in itself indicative of how poorly it fits into the story as given in the long quotation in Chapter 26. Another possibility might therefore be to read this stanza as coming from a version of the fishing story similar to the one found in the Eddic poem *Hymiskviða*, in which Thor visits Þjálfi's parents on his way to the giant Hymir. In the context of *Hymiskviða* (which is independent of the prose account given in *Gylfaginning*) it is completely natural to assume that Þjálfi took some part in the fishing expedition. The stanza might therefore be read as reflecting a version of the story in which Þjálfi provided Thor with support on his journey to Hymir.

The second 'non-Hymir' verse in *Skáldskaparmál*, Chapter 12, 'Vel hafið yðrum eykjum', is ascribed to Bragi. In the previous verse, also ascribed to Bragi, we are told that the serpent stared up at Thor from the waters. 'Vel hafið yðrum eykjum' is notoriously obscure — in his edition Finnur places it among the 'uncertain verses' (ubestemmelige vers) — and the consensus has been to read it in contexts other than the Hymir story as known from *Gylfaginning*. The verse seems to include a reference to Thor's goats — 'eyki' is a draught animal, and Thor's chariot

---

[32] Snorri Sturluson, *Edda*, ed. and trans. by Faulkes, p. 73.
[33] Snorri Sturluson, *Edda*, ed. and trans. by Faulkes, p. 74.

was traditionally drawn by goats — but the kenning 'mæran simbli sumbls' has defied fully satisfactory explanation. Perhaps we can turn again to *Hymiskviða* for help in understanding what is going on. According to the Eddic poem, Thor's journey starts as a mission to fetch a cauldron in which to prepare drink (sumbl) for a feast that Ægir is planning for the gods. Thor sets off from Ásgarðr in his goat-chariot for the home of Hymir, the owner of the cauldron. It is therefore by no means inconceivable that the references to the goats and to 'simbli sumbls', whatever that may mean, may allow us to interpret the verse in terms of Thor's journey to the giant Hymir. Two stanzas later, another fragment ascribed to Bragi (or in one manuscript to Úlfr) contains the kenning for Thor, 'hafra njótr' (goat possessor). In this case there is no doubt about the connection with the fishing expedition. Whatever else, it confirms that in at least one version of the story Thor had his goats somewhere nearby when he went out fishing with Hymir.

The third and final stanza of those that are not usually associated with the fishing expedition, 'Þrøngvir gein við þungum', is generally explained as referring to an incident on Thor's visit to the giant Geirrøðr, when he has to catch a red-hot iron (þungan rauðbita tangar þangs) with his arm-mouth (alinmunni), that is to say his hand. On the basis of this interpretation, Finnur assigns the verse to his reconstruction of *Þórsdrápa* as stanza 16, despite the fact mentioned earlier that it does not appear in the continuous long quotation from *Þórsdrápa* found in three of the manuscripts of *Skáldskaparmál*, Chapter 26. Finnur's interpretation of the stanza is not implausible. But other readings are perhaps possible, taking account of the general context of the verses cited in *Skáldskaparmál*, Chapter 12: the natural interpretation of the verbal phrase *gína við* is 'to gape at', used prototypically of a mouth open wide to take a bait, while *rauðbita* means most literally 'red bite'. Finnur interprets this as part of a metaphor extended further in arm-mouth (alinmunni), that is to say Thor's hand (arm-mouth) catching (swallowing) the red-hot iron. However, it is possibly more natural to see here a more literal interpretation, with the being that is gaping wide at the 'red bite/bit' as the serpent snatching at the bloody ox head on Thor's line. For all its attractiveness, however, it is hard to interpret the rest of the stanza in terms of this image.

We thus have some justification for reading all three of the 'doubtful' verses in *Skáldskaparmál*, Chapter 12 as at least hinting towards the story of Thor's fishing expedition with the giant Hymir. If we then read all the verses cited in *Skáldskaparmál*, Chapter 12 as constituting a continuous narrative, the following storyline emerges (with the reservation that not all the verses have been satisfactorily interpreted in every detail, even if their general meaning is reasonably clear):

— Thor's line was not slack when the Midgard Serpent was pulled up.

— The serpent and Thor became excited. Thjálfi was angry, Thor was successful, and neither was afraid. Thor looked with piercing eyes at the serpent
and the sea came in over the sides of the boat. Thor prepared his tackle. (I
make poetry.) The Midgard Serpent's strike was such that Thor's fists hit
the gunwale. The broad ship was pulled forward. Thor took his hammer
in his right hand when he felt the serpent secure on the hook and gave it
a mighty blow. (Thor has protected Ásgarðr.) The ugly serpent glared up
at Thor from below. (Thor did well with his steeds and the cauldron.) The
serpent was tricked by Thor's bloody bait. The giant lost his nerve in the
face of Thor's great catch. Thor gave the giant a mighty blow with his fist
and struck the serpent's head in the waves.

— These are the images that appear here.

This kind of reading of the verse fragments in Chapter 12 leads to the following
conclusions and questions:

— Thor is accompanied by Thjálfi (as in *Hymiskviða*).

— Thor sees the serpent in the sea and sets his tackle before the serpent
strikes at or swallows the bait.

— Thor hits the serpent twice.

— Hymir panics but we are not told directly if he cuts Thor's line
(as in *Gylfaginning*).

— There is a connection with a cauldron (as in *Hymiskviða*).

— The story is adorned with references to the art and practice of poetry,
Thor's role as protector of the gods, and his success.

— The events are summarized at the end.

— It is unclear whether Thor kills the serpent.

This storyline does not explain all the verses in every detail but, viewed overall, it seems well possible that the poetic fragments cited in *Skáldskaparmál*,
Chapter 12, are meant to form a thematic whole in addition to acting as examples
of two main types of Thor kennings. If so, this would not be a unique instance of
a medieval text being adapted to serve a dual function.

In conclusion then, it seems reasonable to believe that, in addition to their
primary function of illustrating the kinds of kennings that can be used to refer to
Thor in Old Norse skaldic verse, there is an observable tendency to arrange the
sample verses into a thematic narrative order. This raises the question of whether

we are justified in viewing the whole of the *Edda* in this way — whether our understanding of the *Edda* can be enhanced by assuming that the order of the verses cited primarily as illustrative examples of technical aspects of poetics are also arranged with a view to their content. There is much to be said in favour of such an approach. This way we are considering the verses in their original and authentic context rather than second-hand, through the rearranged and reordered constructs of modern scholars who have assigned the individual verses, often on arbitrary grounds, to different poems from different centuries — in the way exemplified by Finnur Jónsson in *Den norsk-islandske skjaldedigtning*. It seems far more advisable to consult the primary source first in our attempt to understand the role of verse in medieval Iceland, rather than to start our analysis with the edited reconstructions, even though they may at times be more readable.

Snorri's prose account of Thor's fishing expedition in *Gylfaginning*, however, cannot have been built entirely upon the 'poetic sources' as we know them from *Hymiskviða* and the skaldic fragments discussed in this paper. This gives us reason to question the received model of Snorri's working practice — of a learned scholar collating and systematizing for the first time fragmentary learning that he found scattered among disparate poetic sources. It seems altogether more natural to assume that he knew both poems and stories. The prose accounts he gives us in the *Edda* should therefore be treated on an equal footing as sources to the poetry he cites to exemplify them — which of course says nothing about how 'authentic' or 'genuine' they are as evidence of religious and mythological thinking in the pre-Christian North.

If we view the *Edda* with this model in mind we need hardly be surprised if there are discrepancies between what Snorri says in different places. If there was still a range of stories and poems about the gods and their activities in oral circulation at the time when Snorri was writing — all of them, presumably, reflecting both earlier beliefs and the perceptions of people at the time — then we have little chance of analysing the poetry *in vacuo* with the aim of identifying different layers and chronological development. Oral poetry is only as old as its latest performance, and even though there are reasons to believe that skaldic poetry was perhaps more 'literary' in this matter than the traditional *Edda* poems, in other words more fixed in wording and attributed to named authors, we still have to take account of the context in which it was preserved. We have, for example, no way of telling if there was some poem from a certain century in which Thor succeeded in killing the serpent, and another poem from a different century in which he did not, if the evidence on which we base such conjectures consists of fragments like those discussed here, selected in order to tell their own independent version of the story (Snorri's version), unlike all others, in a new context that was only constructed for this particular purpose.

There is little point, either, in asking questions about the 'original' version of the myth. More valuable, it seems to me, is to use the sources to draw up a picture of the kind of variation with which people like Snorri were familiar and must have felt quite comfortable. Snorri was most likely well aware that there were different people who told the 'same' stories in different ways in his own time (as in all other times), depending on their knowledge, talent, abilities, and interests, the external conditions of performance, and many other factors. There was never any 'golden age' in the past when everything was unified and correct and truly heathen, only to be corrupted by Christian ideas and learning shortly before it was written down. Neither is it likely that Snorri was the first person to think about this knowledge in a systematic fashion. Snorri's question and the answers he offers on how poets should refer to Thor in their poetry demonstrate a high level of sophistication in the practice of skaldic verse: this was clearly an art that had been honed and polished over the centuries, which required systematic oral training in both its metrical and verbal complexities, as well as in the pre-Christian world view with its varied heritage of mythological narratives and poems that held it all together. Snorri was therefore not creating a universe out of chaos in the *Edda*; what he did there — the systematic arrangement of this body of knowledge — was something generations of professional skalds must have gone through before him, only orally. Snorri's originality lay in putting it all into a book, which laid on him new types of structural demands. But the idea of professional training and the systematization of learning must have existed long before him. Snorri was brought up and trained to become a member of this profession. His written exposition of the oral skills he had acquired as a young man should therefore be seen as a continuation of an ancient tradition, a personal statement rooted in the practice of a long line of skaldic poets going back to the founding fathers of this extraordinary art form that may ultimately have originated under the influence of ancient Irish metres.[34]

---

[34] See Gísli Sigurðsson, *Gaelic Influence in Iceland*, pp. 103–17.

Works Cited

Manuscripts and Archival Documents

Uppsala, Uppsala University Library, De la Gardie 11

Primary Sources

Den norsk-islandske skjaldedigtning, ed. by Finnur Jónsson, 2 vols (København: Gyldendal, 1912–15)

Eddukvæði, ed. by Gísli Sigurðsson (Reykjavík: Mál og menning, 1998)

Snorri Sturluson, *Edda*, ed. and trans. by Anthony Faulkes (London: Dent, 1987)

——, *Edda Snorra Sturlusonar*, ed. by Heimir Pálsson (Reykjavík: Mál og menning, 1988)

——, *Edda Snorra Sturlusonar: Edda Snorronis Sturlæi*, 3 vols (København: Sumptibus Legati Arnamagnæani, 1848–87)

——, *Edda Snorra Sturlusonar: udgivet efter håndskrifterne af Kommissionen for det Arnamagnæanske legat ved Finnur Jónsson*, ed. by Finnur Jónsson (København: Gyldendal, 1931)

Secondary Studies

Aage Kabell, 'Der Fischfang Þórs', *Arkiv för nordisk filologi*, 91 (1976), 124–25

Gísli Sigurðsson, *Gaelic Influence in Iceland: Historical and Literary Contacts; A Survey of Research*, 2nd edn (Reykjavík: University of Iceland Press, 2000)

——, *The Medieval Icelandic Saga and Oral Tradition: A Discourse on Method*, trans. by Nicholas Jones, Publications of the Milman Parry Collection of Oral Literature, 2 (Cambridge, MA: Harvard University Press, 2004)

Some Thoughts on Saxo's Euhemerism

John Lindow*

Background on Saxo

Saxo Grammaticus is the name we now use for the author of a work published in Paris in 1514 with the title *Danorum regum heroumque historia*, and now known almost universally as *Gesta Danorum*. It was based upon a now lost manuscript secured by Christian Pedersen, a canon of Lund, at that time the archbishopric of Denmark (but since the 1658 treaty of Roskilde part of Sweden). Today four manuscript fragments of the work survive, one of them dated to *c.* 1200 and probably the autograph. In his Preface, Saxo tells us that Absalon, bishop of Lund, commissioned the work, and he beseeches Andreas Sunesøn, who succeeded Absalon on the bishop's throne when Absalon died in 1201, to look kindly on the work. Thus the work was begun before 1201 and presumably completed before 1223, when illness compelled Andreas Sunesøn to give up his position as bishop. Exercising extreme caution, the Danish historian Thomas Riis, now something of a senior statesman in Saxo studies, thinks that we can be certain that Saxo was at work on at least one part of his *Historia* before 1202, that the first two books were finished no earlier than 1205, and that the entire work was completed between 1216 and 1219.[1] Since Sven Aggesen mentions Saxo's commission in his own shorter history of Denmark, which ends in 1185 and may have been composed not long thereafter, it is not unlikely that Saxo was at work in the end of the twelfth century, and this would accord with Riis's hyperconservative position.

* John Lindow (lindow@berkeley.edu) is Professor of Scandinavian at the University of California, Berkeley, and the author of *Norse Mythology: A Guide to the Gods, Heroes, Rituals, and Beliefs* (Oxford: Oxford University Press, 2002), with a special interest in the mythological and folk traditions of Scandinavia.

[1] Riis, *Einführung in die Gesta Danorum*, p. 18.

Writing Down the Myths, ed. by Joseph Falaky Nagy, CURSOR 17, (Turnhout: Brepols, 2013)
pp. 241–255   BREPOLS ⬛ PUBLISHERS   10.1484/M.CURSOR-EB.1. 100855

Sven Aggesen called Saxo his *contubernalis*,[2] and Sven was a learned man of the world. Saxo names his father and grandfather as members of the royal retinue, and current thinking is that Saxo was born into this military family around 1160, educated both in Denmark and abroad, and retained as a clerk by Absalon.[3] Since he served both Absalon and Andreas Sunesen, perhaps he was a secular canon at Lund.

Scholarly Appreciation

Saxo's *Historia* was popular when first issued. Erasmus of Rotterdam singled it out for praise, and editions were published in Basle in 1534 and Frankfurt in 1576. Thereafter it became a decidedly Danish taste, until post-Romantic professional scholarship reclaimed it for the study of Germanic and Norse heroic legend and myth — or reclaimed most of it. *Gesta Danorum* comprises sixteen books, but only the first nine are set in pre-Christian Denmark; in Book Nine the conversion occurs. F. York Powell offered commentary on Saxo's 'sources, historical methods, and folklore' within Oliver Elton's 1893 translation of the first nine books,[4] and Paul Herrmann offered a lengthy commentary (1901–22) to the first nine books.[5] The major figure in this line of study, however, is Danish. In his doctoral dissertation, Axel Olrik tried to demonstrate Danish layers in the Nordic legend materials,[6] and his famous two-volume study of Danish heroic legend relied heavily on Saxo alongside the Old Norse materials.[7] After mid-century the pendulum began to swing, and scholars such as Anker Teilgård Laugesen, Inge Skovgaard-Petersen, Kurt Johannesson, and Karsten Friis-Jensen have done much to define the literary and cultural milieu in which Saxo belongs, which is decidedly learned, Latin, and international.[8]

---

[2] Christensen, 'Forholdet mellem Saxo og Sven Aggesen'.

[3] Riis, *Einführung in die Gesta Danorum*, pp. 18–21; see also Kroman, *Saxo og over-leveringen af hans værk*.

[4] Saxo Grammaticus, *The Nine Books of the Danish History*, ed. by Powell.

[5] *Erläuterungen zu den ersten neun Büchern*, ed. by Herrmann, II.

[6] Olrik, *Forsøg på en tvedeling af kilderne*.

[7] Olrik, *Danmarks heltedigtning*; Olrik, *The Heroic Legends of Denmark*.

[8] Laugesen, *Introduktion til Saxo*; Skovgaard-Petersen, 'Saxo, Historian of the Patria'; Skovgaard-Petersen, 'Gesta Danorums genremæssig placering'; Johannesson, *Saxo Grammaticus*; Friis-Jensen, *Saxo Grammaticus as Latin Poet*. But see also Hansen, *Saxo Grammaticus and the Life Of Hamlet*.

The Historical Context

Before turning to a few passages that I think may tell us something about Saxo's mythography, I would like to pause briefly and consider the historical context. Absalon, who commissioned Saxo's work, was archbishop from 1177 until his death in 1201. For almost twenty years before that he had been bishop of Roskilde (and in fact he retained the see when crowned archbishop). It is usually assumed that the mid-century Danish civil war (1147–57) may have given Absalon motivation for commissioning a work that celebrated national unity, since the warring factions were not wholly at peace under the reign of his childhood friend, King Valdemar I. But there was another mid-century event that must have been of interest in Danish ecclesiastic circles, namely the promotion of the see at Niðaróss (now Trondheim) to archiepiscopal status in 1152–53. From around the beginning of the twelfth century, Lund had been the archdiocese for all of Scandinavia, and the elevation of Niðaróss reduced considerably the territory and influence of Lund. Obviously Saxo thought that Lund was important, since he makes the establishment of that archbishopric a typological counterpart of the Birth of Christ.[9] This he does through the arrangement of the books, which has been greatly explicated in the last decades. Essentially they are structured in groups of four: 1–4 before Christ, 5–8 beginning with the Birth of Christ and running up to the end of paganism in Denmark, 9–12 the conversion and early Christian kings, and 13–16 the establishment of the archbishopric down to 1185. The argument turns on 5 and 13, each the first of a group of four.

In support of my suggestion that the establishment of an independent archbishopric in Niðaróss may be one circumstance in the impetus for Absalon to commission Saxo's work is the way Saxo describes the foundation of the archbishopric in Lund: the papal legate sent out to do so

> not only rescued it [Lund] from the hegemony of the Saxons, but he also made her a master in religious matters over Sweden and Norway. Denmark owes much to the benevolence of Rome, which got her not only the right to independence but also supremacy over foreign countries.[10]

---

[9] Skovgaard-Petersen, 'Saxo, Historian of the Patria', p. 69.

[10] XII. 6. 6. 'Nec solam eam [sc. Lundiam] Saxonica ditione eruit [sc. legatur], sed etiam Suetiae Noruagiaeque religionis titulo magistram effecit. Nec parum Dania Romanae benignitati debet, qua non solum liberatatis ius, sed etiam exterarum rerum dominium assecuta est'. Text and translation from Friis-Jensen, 'Saxo Grammaticus's Study of the Roman Historiographers', p. 76.

For the previous century, although Denmark had exercised much independent political power under such renowned Christian kings as Cnut the Great, it had still been under the ecclesiastical control of Hamburg-Bremen, for which originally all the north had been a missionary see. Thus the first half of the twelfth century represented something of a high-water mark for Danish interests, undone not only by the crumbling of the kingdom into separate entities in the middle of the twelfth century but also by loss of ecclesiastical Norway and the Atlantic dependencies. All this was to change again with the ascent to the throne in 1157 of Valdemar I the Great, the Baltic Crusades, and the general strengthening of institutions that would make Denmark from then until the end of the Middle Ages the one true international power in the North.

Niðaróss could become an archbishopric because the remains of Saint Olaf were there, and it was therefore a cult and pilgrimage site. Quite naturally Olaf formed the basis of Norwegian history writing, both in Latin and, famously, in the vernacular. Here it is very much worth recalling that the dedication of the archbishopric included a performance of a vernacular poem honouring St Olaf, Einar Skulason's *Geisli*. Thus, a highly literate Latin history of the Danish *patria* might be viewed as a reaction or antidote to the vernacular celebration of Olaf and Niðaróss. There was already vernacular historical writing in Icelandic by the end of the twelfth century, so how better to belittle that incipient tradition than to embrace the international language of learning and historiography? If this view is correct, Saxo's appropriation of at least some (and in my view probably quite a lot) of Norwegian-Icelandic vernacular tradition, that is, myth and legend, appears to be rather ironic.

Saxo and Snorri

A comparison between Saxo and Snorri thus seems inevitable, and indeed it has been a staple of scholarship.[11] It now seems that both were men of reasonably good families, with some education, with extremely well-tuned literary sensibilities: Snorri's focused on the vernacular, Saxo's on Latin. Like Saxo's *Gesta Danorum*, Snorri's *Heimskringla* begins in prehistory and runs down to the later twelfth century. For both Snorri and Saxo, the gods are just men with magic powers whom people mistakenly came to worship; that is, each operates with a theory

---

[11] An important work, published well after this paper was completed, is *Saxo og Snorre*, ed. by Jørgensen, Friis-Jensen, and Mundal. The excellent essays by Annette Lassen and Else Mundal are especially relevant to my topic.

of euhemerism. Unlike Saxo, however, Snorri confines the gods to the very beginning of *Heimskringla*; Saxo has references to them through Book Eight.

Of course, Saxo nowhere offers a systematization of the sort Snorri performs in
his *Edda*, both for narrative in *Gylfaginning* and for language in *Skáldskaparmál*.
Nor is Saxo interested in the kind of systematization evidently practised by the
compiler of the so-called *Poetic Edda*, in which poems of gods precede poems
of heroes, and within the poems of gods there seems to be an order of a synoptic
poem, Odin poems, a Freyr poem, and Thor poems. Saxo's systematization of the
myths is of an entirely different order, in that it is subservient to the overall aims
of his work. Thus it has been pointed out that the first three books may show a
move from a magical 'Odinized' Hadding through a social and moral outlook in
Suanuita to a reliance on oneself instead of the gods in Hother,[12] and (perhaps
more obviously) that the visits to 'Geruthia sedes' and 'Utgarthia' (in Snorri and
Icelandic tradition visits to Geirrøðr and to Útgarða-Loki), places of darkness and
cold, are set in Book Eight in deliberate opposition to the light and warmth that
the conversion to Christianity will bring in Book Nine — and to create a deliberate parallel to Book XI of the *Aeneid*, in which Aeneas visits his father Anchises in
the underworld and there experiences a vision of the destiny of Rome.

The Mythology

If we accept, then, that Saxo had little interest in the temporal aspects of the
mythology — the mythic past in which the *æsir* created the cosmos, the mythic
present in which they contend with the giants, and the mythic future, in which
Ragnarök destroys and then remakes the world of the gods — what can we say
about Saxo's mythography? Let us begin at the beginning.

Book I opens with Dan, the eponymous proto-king. His great-grandson
Gram ships off his sons to be raised by giants, and at this moment Saxo digresses
on the subject of the uncanny, in this case what he calls *matematici*, perhaps 'nec-
romancers' but more ably rendered 'wizards' by Peter Fisher.

> Horum primi fuere monstruosi generis viri, quos gigantes antiquitas nominavit,
> humanæ magnitudinis habitum eximia corporum granditate vincentes.
>
> Secundi post hos primam physiculandi sollertiam obtinentes artem possedere
> Pythonicam. Qui quantum superioribus habitu cessere corporeo, tantum vivaci
> mentis ingenio præstiterunt. Hos inter gigantesque de rerum summa bellis certa-
> batur assiduis, quoad magi victores giganteum armis genus subigerent sibique non

---

[12] Skovgaard-Petersen, 'The Way to Byzantium', p. 127.

solum regnandi ius, verum etiam divinitatis opinionem consciscerent. Horum utrique per summam ludificandorum oculorum peritiam proprios alienosque vultus variis rerum imaginibus adumbrare callebant illicibusque formis veros obscurare conspectus.

Tertii vero generis homines ex alterna superiorum copula pullulantes auctorum suorum naturæ nec corporum magnitudine nec artium exercitio respondebant. His tamen apud delusas præstigiis mentes divinitatis accessit opinio.[13]

(The first of these were creatures of monstrous size, whom the ancients called giants, far surpassing human beings in bodily size.

Second were those who obtained the leading expertise in haruspicy and were masters of the Delphic art. Although in frame they yielded precedence to the former, they excelled them in acuteness of intellect. Between these and the giants there were interminable battles for supremacy, until the diviners won victory over the monster race and appropriated not only the right to rule but even the reputation of being gods. Both these types, being dexterous in deceiving the eye, were clever at counterfeiting different shapes for themselves and others, and concealing their true appearance under false guises.

The third class, bred from an intermingling of the other two, reflected neither the size nor the magic arts of their parents. Nevertheless minds deluded by their legerdemain believed in their divinity.[14])

Setting aside for a moment the third class, I think we may conclude that Saxo's view of the mythology was very much like Snorri's, or for that matter that of Margaret Clunies Ross or myself. The mythology is a struggle between two groups, here called *gigantes* and *magi*, that is, giants and diviners. The diviners triumph, and here obtain the right to rule; in the mythology we would say that they obtain the goods of the narrative world: objects (many of them magic!), wealth, and women.

In the mythology the two groups are called *jötnar* (sing. *jötunn*) and *æsir* (sing. *áss*). Although the etymology of *jötunn* is disputed, and there seems to me to be little evidence in the mythology that most *jötnar* are physically larger than *æsir*, the modern Scandinavian cognates (Danish *jætte*, Norwegian *jette*, Swedish *jätte*) do refer to beings of large size. And when Saxo writes in the last paragraph of his Prologue about immense stones erected by a civilization of giants, he invokes the trope manifested in Old English as the *eatona gewearc*, with another cognate. (On the other hand, the Finnish loan word *etona* means simply 'bad person').

[13] Saxo Grammaticus, *Saxonis Gesta Danorum*, ed. by Olrik and Ræder, p. 20. I quote from this edition to retain consistency with the Fisher translation.

[14] Saxo Grammaticus, *The History of the Danes*, trans. by Fisher, I, 21–22

Although neither *áss* nor any of the other words for the gods, mostly collective plurals, have to do etymologically with divination, that skill is quite important in the mythology. Obviously it relates first to Odin, whose ability to see the future is paramount, but at various places in the mythology it is assigned to many other figures: Frigg, Freyja, Heimdallr and 'other *vanir*'.[15] However, the point here is not gigantic size versus divination, but an agonistic relationship between two groups, one of which triumphs largely by using mental rather than physical force. If we think of it in that manner, we can fold even Thor — here let us deliberately call him a representative of the Dumézilian second function, force — into Saxo's statement: he overcomes Hrungnir partly through use of a verbal subterfuge (Thialfi gets the giant to nullify his shield by standing on it),[16] and the dwarf Alvíss by getting him to tell stories.[17] And Freyr, a fertility figure (an identification on which both Adam of Bremen and Dumézil could agree), owes his marriage to verbal threats made by his servant Skírnir.

Pretty much everyone who has looked at this passage has reached the conclusion that the first two groups are *jötnar* and *æsir*, giants and gods. But I believe that previous comment has insufficiently stressed that Saxo puts the two groups into the same opposition that forms the very basis of the mythology as we know it from Icelandic sources. And he does so at the very beginning of *Gesta Danorum*. Paul Herrmann referred to this passage as establishing Saxo's theory of the gods,[18] and although Saxo does not put that theory into practice — that is, Saxo's history does not include scenes in which diviners who map directly onto *æsir* overcome giants who map onto the *jötnar* — the theory itself seems secure. Herrmann thought that the three groups were chronological, but I think that Saxo saw the first two as, at one time, having been coterminous.

I wish to argue that the ending of the prologue helps to show how Saxo understood matters. As I mentioned, Saxo invokes the trope of the giants who heaved stones about before we humans were on the scene. But he also brings the concept up to his own time. These are the final words of the prologue.

> Talibus, ut nostri autumant, subitam mirandamque nunc propinquitatis, nunc absentiæ potestatem comparendique ac subterlabendi vicissitudinem versilis corporum status indulget, qui hodieque scrupeam inaccessamque solitudinem, cuius supra mentionem fecimus, incolere perhibentur. Eiusdem aditus horrendi generis

---

[15] *Þrymskviða*, stanza, 15, *Edda: Die Lieder des Codex Regius*, ed. by Kuhn, I, 113.

[16] *Skáldskaparmál*, Snorri Sturluson, *Edda: Skáldskaparmál*, ed. by Faulkes, I, 20–22.

[17] *Alvíssmál*, *Edda: Die Lieder des Codex Regius*, ed. by Kuhn, I, 124–29.

[18] *Erläuterungen zu den ersten neun Büchern*, ed. by Herrmann, pp. 85–89.

periculis obsitus raro sui expertoribus incolumitatem regressumque concessit. Nunc stilum ad propositum transferam.[19]

(Such creatures, so our countrymen maintain, are today supposed to inhabit the rugged, inaccessible waste-land which I mentioned above and be endowed with transmutable bodies, so that they have the incredible power of appearing and disappearing, of being present and suddenly somewhere else. But entry to that land is beset with perils so horrific that a safe home-coming is seldom granted to those who adventure it. Now I shall address my pen to the task in hand.)[20]

These, then, are the supernatural nature beings of Scandinavian legend and folk belief. They live in the uninhabited regions and threaten people who go there. (Saxo's 'rugged inaccessible waste-land' is most likely the wilds of northern Fenno-Scandia, but it might also refer to rock-strewn areas of Denmark, which I would take to be Jutland). These nature-beings are very seldom seen, but when they are (and it is usually at their pleasure), they have human form. Some legends tell that these supernatural beings can even take the form of known members of the community in order to work mischief. Clearly they are the direct descendants of the *jötnar* of the mythology; or to put it another way, the mythology offers a narrative world in the relationship between humans and supernatural beings presents itself as a relationship between gods and giants, and being a mythology, always allows victory to the symbolic humans.

Although I think that the statement about various classes of beings in Book I shows that he knew the mythology, Saxo chooses for the most part to set his story in the real world, where the struggle is between humans and humans, and just occasionally between humans and others. There are indeed two instances in *Gesta Danorum* in which giants carry off humans, both unsuccessfully.

The first case is in the beginning of Book VI. Frodo's son Fridlev, who soon will be King Fridlev II, is in Norway trying to woo a princess. A giant has assumed human shape and carried off Prince Hithin of Telemark, whom he forces to row up a fjord, and three swans and a belt that falls from the sky make this fact known to Fridlev and point out the special outrage of a king serving an inferior. Fridlev intercepts the pair and, with the boy's advice, recites a verse mocking the giant. The verse seems somehow to bind the monster, who apparently puts up no resistance and loses a foot and hand before fleeing in disgrace. So, the human uses the power of words to overcome the giant.

---

[19] Saxo Grammaticus, *Saxonis Gesta Danorum*, ed. by Olrik and Ræder, p. 9.
[20] Saxo Grammaticus, *The History of the Danes*, trans. by Fisher, I, 9.

The second case is a wooing story in Book VII, one which more or less answers to the definition of fairy tale. As far as I can tell Saxo sets it in Götaland, but insofar as the story partakes of fairy tale, the setting is to some extent the fairy tale Neverland. In this narrative, the chaste Sirithia will look no man in the eyes and declares that she will not marry until she does so. Various suitors fail until a giant carries her off, either by bribing a female servant to get her out of the house or by doing so himself in female form. When the giant takes her into the mountain, we see in manifest form the term that Scandinavian folklorists later used to encapsulate all such kidnappings: *bjærgtagning* (literally 'mountain-taking', that is, taking into a mountain).[21] Othar, her most ardent suitor, enters the mountain, kills the giant, and frees her, but she still will not look at him. She then arrives at the house of 'an enormous woman of the woods', presumably a giantess (if we are in Götaland this would be a *skogsrå*) and once again apparently is rescued by Othar. Only in the anticipated third move, when she arrives at the home of Othar's family in disguise, does she lift her gaze and agree to marry Othar.

It would be simple to say, as many do, that Saxo is using plots and devices of the *fornaldarsögur* (literally 'ancient-age sagas'), where heroes roam, the fantastic abounds, and the great game of the gods and the giants is no longer relevant. But to me it seems more clear that he simply thought, or wished his readers to believe, that that game had been played out before King Dan arrived on the scene, or elsewhere. Thus in Book VIII there is a famous reference to the myth of Thor's visit to Geirrøðr and slaying of the giant and his two daughters. In the dark underworld — clearly a world of the dead and not innocent of medieval vision literature, as Mats Malm has shown — Thorkil and his fellow travellers see the perforated body of Geruth and his daughters (here three in number), with their broken backs.[22] Thorkil explains that Thor once (*quondam*) perpetrated the wounds on these giants. Now, we must take Book VIII and especially Thorkil's journey to be set just before the Conversion, and *quondam* is more than a little vague, but certainly Thor's exploits are from the past.

Another indication of the past nature of the mythology is in Saxo's statement of his theory of the euhemerization of the gods in an aside in Book VI.

> Olim enim quidam magicæ artis imbuti, Thor videlicet et Othinus aliique complures miranda præstigiorum machinatione callentes, obtentis simplicium animis, divinitatis sibi fastigium arrogare cœperunt.[23]

---

[21] As captured in the title of H. F. Feilberg's classic monograph, Feilberg, *Bjærgtagen*.

[22] Malm, 'The Otherworld Journeys'.

[23] Saxo Grammaticus, *Saxonis Gesta Danorum*, ed. by Olrik and Ræder, p. 152.

(At one time (*olim*) certain individuals, initiated into the magic arts, namely Thor, Odin and a number of others who were skilled at conjuring up marvellous illusions, clouded the minds of simple men and began to appropriate the exalted rank of godhead.[24])

The following discussion takes on the names of the days of the week, which Saxo shows to be both parallel to and different from the Roman weekday names. He does not try to argue that the Danish names were translated from the Roman ones, as we now know they were. Rather, he uses the genealogical discrepancy between Jupiter as the father of Mercury (*dies Jovis* and *dies Mercurii* — our Thursday and Wednesday) and Odin as the father of Thor in Danish mythology, to show that the Roman gods are not identical with the Danish gods. This discussion puts the Danish gods into the same time frame as the Roman gods and is consistent with Saxo's aim to make of Denmark a northern Roman empire.

Thus far I have argued that Saxo's 'theory of the gods' involved an agonistic relationship between the two groups, giants and diviners, whom we should read as the *jötnar* and *æsir* engaged in the mutual struggles that are at the centre of the mythology as we find it in Icelandic sources. But what of the third group? They are the offspring of the first two, neither large in stature nor as skilled in magic arts as the diviners. Nevertheless, Saxo categorized them, along with the first two groups, as wizards (*matematici*), and they too, like their intelligent rather than large parents, became the object of worship — that is, were euhemerized. I cannot accept the lame suggestion, unsupported, by Herrmann, that they may have been *vanir*, elves, or dwarfs.[25]

The first point to note is that the existence of this group, the result of intermarriage between the first two groups, functions as yet another device to put the battles between giants and diviners in a greatly distant past and thus to keep them out of *Gesta Danorum*. In creating a succession of groups like this in prehistory, Saxo may have been developing, perhaps ironically, parallels to titans and Olympians, but the idea of offspring of the primary mythological groups can perhaps be reconciled with the mythology in the Icelandic sources, as can their euhemerization. A key example here would be the god Týr, who gives us Tuesday and thus would have been known to Saxo, given his excursus on the names of the days of the week. We do not know very much about Týr, but the Eddic poem *Hymiskviða* offers us some enigmatic information about his parentage.[26]

---

[24] Saxo Grammaticus, *The History of the Danes*, trans. by Fisher, I, 170.

[25] *Erläuterungen zu den ersten neun Büchern*, ed. by Herrmann, p. 86.

[26] Hymiskviða, *Edda: Die Lieder des Codex Regius*, ed. by Kuhn, pp. 88–95.

In stanza 5, Týr announces that his father, who lives east of the Élivágar, possesses the kind of cauldron the gods need according to the conceit of the poem. In the conceptual geography of the mythology, east of the Élivágar can only be giant-land. When the lad, presumably Týr, arrives at the hall of Hymir, he encounters a loathsome woman with nine-hundred heads, his grandmother according to a textual conjecture, and also a second woman, all in gold and white-browed, who goes forth to pour beer to her son, Týr. Multiple heads signal *jötnar*, and gold and white signal *æsir*, so I am convinced that this mother is from the *æsir*. Thus, if the loathsome lady is Týr's grandmother, it would be on his paternal side. In the next stanza, the golden white-browed woman addresses Týr, whom the poet has just called her son, as kinsman of giants (*áttniðr jötna*) and announces her intention to protect him from her husband, whose hospitality is not always to be counted on. Indeed, when he arrives home, Hymir is described as malformed (*váskapaðr*) and tyrannical (*harðráðr*), with his beard frozen solid. The family drama goes on when the golden white-browed woman welcomes Hymir home and announces that their son has come to visit (since there is no possessive pronoun, it could be 'my son' or 'your son', but she uses the dual pronoun when saying that they have been expecting him). A few stanzas later the poet makes it explicit by referring to Hymir as an ancient giant (*forn jötunn*). Many people have wrestled with these stanzas and the implications for Týr's parentage, I among them, for what they suggest violates the usual principle that *jötnar* may not possess women from the *æsir*. However, they do offer us one easy way to read Saxo's third group: Týr is apparently indeed the offspring of an alliance between giants and gods, and he was apparently elevated to the status of deity, as the name of the week shows us.

This possible explanation for the third group might be supported with the notion of Odin as the all-father, and therefore a generation ahead of Týr. Odin is also the father of Thor, whose mother Jörð or Earth we might take for a giantess, if only on the basis of size. Thus, we could account for Saxo's third group without, as it were, postulating a third group: group three would be a subset of group two. If this line of reasoning seems unsatisfying, as I realize it may, we can always fall back on Inge Skovgaard-Petersen's suggestion that Saxo postulated group three in order to 'serve as an excuse for speaking of pagan gods through many centuries: of course they were mortal, but having inherited the tricks of their ancestors they could deceive people that they were the original Æsir'.[27]

In even the possibility of reading group three in the light of the Eddic poem *Hymiskviða*, I am crediting Saxo with a quite thorough knowledge of the mythol-

[27] Skovgaard-Petersen, 'The Way to Byzantium', p. 124.

ogy. As I have already mentioned, he knew that Thor had killed Geruth/Geirröðr by throwing a burning ingot through him, and his daughters by breaking their backs. He portrays Odin as a one-eyed schemer whose marriage to Frigg is sometimes contentious. He knows that the gods formed a *collegium*. Beyond the strictly narrative world of the mythology, he knows that Frø/Freyr was associated with Uppland in Sweden and especially with sacrifices there, and he knows that the gods were once associated with Asia, although Saxo makes it Byzantium, a location that Inge Skovgaard-Petersen has explained.[28]

The myth recounted at greatest length by Saxo is that of the death of Baldr.[29] Although much scholarship stressed the differences between Saxo's versions and the Icelandic traditions, Margaret Clunies Ross was able to show convincingly that Saxo works with more or less the same set of stable elements that Icelandic tradition reveals,[30] and that in the end what separates Saxo and Snorri is not what they knew about the mythology but how they chose to present it, each making choices driven by generic considerations.

In his Prologue, Saxo famously praised the men of Thule (Iceland):

Nec Tylensium industria silentio oblitteranda: qui cum ob nativam soli sterilitatem luxuriæ nutrimentis carentes officia continuæ sobrietatis exerceant omniaque vitæ momenta ad excolendam alienorum operum notitiam conferre soleant, inopiam ingenio pensant. Cunctarum quippe nationum res gestas cognosce memoriæque mandare voluptatis loco reputant, non minoris gloriæ iudicantes alienas virtutes disserere quam proprias exhibere. Quorum thesauros historicarum rerum pignoribus refertos curiosius consulens, haud parvam præsentis operis partem ex eorum relationis imitatione contexui, nec arbitros habere contempsi, quos tanta vetustatis peritia callere cognovi.[31]

(The diligence of the men of Iceland must not be shrouded in silence; since the barrenness of their native soil offers no means of self-indulgence, they pursue a steady routine of temperance and devote all their time to improving our knowledge of others' deeds, compensating for poverty by their intelligence. They regard it a real pleasure to discover and commemorate the achievements of every nation; in their judgment it is as elevating to discourse on the prowess of others as to display their own. Thus I have scrutinized their store of historical treasures and composed a considerable part of this present work by copying their narratives, not scorning, where I recognized such skill in ancient lore, to take these men as witnesses.[32])

---

[28] Skovgaard-Petersen, 'The Way to Byzantium'.

[29] On which see Lindow, *Murder and Vengeance among the Gods*.

[30] Clunies Ross, 'Mythic Narrative in Saxo Grammaticus'.

[31] Saxo Grammaticus, *Saxonis Gesta Danorum*, ed. by Olrik and Ræder, p. 5.

[32] Saxo Grammaticus, *The History of the Danes*, trans. by Fisher, I, 5.

In Book XIV, Saxo mentions a specific Icelander, Arnoldus, as in Absalon's retinue, a man expert in antiquity and skilled in narration whom King Valdemar
asks to tell stories while they are on an expedition in western Sjælland, probably
c. 1165–70. This figure was long identified with the Arnaldr Þorvaldsson whom
Skáldatal (a list linking skalds and kings in one manuscript of Snorri's Edda) associates with King Valdemar,[33] but given the current thinking about Saxo's life, he
would not have been born when this incident took place, and we should take it as
Absalon's anecdote, not Arnaldr's. The anecdote is important, however, in that it
puts a king's skald into Absalon's retinue. What is important here, however is not
Arnaldr himself, but rather Arnaldr as one of no fewer than seven skalds whom
Skáldatal assigns to the kings who reigned during Saxo's life: For Valdemar I the
Great, besides Arnaldr, there is Þorsteinn kroppr; for Valdemar's elder son, Knud,
who reigned from 1182–1202, there is Þorgeir Þorvaldsson, and, more tellingly,
for Valdemar's second son, Valdemar II (the Victorious), during whose reign Saxo
completed his history, there are four: Óláfr Þórðarson, Játgeirr Torfason, Þorgeirr
dánaskáld, and Súgandi skáld. The first of these is famous as the author of the
Third Grammatical Thesis, and he probably did not visit Valdemar until 1240 or
so, well after Saxo had completed Gesta Danorum. However, the evidence is manifest: there must have been Icelandic skalds in the courts where Saxo was doing
the research for his history. This is significant because any skald had to be familiar
with the kenning system, both to understand older and other skalds' work, and
to compose his own; and to understand the kenning system was (as Snorri would
show in his Edda) to understand the mythology. In these skalds we have the probable sources for the understanding of the entire mythology I credit to Saxo.

I end with a question. Saxo recounts only one myth at length, namely the
death of Baldr. Although as with all his other mythogical knowledge he turns it
to his immediate use, he nevertheless chose the most important narrative in the
mythology, the linchpin. Was this coincidence, or was it an almost unavoidable
consequence of his deep understanding of the mythology?

---

[33] Bjarni Guðnason, 'The Icelandic Sources of Saxo Grammaticus', p. 80.

Works Cited

Primary Sources

Edda: Die Lieder des Codex Regius nebst verwandten Denkmälern, ed. by Hans Kuhn, rev. by Gustav Neckel, 4th edn, 2 vols (Heidelberg: Winter, 1972)

Saxo Grammaticus, *The Nine Books of the Danish History of Saxo Grammaticus*, ed. by Frederick York Powell, trans. by Oliver Elton (London: Norrœna Society, 1905)

——, *Saxo Grammaticus: The History of the Danes: Books I–IX*, trans. by Peter Fisher, ed. by Hilda Ellis Davidson, 2 vols (Cambridge: Brewer, 1979–80)

——, *Saxonis Gesta Danorum*, ed. by J. Olrik and H. Ræder (Hauniæ: [n.p.], 1931–1957), I: *Textus* (1931)

Snorri Sturluson, *Edda: Skáldskaparmál*, ed. by Anthony Faulkes, 2 vols (London: Viking Society for Northern Research, 1998)

Secondary Studies

Bjarni Guðnason, 'The Icelandic Sources of Saxo Grammaticus', in *Saxo Grammaticus: A Medieval Author between Norse and Latin Culture*, ed. by Karsten Friis-Jensen, Danish Medieval History and Saxo Grammaticus, 2 (København: Museum Tusculanum Press, 1981), pp. 79–93

Christensen, Karsten, 'Forholdet mellem Saxo og Sven Aggesen', in *Saxostudier (Saxo-kollokvierne ved Københavns universitet)*, ed. by Ivan Boserup, Opuscula Graecolatina, 2 (København: Museum Tusculanum, 1975), pp. 128–42

Clunies Ross, Margaret, 'Mythic Narrative in Saxo Grammaticus and Snorri Sturluson', in *Saxo Grammaticus: Tra storiografia e letterature; Bevagna, 27–29 settembre 1990*, ed. by Carlo Santini (Roma: Calamo, 1992), pp. 47–59

Feilberg, Henning Frederik, *Bjærgtagen: studie over en gruppe træk fra nordisk alfetro*, Danmarks folkeminder, 5 (København: Schønberg, 1910)

Friis-Jensen, Karsten, *Saxo Grammaticus as Latin Poet: Studies in the Verse Passages of the Gesta Danorum*, Analecta Romana Instituti Danici, Supplement, 14 (Roma: L'Erma di Bretschneider, 1997)

——, 'Saxo Grammaticus's Study of the Roman Historiographers and his Vision of History', in *Saxo Grammaticus: Tra storiografia e letterature; Bevagna, 27–29 settembre 1990*, ed. by Carlo Santini (Roma: Calamo, 1992), pp. 61–81

Hansen, William F., *Saxo Grammaticus and The Life Of Hamlet: A Translation, History, and Commentary* (Lincoln, NB: University of Nebraska Press, 1983)

Herrmann, Paul, ed., *Erläuterungen zu den ersten neun Büchern der dänischen Geschichte*, 2 vols (Leipzig: Engelmann, 1922)

Johannesson, Kurt, *Saxo Grammaticus: komposition och världsbild i Gesta Danorum*, Lychnos-bibliotek, 31 (Uppsala: Almqvist & Wiksell, 1978)

Jørgensen, Jon Gunnar, Karsten Friis-Jensen, and Else Mundal, eds, *Saxo og Snorre* (København: Museum Tusculanum, 2010)

Kroman, E., *Saxo og overleveringen af hans værk*, Studier fra sprog- og oldtidsforskning, 278 (København: Gad, 1971)

Laugesen, Anker Teilgård, *Introduktion til Saxo* (København: Gyldendal, 1972)

Lindow, John, *Murder and Vengeance among the Gods: Baldr in Scandinavian Mythology*, Folklore Fellows Communications, 262 (Helsinki: Suomalainen Tiedeakatemi, 1997)

Malm, Mats, 'The Otherworld Journeys of the Eighth Book of *Gesta Danorum*', in *Saxo Grammaticus: Tra storiografia e letterature; Bevagna, 27–29 settembre 1990*, ed. by Carlo Santini (Roma: Calamo, 1992), pp. 159–73

Olrik, Axel, *Danmarks heltedigtning: en oldtidsstudie*, 2 vols (København: Gad, 1903–10)

——, *Forsøg på en tvedeling af kilderne til Sakses oldhistorie*, 2 vols (København: Wroblewski, 1892–94)

——, *The Heroic Legends of Denmark*, trans. by Lee M. Hollander, Scandinavian Monographs, 4 (New York: American-Scandinavian Foundation, 1919)

Riis, Thomas, *Einführung in die Gesta Danorum des Saxo Grammaticus* (Odense: University Press of Southern Denmark, 2006)

Skovgaard-Petersen, Inge, 'Gesta Danorums genremæssig placering', in *Saxostudier (Saxo-kollokvierne ved Københavns universitet)*, ed. by Ivan Boserup, Opuscula Graecolatina, 2 (København: Museum Tusculanum, 1975), pp. 20–29

——, 'Saxo, Historian of the Patria', *Mediaeval Scandinavia*, 2 (1969), 54–77

——, 'The Way to Byzantium: A Study in the First Three Books of Saxo's History of Denmark', in *Saxo Grammaticus: A Medieval Author between Norse and Latin Culture*, ed. by Karsten Friis-Jensen, Danish Medieval History and Saxo Grammaticus, 2 (København: Museum Tusculanum, 1981), pp. 121–33

Motivations for
Hittite Mythological Texts

H. Craig Melchert*

For purposes of the following discussion I subsume under the notion 'myth' narratives about deities and/or humans in a past that lies beyond direct knowledge and describes extraordinary events.[1] One may choose to limit 'myth' to those stories that involve deities,[2] and classify those with exclusively human actors as 'legends' or the like. However, the often fragmentary nature of our evidence and the undeniable belief of the Hittites themselves in the routine intervention of deities in human affairs make such a distinction hard to maintain.[3] I will return briefly to the problem of definition and classification in my conclusion. Translations of most of the texts mentioned here are available in Italian in F. Pecchioli Daddi and A. Polvani's *La mitologia ittita* and in English in Harry A. Hoffner Jr's *Hittite Myths* (the latter being more inclusive).[4] These two works also discuss with varying degrees of detail the nature of the respective compositions — discussions that should be compared with others cited below.

Our sources for Hittite myth are limited to the archives of the royal/imperial bureaucracy, whose records include royal annals, treaties, protocols (instructions

* H. Craig Melchert (melchert@humnet.ucla.edu) is A. Richard Diebold Professor of Indo-European Studies and Linguistics at the University of California, Los Angeles, co-author (with Harry A. Hoffner Jr) of *A Grammar of the Hittite Language* (Winona Lake, IN: Eisenbrauns, 2008), and a leading expert on the languages and texts of ancient Anatolia.

[1] Haas, *Die hethitische Literatur*.

[2] For example, Beckman, 'Mythologie'.

[3] For a thoughtful discussion of this problem apropos of one Hittite text, see Gilan, 'How Many Princes Can the Land Bear?'.

[4] *La mitologia ittita*, ed. by Pecchioli Daddi and Polvani; *Hittite Myths*, trans. by Hoffner.

Writing Down the Myths, ed. by Joseph Falaky Nagy, CURSOR 17, (Turnhout: Brepols, 2013)
pp. 257–264   BREPOLS ⬛ PUBLISHERS   10.1484/M.CURSOR-EB.1. 100856

regulating the behaviour of state officials), the state cult, rituals, and scholastic texts for scribal instruction. For us, then, Hittite myth not only exists exclusively in written form, but also has been selectively filtered in that the extant texts must have had some relevance for the governing bureaucracy. Any possible relationship of mythical narratives to an oral tradition among the 'common people' can only be surmised. As defined, Hittite mythological texts fall into three distinct categories according to their role or function in state affairs.

The first group consists of myths ascribed to the Hattians, the autochthonous pre-Indo-European inhabitants of Central Anatolia. The core of the content of these Hattic myths undoubtedly is native Anatolian, but there likely has been some admixture of inherited Indo-European elements in the form in which they are presented to us in the Hittite texts. These Hattic myths form an integral part of state religious festivals (regularly performed rituals to maintain the integrity and prosperity of society, or of rituals performed to resolve crises). As rightly formulated by Beckman: 'The primordial event memorialized in the text served as a paradigm for the resolution of a parallel contemporary problem'.[5]

We have one such myth whose status as part of a fixed state ritual is assured: the 'Myth of Illuyanka'.[6] This myth describes the battle of the Storm-god (chief deity in the Hattic-Hittite pantheon) with an eel-snake dwelling in a watery pit.[7] The latter initially wins, but the Storm-god prevails with the aid of a human who perishes due to his intimate relationship with the deity.

This myth is part of the *furulli* festival of Nerik, a spring festival performed to assure and celebrate the annual renewal of the natural world. See the discussion by Haas and the text opening:[8] *utne-wa māu šešdu nu-wa utnē paḫšanuwan ēšdu nu mān māi šešzi nu* EZEN *purulliya iyanzi*, '"Let the land grow and prosper! Let the land be protected!" In order that (it) grow and prosper, they celebrate the *p.*-festival'.[9]

---

[5] Beckman, 'Mythologie', p. 565.

[6] On which see, in addition to the works cited above, Watkins, 'Le Dragon hittite Illuyankas'; Watkins, *How to Kill a Dragon*, pp. 448–59; Katz, 'How to Be a Dragon in Indo-European'; and Haas, *Die hethitische Literatur*, pp. 97–103.

[7] Katz, 'How to Be a Dragon in Indo-European', p. 324 n. 23.

[8] *Keilschrifttexte aus Boghazköi*, III, text 7, col. 1, ll. 5–8.

[9] My translation follows that of *La mitologia ittita*, ed. by Pecchioli Daddi and Polvani, p. 50, after Stefanini against that of Hoffner and others. The more usual translation 'If/when (it) grows and prospers, they celebrate the *p.*-festival' makes no sense in context, since the fixed annual celebration does not depend on the prosperity of the land, but according to the Hittite belief rather the opposite. Hittite does not have a regular construction for 'final clauses', but

The most famous of the Hattic myths is that of the 'disappearing god',[10] which follows a set plot line: a deity retreats in anger, refusing to perform his or her vital functions, leading to drastic dysfunction in the cosmos (or a part thereof) and the need to induce the deity to return and resume his or her functions. Recitation of the myth (adapted to the case of the specific deity) is accompanied by both divine and human propitiatory rituals and by verbal evocation of the deity. The Hittite term for this ritual type is *mūgawar*, the verbal noun of *mūgā(i)*- 'to induce to action'.[11] The best-known version of the myth is for Telipinu (Hattic for 'great son', that is, of the Storm-god), whose absence leads to widespread famine and sterility, but we have fragments of multiple versions, and there is yet no proven association with a fixed state festival.[12]

A third Hattic myth known as 'When the Moon Fell from the Sky' is to be performed 'when the Storm-god thunders frightfully'.[13] The very fragmentary documentation of this myth leaves its connection with ritual use not fully clear. As *per* Beckman, textual variations in the Hattic myths suggest that they are based on an oral tradition, but it is doubtful that they show any metrical structure.[14]

The second major group of Hittite myths consists of those borrowed (or more accurately adapted) from various Near Eastern sources. I follow Beckman in regarding these as essentially belletristic literature used for the instruction of scribes and perhaps for the entertainment of the Hittite court.[15] These texts may to some extent be subcategorized by source, but this classification must be regarded as provisional for many of the compositions.

Some of the myths are clearly Mesopotamian in origin. The famous story of Gilgamesh is attested in the Hittite archives in both an Akkadian version and a Hittite version based on a Hurrian intermediary. It is clear from the content of the latter despite its fragmentary condition that it is a free adaptation, not a translation. We also find (unfortunately even more fragmentary) manuscripts of the Atrahasīs (which includes a flood narrative) and the story of Gurparanzah (a tale

---

mān may be read here as the particle used to express desire. Thus more literally: 'Would that (it) grow and prosper, (for that) they perform the *p.*-festival'.

[10] Haas, *Die hethitische Literatur*, pp. 103–15.

[11] Thus with Laroche, *La Prière hittite*, pp. 20–24, against all others.

[12] With due respect to Haas, *Die hethitische Literatur*, p. 104.

[13] Haas, *Die hethitische Literatur*, pp. 120–22.

[14] Beckman, 'Mythologie', p. 565. For a different view on the latter point see Haas, *Die hethitische Literatur*, pp. 102 and 105, following deVries.

[15] Beckman, 'Mythologie', p. 565.

of the city of Akkad, the Tigris, and the eponymous hero). Both of these are in Akkadian with a Hittite translation.

Sometimes conventionally labelled 'Canaanite' (in any case Syro-Palestinian) are the story of Elkunirša and Ašertu (relating sexual intrigues about the god El and his wife) and the Tale of Appu (about a wealthy but initially childless man, who after prayer to the Sun-god receives two sons whom he names 'Good' and 'Bad').

Most extensive among the myths adapted by the Hittites are those based on Hurrian precursors. It must be emphasized, however, that the Hurrians are assured only to be the immediate source of transmission to the Hittites. The ultimate origins of the various myths are uncertain and subject to vigorous debate. The largest set of such texts is the 'Kumarbi Cycle', which tells of a multi-generational divine struggle for the kingship of heaven. Its many shared features with Hesiod's theogony surely reflect a Near Eastern, not Indo-European source. These texts are labelled 'songs' in their Hittite versions and almost certainly are in verse.[16]

The Hurro-Hittite 'Song of Release' is an etiological story of the destruction of Ebla, a powerful city state of Syria in the third-second millennia that was destroyed *c.* the sixteenth century BC.[17] It is not yet clear whether this composition is also in verse. Also among the Hurro-Hittite myths belongs the story of Kešši, the hunter.

The third set of myths represents myth in the guise of prehistory. This type is based on the widespread Hittite practice of justifying and motivating current political policy based on past events. Such historical narratives are found in preambles to treaties, both parietal and non-parietal, in the so-called 'apology' of Hattusili III, in the text of Mursili II on the '*tawananna* affair', and others.[18] A desire in some instances to relate the relevant facts 'from the beginning' led beyond the two to three generations available to direct memory and hence a resorting to what we from our perspective would regard as myth.

The clearest example of this sort is the 'Zalpa Narrative'.[19] The extant text first presents a story of prodigious multiple births, exposure of infant boys in baskets

---

[16] See McNeill, 'The Metre of the Hittite Epic'; Durnford, 'Some Evidence for Syntactic Stress in Hittite'; and Melchert, 'Poetic Meter and Phrasal Stress in Hittite'.

[17] On the interpretation of this text (the *editio princeps* is that of Neu, *Das hurritische Epos der Freilassung*), see now Wilhelm, 'Das hurritisch-hethitische "Lied der Freilassung"', and Bachvarova, 'Relations between God and Man', with references.

[18] For translations of the passages in treaties, see *Hittite Diplomatic Texts*, trans. by Beckman.

[19] Translation in *Hittite Myths*, trans. by Hoffner, pp. 81–82.

on a river and their divine rescue, and brother-sister incest. After a significant lacuna we find a few lines referring to the Sun-god (including direct speech by him), followed directly by the beginning of a prosaic historical narrative involving the 'grandfather of the king'. There can be no doubt that the two parts of the text form a single composition. Interpretations diverge widely,[20] but what seems clear is that the text is an attempt to account for an historically attested hostility between Hattusha (the Hittite capital) and Zalpa, a city on Black Sea coast with which there existed some kind of complex (possibly ethnic) prehistorical relationship.

A second example is 'The Bull with the Crumpled Horn', an etiological story of the crossing of the Taurus Mountains.[21] There are surely further examples in texts describing early encounters with the Hurrians (aptly characterized by Laroche as 'récits légendaires')[22] and possibly in the so-called 'cannibal text'.[23] Also worth mentioning are the unassigned *historiolae* and mythologems collected by Haas.[24] As already noted by Haas, the line between 'myth' and 'history' is often blurred.[25] The Zalpa text suggests that the distinction may have been non-existent for Hittites.[26]

We are thus brought back face-to-face with the problem of how we are to define 'myth'. It should be obvious that the threefold classification I have just offered rests entirely on a modern viewpoint, as does the overall selection of compositions to be considered (the latter, I emphasize, generally follows others and

[20] See Watkins, 'The Third Donkey'; Gilan, 'How Many Princes Can the Land Bear?'; Holland and Zorman, *The Myth of Zalpa*; and Zorman, 'CTH 3', and their respective references to still other analyses.

[21] Otten, 'Aitiologische Erzählung von der Überquerung der Taurus'.

[22] Laroche, *Catalogue des textes hittites*, p. 4.

[23] Haas, *Die hethitische Literatur*, pp. 51–54. In an old Hittite text that purports to be a historical narrative we find the tantalizing lines (*Keilschrifttexte aus Boghazköi*, III, text 60, col. 2, ll. 1–5): 'Whatever man arr[ives] among them, they always eat him up. Whenever they see a fat man, they kill him and eat him up'. The preceding context is lacking, so we cannot know to whom 'they' refers, but later in the same text (*Keilschrifttexte aus Boghazköi*, III, text 60, col. 3, ll. 7–9) we find further: 'They seized the mother of Zuppa in Tinisipa. They killed her and ate her up'. See Amir Gilan's thoughtful discussion regarding the difficulty in defining this episode and the entire text as 'fiction' or 'non-fiction' (Gilan, 'Were There Cannibals in Syria?'). We may in this case be dealing with an intentional attempt to characterize a region and its inhabitants as 'the other' by attributing to them a shocking practice.

[24] Haas, *Die hethitische Literatur*, pp. 237–44.

[25] Haas, *Die hethitische Literatur*, p. 20.

[26] Compare Munn, *The Mother of the Gods*, pp. 302–10, on a similar blurring in Herodotus.

is not original with me). It is unlikely that the Hittites themselves perceived the same commonalities among the three types that we do — or at least that they regarded such features from the same perspective. As in the case of trying to classify Hittite 'literature', however, we unfortunately have very little basis for inferring the Hittites' own contextualization of this material. I forgo here any mere speculation in this regard.

Works Cited

Primary Sources

Hittite Diplomatic Texts, trans. by Gary M. Beckman, ed. by Harry A. Hoffner, Writings from the Ancient World, 7, 2nd edn (Atlanta: Scholars, 1999)

Hittite Myths, trans. by Harry A. Hoffner, ed. by Gary M. Beckman, Writings from the Ancient World, 2, 2nd edn (Atlanta: Scholars, 1998)

Keilschrifttexte aus Boghazköi, vols 1–6 (Leipzig: Hinrichs, 1916–1921), vols 7–61 (Berlin: Mann, 1954–2011)

La mitologia ittita, ed. and trans. by Franca Pecchioli Daddi and Anna Maria Polvani (Brescia: Paideia, 1990)

Secondary Studies

Bachvarova, Mary R., 'Relations between God and Man in the Hurro-Hittite "Song of Release"', *Journal of the American Oriental Society*, 125 (2005), 45–58

Beckman, Gary, 'Mythologie. A. II. Bei den Hethitern', in *Reallexikon der Assyriologie und vorderasiatischen Archäologie*, ed. by Erich Ebeling and Bruno Meissner, 11 vols (Berlin: Gruyter, 1928–2010), VIII: *Meek–Mythologie*, ed. by Dietz Otto Edzard (1993–97), pp. 564–72

Durnford, Stephen P. B., 'Some Evidence for Syntactic Stress in Hittite', *Anatolian Studies*, 21 (1971), 69–75

Gilan, Amir, 'How Many Princes Can the Land Bear?—Some Thoughts on the Zalpa Text', *Studi Micenei ed Egeo-anatolici*, 49 (2007), 305–18

——, 'Were There Cannibals in Syria? History and Fiction in an Old Hittite Literary Text', in *Papers on Ancient Literatures: Greece, Rome, and the Near East; Proceedings of the 'Advanced Seminar in the Humanities', Venice International University 2004–2005*, ed. by Ettore Cingano and Lucio Milano, Quaderni del Dipartimento di scienze dell'antichità e del Vicino Oriente, Università Ca' Foscari Venezia, 4 (Padova: Sargon, 2008), pp. 267–84

Haas, Volkert, *Die hethitische Literatur: Texte, Stilistik, Motive* (Berlin: Gruyter, 2006)

Holland, Gary B., and Marina Zorman, *The Myth of Zalpa: Myth, Morality, and Coherence in a Hittite Narrative* (Pavia: Italian University Press, 2007)

Katz, Joshua T., 'How to Be a Dragon in Indo-European: Hittite *illuyankaš* and its Linguistic and Cultural Congeners in Latin, Greek, and Germanic', in *Mír Curad: Studies in Honor of Calvert Watkins*, ed. by Jay Jasanoff, H. Craig Melchert, and Lisi Oliver (Innsbruck: Institut für Sprachwissenschaft der Universität Innsbruck, 1998), pp. 317–34

Laroche, Emmanuel, *Catalogue des textes hittites* (Paris: Klincksieck, 1971)

——, *La Prière hittite: vocabulaire et typologie*, École pratique des hautes études, Section des sciences religieuses, 72 (Paris: Sorbonne, 1964)

McNeill, I., 'The Metre of the Hittite Epic', *Anatolian Studies*, 13 (1963), 237–42

Melchert, Craig H., 'Poetic Meter and Phrasal Stress in Hittite', in *Mír Curad: Studies in Honor of Calvert Watkins*, ed. by Jay Jasanoff, H. Craig Melchert, and Lisi Oliver (Innsbruck: Institut für Sprachwissenschaft der Universität Innsbruck, 1998), pp. 483–94

Munn, Mark, *The Mother of the Gods, Athens, and the Tyranny of Asia: A Study of Sovereignty in Ancient Religion* (Berkeley: University of California Press, 2006)

Neu, Erich, *Das hurritische Epos der Freilassung I: Untersuchungen zu einem hurritisch-hethitischen Textensemble aus Ḫattuša*, Studien zu den Boğazköy-Texten, 32 (Wiesbaden: Harrassowitz, 1996)

Otten, Heinrich, 'Aitiologische Erzählung von der Überquerung des Taurus', *Zeitschrift für Assyriologie*, 55 (1963), 156–68

Watkins, Calvert, 'Le Dragon hittite Illuyankas et le géant grec Typhôeus', *Comptes rendus de séances de l'Académie des inscriptions et Belles-Lettres*, 136 (1992), 319–30

——, *How to Kill a Dragon: Aspects of Indo-European Poetics* (New York: Oxford University Press, 1995)

——, 'The Third Donkey: Origin Legends and Some Hidden Indo-European Themes', in *Indo-European Perspectives: Studies in Honour of Anna Morpurgo Davies*, ed. by John H. W. Penney (New York: Oxford University Press, 2004), pp. 65–80

Wilhelm, Gernot, 'Das hurritisch-hethitische "Lied der Freilassung"', in *Texte aus der Umwelt des Alten Testaments: Ergänzungslieferung*, ed. by Manfried Dietrich and others (Gütersloh: Gütersloher Verlag, 2001), pp. 82–91

Zorman, Marina, 'CTH 3: The Conquest of Zalpa Justified', *Studi Micenei ed Egeo-anatolici*, 50 (2008), 861–70

India and the Graphy o' Myth

Stephanie W. Jamison[*]

As the organizers of the original conference and editor of this volume will attest, I approached the conference in great puzzlement, pestering the organizers for months trying to find out what the word 'mythography' actually meant. My interpretation remains insecure, but insofar as I can tell, especially from the conference brochure, at least for the conference and the subsequent volume there are three crucial parts to 'mythography'.

1. At some point in various cultures (the examples given in the conference blurb were all Western European) the (or a) floating set of traditional stories about gods and heroes gets *collected* and *written down*, and with these actions, the stories get a 'fixed' and canonical form. Though the term mytho*graphy* only references writing, at least as I understand the conference blurb, the *collection* is just as important, as it assembles into a compendium stories that may have been originally independent and/or transmitted separately and for differing purposes, and thereby creates a pseudo-unity.

2. The collection and writing are often done by a single person, or a few individuals, for antiquarian/secular/'patriotic' purposes. I know all those terms, especially the last two, are problematic. But by 'secular' I roughly mean that the collection was not made to serve religious ends (for example, collected by priests for recitation at rituals), and by 'patriotic' I mean that the collection may have been made to celebrate, affirm, or even create an ethnic, cultural, or political identity.

* Stephanie W. Jamison (jamison@humnet.ucla.edu) is Professor of Indo-European Studies, and Asian Languages and Cultures at the University of California, Los Angeles. She is the author of important monographs, including most recently, The Rigveda between Two Worlds (Paris: de Boccard, 2007), and is an expert in the Vedic and epic mythological traditions of India.

Writing Down the Myths, ed. by Joseph Falaky Nagy, CURSOR 17, (Turnhout: Brepols, 2013)
pp. 265–276   BREPOLS 📖 PUBLISHERS   10.1484/M.CURSOR-EB.1. 100857

3. The writing and attendant fixation trigger a 'literary-fication' of the stories. That is, they become available to be self-consciously adapted and reworked and embellished by writers with 'art' on their minds, whatever 'art' means.

If my understanding of the term is anywhere near correct, then my original puzzlement is less puzzling at least to me — for this model has absolutely no applicability to ancient or medieval (or even to some extent modern) India. In what follows, I will discuss the various ways in which the model does not fit India and Indian mythology and how we might modify the model to fit the Indian situation. There is such a rich variety of ways in which India does not fit the above model that it is hard to know where to begin. But I will start by responding very briefly to each of the three points, and enlarge on them thereafter.

1. There is nothing in India that corresponds to the written 'mythological compendia' that form the topic of this conference, without major qualifications.

2. Though there are works that can be considered collections of mythological narratives, they are not the deliberate products of single individuals, and they are never distanced from the culture, to serve other than religious ends.

3. Here is the tricky part: even without the existence of such compendia, there are certain core texts that endlessly furnish subjects for 'high literature', even without the collection and fixation and the repurposing of steps 1 and 2. So, though 3 seems to follow and presuppose 1 and 2 in the terms of the conference, in India 3 can be detached from 1 and 2 and in fact does not require them.

The major reason for the irrelevance of the model is the fact that India avoided the fetishizing of writing, a fetishization that still affects how we all, scholars and non-scholars alike, think about culture and cultures. Long after writing was available and widely used in India, and indeed long after the mythological narratives that are our concern here were put into written form — or forms — , robust oral versions coexisted with and repeatedly gave new and varied form to the written versions of myths. And not just oral traditions precariously preserved off in the corners of 'folk'-dom, but ones forming one strand of erudite and cultivated discourse. There was no sense of a progression, either chronological or logical, from oral to written, nor a 'privileging' of writing and co-opting of oral versions, with the consequent relegation of the oral to the margins and backwaters. So *-graphy of myth* 'writing down the myths', (the terms used by the conference organizers) was not a defining step in literary and cultural history, as it seems to have been elsewhere.

Let me express this in two complementary statements that are somewhat paradoxical at least to Western ears:

1. Fixation does not equal Writing.
2. Writing does not equal Fixation.

To start with the former, probably the most 'fixed' text coming out of ancient and medieval India is the very first one, the *Rig Veda*, a collection of over a thousand hymns to various divinities, which was preserved *entirely orally* for several millennia. The time of the composition of this text is not entirely clear, but the hymns were probably composed over a period of at least several hundred years, and they were collected and ordered into the text we have sometime in the second half of the second millennium BC (say, 1500–1200). The text has been transmitted essentially without variants since then, and elaborate mnemonic devices were developed to ensure that no syllable was lost or changed in its disciplined oral transmission from generation to generation within the various Vedic *śākhās* or schools. It is one of the textual marvels of the entire ancient world. Moreover, each hymn seems to have been frozen in the exact form given it by its poet (who often names himself in the poem) at the time of composition; these are not flexible, ever-changing, and anonymous oral improvizations, but self-consciously crafted, fixed texts, though they were composed using traditional techniques and verbal complexes. In other words, this is not oral composition in the Parry-Lord mode, but a type that oral-formulaic theory seems to have taken little notice of.[1] It is also unclear when the *Rig Veda* was first written down: from the scraps of evidence we have, it was perhaps in the mid- to late first millennium of the Common Era — note the vast chronological distance. Moreover, that writing, whenever it occurred, would have had essentially no effect on the normal, oral transmission of the text within the Vedic schools, transmission that continued, and continues, into modern times (fortunately, since manuscripts are ill-fated in the climate of the subcontinent).

And what about the mythology contained in this *Rig Veda*? Again, its form seems chronologically backwards, at least in terms of the presuppositions of the conference. Rather than naively and straightforwardly telling the stories that will provide the raw material for later artful retellings, counter-tellings, massagings, and manipulations, the Rigvedic poets leap-frogged past the first few steps and arrived at stage 3, when, in the model apparently used by the conference,

---

[1] For further discussion of these issues, see Jamison, *The Rig Veda between Two Worlds*, especially chaps 1 and 2.

the codified mythology becomes available to artistic re-creation. The Rigvedic poets seem to presuppose some sort of standard versions of the various myths *which they never themselves tell*. Instead they just allude to the stories — jumbling their chronology, focusing on and heightening only a single dramatic episode, telescoping the narrative, shining a brief, intense beam on minor characters and incidents not mentioned again, leaving loose ends tantalizingly unresolved — all sorts of postmodern tricks. It is as if the canonical compendia already existed, shared by poets and their audience — both mortals and (this is the important thing) gods. The gods already know their own stories, and a hymn of praise that flat-footedly recounted a god's great deeds would be unpleasing to him — it is the artful manipulation, the creative scrambling, that will catch the divine attention.

To take only one example, the god with the most narrative mythology in this early period is the great warrior god Indra; two of his deeds are especially famed: the smashing of the serpent Vṛtra who was keeping the waters confined, and the opening of the cave named Vala where the dawn cows were imprisoned. There are many many references to these myths, but no direct recountings of them: the closest we come for the Vṛtra battle is the great hymn I. 32, but even there the hymn obsessively keeps circling around and back to the dramatic climax, the smiting of the serpent, while almost pointillistically adding details in the course of the hymn: details about the aftermath, about the preparation for the battle, about the battle itself, dominated by a vivid picture, seen several times from different angles, of the broken serpent immediately after his defeat. The hymn ends with Indra, the great victorious warrior, fleeing in fear after the battle, with the tantalizing question — which has never received a satisfactory answer in the ensuing three and a half millennia: 'Whom did you see, Indra, as the avenger of the serpent when fear came into your heart after you had smashed it | when you crossed over the ninety-nine flowing rivers, like a frightened falcon through the airy realms?' Thus, the story does not end as we expect it to, with the great warrior celebrating his triumph; in fact it does not end at all, but leaves us with the irresolution of an unexpected and almost paradoxical puzzle: the triumphant warrior overcome with fear. The nineteenth-century scholars of the Veda had a tendency to think those 'primitive' poets had not yet figured out how to construct a narrative; the literary movements of the twentieth century have enabled us to recognize the Rigvedic poets as fellow moderns.

And there are worse things in the text: few accounts of any of the myths are as full as the one I have just discussed, and there is also a tendency to trade details among stories, such that, for example, the Vṛtra myth (of the serpent and the waters) and the Vala myth (of the cave and the cows) get conflated, and we are not always sure which story we are in. This is not the result of incompetent or careless story-telling, but of the poets' recognizing deep-structure story patterns that underlie both myths. And even worse (and even more exhilarating) are the dialogue hymns, where we are plunged into a single dramatic moment presumably plucked from a myth, with two or more speakers having a verbal showdown, with no narrative background and no resolution given. Take, for example, the fraught conversation (*Rig Veda*, x. 86) among Indra (the same great warrior), Indra's wife, and a monkey pal of Indra's, who has been causing trouble in the neighbourhood and who, in the course of the hymn, makes crude sexual advances to Indra's wife in Indra's presence — to which she replies with both equivalent crudeness and haughty disdain. Or, hardly less peculiar, the dialogue (*Rig Veda*, x. 10) between the first mortals (or so we surmise), the twins Yama and Yamī, over whether they should commit incest in order to populate the world: she is in favour, he is not. In all these cases, there is presumably a back-story, known to all, but it is never presented to us in that text — though chronologically later texts sometimes set the verses of the hymns into a fuller narrative, one that can seem desperately constructed after the fact. Rigvedic story telling is like Rigvedic formulaic language: it is all deep structure. What we get on the surface are the artful and self-conscious changes rung on the shared store of oral narratives and oral verbal formulae. In other words, the literarification of myth that is supposed to *follow* the collection and writing down of myths is what we *first* encounter in Indian literature.

So much for 'Fixation does not equal Writing'. As for 'Writing does not equal Fixation', let us consider two bodies of texts that are crucial to the study of Indian mythology, the great epics, particularly the *Mahābhārata*, and the purāṇas. For both of these corpora, writing certainly figured far more prominently than in the case of the Veda, but it seems to have the paradoxical effect of almost encouraging variation. Moreover, the narrative style in both corpora, especially the purāṇas, is much more straightforward and less consciously 'literary' than in the Veda: the stories in the purāṇas especially are simply narrated in quite simple Sanskrit.

The epics probably have some chance of being familiar to this audience. The two great epics, the *Rāmāyaṇa* and the *Mahābhārata*, both dating roughly (very roughly) from around the turn of the era (the year zero), each provide what might be termed the most authoritative and influential version of the narrative or sets of narratives that form their core: the story of Rāma and his devoted wife Sītā on the one hand, the story of the great ruinous war among the Bhārata cousins on the other. These stories have inspired vast amounts of literature, high, low, and middlin', across the subcontinent and South and Southeast Asia generally, for the last two millennia or so. (One of the latest and most charmingly bizarre versions of the *Rāmāyaṇa* is the recently released animated film *Sītā Sings the Blues*, made by an American woman who spent some time in India and coincidentally got her heart broken there.) There is no real consensus on the time of composition of the epics, the length of the period of composition, or the time when either text was first written down, in part or in whole, but, given that writing was fully existent in India at least towards the end of the period of the texts' composition, it is not unlikely that writing was involved to some extent fairly early on. But it seems to have had little or no effect on the development of the texts. For we have nothing like a fixed text for either one, especially the *Mahābhārata*, nor is it a mere matter of verbal variants, textual corruptions, and bad readings. There are two *major* recensions of the *Mahābhārata*, the Northern and the Southern, which by some measures differ from each other 'by as much as a third of the full text',[2] each of those two recensions themselves existing in scores of different versions of wildly varying lengths — differing in every possible way and preserved finally in manuscripts in numerous different scripts, from Śāradā in the extreme north to Grantha in the south. As a side note, the sheer extent of the variation in the Indian epic manuscripts contrasts strongly with the Greek epic tradition, and in my opinion makes it less likely that the Homeric epics, as we have them, continued to have an active oral recompositional life in historical times.

One of the great scholarly enterprises of the last century was the production of the critical edition of the *Mahābhārata* in Poona.[3] This was both a magnificent achievement and a somewhat quixotic one, in that the result is not really an Urtext stripped of corruptions and accretions and restored to a pristine original form (nor was that the aim, it should be noted), but a sort of confected compromise, often making the best (or, least worse) choices among a series of incompatible versions. All serious work on the *Mahābhārata* now starts with the critical edition, but all *Mahābhārata* scholars realize that the critical edition represents no text that ever existed in that form.

The purāṇas display this variability in even more acute form. The class of texts known as purāṇas, or 'old (stories)', comes the closest to the mythological compendia we were asked to consider here. They serve as the sources for much of what has been called 'Classical Hindu Mythology',[4] particularly the mythologies of the gods Śiva and Viṣṇu who dominate and divide the landscape of what most people think of as Hinduism, and for the cosmological and cosmogonic doctrines of Classical Hinduism. The purāṇas date in more or less the form or forms we have them from the mid- to late medieval period. There are numerous

---

[2] See Klostermaier, *A Survey of Hinduism*, p. 62.

[3] *The Mahābhārata*, ed. by Sukthankar and others.

[4] See *Classical Hindu Mythology*, ed. by Dimmitt and van Buitenen.

texts identified as major or minor purāṇas, but the traditional number of Great Purāṇas is eighteen, a canonical number in India. However, the lists of the eighteen *Mahāpurāṇas* differ from each other to some extent, and some do not even make it to eighteen. And even enumerating these texts and giving them names is somewhat misleading, for a single title covers a multitude of widely differing texts. There is currently much scholarly debate about whether it is desirable or feasible to attempt to make critical editions of the purāṇas. Though some ambitious attempts at critical editions of purāṇas have appeared in recent years,[5] with reasoned justifications of the enterprise, these seem even more quixotic than the critical edition of the *Mahābhārata*. As Ludo Rocher argues repeatedly in his influential 1986 survey of the purāṇas,[6] the title of a particular purāṇa is a loose cover term for a wide range of versions whose extant manuscripts disagree with each other in major ways, whose extant manuscripts almost surely do not represent the wider range of lost manuscripts, not to mention the material in the long-lived and often still living recitation tradition. He cautions against taking the printed edition of a purāṇa, or the manuscript or manuscripts it is based on, as *the* authoritative version of that purāṇa. Why — because, in his words, 'The principal reason why purāṇic [...] stories can be treated with such a high degree of freedom is that, fundamentally, they do not belong in books,' citing the comment of another scholar (Giorgio Bonazzoli) that 'the purāṇas are still a living and developing tradition,'[7] and himself remarking, 'Nineteenth and twentieth century writings on India provide ample descriptive material on modern purāṇic bards and purāṇic recitals.'[8] In other words, though the purāṇas may be the clos-

---

[5] See, for example, the ongoing project on the Skanda Purāṇa: *The Skandapurāṇa*, I: *Adhyāyas 1–25*, ed. by R. Adriaensen, H. T. Bakker, and H. Isaacson (1998); *The Skandapurāṇa*, IIa: *Adhyāyas 26–31. 14: The Vārāṇasī Cycle*, ed. by H. T. Bakker, and H. Isaacson (2004).

[6] Rocher, *The Purāṇas*.

[7] Rocher, *The Purāṇas*, p. 53.

[8] Rocher, *The Purāṇas*, p. 57. It must be admitted that these views about the fluidity of the purāṇic tradition have been vigorously disputed in recent years, especially by Hans Bakker and the other editors of the Skanda Purāṇa (See especially the introduction in *The Skandapurāṇa*, I: *Adhyāyas 1–25*, ed. by R. Adriaensen, H. T. Bakker, and H. Isaacson (1998), pp. 38–54, and IIa: *Adhyāyas 26–31. 14*, ed. by H. T. Bakker and H. Isaacson (2005), pp. 9–13). While not denying that there are varying versions of the purāṇa, they nonetheless assert that text-critical methods can uncover the Urtext underlying and predating the variant versions. Although the debate is sharp, it is not clear that for the purposes of this paper it is relevant: both sides agree that there exist multiple versions and variants — which is the point I want to make here; the question for the participants in the debate is whether 'Urtext' is a meaningful concept and an achievable goal in conceptualizing the tradition and editing the text.

est we come to the mythological collections we are considering here, and though they have probably existed in written form(s) for hundreds of years, in some cases perhaps a millennium or more, writing has done little to discourage the proliferation of versions and variants or the cross-fertilization with the sturdy tradition of flexible and improvisatory oral recitation.

Another crucial difference between them and the mythological compendia of Western cultures is that they, like the Vedas and the epics, were composed and compiled for religious purposes. They are devotional texts, glorifying the gods whose stories they narrate; indeed, they are generally considered to be 'sectarian': the texts concerning Viṣṇu and his avatars for the benefit of Vaiṣṇavites, those about Śiva and his consort Pārvatī for Śaivites. This Vaiṣṇavite/Śaivite divide highlights another important way in which the history and development of Indian mythology differs from the model of the conference: it shows a process of fission, not fusion. Though in practice the sectarian lines are not always entirely clear in a larger purāṇic text, the general situation is that there are myths about Śiva appropriate for devotees of that god, and myths about Viṣṇu appropriate for his devotees. They do not ordinarily interact; they do not act like members of a 'pantheon', an organized body of divinities who participate in each other's stories. This makes it difficult to imagine how a mythographic enterprise such as the conference envisioned would have proceeded; it would have to have ignored the sectarian lines, the separate lines of tradition, and constructed a big tent for all the divinities to inhabit. Although I realize that part of the point is that the graphic compendia were in part also 'constructed', they seem to start with mythologies that have a certain shared centre. There was nothing like a Mount Olympus at any time in Indian mythological history. Even in Vedic times the gods inhabited their own independent spaces — more like Los Angeles than Mt Olympus. And many of the Vedic gods lack anything resembling mythology: they represent elements of ritual (like Agni, the god 'Fire'; Soma, the deified ritual drink) or ethical/cultural principles (like Mitra, the god 'Alliance'): they may have attributes, but no stories to speak of. Though the gods of the epics tend to present a bit more of a united front, the individualizing tendencies already apparent in the Veda return in force in the purāṇas.

While I am in this contrarian mood, I would like to formulate another Indian paradox. Though narrative mythology is unequally distributed among Indian divinities and there never arose the written mythological compendia under discussion for other cultures, India is a gigantic repository and source of *stories*, assembled in organized collections and disseminated all over the known world from ancient times. Franklin Edgerton famously cited the statement that the story collection known as the *Pañcatantra* has been more widely circulated in

the world as a whole than any book but the Bible — one of those striking formulations that is of course impossible to verify.[9] But, as is well known, versions of
the *Pañcatantra* spread across the known world in medieval times, through Persia
and the Near East all the way to Europe. There are numerous other famous Indic
story collections — *The Tales of the 'Vampire'* (*Vetālapañcaviṃśati*), *The Tales of
the Throne* (*Siṃhāsanadvātriṃśakā*, also known as *Vikramacarita*), *The Tales of
the Parrot* (*Śukasaptati*), and most massive of all, though unfortunately lost in its
original form, the *Bṛhatkathā* or *Great Story*, one version of which comes down
to us as the *Ocean of Story* (*Kathāsaritsāgara*).[10] These story collections are characterized by non-naturalistic elements and organizing principles: the *Pañcatantra* is
populated almost entirely by talking animals, though with a political system rec-
ognizably human (think *Animal Farm*); the *Tales of the Vampire* involves a king
lugging a corpse occupied by a 'vampire', who tells him stories and tricks him into
responding; the *Tales of the Parrot*, a talking parrot of course, who by the lure of
its stories keeps his master's wife from committing adultery while the master is
away. There are frequent supernatural interventions and solutions, and even the
walk-on appearances of various well-known gods. But these story collections are
not, by my definition anyway, mythology. The focus is on the chatty parrot, not
the stray divinity. And the milieu from which these stories were drawn and the
purpose for which they were collected is not mythological either, but relentlessly
secular, with a generally cynical view of power dynamics and with the purpose of
instruction in the craft of governing (*nītiśāstra*): mirrors for princes, as one of the
versions of the *Pañcatantra*, the *Hitopadeśa*, spells out in its framing story of some
lazy princes needing education for their future jobs.[11]

So why did ancient and medieval India, which was otherwise not only story-
mad but mad for story *collections*, fail to make the same sorts of collections of

---

[9] *The Panchatantra Reconstructed*, ed. and trans. by Edgerton, II, 3. Cited also in *The
Pañcatantra*, trans. by Olivelle, p. ix.

[10] See the famous multi-volume English translation: Somadeva Bhaṭṭa, *The Kathá Sarit
Ságara*, trans. by Tawney (orig. pub. 1880–84; edited and reprinted with extensive introductions,
notes, and appendices by N. M. Penzer (Somadeva Bhaṭṭa, *The Ocean of Story*, ed. by Penzer)).

[11] It might be objected that the great collection of Buddhist stories, the *Jātakas*, or stories
of the Buddha's former births (found in various versions in various languages of Buddhism, but
best known in the Pāli version), have a religious purpose. But these tales, in which the Buddha
appears often in animal form, wear their religious trappings very lightly and clearly show their
affinities with the rest of the instructional story literature of India. Each tale is embedded in a
frame story in which the Buddha himself relates the tale and afterwards identifies the participants
and implicitly draws the moral. (The standard English translation of the Pāli collection is *The
Jātaka*, ed. and trans. by Cowell and others.)

their mythological materials? I do not have a real answer to this question, but I wonder if it is not connected to the continual evolution of their religious systems. The three types of text collections we have discussed — the *Vedas*, the *epics*, and the purāṇas — provide us with chronologically arranged snapshots of the religious systems and divinities of what we can loosely call Hinduism: the Vedic period dominated by gods like the powerful warrior Indra; the epic period where the power of Indra and his Vedic ilk has faded, but the narrative mythology still relies on them, while beginning to focus devotion and emotion on up-and-coming gods like Viṣṇu (a minor divinity in Vedic) and Śiva (originally just the epithet, 'Kindly One', of another minor Vedic god, Rudra); and the purāṇic period, where those latter gods have in turn been furnished with elaborate narrative histories — while gods such as Indra still lurk in the narrative background, often providing the plot mechanics that allow the new major gods to shine. Indra is even found all over Buddhist narrative literature under one of his old standard epithets (Pāli *sakka* = Sanskrit *śakra*, 'able one'), despite having no historical claim to this position.

It is almost as if the synchronic fission into sectarian texts devoted to independent divinities had been balanced by an impulse towards diachronic unity and continuity. By the time of the purāṇas, Indra and such gods have lost their awe-inspiring, fearsome divine power, but they hang around to populate the myths of the newly ascendant divinities. In other words, there were no sharp breaks in tradition, at which an inquiring antiquarian mind might be tempted to gather up all the old stories and make sense of them. Despite the radical changes in religious belief and practice, the narrative mythology folds the old gods into the new or newly adapted stories, at least in cameo roles, their old stories sometimes preserved in single-word epithets referring to deeds otherwise long forgotten — even in the epics Indra is known as *vala-vṛtra-han* (the slayer of Vala and Vṛtra), a designation that encapsulates the two Vedic stories mentioned above. Even the 'new' heterodox religious systems of Buddhism and Jainism preserve the gods and heroes of 'Hinduism' in their story literature. This tendency towards preservation *across* religious boundaries seems to contrast sharply with the European situation, in which (as far as I understand it) Christianization seems to have broken the narrative skein and encouraged the 'graphy' of a fading tradition.

* * *

Let me now briefly return to and sum up the contrarian message of this contribution with regard to mythology and writing: *graphy* has little or nothing to do with *myth* in ancient and medieval India — with its form, its content, its transmission, its fixation, its utilization, its adaptation, etc. In fact, in terms of the assumptions of the conference, the meta-history of myth and its verbal form seems to run in reverse: the most fixed and self-consciously artful presentations of myth are in the earliest text — an entirely oral text for which writing was irrelevant even when it finally got written down. And the collection and transmission of myths gets more and more variable — and less and less self-consciously wrought — the later we get: the purāṇas, with their endless variations and their simple narrative style, are the stage we might have expected to start with, but they are the latest of the major sources of mythology in Indian tradition. Moreover, though themed and structured story collections are quite common in India, the stories there collected are not myths, by most definitions, and these collections of folktales never provided the model for similar collections of mythic material.

Works Cited

Primary Sources

Classical Hindu Mythology: A Reader in the Sanskrit Puranas, ed. and trans. by Cornelia Dimmitt and J. A. B. van Buitenen (Philadelphia: Temple University Press, 1978)

The Jātaka, or Stories of the Buddha's Former Births, ed. and trans. by E. B. Cowell and others, 6 vols (Cambridge: Cambridge University Press, 1895–1913)

The Mahābhārata: For the First Time Critically Edited, ed. by Vishnu S. Sukthankar and others, 19 vols (Pune: Bhandarkar Oriental Research Institute, 1933–66)

The Panchatantra Reconstructed: An Attempt to Establish the Lost Original Sanskrit Text of the Most Famous of Indian Story-Collections on the Basis of the Principal Extant Versions, ed. and trans. by Franklin Edgerton, American Oriental Series, 2–3, 2 vols (New Haven: American Oriental Society, 1924)

The Pañcatantra: The Book of India's Folk Wisdom, trans. by Patrick Olivelle (Oxford: Oxford University Press, 1997)

Siṃhāsanadvātriṃśakā: Vikrama's Adventures; or, The Thirty-Two Tales of the Throne. A Collection of Stories about King Vikrama (Vikrama-charita or Sinhasana-dvatriņçaka), ed. and trans. by Franklin Edgerton (Cambridge, MA: Harvard University Press, 1926)

The Skandapurāṇa: Critically Edited with Prolegomena and English Synopsis, 2 vols to date (Groningen: Fortson, 1998–2005)

Somadeva Bhaṭṭa, *The Kathā Sarit Ságara: or, Ocean of the Streams of Story*, trans. by C. H. Tawney, 2 vols (Kolkata: [n. pub.], 1880–84)

——, *The Ocean of Story: Being C. H. Tawney's Translation of Somadeva's Kathā Sarit Ságara*, ed. by N. M. Penzer, 10 vols (London: Sawyer, 1924–28)

Śukasaptati: Shuka Saptati: Seventy Tales of the Parrot, trans. by Aditya Narayan Dhairyasheel Haksar (New Delhi: HarperCollins, 2000)

Vetālapañcaviṃśati: Jambhaladatta's Version of the Vetālapañcaviṃśati, ed. and trans. by Murray Barnson Emeneau, American Oriental Series, 4 (New Haven: American Oriental Society, 1934)

Secondary Studies

Jamison, Stephanie W., *The Rig Veda between Two Worlds*, Publications de l'Institut de Civilisation Indienne, 74 (Paris: Collège de France, 2007)

Klostermaier, Klaus K., *A Survey of Hinduism*, 3rd edn (Albany: SUNY Press, 2007)

Rocher, Ludo, *The Purāṇas*, in *A History of Indian Literature*, ed. by Jan Gonda, 10 vols (Wiesbaden: Harrassowitz, 1973–87), 2, fasc. 3 (1986)

MYTH AND COUNTER-MYTH
IN EARLY MODERN JAPAN

William M. Bodiford*

Japan's early modern period drew to a close in 1868 when the new Meiji regime forced the last shogun (military ruler) out of power and proclaimed a new government of direct rule by the Heavenly Sovereign (*tennō*, a title usually rendered in English as 'emperor'). This transition of power is well known, and its causes and consequences have been examined in numerous publications, both scholarly and popular. But except for a few notable exceptions, its religious dimensions remain largely unexplored.[1] Few people realize that the overthrow of the Tokugawa family, which had ruled as shoguns since 1603, entailed the fall of the Tokugawa's pantheon and its replacement by another. Until the end of the Pacific War in 1945, the new pantheon, led by the Sun Goddess with the Heavenly Sovereign as her ruling descendant on earth, constituted the national essence (*kokutai*) of Japan. The Japanese government proclaimed that all subjects of the throne must participate in Shintō rituals dedicated to this pantheon as an expression of patriotic duty, regardless of individual religious beliefs. Government schools taught the story of this pantheon not as myth, but as the

* William M. Bodiford (bodiford@ucla.edu) is Professor of Asian Languages and Literatures at University of California, Los Angeles, the author of *Sōtō Zen in Medieval Japan* (Honolulu: University of Hawaii Press, 2008), and a noted authority on Japanese religious traditions.
This essay is based on a lecture presented at UCLA for the conference 'Writing Down the Myths: The Construction of Mythology in Classical and Medieval Traditions' in 2009. The author wishes to thank everyone involved in the conference, especially Professor Nagy, for their encouragement.

[1] For important correctives to the standard historical narrative, see Grapard, 'Japan's Ignored Cultural Revolution'; Collcutt, 'Buddhism: The Threat of Eradication'; and Ketelaar, *Of Heretics and Martyrs in Meiji Japan*, pp. 43–86.

Writing Down the Myths, ed. by Joseph Falaky Nagy, CURSOR 17, (Turnhout: Brepols, 2013)
pp. 277–309   BREPOLS ☙ PUBLISHERS   10.1484/M.CURSOR-EB.1. 100858

factual history of Japan. People who denied or disrespected it risked imprisonment or even death.[2]

Long after Japan had become one of the world's major industrial and military powers, therefore, mythology remained of vital importance. It shaped lives, provided ideological justification for government policies, and even demanded the ultimate sacrifice. The mythology of the Sun Goddess and her Heavenly Sovereign proved so powerful and durable for such a long period that today many people assume that it must have always existed, or that even if pushed aside for awhile its return to prominence must have been inevitable. Within the broad sweep of Japanese history, however, we can discern many alternative mythologies. Competition for power generated both myths and counter-myths. Though many alternative myths have become all but forgotten, their power erased by the events of the past century and a half, they still can teach us much about Japanese culture.[3] They remind us that history is not teleological, but contingent upon circumstance and chance. Below I present one such counter-myth which also illustrates how the writing — and printing — of a myth can reframe it and give it new power.

Two authors, one obscure and forgotten, the other well known and celebrated, can serve to illustrate myth and counter-myth in Early Modern Japan. The forgotten author is a Buddhist priest named Jōin (1682–1739), who attained positions of influence within the highest levels of political power. He served as a tutor for members of the royal family and as a chief ritualist for the shogun. Around 1728 Jōin composed several essays in which he explained how the Tokugawa shoguns ruled as divine kings, sanctified by gods. Although not formally structured as such, his ideas can be seen as a Buddhist justification for the divine right to rule. Jōin composed his essays as ecclesiastical secrets, to be used by the Buddhist clerics in service to the Tokugawa family. They were not published until the first half of the twentieth century, long after the Tokugawa had lost power.[4]

The celebrated author is a private physician named Motoori Norinaga (1730–1801),[5] who became one of the founding figures of the academic and social movement that subsequent scholars (but not Motoori) labelled *kokugaku*

---

[2] 'Subjects of the throne' included the residents of annexed lands, such as Taiwan and Korea. Regarding *kokutai*, see *Kokutai no Hongi*, ed. by Hall. On Shintō, educational practices, and freedom of religion, see Hardacre, *Shintō and the State*, pp. 21–41, 79–99, 114–32.

[3] For useful introductions to alternative myths, see Yamamoto, *Chūsei shinwa*; and Iyanaga, 'Medieval Shintō'.

[4] Regarding Jōin, see Bodiford, 'Matara', pp. 242–44.

[5] The names of Asian individuals appear in Asian word order, surname first.

(a term translated literally as 'national learning' and interpretively as 'nativism').[6] Motoori wrote *Kojiki-den* (Conveying the Ancient Accounts). In this massive work of forty-four books, Motoori developed a new way of reading (and writing) Japanese literature that allowed him to reconstruct the language of the gods. Just as important, he published his reconstructions: Books I–V in 1790, Books IV–XI in 1792, Books XII–XVII in 1797, and Books XVIII–XLIV posthumously in 1822.[7] In conveying the *Kojiki* (Ancient Accounts), Motoori established its meaning, transformed the way that Japanese understand their past, and determined how all subsequent scholars interpret the texts of premodern Japan. So great has been Motoori's influence on the way we imagine Japan's past, that it has become difficult to even consider other alternatives.[8] We can gain some sense of Motoori's inventiveness in light of Jōin's arguments, which though typical of his time would strike most Japanese of today as novel.

Jōin's Theory of Buddhist Kingship as Sanctified by the Gods

Jōin wrote his essays on Buddhist Kingship to explain the significance of an earlier event. In 1617 Tokugawa Ieyasu (1542–1616), the founder of the Tokugawa family of shoguns, was enshrined as a Buddhist god named Tōshō Dai Gongen (The Great Avatar Illuminating the East). He was also known as Shinkun (The Divine King). All branches of the Tokugawa family as well as the other major ruling warlords (*daimyō*) participated in regular rituals to propitiate this god and to bring peace to the realm and ensure the prosperity of their descendants (*kokka anzen, shison hanjō*). Successful policies demonstrated divine favour while opposition or deviation invited divine retribution.[9] The name 'Tōshō' clearly smacks of Tenshō Daijin (The Great Deity Illuminating the Heavens), the name by which

[6] Regarding the term *kokugaku*, see Breen, 'Nativism Restored', pp. 429–33, and Burns, *Before the Nation*, pp. 231–32.

[7] Wehmeyer, 'Biographical Introduction', pp. 2, 11 n. 1. For a standard introduction to Motoori, see Matsumoto, *Motoori Norinaga*. Regarding his approach to language, see Sakai, *Voices of the Past*, pp. 255–63. Regarding his impact on the Early Modern construction of Japanese self identity, see Burns, *Before the Nation*, pp. 68–101.

[8] As noted by Burns, *Before the Nation*, p. 35, Motoori's assertions about the *Kojiki*, from his guides to pronunciation to his interpretive framework, 'have all but achieved the status of fact'. The *Kojiki* is sometimes described as a 'chronicle', but I prefer 'accounts' because the text rarely mentions dates or chronology. Regarding the significance of the *Kojiki*'s lack of temporality, see Kōnoshi, *Kanji tekisuto to shite no Kojiki*, pp. 101–08, 114–16.

[9] Boot, 'The Religious Background of the Deification of Tokugawa Ieyasu'.

the Sun Goddess was most commonly known. Just as rule by the royal family had been legitimated by a divine ancestor (Tenshō), rule by the shoguns likewise was being so legitimated by Tōshō. To drive home this point, the Buddhist religious ceremonies in honour of Tōshō were led by a Buddhist cleric whose position could be held only by a royal prince of the highest rank. In other words, the son of the Heavenly Sovereign led the nation in worshiping the Divine King.[10]

One of these royal princes, Kōgan *Hōshinnō* (1697–1738), asked Jōin to explain the Buddhist doctrines that justified the apotheosis of Tokugawa Ieyasu. Jōin responded by presenting the prince with three essays: *Sannō ichijitsu shintō kuden go sōshō hiki* (Secret Initiations in the Tendai Buddhist One-Reality Doctrines of the Gods), *Tenrin shōō shō* (Noble Wheel-Turning King), and *Tenrin shōō shō naiden* (Private Commentary on the Noble Wheel-Turning King).[11] Jōin's essays touch on many topics related to the roles played by gods in promoting Buddhism, protecting rulers, and securing prosperity for the realm. Here I want to summarize only his comments on kingship.

Jōin bases his explanations on a Buddhist scripture called the *Golden Light Sūtra*.[12] It teaches a 'righteous doctrine' (*shōron*) by which a king can establish a successful dynasty.[13] First, a ruler must promote the *Golden Light Sūtra*, support the Buddhist clergy, and teach Buddhist morality. In so doing, the king will gain the favour of the Four Heavenly Kings (*shi tennō*; the gods of the four directions) and of innumerable other gods, goddesses, demons, and deities of the heavens

---

[10] Bodiford, 'When Secrecy Ends', pp. 313–15.

[11] Available in: *Tendaishū zensho*, ed. by Tendai, XII, 253–59, 261–77, and 279–307, respectively. The clerical title *hōshinnō* designates legitimate royal sons who become Buddhist monks. The word 'noble' (*shō*) represents the East Asian translation of the Sanskrit *ārya* (honourable, superior, sacred, etc.) and describes things or people of superior spiritual or religious value from a Buddhist perspective. A wheel-turning king (Sanskrit: *cakavartin*) is a Buddhist monarch who turns the wheel of righteousness.

[12] East Asian Buddhists use two version of the *Golden Light Sūtra*: the *Jīnguāngmíng jīng*, in nineteen chapters, trans. *c.* 414–421 by Dharmakṣema (Tánwúchèn, 385–433); and the *Jīnguāngmíng zuìshèngwàng jīng* in thirty-two chapters, trans. 703 by Yìjìng (635–713). Both are available in: *Taishō shinshū daizōkyō*, ed. by Takakusu, T nos 663 and 665, respectively. R. E. Emmerick provides an English translation from a Sanskrit text similar in structure and content to the Dharmakṣema version; see *The Sūtra of Golden Light*, trans. by Emmerick. I have not been able to consult *This Most Excellent Shine of Gold*, ed. by Skjærvø.

[13] Jōin's assertions are found throughout the essays cited above, but especially see *Tendaishū zensho*, ed. by Tendai, XII, 254b, 256b, 261b–262b, 265b, 302a. The righteous doctrine corresponds to chap. 11, 'Zhènlùn pǐn', of Dharmakṣema's translation (the version cited by Jōin), to chap. 20, 'Wángfǎ zhènglùn pǐn', of Yìjìng's translation, and to chap. 12, 'Instruction Concerning Divine Kings', of *The Sūtra of Golden Light*, trans. by Emmerick.

and earth. These supernatural beings will give protection, defence, and welfare to the human king and cause him to be respected, revered, honoured, and praised. Moreover, they will prevent any hostile armies from threatening that king's territory.[14] Finally, by establishing righteousness and ruling according to the will of the gods, the king himself becomes godlike. Thus, the scripture says that although the king is gestated in a human womb, because he is blessed by the gods he and his descendants will be regarded as being of heavenly birth (that is, as gods or 'sons of heaven', *tenshi*).[15] Jōin asserts that these euhemeristic policies constitute the universal Doctrine of the Gods (Shintō) used by the founders of successful dynasties across Asia in India, China, and Japan.[16]

Jōin explains that Jinmu (Divine Warrior), the founder of Japan's royal family, used this Shintō to elevate his ancestor to divine status as Tenshō Daijin. The royal family ruled successfully for hundreds of years until the middle of the ninth century, when the Fujiwara family assumed control of the government by becoming hereditary regents (*sekkan ke*). To ensure the success of their rule, they used this Shintō to elevate the founder of their family, Fujiwara Kamatari (614–669), to divine status as Danzan Gongen (The Avatar of Consultation Mountain). Thereafter the Fujiwara family ruled successfully for about five hundred years until the middle of the fourteenth century. Subsequently, after a long period of civil unrest and lawlessness, in 1603 Tokugawa Ieyasu restored peace to the land by establishing a new government with his family as hereditary shoguns. The Tokugawa family used this same Shintō to elevate Ieyasu to divine status as Tōshō Dai Gongen. The apotheosis of Ieyasu, therefore, represents just another example of a pattern of Shintō rulership with well established precedents across Asia and in Japan. Jōin praises it as the only way to insure the success of the new Tokugawa dynasty and the prosperity of the country.[17]

---

[14] See *Taishō shinshū daizōkyō*, ed. by Takakusu, chap. 6, Dharmakṣema's translation, chap. 12, 'Sì tiānwáng pǐn'; Yìjìng's translation 'Sì tiānwáng húguó pǐn'; and *The Sūtra of Golden Light*, trans. by Emmerick, chap. 6, 'The Four Great Kings'.

[15] *Taishō shinshū daizōkyō*, ed. by Takakusu, Dharmakṣema's translation, chap. 11, 'Zhènlùn pǐn' (T no. 663, XVI, 347a); Yìjìng's translation, chap. 20, 'Wángfǎ zhènglùn pǐn' (T no. 665, XVI, 442b); and *The Sūtra of Golden Light*, trans. by Emmerick, chap. 12, 'Instruction Concerning Divine Kings', p. 58.

[16] *Tendaishū zensho*, ed. by Tendai, XII, 256b–57b, 286b–87a, 293a–94b, 299b, 303b.

[17] *Tendaishū zensho*, ed. by Tendai, XII, 254b, 300b–02a. Danzan is an alternative name for Tōnomine, the mountain where Fujiwara Kamatari is said to have advised Tenji, an early member of the royal family who supposedly reigned from 668 to 671. When the Meiji regime came to power, Tōnomine was converted from a Buddhist monastery into a Shintō shrine. For

Jōin's explanation is not without foundation. The *Nihon shoki* (History of Japan) and *Shoku Nihongi* (Continued Chronicle of Japan), the first two of Japan's official dynastic histories (compiled in 720 and 797, respectively), record nine occasions (during years 676, 680, 686, 692, 694, 696, 702, 703, 705) prior to 720 when the court commanded the *Golden Light Sūtra* to be chanted throughout the land. During this same period — identified by Herman Ooms as the 'Tenmu Dynasty' when the royal family first exerted control over the centralized reigns of power — the official histories mention other Buddhist scriptures by name no more often than twice each.[18] Clearly the *Golden Light Sūtra* was the single most important scripture for Japan's early rulers. Moreover Jōin's theory of divine kingship rests on a broad comparative method. He cites numerous Chinese texts not just for other precedents but also to demonstrate that the same techniques of divine kingship exist across Asia. 'Shintō', thus, refers not to a unique Japanese religion but to the religious sanction of rulership in general. His historical consciousness is especially noteworthy. Jōin recognizes that as governments and social institutions evolve, the conception of the gods linked to those institutions also must change. The progression from Tenshō Daijin, to Danzan Gongen, to Tōshō Dai Gongen neatly corresponds to stages of Japanese history. Finally, his ideas fit into a broader Buddhist discourse that describes gods as being important primarily for worldly (*seken*) ends such as economics and politics, not for other-worldly (*shusseken*) goals such as religious salvation.[19]

Textual Issues

Motoori probably never heard of Jōin nor saw Jōin's secret essays. But Motoori certainly must have heard ideas similar to those of Jōin. He lived during an age when many different theories and practices circulated under the label 'Shintō', some proclaimed publically and others (like Jōin's) taught secretly only during

details of the destruction wrought by this conversion, see Grapard, 'Japan's Ignored Cultural Revolution', pp. 247–65.

[18] Based on electronic searches of the *Rikkokushi*. See the entries for the following dates (year. month. day): 676. 11. 20, 680. 5. 1, 686. 7. 8, 692. 5. 3, 694. 5. 11, 696. 12. 1, 702. 12. 13, 703. 6. 13, 705. 4. 1. Tenmu (Heavenly Warrior) reigned from 672 to 686. The title 'Heavenly Sovereign' (*tennō*) probably came into use during or shortly after his reign. Ooms, *Imperial Politics and Symbolics*, pp. 46–48.

[19] Jōin, in *Tendaishū zensho*, ed. by Tendai, XII, 261a, 274a. Regarding the worldly (*laukika*) versus other-worldly (*lokottara*) distinction in Buddhism, see Ruegg, *The Symbiosis of Buddhism with Brahmanism/Hinduism*.

private initiations.[20] Motoori wrote his commentary on the *Kojiki* to sweep away those competing explanations of the gods. That he (and his followers) so thoroughly swept them aside was due in no small part to the way he confronted three textual obstacles: the prestige of the *Nihon shoki*, the obscurity of the *Kojiki*, and new trends in the markup and analysis of Chinese texts.

Motoori began writing his *Kojiki-den* in 1764. At that time, anyone who wanted to learn about the gods of ancient Japan normally would read the first two books (out of thirty total) of the *Nihon shoki*, which describe the activities of the gods during the Divine Age (*jindai*). These first two books were published in 1599 by the royal command of the Heavenly Sovereign Go-Yōzei on printing presses with movable type newly acquired from Korea (see Figure 8). For an early text, the *Nihon shoki* has a remarkably well-established pedigree. Its presentation to the court during the year 720 is duly recorded in the *Shoku Nihongi*, Japan's second official dynastic history. Court scholars regularly presented lectures on it, based on which they compiled at least six commentaries between the years 812 to 965.[21] Because of its royal sponsorship and established textual history, the *Nihon shoki* enjoyed unassailable authority.

At the same time, because the *Nihon shoki* conforms to Chinese historiographic conventions it can be evaluated in terms of other Chinese texts. It borrows vocabulary, concepts, and entire passages from Chinese sources. The first line, for example, famously weaves together the genesis story from the *Huáinánzi* (*c.* second century BCE) and the idea of the cosmic egg from the *Sānwŭ lìjì* (*c.* CE 280). Based on these sources it presents a cosmology, animated by the alternating succession of yin and yang, which fits easily into Buddhist, Confucian, or Daoist interpretive frameworks. In a series of court lectures during the years 1455 to 1457, for example, Ichijō Kaneyoshi (1402–1481) explained the gods of the *Nihon shoki* by citing the *Kusharon* (that is, *Abhidharma kośa*), a Buddhist guide to cosmology.[22] Jōin did likewise.[23] As long as the *Nihon shoki* provided the most authoritative account of the Japanese gods, the significance of those gods would continue to be debated in light of Chinese and Buddhist sources.

When the *Kojiki* (three books total) first appeared in print, in 1644, it appeared to be an unlikely alternative source of information about the gods. It

---

[20] Endō, 'The Early Modern Period'.

[21] Kōnoshi, *Kojiki to Nihon shoki*, pp. 173–76.

[22] Kōnoshi, *Kojiki to Nihon shoki*, pp. 35–41, 114–20, 175–78. The lectures by Ichijō Kaneyoshi formed the basis of the commentary known as the *Nihon shoki sanso*.

[23] *Tendaishū zensho*, ed. by Tendai, XII, 264a.

included a preface written in the style of a memorial which supposedly had been presented along with the rest of the text to the court in 712 (eight years prior to the *Nihon shoki*). But no other sources attest that this event occurred or that such a text then existed. It is mentioned neither in the official dynastic histories nor by other early records. The word *kojiki* appears in the *Man'yōshū* (the court-sponsored collection of poetry compiled *c.* 760), but in a way that could be interpreted as a generic term ('ancient accounts') rather than as a proper name. The *Kojiki* disagrees with the *Nihon shoki* on many fundamental details. It counts the reigns of the ancient rulers differently, omitting Jingū (no. 15 in the *Nihon shoki*). The *Kojiki* generally lacks dates, but it gives the age for twenty-two rulers and the dates of death for ten of them (out of thirty-three total). Not a single one of its figures agree with those of the *Nihon shoki*. More important, its account of the gods also diverges in many important respects. Only in the *Kojiki*, for example, is it the Sun Goddess who decrees that her descendants must rule over the lands below.[24] These discrepancies can be interpreted as evidence that the *Kojiki* reflects the views of later authors who supported a political agenda at odds with the *Nihon shoki*.

Medieval period manuscripts of the *Kojiki* could be found (the earliest one was copied by Buddhist monk Ken'yu in 1372), but their existence proved little. They were just one example of a larger genre, texts with titles such as *Gochinza hongi* (Mainline Chronicle of our Deities), *Kujiki* (Former Chronicles), *Hōki hongi* (Mainline Chronicle of the Jeweled Foundation), each one of which purported to record ancient histories of the gods. During the early modern period *Kokugaku* scholars identified anachronisms in every one of these texts and denounced them as apocryphal.[25] Initially, the *Kojiki* was regarded likewise. In 1750 the scholar Tada Yoshitoshi (1698–1750) published *Nihon jindai ki* (Accounts of Japan's Divine Age) in which he noted that the preface of the *Kojiki* does not conform to the literary norms for court documents and that the rustic format of its historical accounts could never have been accepted by the court. Likewise in 1768 Kamo no Mabuchi (1697–1769) — the scholar under whom Motoori studied the lan-

---

[24] Regarding dates, see Kōnoshi, *Kanji tekisuto to shite no Kojiki*, pp. 114–16. Regarding differences in the accounts of the gods, see Kōnoshi, *Kojiki to Nihon shoki*, pp. 126–33.

[25] Ken'yu's copy of the *Kojiki* also is known as the Shinpukuji edition, after the alternative name of the Buddhist temple (Ōsu Kannon Hōshōin, Nagoya) where it was discovered. Today the *Kujiki* is commonly referred to as the *Sendai kuji hongi*. Regarding this text, see Bentley, *The Authenticity of 'Sendai kuji hongi'*, and the book review: Teeuwen, 'Sendai Kuji Hongi'. Regarding the *Gochinza hongi* and *Hōki hongi*, see the account of Yoshimi Yukikazu (1673–1716) in Teeuwen, *Watarai Shintō*, pp. 313–42.

guage of the *Man'yōshū* — sent a letter to Motoori in which he asserted that the *Kojiki*'s preface must be a forgery added later.[26]

The third textual obstacle, new academic norms for the treatment of Chinese texts, requires a more detailed explanation since this topic rarely receives the attention it deserves. In 1912 the Japanese Ministry of Education issued guidelines to standardize the way that Chinese texts (*kanbun*) can be translated into a Japanese format (a process generally known as *kundoku*).[27] The guidelines result in what Roy Andrew Miller calls a 'chaste' style, one which sacrifices meaning and understanding for conciseness.[28] This style is used in all school textbooks, reference works, college entrance exams, and editions of Chinese texts published for a general audience. It has become so ubiquitous that today many people do not realize that other formats exist. Too often even scholars assume that any deviation from the official style, whether today or in former times, is simply incorrect.

Prior to the Tokugawa period, however, literate Japanese parsed Chinese texts in many different ways.[29] Certain court families (known as *hakase ke* or *dōshō ke*) each maintained secret and unique traditions regarding such basic issues as how to punctuate a text, when to pronounce glyphs phonetically (*on*) as Chinese terms or when to gloss (*kun*) them with equivalent Japanese words, and how to rearrange the Chinese word order (subject verb object) so as to reflect Japanese syntax (subject, object, verb).[30] Japanese Buddhists favoured a hybrid style in which the same passages might be parsed twice, once in Chinese word order with Chinese phonetics (for chanting aloud), and again with Japanese glosses

[26] Ōwa, *Shinpan Kojiki seiritsu kō*, pp. 27–31 (see also Ōwa, *Kojiki seiritsu kō*, and Ōwa, *Kojiki seiritsu kō*, rev. edn). Ōwa presents the most comprehensive account of the questions raised regarding the authenticity of the *Kojiki*. The *Man'yōshū*, like the *Kojiki*, is written entirely in Chinese glyphs. Kamo no Mabuchi taught Motoori how to decipher the Chinese so as to reconstruct the Japanese diction and prosody of the poems.

[27] The text of the 1912 guidelines ('Kanbun jugyō ni kansuru chōsa hōkoku' [Announcement of (the Results of) Our Investigation Regarding the Teaching of Chinese Texts], in *Kanpō* [Official Announcements], no. 8630) is available online, Tokyo, Nishōgakusha University, Department of Japanese Kanbun Instruction (<http://www.nishogakusha-kanbun.net/kanp8630.pdf> [accessed February 2010]).

[28] Miller, *The Japanese Language*, p. 120.

[29] For a standard historical account of the methods used to markup Chinese texts, see Nakada, *Kotenbon no kokugogakuteki kenkyū* and Nakada, *Kotenbon no kokugogakuteki kenkyū*, rev. edn, pp. 87–173.

[30] This usage of the term '*kun*' (literally, 'to instruct') comes from the Chinese *xùngǔ* (Japanese, *kunko*), which refers to textual glosses that use a familiar word to explicate an archaic or unfamiliar one.

and syntax.[31] Buddhists, especially the esoteric lineages on Mount Hiei, could be extremely creative in their Japanese glosses. They would parse the same passage several different ways (*jikunshaku*), read complex Chinese glyphs in terms of their component elements (*jizōshaku*), or interpret them as homophones for other words (*tenshōshaku*), all in order to reveal multiple hidden layers of meaning.[32] Whether secular or Buddhist, however, all of these textual techniques comprised trade secrets that could be revealed only to select disciples.

Idiosyncratic methods of analysing Chinese texts (and the secret initiations which shielded them from critical scrutiny) largely ended after 1624. That year saw the publication of *Keian oshō kahō waten* (Reverend Keian's Method of Japanese Markup), detailed instructions on how to markup Chinese Confucian texts for reading aloud in Japanese.[33] Keian Genju (1427–1508), the author of the instructions, was a Zen monk who had spent seven years studying in China from 1467 to 1473. He was the first Japanese to lecture on the *Sìshū jízhù* (*Collected Annotations on the Four Books*) — the Confucian commentaries by Zhū Xī (1130–1200) which then served as the basis for the Chinese civil service examinations. Keian had rejected previous Japanese methods of marking Chinese texts as inadequate for expressing Zhu Xi's interpretations. The following year, in 1625, a complete set of the *Sìshū jízhù* appeared in print with full textual markup by Bunshi Genshō (also known as Nanpo; 1555–1620), a Zen monk in Keian's lineage. This edition became such a bestseller (reprinted in 1626, 1631, 1643, 1649, 1650, and 1659) that Keian's method of markup became known as 'Bunshi Marks' (*bunshi ten*).[34]

---

[31] This textual technique is known as *monzen yomi*. Outside of Buddhist contexts, it is also commonly used for Japanese editions of the Chinese *Thousand Character Classic* (*Qiānzì wén*). For a detailed example, see Miller, *The Japanese Language*, pp. 118–19.

[32] Maeda Eun, *Bukkyō kokinhen ippan*; reprinted in Maeda Eun, *Bukkyō kokinhen ippan* (1931–32), pp. 389–93.

[33] I use the term 'markup' (rather than 'punctuate') because *wakun* (or *kunten* as it is more commonly known today) consists of textual instructions concerning both lexicographical meaning and syntactical relationships. These instructions can appear with or without punctuation marks (that is dots or circles to separate sentences and clauses). Regarding Keian, see Kawase, 'Keian oshō kahō wakun ni tsuite', pp. 45–53. The text of Keian's instructions, which gives its date of composition as the year 1501, is reprinted on pp. 55–72 of this article.

[34] The version of the *Sìshū jízhù* with Bunshi's markup usually is known as the *Taikai shisho shūchū* (Large [Print] Edition of the Collected Annotations on the Four Books). It was prepared for publication by Bunshi's disciple, Tomari Jochiku (1570–1655), the same person who published the *Keian oshō kahō wakun* one year earlier. For a useful overview of Bunshi's career, with reprint dates for the *Taikai shisho shūchū*, see Takatsu, 'Kinsei Ryūkyū ni okeru

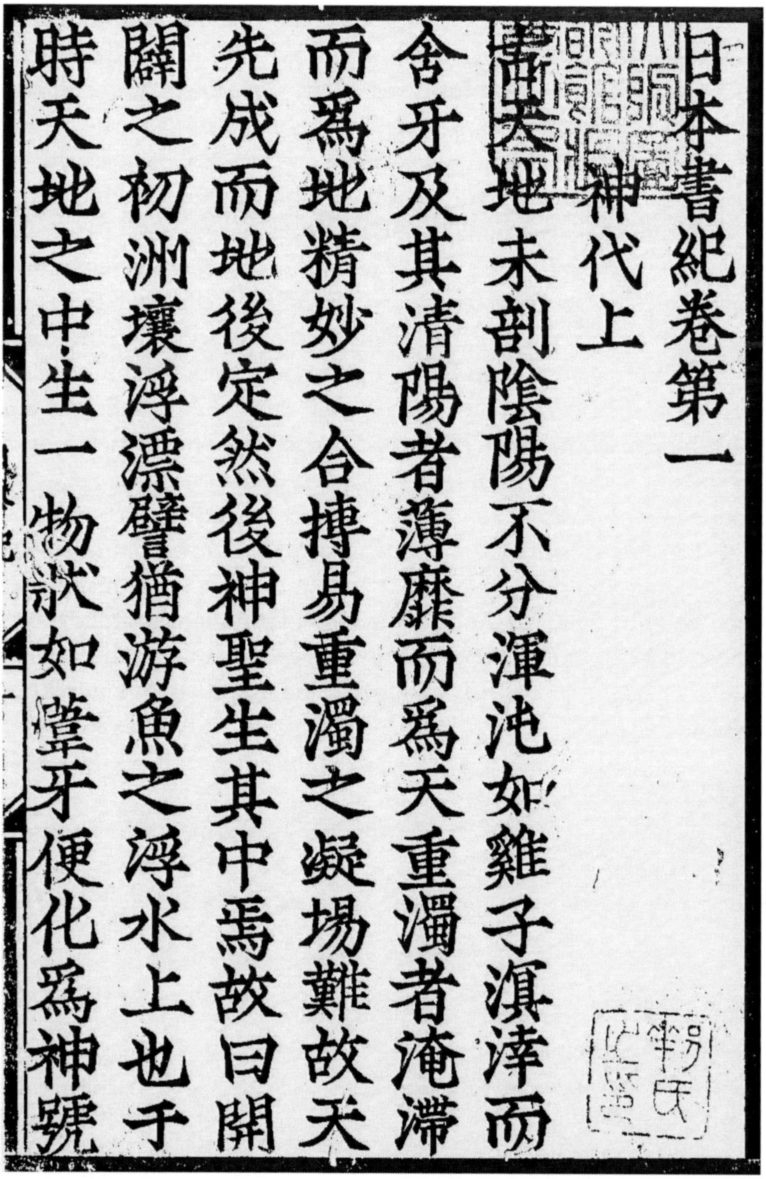

日本書紀巻第一
神代上
古天地未剖陰陽不分渾沌如雞子溟涬而
含牙及其清陽者薄靡而爲天重濁者淹滯
而爲地精妙之合摶易重濁之凝場難故天
先成而地後定然後神聖生其中焉故曰開
闢之初洲壤浮漂譬猶游魚之浮水上也于
時天地之中生一物狀如葦牙便化爲神號

Figure 8. *Nihon Shoki Jindai Kan* (History of Japan: Books on the Divine Age), printed by the royal command of Go-Yōzei (1572–1617), movable-type edition, bk I, leaf 1r. 1599. Osaka, Osaka Prefectural Nakanoshima Library, Kichōsho Gazō Database. Available online at <http://www.library.pref.osaka.jp/lib/collect/kichosho.html>. Reproduced with permission. The first line (col. 3) says: 'Antiquity: Heaven and Earth not yet sundered, Yin and Yang not divided, just [featureless] potentiality (*húndùn*) like a chicken egg [...]'.

As Confucian learning moved out of Zen monasteries and into public academies, however, subsequent Confucian scholars revised Keian's rules. They quibbled over the minor details of his instructions regarding when Chinese glyphs should be read phonetically (*on*) or glossed (*kun*) with Japanese words, what glosses should be standard for each Chinese grammatical particle, and so forth. Most of all, they debated his rule that most (but not all) Chinese grammatical particles should be assigned a Japanese phonetic representation even when the inflexion of the other Japanese glosses convey the same meaning, and thus render the Chinese glyph redundant. Subsequent Confucian scholars insisted that every Chinese glyph must be represented by its own unique phonetic element. They wanted to prevent anyone from failing to memorize even a single glyph that had been written by the sages of China. Accordingly they published their own editions of the Chinese texts, with revised Japanese markup. Some of the more influential methods were the 'Dōshun Marks' of Hayashi Razan (1583–1657), the 'Ka Marks' of Yamazaki Anzai (1618–1682), and the 'Gotō Marks' of Gotō Shizan (1721–1782).[35] Each of these published methods build on their predecessors, introducing more standardization and conciseness, in a process of evolution which ultimately culminated in the official Ministry of Education guidelines of 1912.

The publishing record reflects this evolution in textual methodologies. The *Nihon shoki jindai kan* published in 1599 includes neither punctuation nor markup (see Fig. 8). The *Kojiki* published in 1644 still lacks punctuation but includes full Japanese markup, with lexicographical glosses on the right side of each column of Chinese glyphs to indicate the meaning of words as well as syntactical markup on the left side to indicate the reordering of the words for reading sentences as Japanese (see Figs 9 and 11). This markup can tell us only how the editor who added it (and perhaps subsequent readers) interpreted and pronounced the text, but not how earlier generations of readers might have done so.[36]

---

kanseki juyō', pp. 9–11. For an English-language account, see Steben, 'The Transmission of Neo-Confucianism', pp. 44–46.

[35] Nakada, *Kotenbon no kokugogakuteki kenkyū*, pp. 157–73. Wai-ming Ng provides a handy table which lists eighteen individual Confucian scholars whose versions of the *Yijīng* (*Book of Changes*) and its commentaries, each with their own methods of textual markup (not 'punctuation' as stated by Ng), were published from 1626 (Bunshi's version) to 1859; see Ng, *The 'I Ching' in Tokugawa Thought and Culture*, p. 33.

[36] The 1644 edition states that it was published by the Fūgetsudō bookshop in Kyoto by Fūgetsu Munemoto, but the name of the editor is not given. The markup reflects earlier *Kojiki* manuscripts in the so-called Urabe filiation, named for the Urabe (also known as Yoshida) family of hereditary celebrants with which it is associated. The earliest manuscript in this group, copied by Yoshida Kanenaga (1467–1536) in 1522, has very little markup. The next earliest

The 1644 markup indicates that the editor interpreted the *Kojiki* solely based on the Chinese glyphs with which it is written. As long as the *Kojiki* was construed in terms of this orthodox Confucian style of *kundoku*, it would be regarded at best as a poor, rustic cousin to the *Nihon shoki* and at worst as a medieval forgery.

The Language of the Gods

Motoori Norinaga rescued the *Kojiki* from its critics and placed it at the fountainhead of Japanese culture by reading it as the ancient language of the gods. Motoori's life and intellectual context have been discussed elsewhere.[37] Here I wish to focus on his approach to reading and rewriting the *Kojiki* as explained in Book One of his *Kojiki-den*, which is now available in English translation.[38] This book summarizes the following methodology, which Motoori applies to the *Kojiki* as a whole. First, Motoori portrays the superior Chinese style of the *Nihon shoki* as its greatest defect. He interprets the seemingly inferior Chinese of the *Kojiki* as evidence of its compiler's sincere efforts to transcribe accurately the heretofore oral narratives of the gods in a foreign medium. He argues that in terms of the accuracy of its archaic transcriptions, the *Kojiki* is superior to the *Nihon shoki*. Then, he explains how to reconstruct the ancient language underlying that transcription. In short, Book One provides for the *Kojiki* what Keian Genju previously had provided for Chinese Confucian texts, namely, detailed instructions for converting their Chinese linguistic structures into Japanese. This time, though, it would be a different kind of Japanese.

manuscript was copied by Bonshun (1553–1632), a Buddhist monk who was the son of Yoshida Kanemigi (1516–73). It includes markup very similar to the 1644 printed version, as does the 1638 manuscript by an otherwise unknown person named Ujitsune (or Ujinawa). Manuscripts in the Ise filiation (named for the Kōkōji Buddhist temple in Ise), in contrast, were copied by Buddhist monks: Ken'yu in 1372, Dōka in 1381, Dōshō in 1424, and Shun'yu in 1426. Ken'yu's copy has no markup and the others in this textual lineage very little. Textual historians assume that the Buddhists were more faithful scribes and that their copies more accurately preserve the original format of the texts. The Bonshun MS and the 1638 Ujitsune MS are available online: Nara, Sakamoto Ryūmon Bunko, Ujitsune MS; and Tokyo, Kokugakuin UL, Bonshun MS.

[37] Matsumoto, *Motoori Norinaga*, pp. 76–119; Sakai, *Voices of the Past*, pp. 255–63; and Burns, *Before the Nation*, pp. 35–101.

[38] Motoori, *Kojiki-den, Book 1*, trans. by Wehmeyer. Also see the helpful book review Bentley, 'Review of *Kojiki-den: Book 1*'. Bentley points out many inconsistencies in Wehmeyer's historical romanizations, but readers should also be warned that her spellings of modern Japanese words and proper names are just as unreliable.

Motoori's objections to the *Nihon shoki* began with its title. The fact that it is named 'The History of Japan' already indicates that it was written from a Chinese point of view, for a Chinese audience. Chinese dynasties have come and gone. Accordingly, the successive histories written about them include the name of the dynasty they depict in their titles. For Motoori, a history of Japan with its everlasting royal family, written for a Japanese audience has no need to even mention the name 'Japan'. Accordingly, the simple title of the *Kojiki* (Ancient Accounts) is 'quite splendid'.[39] From its title onwards, the *Nihon shoki* uses the language of China to describe Japanese affairs, the words of later times in regard to earlier events, creating endless distortions. Motoori explains that in Japan people describe things as they actually are, whereas Chinese literary style demands abstract embellishments (p. 22). Thus, in the *Kojiki* people speak of sky (*ame*) and ground (*tsuchi*), not Firmament and Terra (Chinese, *gānkūn*; Japanese, *kenkon*) as in the *Nihon shoki*. Instead of the yin and yang of the *Nihon shoki*, the *Kojiki* speaks of woman (*me*) and man (*wo*) (pp. 38–39).

Motoori objects to the yin and yang at the beginning of the *Nihon shoki* not just as a foreign embellishment, but also because it leads Japanese away from reality towards the artificial. Unlike the authentic accounts of antiquity preserved in Japan, Chinese individuals invented their stories about the beginning of the cosmos (pp. 35–36). Chinese describe heaven in anthropomorphic terms — in phrases such as 'heaven's mandate', the 'will of heaven' (etc.) — because they have no knowledge of the Divine Age. The Japanese, in contrast, know real gods, with real bodies, who live in the sky, not in an abstract Chinese-style heaven. For this reason, one must not mistakenly assume that the Chinese glyph for writing 'heaven' (*tiān*; Japanese, *ten*) represents the same idea as the archaic Japanese vernacular word for 'sky' (*ame*) (pp. 43–44). In this way, Motoori draws a sharp contrast between Chinese writing, which he describes as an art of cunning and artifice, and the ancient oral traditions of Japan, in which meaning (*kokoro*), event (*koto*), and language (*kotoba*) correspond with one another (pp. 21–22).

Motoori acknowledges that the *Kojiki* is written in literary Chinese (p. 75), but he cites its preface to argue that it was compiled as a transcription of an oral recitation for the purpose of preserving the Japanese language of antiquity.[40] He

---

[39] Motoori, *Kojiki-den, Book I*, trans. by Wehmeyer, p. 65; also see p. 34. Hereafter paranthetical notations refer to this source.

[40] Here the term 'literary Chinese' translates the word '*kanbun*'. Modern scholars frequently distinguish the literary Chinese composed in Japan from that composed by Chinese authors. Wixted, '*Kanbun*', for example, argues that *kanbun* composed in Japan should be called 'Sino-Japanese' so that the designation 'Chinese' can be reserved for 'Chinese traditional texts written

asserts that the *Kojiki* had been compiled on the royal command of the Heavenly Sovereign Tenmu because the sovereign was 'saddened' (p. 142) at the prospect that the adoption of Chinese writing might cause future generations of Japanese to forget their ancient language. The Chinese diction of the *Kojiki* might seem stylistically inferior, but its irregularities demonstrate the dedication with which its compiler strove to transcribe the ancient accounts accurately (p. 79). One must respect this original intent by reading the *Kojiki* with Japanese pronunciations as a Japanese text (p. 141), not Chinese.[41] Toward this goal, Motoori carefully catalogs the semantic structures found within the *Kojiki*, identifying how it uses Chinese glyphs to represent (*a*) pure Japanese in phonetic transcription, (*b*) the style of ancient Japanese, (*c*) a hybrid style of ancient Japanese with Chinese influences, and (*d*) pure Chinese (pp. 80–82).

Linguistically, Motoori's most influential accomplishment lies in his exhaustive analysis of the Chinese glyphs used in the *Kojiki* for the phonetic transcriptions of archaic Japanese words (pp. 95–119). He carefully documents regularities in the phonetic spelling of many key words, in which glyphs that represent the same phonic element today in fact are differentiated from one another. He deduces from this evidence that the glyphs originally must have represented separate sets of sounds, which the Japanese of later centuries ceased to distinguish (pp. 112–13). Motoori points out that similar spelling regularities also exist in the *Nihon shoki* and the *Man'yōshū*, but that neither of these texts maintain the same level of consistency and accuracy as does the *Kojiki* (pp. 108, 114). Here he

---

by Chinese' (p. 23). Likewise, Rabinovitch, 'An Introduction to Hentai Kambun', p. 99 and Aldridge, 'Principles of *Hentai Kanbun* Word Order', p. 207 follow the lead of mainstream Japanese historians by referring to Chinese literature composed in Japan as '*hentai kanbun*' ('non-standard' or 'variant' *kanbun*), while Kōnoshi, *Kanji tekisuto to shite no Kojiki*, pp. 43–49 advocates the term '*hi kanbun*' ('non-Chinese') to clearly indicate that *kanbun* composed in Japan is an artificial language which conveys fully neither Japanese nor Chinese. This manner of distinguishing *kanbun* by its Chinese or Japanese origin, however, represents a modern historiography which postdates Motoori. Also, the assumption that premodern Japanese *kanbun* always was intended to be read only in *kundoku* style (Rabinovitch, 'An Introduction to Hentai Kambun', p. 110; Aldridge, 'Principles of *Hentai Kanbun* Word Order', p. 207) needs to be reexamined. Evidence suggests that many premodern Buddhist texts composed in Japan once were read in Chinese word order. Regarding the distinction between Chinese and Japanese *kanbun*, see Aldridge, 'Principles of *Hentai Kanbun* Word Order'; Rabinovitch, 'An Introduction to Hentai Kambun'; Wixted, 'Kanbun'.

[41] Space precludes addressing this topic here, but Kōnoshi Takamitsu argues that the phonetic notes in the *Kojiki* primarily serve to resolve issues of grammatical interpretation, not pronunciation. See Kōnoshi, *Kanji tekisuto to shite no Kojiki*, pp. 78–81.

found irrefutable documentation of the *Kojiki*'s superiority. The exhaustive precision with which Motoori presents this analysis lends his entire commentary an aura of rigour and authority (an aura that was only enhanced in subsequent centuries when modern linguists used the same data to model the sound system of Old Japanese).[42] This aura of authority not only made Motoori's criticisms of the *Nihon shoki* seem more persuasive, but also lent greater credibility to his ultimate project: reading the *Kojiki* as the ancient language of the gods.

Motoori states his project directly: 'One should [...] read the text seeking the pure language of antiquity, without any contamination by the Chinese style' (p. 145). In this process, one must be willing to discard the Chinese glyphs with which the text was written. He describes them as 'makeshift items which were simply attached to the text' (p. 145), lacking any reality or deeper meaning. Instead of literal faithfulness to the Chinese glyphs, one should simply 'determine what were the words of [the original recitalist] and assign a reading [in other words, Japanese gloss] based on the sensibilities of antiquity' (p. 151). In this process, one should give special weight to phonetic transcriptions of ancient Japanese words and use them as much as possible. Longer forms of ancient words are preferable to shorter forms or abbreviated transcriptions. Thus, where a phrase written in Chinese conveys the same meaning as does a phrase written elsewhere in the language of antiquity, one should always substitute the Japanese version for the original Chinese glyphs (pp. 151–53). The same exercise applies to passages written completely in Chinese for which no Japanese version is attested. Motoori instructs readers not to rely on the Chinese glyphs, but: 'rather obtain an understanding of the meaning, and assign a reading in the language of antiquity which is appropriate to the tenor of the passage' (p. 154).

To understand how this method works in practice, consider the example of the word '*akujin*' (Chinese, '*èshén*'; hateful or evil spirits).[43] This term occurs in the *Kojiki* as part of a passage about how the god Susanoo (also spelled 'Susanowo') cried endlessly upon the loss of his mother, Izanami. As a result, the text tells us, the world was filled with the sounds of hateful spirits like the flies that swarm in the fifth month.[44] The 1644 edition of the text glosses '*akujin*' with the Japanese phrase '*ashiki kami*' (unpleasant or mean deity).[45] This gloss is a standard Japanese

---

[42] See Wehmeyer's note, Motoori, *Kojiki-den, Book 1*, trans. by Wehmeyer, pp. 138–140 n. 168.

[43] This example is discussed by Kōnoshi, *Kojiki to Nihon shoki*, pp. 12–14.

[44] *Kojiki*, ed. by Kōnoshi, pp. 54 (Chinese text), 55 (translation).

[45] Tokyo, Waseda UL, ri05 09177, bk 1, leaf 16ᵛ.

markup for this Chinese term. It occurs not just in the 1644 edition of the *Kojiki*, but also in earlier manuscript versions and in a 1687 printed edition annotated by Deguchi (also known as Watarai) Nobuyoshi (1615–1690).[46]

Motoori, however, rejects '*ashiki kami*'. He takes his gloss from another *Kojiki* passage which discusses the deliberations among the heavenly gods for subduing the lands below. In this passage, one of the gods remarks that those lands seem to have many '*kō shin koku jin*'.[47] The 1644 edition of the text glosses the first two Chinese glyphs in rebus fashion as phonetic transcriptions for the Japanese adjectival compound '*ara-buru*' (unruly, or violent) and translates the second two glyphs into Japanese as '*kunitsu kami*' (earthly deities).[48] Motoori then uses three of the four elements from this gloss in the form of '*ara-buru kami*' as his gloss for *akujin*. His commentary further states that this same gloss applies to Chinese glyphs for related terms such as 'malicious ghosts' (*jaki*; Chinese, *yéguǐ*). Note that Motoori's gloss lacks any linguistic basis whatsoever.[49] It is not the case that he merely interprets the glyphs '*akujin*' as '*ara-buru kami*', but rather that he asserts that the original recitation must have used the words '*ara-buru kami*'. Instead of glossing the words actually found in the text, in effect he replaces them with what he believes the compiler of the text should have written.

When glossed in this way, every Chinese term in the *Kojiki* becomes nothing more than a linguistic placeholder for a vernacular Japanese word.[50] A search

---

[46] Tokyo, Kokugakuin UL, Bonshun MS, bk 1, leaf 20ᵛ; Nara, Sakamoto Ryūmon Bunko, Ujitsune MS, bk 1, leaf 14ʳ, dated 1638; Deguchi Nobuyoshi, *Gōtō Kojiki*, 1687 edition, Tokyo, Waseda UL, Bunko17 w0199.

[47] *Kojiki*, ed. by Kōnoshi, pp. 98 (original text), 99 (translation).

[48] By 'rebus fashion' I refer to a kind of phonetic transcription based not on the pronunciation of the Chinese glyphs themselves, but on the sounds represented by their Japanese translations. Imagine, for example, that one could write the Chinese glyphs '*zhú*' and '*bòhe*' (words for the biological plants 'bamboo' and 'mint') as a phonetic transcription for the English word 'bamboozlement'. In the Japanese text, the glyph *kō* (Chinese, *huáng*) means 'rough, uneven' (Japanese, *ara*), while the glyph '*shin*' (Chinese, *zhèn*) is the verb 'to shake' (Japanese, *furu*). Together they transcribe a single word consisting of the first part of a verb (*ara*) plus its inflected adjectival ending (*buru*), forming '*araburu*' ('unruly' or 'violent'). See Tokyo, Waseda UL, ri05 04868, bk 1, leaf 39ʳ.

[49] Kōnoshi, *Kojiki to Nihon shoki*, p. 14.

[50] At about this same time authors of social satire had begun to exploit the gap between Chinese terms and their vernacular Japanese glosses for humorous effect. See Ariga, 'The Playful Gloss', pp. 320–35. Note also how Ariga discusses the *Kojiki* (pp. 311–12) only as an ancient text without consideration of the contemporaneous transformations of its glosses. Even textual scholars who accept 712 as the date of the *Kojiki*'s composition do not assert with certainty

for the Chinese glyphs for '*akujin*' (that is, '*ashiki kami*' or '*èshén*') will produce hundreds of examples in the classical literature of China and Japan as well as in the Chinese translations of the Buddhist scriptures from India. One can easily compare and contrast the literary and religious implications of this term in its Indian, Chinese, and Japanese contexts. But outside of Motoori's *Kojiki-den* it is impossible to find the word '*ara-buru kami*'. By reading (that is to say, rewriting) the *Kojiki* in this fashion, Motoori divorces the *Kojiki*'s narrative from its Asian cultural milieu. All Chinese and Buddhist influences or parallels disappear. He forces us to read the *Kojiki* only in its own context and that of a limited number of other early Japanese texts (for example the *Man'yōshū*) that can be glossed with similar techniques. The gods of Japan's Divine Age become unique. In fact, they are no longer 'gods' but belong to the *sui generis* category '*kami*'.[51] No longer can Tenshō Daijin (Heavenly Illuminating Great God) be compared to Danzan Gongen or Tōshō Dai Gongen, as Jōin does. Instead, the Chinese glyphs for Tenshō Daijin must assume the pronunciation by which we know them today: Amaterasu Ōkami (Majestic Deity Shinning in the Sky; or, more simply, the Sun Goddess).

The above style of reading and rewriting alters the text in ways that extend beyond the linguistic. It transforms it both conceptually and chronologically. When one reads the text, as Motoori instructs, by 'seeking the pure language of antiquity without any contamination by the Chinese style' (p. 145), one must imagine another text, an original verbal recitation, as existing behind the written text.[52] The narrative of the gods conveyed by the original verbal recitation must predate the adoption of Chinese writing in Japan.[53] If Chinese influences or literary motifs occur in this narrative, they must be later accretions. As such, they are to be ignored or devalued. Jōin's quotations from the *Golden Light Sūtra*, therefore, become meaningless as long as readers imagine the *Kojiki* as a source for an early oral narrative predating the adoption of Buddhism by Japan's ruling elites.

---

whether the phonetic notes (*kunchū*; Ariga, 'The Playful Gloss', p. 312, fig. 1) embedded in its text date just as early or were added by later copyists. See Seeley, *A History of Writing in Japan*, p. 45 n. 15.

[51] It once was common for introductory accounts of Japanese religions to include statements such as this one: 'Because there is no exact English equivalent for the word *kami*, it will be used throughout the text without translation'. See Earhart, *Japanese Religion: Unity and Diversity*, p. 8. Regarding Motoori's view of *kami*, see Matsumoto, *Motoori Norinaga*, pp. 82–95.

[52] Kōnoshi, *Kanji tekisuto to shite no Kojiki*, pp. 178–83.

[53] Sakai describes the results of this reconceptualization as placing the Kojiki out of historical time and into an imaginary realm 'beyond history'; see Sakai, *Voices of the Past*, p. 259.

Visualizing the Language of the Gods

Motoori's transformation of the *Kojiki* extended to its visual representation. We can see this transformation with our own eyes, but to do so we must examine the page layout of the 1644 edition with its original Chinese text and Japanese markup. Then we must contrast it to the page layout of the *Kojiki-den*, published in 1790. We will begin with a simple example, the very first line of the *Kojiki*. In the 1644 edition (see Fig. 9, cols 1–2) this line appears as:

アメツチノ		ハシメテヒラクル			トキ		タカマノハラニ		ナリイツル		カミヲ	マウス
天	地	初	發	之	時	於	高	天	原 _	成	神	名 _
1	2	3	4	5	6	7	8	9	10	11	12	13

アマノ		ミナカヌシノ			カミト	
天	之	御	中	主	神 _
14	15	16	17	18	19

When shifted from a vertical layout to a horizontal one, its textual components line up as follows. The top row of small glyphs convey lexicographical glosses in Japanese *katakana* syllabary. The middle row of large glyphs consist of the original Chinese text. Interspersed between some of the larger Chinese glyphs, this row also contains smaller subscript Chinese glyphs, which convey Japanese syntactical markup for the reordering of the words. Finally, the bottom row consists of numerals I have added to aid readers in following how the reordering occurs.

We can see that the 1644 edition already provides readers with extensive markup. The lexicographical glosses cover almost the entire text. Especially note how they clump together with wide gaps between the combinations. This layout ties individual glosses to specific Chinese glyphs or combinations of glyphs. The large Chinese glyphs serve to convey the primary meaning, while the Japanese markup plays only a secondary role as an aid for the reader. We can also see that the syntactical markup suggests only minor reordering of the text. If we romanize this line in accordance with its accompanying markup, the result will be as follows:

ametsuchi hajimete hirakuru no toki takama-no-hara ni nari-itsuru kami wo
1, 2   3   4   5   6   8, 9, –, 10   7   11   12   –

ama-no-minakanushi no kami to mōsu
14, 15, 16, 17, 18   –   19   –   13

Again I have added numerals underneath the text to show how the individual Japanese words correspond to the original Chinese glyphs. Two textual inversions occur, with glyphs 7 and 13 relocated in the Japanese version. The dash (–) indicates where a Japanese lexicographic element (usually a grammatical particle) is

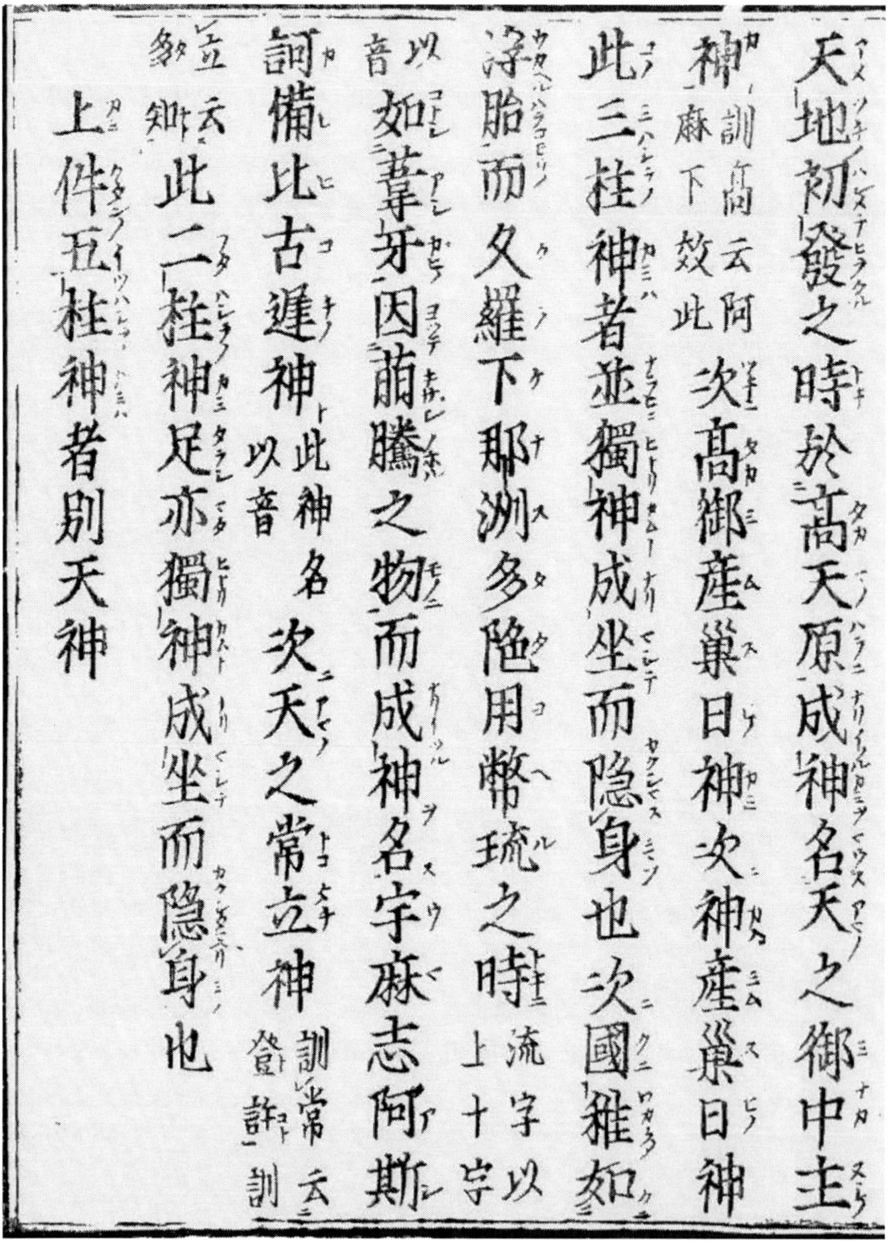

Figure 9. *Kojiki* (Ancient Accounts), 1644 edition, bk 1, leaf 4ᵛ. 1644.
Tokyo, Waseda UL, ri05 04868. Reproduced with permission.
Line 1 (cols 1–2) says: 'At the time when heaven and earth began to burst forth, on the high heavenly plain there developed a god called the god who rules the August Centre of the Heavens.'

added for sense, even though no corresponding glyph exists in the original Chinese. Notice that the exact same set of numerals appear beneath the Chinese glyphs and beneath their corresponding Japanese romanization. In this Japanese markup, every Chinese glyph in the original text generates a corresponding Japanese phonetic element or word. In this regard the 1644 edition conforms to the orthodox style of markup advocated by Japanese Confucians. Finally, a literal-minded translation that adheres to the style indicated by the markup would be similar to: 'At the time when heaven and earth began to burst forth, on the high heavenly plain there developed a god called the god who rules the August Centre of the Heavens'.

The same line in the *Kojiki-den* (see Fig. 10, cols 3–4) appears as follows:

アメ　ツチノ　ハジメ　ノ　トキ　　タ カマノハラ ニ ナリマセル カミ ノ ミナ ハ
天　地　初　發　之　時。於　高　天　原　成　神　名。
1　　2　　3　　4　　5　　6　　7　　8　　9　　10　　11　　12　　13

アメ　ノ　ノ　ミ　ナ　カ　ヌシノ　カミ
天　之　御　中　主　神。
14　　15　　16　　17　　18　　19

Here we encounter a very different style of markup. The lexicographical glosses in the top row cover the entire Chinese text, but in such a way as to avoid being directly associated with specific Chinese glyphs. The original Chinese text has punctuation marks (that is, small circles), but no smaller subscript Chinese glyphs to indicate any Japanese syntactical markup. Their absence suggests to the reader that the original text requires no reordering of the words to be understood as Japanese. To see if that suggestion is correct, we can romanize the text in Japanese as indicated by the markup:

ametsuchi no hajime no toki, takama-no-hara ni narimaseru kami no mina wa,
1, 2　　–　　3　　5　　6　　　8, 9, –, 10　　–　　11　　12　　–　　13　　–

ama-no-minakanushi no kami,
14, 15, 16, 17, 18　　–　　19

In fact, the Japanese version now follows the same word order as in the original Chinese text. The significant alterations occur elsewhere. Note that the Japanese version provides no phonic elements for two Chinese glyphs, numbers 4 and 7. The second one is a Chinese grammatical particle ('*yú*'; Japanese, '*o*'), which according to the initial version of Keian Genju's rules for Japanese markup can be skipped provided that the original sense of the sentence is maintained.[54] The

---

[54] *Keian oshō kahō waten* (1501), reprinted in Kawase, 'Keian oshō kahō wakun ni tsuite', p. 60: 'Ni woite to yomanu tokoro ari'.

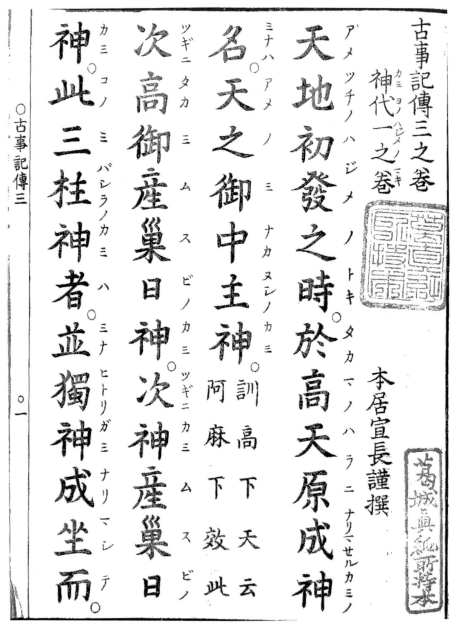

Figure 10. *Kojiki-den* (Ancient Accounts Conveyed), by Motoori Norinaga (1730–1801),
undated reprint of 1790 edition, bk III, leaf 1ʳ. Tokyo, Waseda UL, ri05 09177.
Reproduced with permission. Line 1 (cols 3–4) says: 'At the time when the sky and land began,
the honourable title of the kami formed on the high plains is the Sky's August Central Ruling Kami'.

other glyph (no. 4), however, represents a verb, 'to burst forth' (Chinese, '*fā*'; Japanese, '*hotsu*'). It cannot be omitted without changing the sense of the sentence. In his commentary, Motoori, merely asserts that this word is superfluous, leaving the reader to guess what the reason might be for omitting it.[55] Following Motoori's gloss, we can now translate this line as: 'At the time when the sky and land began, the honourable title of the *kami* formed on the high plains is the Sky's August Central Ruling Kami'.

Merely from the English translations, we can gain some idea of how Motoori overcame the differences between Chinese (subject, verb, object) and Japanese (subject, object, verb) word order. Much like one finds in translations by college students in elementary foreign language classes, Motoori not only omits some words, but he assigns unexpected grammatical functions to the others that he does translate. In this case, the Chinese glyph (no. 13) that the 1644 edition glosses as the verb '*mōsu*' (to call as), Motoori interprets as the noun '*mina*' (honourable title). As a noun it can stay in its original location, without having to be moved to the end of the sentence where one normally would expect to find a Japanese verb. It spite of its awkward style, the end result nonetheless conveys much of the same sense as does the 1644 version.

To see how this approach works with a longer, more complex sentence, consider the following line. It occurs just after the two gods Izanagi and Izanami have descended to the island they created and established their household. Izanagi (the male) asks Izanami (the female) if they should mate to populate this new world. In the 1644 edition (see Fig. 11, cols 3–4) Izanagi poses his question as follows:

カレニ	モテ	コノ	アカミ		ナリアマル		ヲ	サシ フサイテ	イマシノミ	
故	以二	此	吾	身	成	餘	處	判下塞	汝	身
1	2	3	4	5	6	7	8	9　10	11	12

	ル	ヲ		セン	ナリナスヿヲ	クニ	ツチヲ	ウムヿ	イカン	
不二	成	合一	處上	而	爲レ	生二	成	國	土一	生 奈 何
13	14	15	16	17	18	19	20	21	22	23　24　25

Compared to the previous example, the Japanese syntactical markup (in other words the smaller Chinese glyphs interspersed between some of the larger ones)

---

[55] *Kojiki den*, undated reprint of 1790 edition, Tokyo, Waseda UL, ri05 09177, bk III, leaf 4ʳ. In the notes to their translation of the *Kojiki*, Kōnoshi and Yamaguchi gloss this glyph (Chinese, *fā*; Japanese, *hotsu*) with the Japanese word '*araharu*' (to appear). They explain (*Kojiki*, ed. by Kōnoshi and Yamaguchi, p. 28 n. 1) that this glyph traditionally as been glossed either as '*hiraku*' (that is, the gloss used in the 1644 edition) or as '*okoru*', but neither of those glosses are appropriate because these words also gloss '*fā*' when it appears in Chinese texts that discuss yin and yang cosmogonic theories.

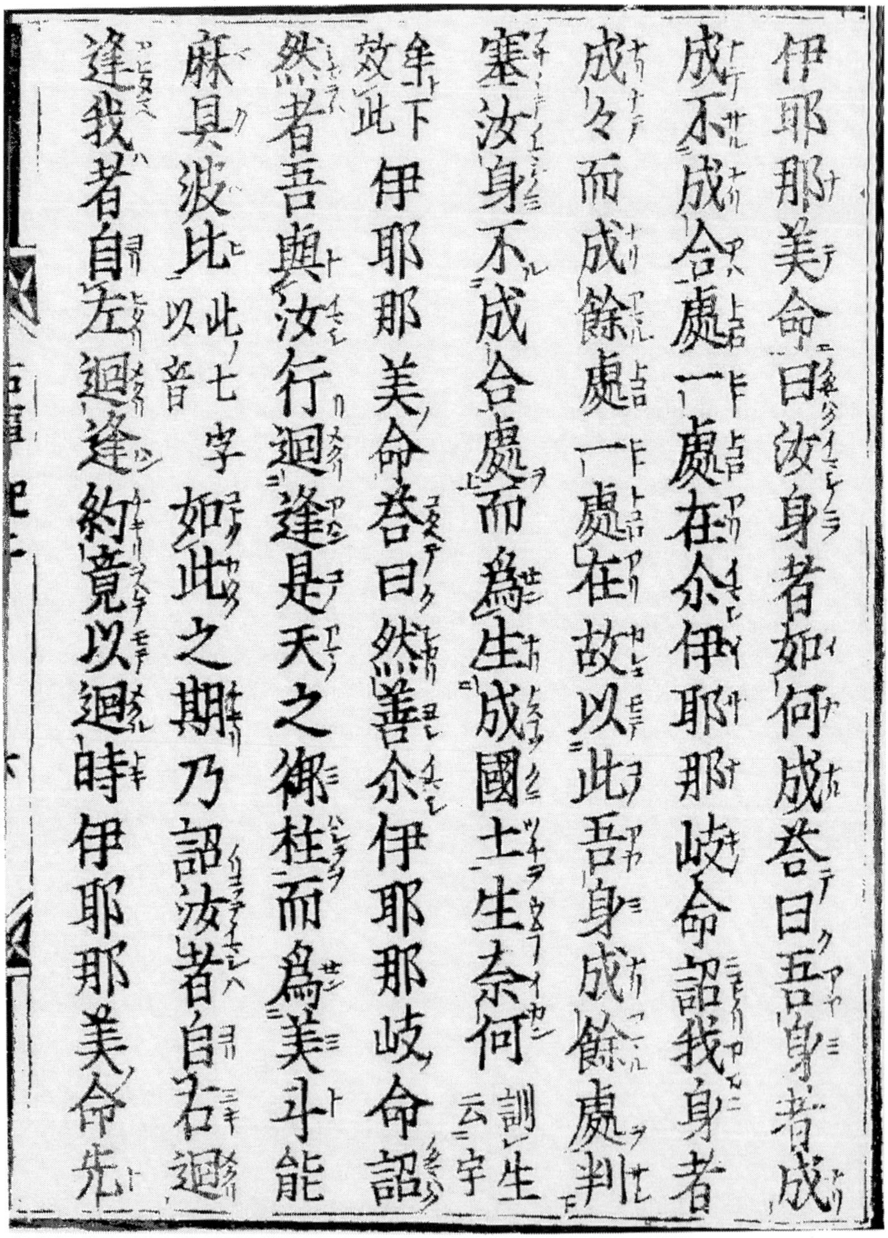
伊耶那美命曰汝身者如何成荅曰吾身者成
成不成合處一處在尒伊耶那岐命詔我身者
成々而成餘處一處在故以此吾身成餘處刺
塞汝身不成合處而爲生成國土生奈何訓生云宇
下效此 伊耶那美命荅曰然善尒伊耶那岐命詔
然者吾與汝行廻逢是天之御柱而爲美斗能
麻具波比此七字以音 如此之期乃詔汝者自右廻
逢我者自左廻逢約竟以廻時伊耶那美命先

Figure 11. *Kojiki* (Ancient Accounts), 1644 edition, bk I, leaf 6r. 1644.
Tokyo, Waseda UL, ri05 04868. Reproduced with permission. Cols 3–4 say:
'With this excessive part of my body, I will plug the incomplete part of your body, thereby producing and forming the bounded realm. Producing [in this manner] is alright?'

appears much more complex. While the word order in that earlier line of nineteen glyphs requires only two inversions, this line with only six more glyphs requires a total of five, more than twice as many. If romanized according to the 1644 markup, Izanagi's question assumes the following form:

kare ni kono aga-mi nari-amaru tokuro wo mote imashi-no-mi nari-awa-zaru
 1   -   3   4, 5   6, 7   8   -   2   11, -, 12   14, 15, 13

tokuro wo sashi-fusai-te kuni tsuchi wo umi-narinasu koto wo nasen umu koto i-kan
 16   -   9, 10, 17   21, 22   -   19, 20   -   -   18   23   - 24, 25

Once again note that every Chinese glyph in the original text generates a corresponding Japanese word as dictated by the orthodox Confucian style of markup. A somewhat stilted, overly literal translation in accordance with this markup might render Izanagi's question as: 'With this excessive part of my body, I will plug the incomplete part of your body, thereby producing and forming the bounded realm. Producing [in this manner] is alright?'

The same line in the *Kojiki-den* (see Fig. 12, cols 3–5) appears as follows:

カレ コノ アガミ ノ ナリアマ レ ル トコロ ヲ   ナ ガミ ノ ナリア ハ ザ ル トコロ
故 以 此 吾 身 成 餘 處。 刺 塞 汝 身 不
1   2   3   4   5   6   7   8   9   10 11 12 13

       ニ サ シ フタ ギテ   クニ ウミ ナ サ ム ト オフ ハイ カ ニ ト ノリタマ ヘ バ
成 合 處 而。 爲 生 成 國 土 奈 何。
14 15 16 17   18 19 20 21 22 24 25

Just as before, the lexicographical glosses in the top row cover the entire Chinese text in a smooth regular pattern, while the Chinese text itself appears undisturbed by any Japanese syntactical markup. At first glance, it appears that we have encountered exactly the same grammatical features as seen previously in the first line of the *Kojiki*. Readers who focus their attention solely on the Japanese *katakana* syllabary of the glosses (that is, the vast majority of Japanese readers) would likely assume from its appearance that the Chinese text and the Japanese glosses have exactly the same word order. Appearances, however, can be misleading.

Before examining the markup more carefully, first note that one Chinese glyph (no. 23) is missing. As stated earlier, Motoori asserts that no other early Japanese text can rival the *Kojiki* for its accuracy (pp. 108 and 114). At the same time (p. 109) he states that where errors do exist, they must have resulted from careless copyists. In his version of the text he corrects those so-called copyist errors by replacing Chinese glyphs or deleting them. Motoori's claim for superior textual accuracy, therefore, cannot be accepted uncritically. It rests on his cor-

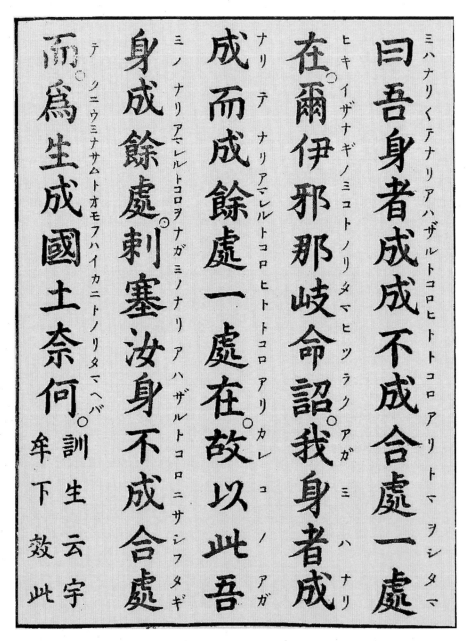

Figure 12. *Kojiki-den* (Ancient Accounts Conveyed), by Motoori Norinaga (1730–1801), undated reprint of 1790 edition, bk IV, leaf 14ᵛ. Tokyo, Waseda UL, ri05 09177. Reproduced with permission. Cols 3–5 say: 'With this excessive part of my body, I will plug the incomplete part of your body, with the intention of giving birth to the domain. Please do tell if it is acceptable'.

rected version of the text. Since no early manuscripts exist, neither he nor anyone else can determine with absolute certainty which glyphs might be the errors of a copyist. Textual emendations to the *Kojiki* should receive the utmost scrutiny.

Now we can examine how Motoori's markup treats the remaining Chinese glyphs. When romanized according to his markup, Izanagi's question assumes the following form:

kare kono aga-mi no nari-amaru tokoro wo, naga-mi no nari-awa-zaru tokoro
1   3   4,5   –   6,7   8   –   11,12   –   14,15,13   16

ni sashi-futagi-te, kuni umi nasamu to omou wa i-ka ni to nari-tamaeba,
–   9,10,17   21   19   20   –   18   – 24,25 – –   –, –

Motoori's Japanese version provides no corresponding Japanese words for two glyphs (nos 2 and 22), not to mention the one he deleted (no. 23). Otherwise, it has the exact same Japanese word order as dictated by the markup in the 1644 edition. That edition specifies five inversions (for glyphs 2, 9–10, 13, 18, and 19–20). Motoori's markup produces four inversions (glyphs 9–10, 13, 18, and 19–20). The only reason his text has one less, is because he skips glyph no. 2. The average reader, however, is unlikely to notice the inversions in Motoori's text. His style of markup provides no indication of their existence. When Japanese readers compare these two lines from the 1644 *Kojiki* and Motoori's *Kojiki-den*, what most likely will notice is the difference in politeness. The sentence in the 1644 edition ends with an abrupt Chinese-style question word: '*ikan*'. Motoori renders the same word as a more gentle-sounding Japanese phrase: '*ika ni to naritamaeba*'. With this minor difference and the omission of a couple of words, the resulting English translation remains similar to the previous version: 'With this excessive part of my body, I will plug the incomplete part of your body, with the intention of giving birth to the domain. Please do tell if it is acceptable.'

This example demonstrates that Motoori's rereadings of the *Kojiki* do not, as frequently asserted, represent his categorical rejection of the established Japanese techniques (*wakun*) for transforming Chinese texts into Japanese prose.[56] They merely create the illusion of his having done so. So great is this illusion that it radically transforms the text, not necessarily by profoundly altering the meaning of any individual sentence, but by shifting its cultural context. Just as is the case with his practice of replacing Chinese vocabulary with seemingly ancient and pure Japanese words, the visual layout reverses the relationship between the Chinese glyphs and the supplied Japanese gloss. The 1644 edition presents itself to the

---

[56] For the assertion that Motoori rejected *wakun*, see Sakai, *Voices of the Past*, pp. 257, 262.

reader as an unmistakably Chinese text, with the Chinese glyphs as primary and the supplied glosses and markup merely as supplementary aids to comprehension. Motoori's version presents the Japanese gloss as the real text. The Chinese glyphs still appear, but only for those curious about the original anagram which had concealed the ancient Japanese oral narrative hidden within. The presence of Chinese glyphs merely confirms the historical authenticity of the ancient Japanese speech. They are not to be read as themselves. The lack of any Japanese syntactical markup would discourage readers from making the effort to do so. In this way the visual layout of every page serves to confirm the original Japanese identity of the underlying narrative.

In 1803 Motoori's version of *Kojiki* text with its innovative running gloss and lack of syntactical markup was published as a stand-alone book, without the accompanying commentary. It appeared in print some nineteen years before the bulk (Books XVIII–XLIV) of Motoori's commentary did so. The publication of this version, titled *Kokun Kojiki* (Kojiki with Ancient Glosses), so many years prior to the remainder of Motoori's commentary implies that his Japanese reconstruction of the Chinese text needed no further justification. Without any commentary, the *Kokun Kojiki* provides only the Japanese gloss to aid readers. This version thus conveys even more forcibly the impression that the *Kojiki* can be nothing other than a transcription of ancient Japanese speech. The visual transformation of the text reached its ultimate conclusion in 1874, when Sakata Kaneyasu (1820–1890) published *Kana Kojiki* (Phonetic Kojiki), which presents the text of the *Kojiki* as being written in the Japanese syllabary with Chinese glyphs here and there to phonetically transcribe proper names. No longer was the *Kojiki* merely imagined as a work written in Japanese, it had become one. Most significant of all, it had become — within less than a hundred years after the publication of Motoori's commentary — accepted as the first and oldest book written in Japanese.[57]

Writing Myths

Both Jōin and Motoori wrote new myths for the new realities of their own times. With age these myths grew stale and lost their vitality. Jōin and his myths faded into obscurity. Motoori and his myths, though, in some ways still resonate or echo today. Motoori opened a door to a new way of imagining Japan, a Japan of

---

[57] Even W. G. Aston (1841–1911), who completed his authoritative translation of the *Nihon shoki* in 1896, could make this assertion in Aston, *A History of Japanese Literature*, p. 18.

independent and pristine beginnings, the allure of which still lingers. Looking through that door, his followers (and the subsequent generations who followed them) developed new ways of viewing themselves. They wrote new myths, which refashioned and extended the ones formulated by Motoori: the myth of an unbroken ruling dynasty which transformed the Heavenly Sovereign into a head of state; the myth of an original native religion (Shintō) which absorbs external influence while retaining its inner essence unchanged; the myth of a native language (*kokugo*) which unites all Japanese, in all geographic regions past and present; and the myth of a national literature with its own ancient classes written in that language.[58] Over time these narratives coalesced and contributed to the mega-myth (now called 'ideology') of the modern nation state.[59] This process did not begin with Motoori, and he certainly did not determine its course. But his handwriting appears in all of its features mentioned above. They presented themselves in the configurations that we find familiar even today because of the new techniques with which Motoori wrote or, rather, rewrote and printed mythology.

[58] Regarding language and literature, esp. see Lee, *The Ideology of Kokugo*; Isomae, 'Reappropriating the Japanese Myths'; and Kōnoshi, 'Constructing Imperial Mythology', trans. by Joko.

[59] Gluck, *Japan's Modern Myths*, esp. pp. 73–101, 138–56. For a comparative perspective on the roles that the recovery of ancient vernacular languages and literatures (especially myths) played in European constructions of nationalism, see Lincoln, *Theorizing Myth*, pp. 47–137.

Works Cited

Manuscripts and Archival Documents

Nara, Sakamoto Ryūmon Bunko, Ujitsune MS, Sakamoto Ryūmon Bunko Digital Image Collection <http://mahoroba.lib.nara-wu.ac.jp/y05/html/103/index.htm> [accessed 20 February 2010]

Tokyo, Kokugakuin University Library, Bonshun MS, Kokugakuin University Digital Library <http://kaiser.kokugakuin.ac.jp/digital/diglib.html> [accessed 20 February 2010]

Tokyo, Waseda University Library, Bunko17 w0199 <http://www.wul.waseda.ac.jp/kotenseki/html/bunko17/bunko17_w0199/index.html> [accessed 14 July 2009]

Tokyo, Waseda University Library, ri05 09177 <http://www.wul.waseda.ac.jp/kotenseki/html/ri05/ri05_09177/index.html> [accessed 14 July 2009]

Tokyo, Waseda University Library, ri05 04868 <http://www.wul.waseda.ac.jp/kotenseki/html/ri05/ri05_04868/index.html> [accessed 14 July 2009]

Primary Sources

Taishō shinshū daizōkyō [Taishō Edition of the Great Library of Buddhist Scriptures], ed. by Takakusu Junjirō and Watanabe Kaikyoku (Tokyo: Daizōkyōkai, 1924–35)

Kojiki, ed. by Kōnoshi Takamitsu and Yamaguchi Yoshinori, Shinpen Nihon Koten Bungaku Zenshū [New Edition of the Complete Works of Japanese Classical Literature], 1 (Tokyo: Shōgakkan, 1997)

Kokutai no Hongi: Cardinal Principles of the National Entity of Japan, ed. by Robert King Hall, trans. by John Owen Gauntlett (Cambridge, MA: Harvard University Press, 1949)

Maeda Eun, *Bukkyō kokinhen ippan* [A Class on Buddhism, Then and Now] ([n.p.]: [n.pub.], 1900)

——, *Bukkyō kokinhen ippan* [A Class on Buddhism, Then and Now], in Maeda Eun, *Maeda Eun zenshū* [Complete Works of Maeda Eun], 8 vols (Tokyo: Shunjūsha, 1931–32), I, pp. 355–410

This Most Excellent Shine of Gold, King of Kings of Sutras: The Khotanese Suvarabhāsottamasūtra, ed. by Prods Oktor Skjærvø, 2 vols (Cambridge, MA: Harvard University, Dept. of Near Eastern Languages and Civilizations, 2004)

Motoori Norinaga, *Kojiki-den, Book 1*, trans. by Ann Wehmeyer, with preface by Naoki Sakai (Ithaca: East Asia Program, Cornell University, 1997)

Rikkokushi [Six Dynastic Histories], Nihon Kodai Shiryō Honbun Deeta [Database of Original Sources for Japanese Ancient History] <http://ifs.nog.cc/kodaishi-db.hp.infoseek.co.jp/> [accessed 6 August 2012]

The Sūtra of Golden Light: Being a Translation of the Suvarabhāsottamasūtra, trans. by R. E. Emmerick (London: Luzac, 1970)

Tendaishū zensho [Collected Works of Tendai Buddhism], ed. by Tendai Shūten Kankōkai, 25 vols (Tokyo: Daiichi Shobō, 1935–37)

Secondary Studies

Aldridge, Edith, 'Principles of *Hentai Kanbun* Word Order: Evidence from the *Kojiki*', in *Language Change in East Asia*, ed. by Thomas E. McAuley (Richmond: Curzon, 2001), pp. 207–32

Ariga, Chieko, 'The Playful Gloss: *Rubi* in Japanese Literature', *Monumenta Nipponica*, 44 (1989), 309–335

Aston, William George, *A History of Japanese Literature* (New York: Appleton, 1899; repr. Tokyo: Tuttle, 1972)

Bentley, John R., *The Authenticity of 'Sendai kuji hongi': A New Examination of Texts, with a Translation and Commentary*, Brill's Japanese Studies Library, 25 (Leiden: Brill, 2006)

——, 'Review of *Kojiki-den: Book I*', *Monumenta Nipponica*, 53 (1998), 120–22

Bodiford, William M., 'Matara: A Dream King between Insight and Imagination', *Cahiers d'Extrême-Asie*, 16 (2006–07 [2010]), 233–62

——, 'When Secrecy Ends: The Tokugawa Reformation of Tendai Buddhism and its Implications', in *The Culture of Secrecy in Japanese Religion*, ed. by Bernhard Scheid and Mark Teeuwen (New York: Routledge, 2006), pp. 309–30

Boot, Willem. J., 'The Religious Background of the Deification of Tokugawa Ieyasu', in *Rethinking Japan*, ed. by Adriana Boscaro, Franco Gatti, and Massimo Raveri, 2 vols (New York: St. Martin's, 1990–91), II: *Social Sciences, Ideology, and Thought* (1991), pp. 331–37

Breen, John, 'Nativism Restored', *Monumenta Nipponica*, 55 (2000), 429–39

Burns, Susan L., *Before the Nation: Kokugaku and the Imagining of Community in Early Modern Japan* (Chapel Hill: Duke University Press, 2003)

Collcutt, Martin, 'Buddhism: The Threat of Eradication', in *Japan in Transition: From Tokugawa to Meiji*, ed. by Marius B. Jansen and Gilbert Rozman (Princeton: Princeton University Press, 1986), pp. 143–67

Earhart, H. Byron, *Japanese Religion: Unity and Diversity*, 3rd edn (Belmont: Wadsworth, 1982)

Endō Jun, 'The Early Modern Period: In Search of a Shinto Identity', in *Shinto: A Short History*, ed. by Inoue Nobutaka and others, trans. by Mark Teeuwen and John Breen (London: Routledge Curzon, 2003), pp. 108–58

Gluck, Carol, *Japan's Modern Myths: Ideology in the Late Meiji Period* (Princeton: Princeton University Press, 1985)

Grapard, Allan G., 'Japan's Ignored Cultural Revolution: The Separation of Shinto and Buddhist Divinities in Meiji (*shimbutsu bunri*) and a Case Study: Tōnomine', *History of Religions*, 23 (1984), 240–65

Hardacre, Helen, *Shintō and the State, 1868–1988* (Princeton: Princeton University Press, 1989)

Isomae Jun'ichi, 'Reappropriating the Japanese Myths: Motoori Norinaga and the Creation Myths of the *Kojiki* and *Nihon Shoki*', trans. by Sarah E. Thal, *Japanese Journal of Religious Studies*, 27 (2000), 15–39

Iyanaga Nobumi, 'Medieval Shintō as a Form of "Japanese Hinduism": An Attempt at Understanding Early Medieval Shintō', *Cahiers d'Extrême-Asie*, 16 (2006–07 [2010]), 263–303

'Kanbun jugyō ni kansuru chōsa hōkoku' [Announcement of (the Results of) Our Investigation Regarding the Teaching of Chinese Texts], in *Kanpō No. 8630* [Official Announcements No. 8630], issued by the Monbushō 1912; undated repr. <http://www.nishogakusha-kanbun.net/kanp8630.pdf> [accessed 23 February 2010]

Kawase Kazuma, 'Keian oshō kahō wakun ni tsuite', *Aoyama Gakuin Joshi Tanki Daigaku Kiyō*, 13 (1959), 35–72

Ketelaar, James Edward, *Of Heretics and Martyrs in Meiji Japan: Buddhism and its Persecution* (Princeton: Princeton University Press, 1993)

Kōnoshi Takamitsu, 'Constructing Imperial Mythology: *Kojiki* and *Nihon shoki*', trans. by Iori Joko, in *Inventing the Classics: Modernity, National Identity, and Japanese Literature*, ed. by Haruo Shirane and Tomi Suzuki (Stanford: Stanford University Press, 2000), pp. 51–67, 255–58

——, *Kanji tekisuto to shite no Kojiki* [The Kojiki as a Chinese Text] (Tokyo: Tōkyō Daigaku Shuppankai, 2007)

——, *Kojiki to Nihon shoki: 'Tennō shinwa' no rekishi* [The Kojiki and Nihon shoki: A History of 'Heavenly Sovereign Mythology'] (Tokyo: Kōdanasha, 1999)

Lee Yeounsuk [Yi Yŏn-suk], *The Ideology of Kokugo: Nationalizing Language in Modern Japan*, trans. by Maki Hirano Hubbard (Honolulu: University of Hawaii Press, 2010)

Lincoln, Bruce, *Theorizing Myth: Narrative, Ideology, and Scholarship* (Chicago: University of Chicago Press, 1999)

Matsumoto Shigeru, *Motoori Norinaga, 1730–1801* (Cambridge, MA: Harvard University Press, 1970)

Miller, Roy Andrew, *The Japanese Language* (Chicago: University of Chicago Press, 1967)

Nakada Norio, *Kotenbon no kokugogakuteki kenkyū, sōron hen* [Japanese Language Studies on the Markup of Old Texts, Comprehensive Edition] (Tokyo: Benseisha, 1954)

Nakada Norio, *Kotenbon no kokugogakuteki kenkyū, sōron hen* [Japanese Language Studies on the Markup of Old Texts, Comprehensive Edition], rev. edn (Tokyo: Benseisha, 1979)

Ooms, Herman, *Imperial Politics and Symbolics in Ancient Japan: The Tenmu Dynasty, 650–800* (Honolulu: University of Hawaii Press, 2009)

Ōwa Iwao, *Kojiki seiritsu kō* [Considering the Origins of the Kojiki] (Tokyo: Daiwa Shobō, 1975)

——, *Kojiki seiritsu kō* [Considering the Origins of the Kojiki], rev. edn (Tokyo: Daiwa Shobō, 1997)

——, *Shinpan Kojiki seiritsu kō* [Considering the Origins of the Kojiki], new edn (Tokyo: Daiwa Shobō, 2009)

Rabinovitch, Judith N., 'An Introduction to Hentai Kambun [Variant Chinese], a Hybrid Sinico-Japanese used by the Male Elite in Pre-Modern Japan', *Journal of Chinese Linguistics*, 24 (1996), 98–127

Ruegg, David Seyfort, *The Symbiosis of Buddhism with Brahmanism/Hinduism in South Asian and of Buddhism with 'Local Cults' in Tibet and the Himalayan Region* (Wien: Österreichische Akademie der Wissenschaften, 2008)

Sakai, Naoki, *Voices of the Past: The Status of Language in Eighteenth Century Japanese Discourse* (Ithaca: Cornell University Press, 1991)

Seeley, Christopher, *A History of Writing in Japan* (Leiden: Brill, 1991)

Ng Wai-ming, *The 'I Ching' in Tokugawa Thought and Culture* (Honolulu: University of Hawaii Press, 2000)

Steben, Barry D., 'The Transmission of Neo-Confucianism to the Ryukyu (Liuqiu) Islands and Its Historical Significance: Ritual and Rectification of Names in a Bipolar Authority Field', *Sino-Japanese Studies*, 11.1 (1998), 39–60

Takatsu Takashi, 'Kinsei Ryūkyū ni okeru kanseki juyō' [The Adoption of Chinese Texts in the Early Modern Ryūkyū Islands], *Anmi Nyuuzuretaa*, 5 (2004), 7–11

Teeuwen, Mark, '*Sendai Kuji Hongi*: Authentic Myths or Forged History?', *Monumenta Nipponica*, 62 (2007), 87–96

——, *Watarai Shintō: An intellectual history of the Outer Shrine in Ise* (Leiden: Research School, Centre for Non-Western Studies, Leiden University, 1996)

Wixted, John Timothy, '*Kanbun*, Histories of Japanese Literature, and Japanologists', *Sino-Japanese Studies*, 10 (1998), 23–31

Wehmeyer, Ann, 'Biographical Introduction', in Motoori Norinaga, *Kojiki-den, Book 1*, trans. by Ann Wehmeyer, with preface by Naoki Sakai (Ithaca: East Asia Program, Cornell University, 1997), pp. 1–14

Yamamoto Hiroko, *Chūsei shinwa* [Myths of Medieval Japan] (Tokyo: Iwanami Shoten, 1998)

INDEX

CURSOR MUNDI

All volumes in this series are evaluated by an Editorial Board, strictly on academic grounds, based on reports prepared by referees who have been commissioned by virtue of their specialism in the appropriate field. The Board ensures that the screening is done independently and without conflicts of interest. The definitive texts supplied by authors are also subject to review by the Board before being approved for publication. Further, the volumes are copyedited to conform to the publisher's stylebook and to the best international academic standards in the field.

Titles in Series

Chris Jones, *Eclipse of Empire? Perceptions of the Western Empire and its Rulers in Late-Medieval France* (2007)

Simha Goldin, *The Ways of Jewish Martyrdom* (2008)

Franks, Northmen, and Slavs: Identities and State Formation in Early Medieval Europe, ed. by Ildar Garipzanov, Patrick Geary, and Przemyslaw Urbanczyk (2008)

William Walker, *'Paradise Lost' and Republican Tradition from Aristotle to Machiavelli* (2009)

Carmela Vircillo Franklin, *Material Restoration: A Fragment from Eleventh-Century Echternach in a Nineteenth-Century Parisian Codex* (2010)

Saints and their Lives on the Periphery: Veneration of Saints in Scandinavia and Eastern Europe (c.1000-1200), ed. by Haki Antonsson and Ildar Garipzanov (2010)

Approaching the Holy Mountain: Art and Liturgy at St Catherine's Monastery in the Sinai, ed. by Sharon E. J. Gerstel and Robert S. Nelson (2011)

'This Earthly Stage': World and Stage in Late Medieval and Early Modern England, ed. by Brett D. Hirsch and Christopher Wortham (2011)

Alan J. Fletcher, *The Presence of Medieval English Literature: Studies at the Interface of History, Author, and Text in a Selection of Middle English Literary Landmarks* (2012)

Vehicles of Transmission, Translation, and Transformation in Medieval Textual Culture, ed. by Robert Wisnovsky, Faith Wallis, Jamie C. Fumo, and Carlos Fraenkel (2012)

Claudio Moreschini, *Hermes Christianus: The Intermingling of Hermetic Piety and Christian Thought* (2012)

The Faces of the Other: Religious Rivalry and Ethnic Encounters in the Later Roman World, ed. by Maijastina Kahlos (2012)

Barbara Furlotti, *A Renaissance Baron and his Possessions: Paolo Giordano I Orsini, Duke of Bracciano (1541–1585)* (2012)

Rethinking Virtue, Reforming Society: New Directions in Renaissance Ethics, c.1350 – c.1650, ed. by David A. Lines and Sabrina Ebbersmeyer (2013)

In Preparation

Luigi A. Berto, *The Political and Social Vocabulary of John the Deacon's 'Istoria Veneticorum'*

Wendy Turner, *Care and Custody of the Mentally Ill, Incompetent, and Disabled in Medieval England*

Tanya Lenz, *Dreams, Medicine, and Literary Practice: Exploring the Western Literary Tradition Through Chaucer*

Charles Russell Stone, *From Tyrant to Philosopher-King: A Literary History of Alexander the Great in Medieval and Early Modern England*